BEST PRACTICES IN WRITING INSTRUCTION

Also available

Handbook of Writing Research
Edited by Charles A. MacArthur,
Steve Graham, and Jill Fitzgerald

Best Practices in
WRITING
INSTRUCTION

SECOND EDITION

Edited by
Steve Graham
Charles A. MacArthur
Jill Fitzgerald

THE GUILFORD PRESS
New York   London

© 2013 The Guilford Press
A Division of Guilford Publications, Inc.
72 Spring Street, New York, NY 10012
www.guilford.com

Printed in the United States of America

This book is printed on acid-free paper.

Last digit is print number: 9   8   7   6   5   4   3   2

Library of Congress Cataloging-in-Publication Data

Best practices in writing instruction / edited by Steve Graham, Charles A.
MacArthur, and Jill Fitzgerald. — Second edition.
    pages ; cm
  Includes bibliographical references and index.
  ISBN 978-1-4625-1008-5 (pbk. : alk. paper) — ISBN 978-1-4625-1009-2
(cloth : alk. paper)
  1. English language—Composition and exercises—Study and teaching
(Elementary) 2. English language—Composition and exercises—Study
and teaching (Secondary) I. Graham, Steve, 1950– II. MacArthur,
Charles A. III. Fitzgerald, Jill.
  LB1576.B487 2013
  372.6—dc23
                                                          2013002118

To my better three-quarters;
in other words, to my wife, Karen Harris
—STEVE GRAHAM

To my wife, Dorothy Hsiao,
and my three boys, Alexander, Peter, and Daniel
—CHARLES A. MACARTHUR

To my children,
Kenneth Craig Jackson and Kristen Michelle Miller,
and my granddaughter, Lorine Winifred Miller
—JILL FITZGERALD

About the Editors

Steve Graham, EdD, is the Warner Professor in the Mary Lou Fulton Teachers College at Arizona State University. His research focuses on identifying the factors that contribute to writing development and writing difficulties, developing and validating effective instructional procedures for teaching writing, and the use of technology to enhance writing performance. Dr. Graham is a past editor of *Exceptional Children* and *Contemporary Educational Psychology* and a current editor of the *Journal of Writing Research*. He is the author or editor of numerous books on writing instruction and research and is a series editor of *What Works for Special-Needs Learners*, published by The Guilford Press. Dr. Graham was a member of the Adolescent and Adult Literacy Panel of the National Research Council and the Research Advisory Panel and Early History Panel of the National Writing Project. He has received many awards, including the Career Research Award from the Council for Exceptional Children, and was elected a Fellow of the American Educational Research Association in 2012.

Charles A. MacArthur, PhD, is Professor of Special Education and Literacy in the School of Education at the University of Delaware. A former special education teacher, he teaches courses on literacy problems, writing instruction, and assistive technology. Dr. MacArthur's major research interests include writing development and instruction for struggling writers, adult literacy, development of self-regulated strategies, and applications of technology to support reading and writing. He is currently principal investigator of a research project developing a writing curriculum for college basic writing, and coprincipal investigator of a study of writing instruction in first grade. Dr. MacArthur is a former coeditor of the *Journal of Special*

Education and is on the editorial boards of several other journals. He is the author of more than 100 articles and book chapters and the editor of several books, including the *Handbook of Writing Research* (coedited with Steve Graham and Jill Fitzgerald).

Jill Fitzgerald, PhD, is Distinguished Research Scientist at MetaMetrics in Durham, North Carolina, and Professor Emerita at The University of North Carolina at Chapel Hill, where she is currently Adjunct Research Professor in the School of Education. A former primary-grades teacher and reading specialist, Dr. Fitzgerald taught university courses in reading and writing education at the undergraduate and graduate level for more than 30 years. Her research interests center on literacy issues for multilingual learners and understanding text complexity. Dr. Fitzgerald is the author of more than 100 articles and books, is associate editor of the *Journal of Educational Psychology*, and serves on the editorial boards of several national and international journals. She is a recipient of the Outstanding Review of Research Award from the American Educational Research Association and the Dina Feitelson Research Award from the International Reading Association. In 2011, Dr. Fitzgerald was inducted into the Reading Hall of Fame. Currently she is a consultant to a Chilean federal government project designed to help teachers learn how to assess young children's reading abilities.

Contributors

Pietro Boscolo, PhD, Department of Developmental Psychology and Socialization, University of Padua, Padua, Italy

Robert C. Calfee, PhD, Graduate School of Education, Stanford University, Stanford, California

David L. Coker, Jr., EdD, School of Education, University of Delaware, Newark, Delaware

Ralph P. Ferretti, PhD, School of Education, University of Delaware, Newark, Delaware

Carmen Gelati, PhD, Department of Psychology, University of Milan–Bicocca, Milan, Italy

Steve Graham, EdD, Division of Educational Leadership and Innovation, Mary Lou Fulton Teachers College, Arizona State University, Tempe, Arizona

Karen R. Harris, EdD, Division of Educational Leadership and Innovation, Mary Lou Fulton Teachers College, Arizona State University, Tempe, Arizona

Rachel Karchmer-Klein, PhD, School of Education, University of Delaware, Newark, Delaware

Perry D. Klein, PhD, Faculty of Education, University of Western Ontario, London, Ontario, Canada

Cindy Lassonde, PhD, Department of Elementary Education and Reading, State University of New York at Oneonta, Oneonta, New York

William E. Lewis, PhD, School of Education, University of Delaware, Newark, Delaware

Charles A. MacArthur, PhD, School of Education, University of Delaware, Newark, Delaware

Tina Matuchniak, MA, School of Education, University of California, Irvine, Irvine, California

Anne McKeough, PhD, Faculty of Education, University of Calgary, Calgary, Alberta, Canada

Roxanne Greitz Miller, EdD, Graduate School of Education, Chapman University, Orange, California

George E. Newell, PhD, College of Education and Human Ecology, The Ohio State University, Columbus, Ohio

Carol Booth Olson, PhD, School of Education, University of California, Irvine, Irvine, California

Dolores Perin, PhD, Teachers College, Columbia University, New York, New York

Janet C. Richards, PhD, College of Education, University of South Florida, Tampa, Florida

Bruce Saddler, PhD, Department of Educational and Counseling Psychology, University at Albany, State University of New York, Albany, New York

Robin Scarcella, PhD, School of Humanities, University of California, Irvine, Irvine, California

Bob Schlagal, PhD, Department of Language, Reading, and Special Education, Reich College of Education, Appalachian State University, Boone, North Carolina

Timothy Shanahan, PhD, Department of Curriculum and Instruction, University of Illinois at Chicago, Chicago, Illinois

Gary A. Troia, PhD, Department of Counseling, Educational Psychology, and Special Education, Michigan State University, East Lansing, Michigan

Jennifer VanDerHeide, MEd, College of Education and Human Ecology, The Ohio State University, Columbus, Ohio

Melissa Wilson, PhD, College of Education and Human Ecology, The Ohio State University, Columbus, Ohio

Amy Meichi Yu, BSc, Faculty of Education, University of Western Ontario, London, Ontario, Canada

Preface

We are pleased to present the second edition of *Best Practices in Writing Instruction*. The first edition was designed to help teachers become more effective at teaching writing. It presented evidence-based practices for enhancing the writing of students at all levels—elementary through high school. It also provided effective strategies for teaching writing to multilingual students and students with special needs.

The second edition continues to provide practical examples of best practices in writing instruction across the grades, but each chapter has been fully revised so that it addresses the writing skills and applications stressed in the Common Core State Standards (CCSS), and includes the newest and most effective instructional procedures for teaching writing to a broad array of children and youth. In addition to the extensive chapter revisions, the book now begins with a chapter by Graham and Harris on designing an effective writing program, which provides a structure that links the other 16 chapters together. We have added new chapters on (1) teaching argumentative writing (Ferretti and Lewis), (2) teaching informative writing (Newell, VanDerHeide, and Wilson), (3) using writing as a tool for supporting learning in the academic disciplines (Klein and Yu), (4) writing about text in a literacy-enhancing way (Shanahan), and (5) improving students' writing skills for college and the workplace (Perin). The chapter on technology (Karchmer-Klein) was extensively revised so that it also addresses the demands created by the CCSS. Finally, we invited new authors to write chapters on best practices in planning for writing (Lassonde and Richards), teaching writing to English learners (Olson, Scarcella, and Matuchniak), and teaching writing to students with special needs within a response-to-intervention framework (Troia).

Of course, we also want to thank and acknowledge the authors who revised their chapters from the first edition: on writing instruction in preschool and kindergarten (Coker), teaching narrative writing (McKeough), evaluation and revision (MacArthur), sentence construction skills (Saddler), handwriting and spelling (Schlagal), promoting motivation (Boscolo and Gelati), and assessment (Calfee and Miller). We believe that the second edition is practical, research-based, and responsive to the CCSS. The instructional methods included in this book will be helpful to experienced and novice language arts and content-area teachers. They can be used in language arts and writing instruction courses as well as staff development workshops that focus on writing and literacy development, and they should be of value to school principals, writing specialists, and others involved in administering or delivering writing instruction to children and adolescents.

Contents

PART III.   STRATEGIES FOR TEACHING AND LEARNING IN WRITING

PART IV.   SPECIAL POPULATIONS

BEST PRACTICES IN WRITING INSTRUCTION

PART I

Designing Writing Programs

Chapter 1

Designing an Effective Writing Program

STEVE GRAHAM
KAREN R. HARRIS

Since the publication of the first edition of *Best Practices in Writing Instruction* (Graham, MacArthur, & Fitzgerald, 2007), little has changed in how writing is taught in the majority of classrooms in the United States. Teachers report they devote little time to teaching writing beyond grade three, and students do little writing in or out of school for academic purposes (Applebee & Langer, 2011; Gilbert & Graham, 2010; Kiuhara, Graham, & Hawkens, 2009). This stands in stark contrast to the other members of the three R's, reading and mathematics, subjects in which schools and teachers have devoted considerable effort to improving students' performance.

The general lack of attention to improving writing instruction nationwide during this and the last decade should not distract from the phenomenal job that many schools and teachers do when teaching writing. Rather, what these educators have accomplished illustrates what is possible when we squarely focus our efforts on providing effective writing instruction. In fact, it is clear that we now have the instructional "know-how" needed to ensure that students become skillful writers. Recent reports from the Carnegie Corporation of New York (Graham, Harris, & Hebert, 2011; Graham & Hebert, 2010; Graham & Perin, 2007a) and the Institute of Education Sciences (Graham et al., 2012) show we possess many tools for improving the quality of students' writing. Writing, in turn, enhances students' learning as well as their ability to read effectively.

It is especially important at this time that we focus our will on bringing these best practices in writing instruction more fully into all classrooms. We stand at a unique moment in the history of writing instruction in schools in the United States. Forty-six states have agreed to implement the Common Core State Standards (CCSS; National Governors Association & Council of Chief State School Officers, 2010). These standards make writing and writing instruction a central element of the school reform movement (Graham, 2013). Learning to write and writing to learn are strongly emphasized in the CCSS, as students are expected to learn how to write for multiple purposes (e.g., to persuade, to inform, and to narrate) and use writing to recall, organize, analyze, interpret, and build knowledge about content or materials read across discipline-specific subjects. In effect, a basic goal of the CCSS is to revolutionize how writing is taught in today's schools and classrooms.

The CCSS provide benchmarks for writing skills and applications that students are expected to master and apply in kindergarten through grade 12. As with all maps of this nature, teachers need to be aware of problems that potentially limit the impact of the CCSS (Graham, 2013). A primary issue is that many of the writing benchmarks are simply educated guesses as to what students should be able to achieve at particular grades. These objectives lack precision and accuracy and encourage the belief that the same goals are appropriate for all students at each grade. We think this is misguided, as some goals will be too easy and others too hard, depending upon the veracity of the benchmark and the competence of the student. A slavish reliance on such objectives is likely to result in situations where students underachieve because the goal was too easy or fail to achieve because the goal was unrealistic. As a result, the value of the CCSS as a roadmap for teachers will be limited if they do not understand why writing is important, how it develops, and how to teach it effectively.

This chapter and *Best Practices in Writing Instruction* as a whole address each of these assumptions. We think that if teachers know *why writing is important*, they will invest the energy and time needed to develop an excellent writing program (and correspondingly achieve the CCSS writing standards). If they understand *how writing develops*, they will approach writing instruction and the CCSS benchmarks in a flexible and reasonable manner. If they possess *effective tools for teaching writing*, they will appropriately adapt and likely extend goals of the CCSS goals for writing. We address each of these assumptions in turn in this chapter, drawing attention to other chapters in this volume that address each assumption more specifically.

Is Writing Important?

The answer to this question is an unqualified YES! First, writing is an extremely versatile tool that is used to accomplish a variety of goals

(Graham, 2006a). It provides a mechanism for maintaining personal links with family, friends, and colleagues when we are unable to be with them in person. We use writing to share information, tell stories, create imagined worlds, explore who we are, combat loneliness, and chronicle our experiences. Writing can even make us feel better, as writing about our feelings and experiences can benefit us psychologically and physiologically (Smyth, 1998).

Second, writing provides a powerful tool for influencing others. Books like *Uncle Tom's Cabin* provided a catalyst for antislavery beliefs in 19th-century America, whereas *The Jungle* by Upton Sinclair changed the way we think about food preparation. The persuasive effects of writing are so great that many governments ban "subversive" documents and jail the offending authors.

Third, writing is an indispensable tool for learning and communicating. We use writing as a medium to gather, preserve, and transmit information. Just as important, writing about what we are learning helps us understand and remember it better. The permanence of writing makes ideas we are studying readily available for review and evaluation, its explicitness encourages establishing connections between these ideas, and its active nature fosters the exploration of unexamined assumptions (Applebee, 1984). The impact of writing on learning was captured in two recent meta-analysis (Bangert-Drowns, Hurley, & Wilkinson, 2004; Graham & Perin, 2007a), which found that writing about content material enhanced students' learning in social studies, science, mathematics, and the language arts. Two examples of a writing-to-learn activity are presented in Figure 1.1 (see also Perin, Chapter 3; Ferretti & Lewis, Chapter 5; Newell, VanDer-Heide, & Wilson, Chapter 6; and Klein & Yu, Chapter 7, this volume, for additional guidelines and examples).

Fourth, students understand material they read better if they write about it. As with writing about concepts presented in science or other content classes, writing about material read provides students with a tool for visibly and permanently recording, analyzing, connecting, personalizing, and manipulating key ideas from text. This has a strong impact on making text read more memorable and understandable (Graham & Hebert, 2010, 2011). This is the case for students in general, and those who are weaker readers and/or writers in particular. It is also the case for narrative and expository text and materials students read for language arts, science, and social studies. Two examples of writing activities that improve students' comprehension of text in scientific studies are presented in Figure 1.2 (see also Shanahan, Chapter 14, this volume).

Fifth, teaching students to write improves their reading skills. While reading and writing are not identical skills, they both rely on a common fund of knowledge, processes, and skills (Fitzgerald & Shanahan, 2000). Consequently, instruction that improves writing skills and processes improves reading skills and processes. Reading is also improved by having students engage in the process of composing text (Tierney & Shanahan, 1991). Writers gain insights about reading by creating text for an audience to read. When they write, students must make their assumptions and premises explicit as well as observe the rules of logic, making them more aware of these same issues in the material they read. Support for both of these premises was obtained in a meta-analysis by Graham and Hebert (2010, 2011) who found that:

- Teaching spelling improved students' word reading skills.
- Teaching spelling and sentence constructions skills increased students' reading fluency.
- Implementing multicomponent writing instructional programs, such as the process writing approach or skills-based writing instructions, increased how well students comprehended text read.
- Increasing how much students write led to better reading comprehension.

Grade 5: Walt Longmire, a fifth-grade teacher, began an experiment on buoyancy by directing his students to look at the objects they would test (celery stick, wood, rock, Styrofoam, rubber ball, and key). Each child partnered with another student and wrote a prediction for each item, specifying if it would sink to the bottom in a tank of water, float on top of it, or be suspended in between. They had to explain the rationale for each prediction. After discussing these predictions as a class, students conducted the experiments and made notes about what happened to each item as it was placed in the water. Students then reexamined their predictions and explanations, and revised them in writing as necessary. The class discussed the experiment as well as the revised predictions and explanations, drawing several general observations about buoyancy. Students recorded these in in their science journal (Graham, 2013).

Grade 11: Beatrice Linwood an 11th-grade social studies teacher in Montana had her class watch two films: one about the response of Dutch citizens to the Nazi's practice of making Jewish people wear a red star, another about the reaction of people in Germany to the same practice. As they watched the film, students were asked to take notes on how people in each country reacted to this practice, and why they thought they reacted in their respective manners. After viewing each film, the class discussed their notes and their reactions to the films. They were then asked to write a two-page paper about what would happen in present-day Montana if illegal immigrants were forced to wear a similar star. They shared and discussed their conclusions from their paper the next day.

FIGURE 1.1. Examples of writing-to-learn activities.

Grade 3: Alfredo Coda taught his third-grade students how to write questions about the stories they were reading in language arts. He started by having them read a short story, and then modeled how to generate and answer who, what, when, where, and why questions about the material read. As he modeled how to write each question he explained why each was important. Next, students read several additional stories and helped Mr. Coda generate and answer these same kinds of questions. Each student paired with another student and did the same thing. Each student shared his or her favorite question with the class. The final activity involved having students write their own questions and give them to a peer to answer after they read the text for which the questions were developed. The student who answered the questions gave the other student feedback on the quality of each question, indicating what he or she liked or how the question could be changed to make it better. This exercise was repeated several times until students had mastered this skill.

Grade 10: Sancho Saizarbitoria, a 10th-grade social studies teacher, asked his students to read and take notes on two-page descriptions of governments in four countries (two were republics and two were representative democracies). He then defined with the students each of these two forms of government, and the class identified which of the four countries were republics and which were representative democracies. He then asked them to write a two-page paper comparing and contrasting the two forms of government, indicating which they thought was best about each and why. He read their papers that evening, and after returning them the next day, they discussed misperceptions about what were evident in the papers and further explored the advantages and disadvantages of the two forms of government.

FIGURE 1.2. Examples of writing-to-read activities.

As this brief discussion shows, writing is a flexible, versatile, and powerful tool. Writing helps students learn and it can help them become better readers (though research clearly indicates that both writing and reading competence will require substantial instruction in each separately as well as in combination). Students can use writing to help them better understand themselves. Writing also allows them to communicate with, entertain, and persuade others.

How Does Writing Develop?

While our understanding of how writing develops is not complete, we know enough to be certain that the road from novice to competent writer is strongly influenced by the context in which writing takes place and changes in students' writing skills, strategies, knowledge, and motivation (Graham, 2006a). First, writing is a social activity involving an implicit or explicit dialogue between writer(s) and reader(s). It also takes place in a broader context where the purposes and meaning of writing are shaped by cultural, societal, and historical factors. For instance, written discourse differs considerably among a group of friends tweeting to each other versus the types of academic text students are expected to write at school (Nystrand, 2006).

Writing is more than a social activity, however, as it requires the application of a variety of cognitive and affective processes. It is a goal-directed and self-sustained cognitive activity requiring the skillful management of the writing environment; the constraints imposed by the writing topic; the intentions of the writer(s); and the processes, knowledge, and skills involved in composing (Zimmerman & Reisemberg, 1997). Writers must juggle and master a commanding array of skills, knowledge, and processes, including knowledge about topic and genre; strategies for planning, drafting, revising, editing, and publishing text; as well as the skills needed to craft and transcribe ideas into sentences that convey the author's intended meaning. With the ongoing development of new ways of composing that can include visual and auditory information, this process has become even more demanding. Consistent with the conceptualizations above, two basic approaches have dominated much of the discussion about how writing develops. One viewpoint focuses on how context shapes writing development (Russell, 1997), whereas the other concentrates mostly on the role of cognition and motivation in writing (Hayes, 1996). Scholars of writing generally align themselves with one conceptualization or the other. We believe this is a mistake, as writing development (or instruction for that matter) cannot be adequately understood without considering both points of view. When we ask teachers about their writing practices, we find that they also think both points of view are essential, as evidenced by how they teach writing and what they believe about it (Cutler & Graham, 2008; Graham, Harris, Fink, & MacArthur, 2002).

Writing Development and Context

The contextual view of writing development in the classroom is aptly illustrated in a model developed by Russell (1997). A basic structure in this model is the activity system, which includes how actors (a student, pair of students, student and teacher, or class—perceived in social terms and taking into account the history of their involvement in the activity system) use concrete tools, such as paper and pencil or word processing, to accomplish an action leading to an outcome, such as writing a story or explaining how to apply a scientific principle. The outcome is accomplished in a problem space where the actors use writing tools in an ongoing interaction with others (peers and teachers) to shape the paper that is being produced over time in a shared direction.

A second basic structure in this model is the concept of genre. These are "typified ways of purposefully interacting in and among some activity system(s)" (Russell, 1997, p. 513). These typified ways of interacting become stabilized via regularized use of writing by and among students, creating a generally predictable approach for writing within a classroom (e.g., in some classes this takes the form of selecting a topic, planning, drafting, revising, editing, and publishing). These are conceived as only temporarily stabilized structures, however, because they are subject to change depending upon the context. For example, a new student entering a classroom with an established activity system for writing may appropriate some of the routinized tools used by his classmates, such as creating a semantic web for organizing writing ideas before drafting a paper. In turn, the new student may change typified ways of writing in a classroom, as other students in the class adapt unfamiliar routines applied by their new classmate, such as "free writing' ideas about the topic before creating a first draft of the paper.

While we are mostly concerned in this chapter with how Russell's (1997) model plays out in the classroom, it is not limited to that single context. Macrolevel activity systems involving culture, institution, family, and society shape what happens as well. An easy way to illustrate this is through the consequences of high-stakes testing for writing. Most states require high-stakes writing tests yearly with students in specific grades. This institutional action increases the amount of time devoted to teaching writing, at least during the years when it is tested (Graham et al., 2011). Not all of the effects of such testing are positive, however. Hillocks (2002) reported that it restricted writing instruction to what is measured. For instance, if narrative writing is tested in fourth grade, writing instruction may well be limited to this genre. Our experiences in schools substantiate this concern.

Writing Development and Cognitive/Motivational Capabilities

The cognitive/motivational view of writing development concentrates primarily on the individual writer and the mental and affective processes involved in composing text. This approach can be illustrated through a model of skilled writing developed by Hayes (1996). His model identifies the mental moves and motivational resources writers draw on as they compose text. These include the mental processes of text interpretation, reflection, and text production. Writers draw on these cognitive processes to create a representation of the writing task, develop a plan to complete it, draw conclusions about the audience and possible writing content, use cues from the writing plan or text produced so far to retrieve needed information from memory, turn these ideas and information into written sentences, and evaluate plans and text and modify them as needed. It also includes long-term memory (knowledge of the writing topic and audience as well as vocabulary, linguistic, morphological, and genre knowledge, including schemas for carrying carry out particular writing tasks), working memory (which serves as an interface between cognitive processes, motivation, and memory, providing a mental place for holding information and ideas for writing as well as carrying out mental operations that require the writer's conscious attention), and motivation (the goals, predispositions, beliefs, and attitudes that influence the writer and the writing process).

As Hayes's model shows, skilled writers are strategic, motivated, and knowledgeable about the craft of writing. Not as explicitly identified in Hayes's (1996) model are the skills and abilities writers use to transform ideas into sentences that are then translated into text through handwriting, typing, and spelling. The goal of writing instruction should be for students to be facile at developing sentences and extended text that clearly convey meaning and reflect the writer's intentions, as well as to automatize the transcription skills of handwriting, typing, and spelling so that they require little conscious attention on the part of the developing writer.

Russell's (1997) and Hayes's (1996) models provide a good roadmap for what we must attend to when designing an effective writing programs for students from kindergarten through grade 12 (one that complements and extends the CCSS). It is important to create a writing context in which students can flourish. This goal includes developing typified routines that facilitate writing development as well as addressing motivation and affect related to the writing process. It is also important to make sure students acquire the skills, strategies, knowledge, and will needed to become skilled writers (though such development over time is not fully understood). In the next section we identify best practices for achieving both of these goals, and make connections to other chapters in the book where specific best practices are described in greater detail.

What Are Best Practices in Writing Instruction?

Daniel Walker, the 1999 Alaska Teacher of the Year, rightly noted, "Teaching is brain surgery without breaking the skin. It should not be entered into lightly" (Sennette, 2003). This is especially true for the teaching of writing, as it is a very complex and demanding activity. How, then, can we identify best practices in the teaching of writing?

One possible source for identifying best practices in writing is to draw on the wisdom of professional writers. These highly skilled writers have offered many suggestions about how to teach writing over the centuries, ranging from Mark Twain's famous advice, "When you catch an adjective, kill it," to Winston Churchill's admonishment, "Short words are the best, and old words when short are the best of all." While professional writers surely possess considerable wisdom about writing, their advice is most often aimed at other skilled writers who seek to make writing their profession too. Consequently, we do not draw on this advice as a source for best practices for teaching developing writers in this chapter.

Another possible source for best practices comes from those who teach developing writers. Throughout their careers, teachers acquire incredible insights into how to teach students to write (see, e.g., Atwell, 1987, and Graves, 1983). The drawback to this approach to identifying best practices is that it is difficult to separate the "wheat from the chaff" to use a colloquial expression (Graham, 2010). There is usually no direct evidence showing which of the many methods a teacher uses is responsible for changes in students' writing. When evidence is provided for a specific method, it commonly takes the form of a testimonial, as the writing of selected students is presented to show that a method works. This makes it difficult to determine if the evidence provides a typical or an atypical picture of the method's impact. Moreover, if a method is drawn from the experiences of a single teacher (regardless of how effective that teacher is), there is no way to predict if it will be effective with other teachers.

To address these limitations, one way we identify best practices in this chapter is by examining the methods that exceptional teachers of literacy commonly apply when teaching writing (Graham & Perin, 2007b). This decision addresses the evidence issue above (at least in part), as students of these teachers made exceptional gains in their writing development. It also addresses the single teacher issue, as we only considered an instructional method a best practice if it was applied across most of the available studies of exceptional teachers. While our approach cannot establish that a particular method is solely responsible for improvements in students' writing, it is reasonable to assume that practices that are commonly applied by exceptional writing teachers are potentially more important than those applied idiosyncratically.

This teacher-based approach to identifying best practices should not distract or take away from the potential power or effectiveness of methods that you have established as effective in your own classroom. In fact, what we hope you do is combine these methods with the best practices identified in this chapter and throughout the book.

A third source for best practices can be drawn from scientific studies testing the effectiveness of specific writing practices. This provides a relatively trustworthy approach for identifying best practices, as such testing provides evidence on whether a procedure enhanced students' writing. It further makes it possible to determine how much confidence can be placed in the findings. As a result, the best practices identified in this chapter are also based on methods shown to be effective in scientific studies where writing outcomes were reliably assessed.

It must be noted that the scientific testing of instructional practices is not without its own problems. A scientifically validated practice is only as good as the evidence supporting it, and just because an instructional method was effective in multiple research studies does not guarantee that it will be effective in all other situations. There is hardly ever a perfect match between the conditions under which a writing method was implemented in a scientific study and the conditions in which it will subsequently be applied in your classroom (Graham, McKeown, Kiuhara, & Harris, 2012). The safest course of action is to monitor the effects of any best practice from this chapter you implement in your class to be sure it works with your students.

In the next sections, we identify teacher-based and scientifically based best practices that can be used to create an effective writing program. We structure the presentation of these practices so that they are responsive to what we know about writing development from a contextual as well as a cognitive/affective/motivational viewpoint. This includes creating a writing environment in which students can flourish and making sure they develop the skills, strategies, knowledge, and motivation needed to become skilled writers. We address each of these topics separately, with the exception of motivation, which is primarily addressed in the section on creating a supportive classroom environment. Teacher-based best practices are drawn from an analysis of studies examining the writing practices of exceptional literacy teachers conducted by Graham and Perin (2007b), whereas scientifically based practices are taken from comprehensive reviews of scientific studies testing specific instructional writing methods (Bangert-Drown, 1993; Goldberg, Russell, & Cook, 2003; Graham, 2006b; Graham et al., 2012; Graham & Harris, 2003; Graham et al., 2011; Graham, Harris, & McKeown, 2013; Graham et al., in press; Graham & Perin, 2007a, 2007c; Hillocks, 1986; Morphy & Graham, 2012; Rogers & Graham, 2008; Sandmel & Graham, 2011).

Create a Supportive Classroom Where Writing Development Can Flourish

Writing is hard work and learning to write well is even harder. Students are less likely to put forth their best efforts when writing or learning to write if they view the classroom as an unfriendly, chaotic, high-risk, or punitive place. Many students evidence mental withdrawal or evasion of productive work in such situations (Hansen, 1989). This makes it especially important to develop a classroom writing environment that is interesting, pleasant, and nonthreatening, where the teacher supports students and students support each other. This viewpoint is also evident in the classrooms of highly effective literacy teachers (Graham & Perin, 2007b), where they:

- Are enthusiastic about writing and the teaching of writing, establishing a stimulating mood during writing time.
- Make students' writing visible by encouraging them to share it with others; displaying it on the wall; and publishing it in anthologies, books, or other classroom collections.
- Create a positive environment in which students are encouraged to try hard, to believe that the writing skills and strategies they are learning will permit them to write well, and to attribute success to effort and the tactics they are learning (also see Boscolo & Gelati, Chapter 12, this volume).
- Set high but realistic expectations for students, encouraging them to surpass previous efforts or accomplishments.
- Provide just enough support to students so they can make progress or carry out writing tasks, but encourage them to act in a self-regulated fashion, doing as much as they can on their own.
- Adapt writing assignments and instruction so that they are appropriate to the interests and needs of their students (see also Olson, Scarcella, & Matuchniak, Chapter 16, and Troia, Chapter 17, this volume).
- Keep students engaged by involving them in thoughtful activities (such as gathering information for their composition) versus activities require less thoughtfulness (such as completing a workbook page that can be finished quickly, leaving many students disengaged).
- Create classroom routines that promote positive interactions among students.

Many of these same teacher-based best practices are also evident in the process approach to writing. This includes the following motivating and supportive practices: writing for real audiences; encouraging personal responsibility and ownership of writing projects; promoting high levels of student interactions, creating a pleasant and positive writing environment; and encouraging self-reflection and evaluation. It is important to keep in mind that this approach to teaching writing involves other instructional components such as creating routines in which students are asked to plan, draft, revise, and edit their text. While scientific studies testing the process approach do not provide evidence on the effectiveness of specific aspects of this method, such as the motivational and supportive practices identified above, the available research demonstrates that this overall approach does improve how well students in grades 1 to 12 write (see Sandmell & Graham, 2011, for a review of scientific studies).

Three specific writing practices that are supported by scientific testing are praise, goal setting, and creating instructional arrangements where students write together (see reviews by Graham et al., 2011; Graham et al., in press; Graham & Perin, 2007c; Rogers & Graham, 2008). When teachers reinforce a positive feature of students' writing, such as good word choice, students are more likely to make such choices in future papers. When providing such praise, it is important to be specific about what you like.

Providing students with clear, specific, and reasonably challenging goals improves the quality of what they write. Examples of such goals include:

- Asking elementary grade students to add three new ideas to their paper when revising it.
- Asking middle school students to address both sides of an argument when writing, providing three or more reasons to support their point of view, and countering at least two reasons supporting the opposing view.

For both elementary and secondary students, creating arrangements where students work together to plan, draft, revise, or edit a composition improves the quality of what they write (see also Lassonde & Richards, Chapter 8, and MacArthur, Chapter 9, this volume). The key to creating such routines is to provide students with specific directions and guidelines for what they will do when working together and to directly teach them how to apply these procedures. An example of peers working together to compose a composition is provided in Figure 1.3.

We believe the most critical element in creating an environment where students can prosper and grow as writers is for them to write. The basic premise underlying this assumption is that students need to write frequently and regularly to become comfortable with writing, develop their ideas as

---

Lonnie Bird taught his third-grade students how to work with another peer to plan, draft, revise, and edit their papers. Students were taught to work together as partners as they composed. He modeled and they practiced how to help each other with a variety of basic writing tasks including generating ideas, creating a draft, rereading essays, editing essays, choosing the best copy, and evaluating the final product. As they jointly composed papers, he monitored, prompted, and praised students and addressed their concerns. Based on Yarrow & Topping (2001).

FIGURE 1.3. Example of students working together to compose a composition.

they write, and further hone their skills as writers. Surprisingly, students spend very little time writing in school. When they do write, their writing is rarely longer than a single paragraph (Applebee & Langer, 2011; Gilbert & Graham, 2010; Kiuhara et al., 2009). Highly effective literacy teachers, however, recognize that writing is essential, as youngsters in their classrooms (Graham & Perin, 2007c):

- Write often and for many different purposes, including to inform, persuade, and entertain (see also McKeough, Chapter 4; Ferretti & Lewis, Chapter 5; and Newell, VanDerHeide, & Wilson, Chapter 6, this volume).
- Write frequently across the curriculum (see also Perin, Chapter 3, and Klein & Yu, Chapter 7, this volume).

These teacher-based best practices are supported by scientific experiments showing that increasing the frequency of elementary grade students' writing improves how well they write (Graham et al., in press) and writing about material read or presented in content classes improves learning (Bangert-Drowns et al., 2004; Graham & Hebert, 2010, 2011; Graham & Perin, 2007a). We also think it is important for students to:

- Write for real audiences and purposes (see Figure 1.4 for an example).
- Make personal choices about what they write, including encouraging them to develop unique interpretations of assigned writing topics.
- Write for extended periods of time about single topics.

Developing a supportive writing environment also requires some consideration of the tools students use when writing. Many schools still use 19th-century writing tools such as pencil and paper, even though scientific studies demonstrate that students in grades 1 to 12 show greater improvement in their writing over time when they use word processing to write at school versus writing by hand (Bangert-Drowns, 1993; Goldberg et al., 2003; Morphy & Graham, 2012). Word processors have a number of advantages over writing by hand, as electronic text is legible; electronic text can easily be deleted, added to, rewritten, or moved; word processors are bundled with other software such as spell checkers or speech synthesis that can support the writer; and word processors can be connected to the web and other programs in which students can gather material for what they write as well as share their text with others. Despite these advantages, students still do most of their writing for school by hand (Cutler & Graham, 2008; Gilbert & Graham, 2010; Kiuhara et al., 2009). We obviously need

Victoria Moretti and her class of fourth-grade students in Virginia planned a project to help save the Chesapeake Bay (Graham, 2013). They set out to clean a stream that ran behind their school and whose water eventually fed the bay. The class carried out a variety of writing tasks to help them meet their objective, including:

- Writing letters to the mayor and town council indicating why it was important that the bay become cleaner, how they were helping to make this a reality, and what the mayor and town council could do.
- Writing letters to two local newspapers indicating why local streams, rivers, and estuaries must be kept clean.
- Writing and performing a play for younger students at the school, showing what happens to fish and other wildlife when streams are polluted.
- Writing key message on placards for a "Save-the-Bay" rally held at a local mall.
- Creating a list of activities for creating a cleaner bay (after interviewing parents, accessing online resources, and contacting environmental experts).

FIGURE 1.4. Example of writing for a real purpose.

to move writing instruction more squarely into the 21st century, making it possible for our students to take advantage of word processing and other electronic methods for composing (see Chapter 13).

Finally, teacher assessment is essential to creating a supportive writing environment. When teachers monitor their students' progress as writers, they can adjust classroom practices to meet the collective as well as the individual needs of their students. When they provide students with feedback, they facilitate the learning of writing skills, strategies, or knowledge by helping students evaluate their progress and determine if they need to exert more effort to be successful (Pass, Van Merrienboer, & Van Gog, 2012). Scientific studies have demonstrated that both of these assessment activities enhance students' writing performance (Graham et al., 2011; see Calfee & Miller, Chapter 15, this volume, for additional information on best practices in writing assessment).

Teach Writing Strategies

Writers employ a variety of strategies to help them manage the writing process and to create and improve what they write (Zimmerman & Riesemberg, 1996). These strategies include goal setting and planning (e.g., establishing rhetorical goals and tactics to achieve them), seeking information (e.g., gathering information for writing), record keeping (e.g., making notes), organizing (e.g., ordering notes or text), transforming (e.g., visualizing a character to facilitate written description), self-monitoring (e.g., checking to see if writing goals are met), reviewing records (e.g., reading notes or the text produced so far), self-evaluating (e.g., assessing the quality of text or proposed plans), revising (e.g., modifying text or plans for writing), self-verbalizing (e.g., saying dialogue aloud or personal articulations about what needs to be done), rehearsing (e.g., trying out a scene before writing it), environmental structuring (e.g., finding a quiet place to write), time planning (e.g., estimating and budgeting time for writing), and self-consequating (e.g., going to a movie as a reward for completing a writing task).

Highly effective teachers emphasize the use and teaching of such strategies (Graham & Perin, 2007b), as they:

- Encourage students to treat writing as a process.
- Teach students strategies for planning, drafting, revising, and editing text.

The practice of explicitly teaching students strategies for planning, drafting, evaluating, and revising text is supported by scientific experiments showing that such instruction strongly improves the quality of writing produced by students in grades 1 to 12 (see reviews by Graham, 2006b; Graham & Harris, 2003; Graham et al., 2011, 2013). Strategies that improve students' writing performance range from more general processes such as brainstorming or semantic webbing (which can be applied across genres) to planning and revising strategies designed for specific types of writing, such as writing an explanation or writing to persuade (see also Lassonde & Richards, Chapter 8, and MacArthur, Chapter 9, this volume).

At the most basic level, writing strategies instruction involves the teacher explaining the purpose and rationale of the strategy (as well as when and where to use it); modeling how to use the strategy (often multiple times); providing students with assistance in applying the strategy until they can apply it independently and effectively; and facilitating continued and adaptive use of the strategy (again through explanation, modeling, and guided practice). This basic routine for teaching writing strategies is enhanced when students are shown how to regulate the planning, drafting, revising, or editing strategies taught (see Graham et al., 2013). This includes teaching them how to set goals for learning and using the strategies as well as monitoring the impact the strategy use has on their writing. The advantage of making such gains visible to students is that it is motivating and increases the likelihood they will use the strategy in the future. Figure 1.5 presents an example of a strategy for planning and drafting an essay and provides a brief description of the basic procedures used to teach it (We refer readers to Graham & Harris, 2005, and Harris, Graham, Mason, &

> Henry Bear taught his 10th-grade class the following strategies for planning and drafting an essay (based on De La Paz & Graham, 2002):
>
> - PLAN (*P*ay attention to the prompt, *L*ist the main idea, *A*dd supporting ideas, *N*umber your ideas)
> - WRITE (*W*ork from your plan to develop your thesis statement, *R*emember your goals, *I*nclude transition words for each paragraph, *T*ry to use different kinds of sentences, and *E*xciting, interesting, $10,000 words).
>
> He taught these strategies using the self-regulated strategy development model (based on Harris et al., 2008). It includes the following six stages of instruction:
>
> - *Develop background knowledge*. Students were taught background knowledge needed to use the strategy successfully.
> - *Describe it*. The strategy as well as its purpose and benefits was described and discussed.
> - *Model it*. Henry Bear modeled how to use the strategy.
> - *Memorize it*. The students memorized the steps of the strategy and the accompanying mnemonics.
> - *Support it*. Henry Bear supported students' use of the strategy, providing assistance as needed.
> - *Independent use*. Students used the strategy with few or no supports.
>
> Students were also taught a number of self-regulation skills (including goal setting, self-monitoring, self-instruction, and self-reinforcement) to help them manage the writing strategies, the writing process, and their behavior.

FIGURE 1.5. Strategy for planning and drafting an essay.

Freidlander, 2008, for other scientifically validated writing strategies and a more complete description of the self-regulated strategy development model used to develop these strategies).

Help Students Acquire the Knowledge Needed to Write Effectively

Two types of knowledge that are especially important to writers are knowledge about the writing topic and knowledge about the genre(s) in which the writer will present this topic information. In a recent study (Olinghouse, Graham, & Gillespie, 2012), we found that both types of knowledge made a unique and significant contribution to predicting the quality of students' writing across different genres. This observation is buttressed by scientific intervention studies showing that methods used to help students access or organize topic knowledge in advance of writing improves the quality of what they write, whereas methods used to enhance students' knowledge of genres and the characteristics of good writing result in better text (see Graham et al., 2013; Graham & Perin, 2007c).

One scientifically based best practice for helping students acquire information to write about is prewriting activities. With these types of activities, students locate information through brainstorming, reading, or other informational-gathering procedures. They may also use a graphic organizer to help them structure this information. Another means for acquiring possible writing content is through inquiry. This is characterized by setting a clearly specified goal for the writing task (e.g., describe the actions of people), analyzing concrete and immediate data to obtain information needed to complete the task (e.g., observe one or more peers during specific activities), using specific strategies to conduct the analysis (e.g., retrospectively ask the person being observed the reason for their action), and applying what was learned (e.g., write a story where the insights from the inquiry are incorporated into the composition).

Two scientifically based best practices for acquiring information about specific genres or the characteristics of good writing include (1) teaching students about the characteristics of specific types of text (e.g., stories have a setting, starting event, characters, actions, resolution, and so forth) and (2) providing them with good models for the types of writing they are expected to create (see Figure 1.6 and McKeough, Chapter 4, this volume). Both activities have a positive impact on the quality of what students write (Graham et al., 2013; Graham & Perin, 2007c).

Dorothy Caldwell, a seventh-grade teacher, initiated a discussion with her class about the characteristics of a good persuasive paper. As they generated ideas, she listed them on a white board, providing a label for common persuasive elements such as claim and evidence. Next, they read an especially strong persuasive essay together and talked about the characteristics of the text that made it so convincing. They then conducted a "persuasive element hunt" as they read other persuasive essays to find and discuss other persuasive elements. These were also listed on the white board. Again, Mrs. Caldwell provided labels for these elements or characteristics (e.g., "transition words"). Using the first persuasive essay as a model, students were asked to generate their own persuasive essay on whether people should be allowed to use their cell phone at school. They shared their essay with one or more peers (and in some instances with the class), receiving feedback on what worked and how they could make it even better. As they developed additional essays, they were encouraged to go beyond the initial models they used as a guide.

FIGURE 1.6. Teaching students about the characteristics of a good persuasive paper.

Teach Foundational Writing Skills

Skilled writers rarely think about handwriting, typing, or spelling. They execute these skills correctly and with little to no conscious attention. Until they are mastered, these skills create several undesirable consequences for developing writing. One, misspellings and difficult-to-read handwriting makes text more difficult to read, and readers are more negative about the ideas in such text (Graham et al., 2011). Two, having to devote conscious attention to handwriting, typing, and spelling interferes with other writing processes (Scardamalia & Bereiter, 1986). For instance, having to switch attention to think about how to spell a word can lead the writer to forget ideas or plans held in working memory.

It is best to teach these transcription skills early, as children who experience difficulties with them may avoid writing and develop a mind-set that they cannot write (Berninger, Mizokawa, & Bragg, 1991). Scientific studies show that teaching handwriting, spelling, and typing to children in the primary grades has a positive impact on their writing (Graham et al., 2013). In effect, interference from these skills is lessened, as children become increasingly fluent and correct in executing them. Figure 1.7 presents an example of best practices for spelling (see also Schlagel, Chapter 11, this volume, for best practices in handwriting and spelling).

A major part of a writer's effort when drafting text is involved in transforming ideas into the words and syntactic structures that convey the author's intended meanings. These goals include constructing sentences as well as using appropriate grammar, punctuation, capitalization, and so forth. Scientific studies show that teaching such sentence constructions

---

Every 2 weeks, Cady Longmire introduces her second-grade class to two contrasting spelling patterns (e.g., short vowels /a/ and /o/; short and long /a/; or long vowels /ay/ and /ai/). These patterns are introduced through a word-sorting activity, in which she sorts words involving the two patterns into different piles. She provides students with hints on why each card is placed in a particular pile (e.g., emphasizing a specific sound in a word), leading students to discover and specifically state (with her help) the rule underlying the spelling patterns. During the next 2 weeks, students:

- Search for words in their reading and writing that fit the patterns.
- Learn to spell common words that fit the patterns by playing games (e.g., tic-tac-toe spelling).
- Build words with the patterns by adding consonants, blends, or diagraphs to rimes representing the patter (e.g., the rime *at* for short /a/).

FIGURE 1.7. Teaching spelling skills.

skills not only improves the sentences students write (Andrews et al., 2006), but the quality of the text they produce (Graham et al., 2013; Graham & Perin, 2007c). Such instruction typically involves teaching students how to combine simpler sentences into more sophisticated ones. With this approach, the teacher models how to combine two or more sentences into a more complex one. Students practice combining similar sentences to produce the same type of sentence the teacher did. Students then apply the sentence-combining skill in text they produce (see also Saddler, Chapter 10, this volume).

It is also helpful to teach students strategies for writing different types of paragraphs, as this improves their ability to create such constructions (Rogers & Graham, 2008). An example of such a strategy involves procedures for developing a paragraph with an opening sentence, sentences that provide details related to the opening sentence, and a closing or passing sentence (to the next paragraph).

Bringing It All Together

As this chapter shows, the teaching of writing is not a simple task nor should it be the province of amateurs. A good starting point in designing an effective writing program is to determine how you will create a supportive writing environment. This task includes thinking about how to create a pleasant and supportive writing environment; what needs to be done to enhance students' motivation to write; how students will support each other in a positive manner; and how assessment, evaluation, and feedback will be used in your classroom.

One critical issue to consider is what genres students need to develop competence in across the elementary, middle, and high school grades. At the end of elementary school, students should be well prepared for the demands of middle school, and similarly, at the end of middle school, students should be well prepared for the demands of high school. Then, it is important to determine what types of writing you want students to engage in during the course of the school year and exactly how writing will be used to support reading and learning. We then suggest that you think about what students need to learn about each of these forms or genres of writing. Consideration must also be given to the types of writing strategies (planning, drafting, revising, and editing) your students should master to use these forms of writing effectively as well as the foundational skills (handwriting, typing, spelling, sentence construction, paragraph construction) that are still require instruction.

Once you know what types of writing you plan to emphasize, how students will use writing to support reading and learning, and what you will

teach, preliminary plans must be made as to how much time will be allotted to each aspect of the writing program (balancing the amount of time
devoted to writing and instruction); how all of this will be sequenced; and
how specific strategies, knowledge, and skills will be taught.

We further encourage you to think about the role of word processing
and other 21st-century writing tools in your program; the types of adaptations that you might need to make for students in your classroom; and how
your writing program will connect to what other teachers in the school are
doing and the community at large. Like writing, planning a writing program is a recursive and messy process that changes and must be at times
reconceptualized as it unfolds. While there is no perfect writing program,
this chapter and the book provide you with a wide variety of best practices
for helping all students become skilled writers.

References

Andrews, R., Torgerson, C., Beverton, S., Freeman, A., Locke, T., Low, G., et
al. (2006). The effects of grammar teaching on writing development. *British
Educational Research Journal, 32,* 39–55.

Applebee, A. (1984). Writing and reasoning. *Review of Educational Research, 54,*
577–596.

Applebee, A., & Langer, J. (2011). A snapshot of writing instruction in middle and
high schools. *English Journal, 100,* 14–27.

Atwell, N. (1987). *In the middle: Reading, writing, and learning from adolescents.*
Portsmouth, NH: Heinemann.

Bangert-Drowns, R. L. (1993). The word processor as an instructional tool: A
meta-analysis of word processing in writing instruction. *Review of Educational Research, 63,* 69–93.

Bangert-Drowns, R. L., Hurley, M. M., & Wilkinson, B. (2004). The effects of
school-based writing-to-learn interventions on academic achievement: A
meta-analysis. *Review of Educational Research, 74,* 29–58.

Berninger, V., Mizokawa, D., & Bragg, R. (1991). Theory-based diagnosis and
remediation of writing disabilities. *Journal of School Psychology, 29,* 57–79.

Cutler, L., & Graham, S. (2008). Primary grade writing instruction: A national
survey. *Journal of Educational Psychology, 100,* 907–919.

De La Paz, S., & Graham, S. (2002). Explicitly teaching strategies, skills, and
knowledge: Writing instruction in middle school classrooms. *Journal of Educational Psychology, 94,* 687698.

Fitzgerald, J., & Shanahan, T. (2000). Reading and writing relations and their
development. *Educational Psychologist, 35,* 39–50.

Gilbert, J., & Graham, S. (2010). Teaching writing to elementary students in grades
4 to 6: A national survey. *Elementary School Journal, 110,* 494–518.

Goldberg, A., Russell, M., & Cook, A. (2003). The effect of computers on student
writing: A meta-analysis of studies from 1992 to 2002. *Journal of Technology,*

Learning, and Assessment, 2. Retrieved from *http://escholarship.bc.edu/jtla/vol2/1*.

Graham, S. (2006a). Writing. In P. Alexander & P. Winne (Eds.), *Handbook of educational psychology* (pp. 457–478). Mahwah, NJ: Erlbaum.

Graham, S. (2006b). Strategy instruction and the teaching of writing: A meta-analysis. In C. A. MacArthur, S. Graham, & J. Fitzgerald (Eds.), *Handbook of writing research* (pp. 187–207). New York: Guilford Press.

Graham, S. (2010). Teaching writing. In P. Hogan (Ed.), *Cambridge encyclopedia of language sciences* (pp. 848–851). Cambridge, UK: Cambridge University Press.

Graham, S. (2013). Writing standards. In L. M. Morrow, K. K. Wixson, & T. Shanahan (Eds.), *Teaching with the Common Core standards for English language arts, Grades 3–5* (pp. 88–106). New York: Guilford Press.

Graham, S., Bollinger, A., Booth Olson, C., D'Aoust, C., MacArthur, C., McCutchen, D., et al. (2012). *Teaching elementary school students to be effective writers: A practice guide*. Washington, DC: National Center for Education Evaluation and Regional Assistance (NCEE), Institute of Education Sciences, U.S. Department of Education. Retrieved from *http://ies.ed.gov/ncee/wwc/publications/practiceguides*.

Graham, S., & Harris, K. R. (2003). Students with learning disabilities and the process of writing: A meta-analysis of SRSD studies. In H. L. Swanson, K. R. Harris, & S. Graham (Eds.), *Handbook of learning disabilities* (pp. 383–402). New York: Guilford Press.

Graham, S., & Harris, K. R. (2005). *Writing better: Teaching writing processes and self-regulation to students with learning problems*. Baltimore: Brookes.

Graham, S., Harris, K. R., Fink, B., & MacArthur, C. A. (2002). Primary grade teachers' theoretical orientations concerning writing instruction: Construct validation and a nationwide survey. *Contemporary Educational Psychology, 27*, 147166.

Graham, S., Harris, K. R., & Hebert, M. (2011). *Informing writing: The benefits of formative assessment*. Washington, DC: Alliance for Excellence in Education.

Graham, S., Harris, K. R., & McKeown, D. (2013). The writing of students with learning disabilities, meta-analysis of self-regulated strategy development writing intervention studies, and future directions: Redux. In L. Swanson, K. R. Harris, & S. Graham (Eds.), *Handbook of learning disabilities* (2nd ed., pp. 405–438). New York: Guilford Press.

Graham, S., & Hebert, M. (2010). *Writing to reading: Evidence for how writing can improve reading*. Washington, DC: Alliance for Excellence in Education.

Graham, S., & Hebert, M. (2011). Writing-to-read: A meta-analysis of the impact of writing and writing instruction on reading. *Harvard Educational Review, 81*, 710–744.

Graham, S., MacArthur, C., & Fitzgerald, J. (2007). *Best practices in writing instruction*. New York: Guilford Press.

Graham, S., McKeown, D., Kiuhara, S., & Harris, K. R. (2012). A meta-analysis of writing instruction for students in the elementary grades. *Journal of Educational Psychology, 104*(4), 879–896.

Graham, S., & Perrin, D. (2007a). *Writing next: Effective strategies to improve writing of adolescent middle and high school.* Washington, DC: Alliance for Excellence in Education.

Graham, S., & Perrin, D. (2007b). What we know, what we still need to know: Teaching adolescents to write. *Scientific Studies in Reading, 11,* 313–336.

Graham, S., & Perrin, D. (2007c). A meta-analysis of writing instruction for adolescent students. *Journal of Educational Psychology, 99,* 445–476.

Graves, D. (1983). *Writing: Teachers and children at work.* Exeter, NH: Heinemann.

Hansen, D. (1989). Lesson evading and lesson dissembling: Ego strategies in the classroom. *American Journal of Education, 97,* 184–208.

Harris, K. R., Graham, S., Mason, L., & Friedlander, B. (2008). *Powerful writing strategies for all students.* Baltimore: Brookes.

Hayes, J. (1996). A new framework for understanding cognition and affect in writing. In M. Levy & S. Ransdell (Eds.), *The science of writing: Theories, methods, individual differences, and applications* (pp. 1–27). Mahwah, NJ: Erbaum.

Hillocks, G. (1986). *Research on written composition: New directions for teaching.* Urbana, IL: National Council of Teachers of English.

Hillocks, G. (2002). *The testing trap: How state writing assessments control learning.* New York: Teachers College Press.

Kiuhara, S., Graham, S., & Hawken, L. (2009). Teaching writing to high school students: A national survey. *Journal of Educational Psychology, 101,* 136–160.

Morphy, P., & Graham, S. (2012). Word processing programs and weaker writers/readers: A meta-analysis of research findings. *Reading and Writing: An Interdisciplinary Journal, 25,* 641–678.

National Governors Association & Council of Chief State School Officers. (2010). *Common Core State Standards for English language arts & literacy in history/social studies, science, and technical subjects.* Washington, DC: Authors. Retrieved from *www.corestandards.org.*

Nystrand, M. (2006). The social and historical context for writing research. In C. A. MacArthur, S. Graham, & J. Fitzgerald (Eds.), *Handbook of writing research* (pp. 11–27). New York: Guilford Press.

Olinghouse, N., Graham, S., & Gillespie, A. (2012, February). *The role of discourse and content knowledge in the narrative, persuasive, and informational writing of fourth grade students.* A presentation at the Pacific Coast Research Conference, Coronado, CA.

Paas, F., Van Merrienboer, J., & Van Gog, T. (2012). Designing instruction for the contemporary learning landscape. In K. R. Harris, S. Graham, & T. Urdan (Eds.), *APA educational psychology handbook* (Vol. 3, pp. 335–358). Washington, DC: American Psychological Association.

Rogers, L., & Graham, S. (2008). A meta-analysis of single subject design writing intervention research. *Journal of Educational Psychology, 100,* 879–906.

Russell, D. (1997). Rethinking genre in school and society: An activity theory analysis. *Written Communication, 14,* 504–554.

Sandmel, K., & Graham, S. (2011). The process writing approach: A meta-analysis. *Journal of Educational Research, 104*, 396–407.

Scardamalia, M., & Bereiter, C. (1986). Written composition. In M. Wittrock (Ed.), *Handbook of research on teaching* (3rd ed., pp. 778–803). New York: Macmillan.

Sennett, F. (2003). *Teacher of the year.* Chicago: Contemporary Books.

Smyth, J. (1998). Written emotional expression: Effect sizes, outcome types, and moderating variables. *Journal of Consulting and Clinical Psychology, 66*, 174–184.

Tierney, R., & Shanahan, T. (1991). Research on the reading–writing relationship: Interactions, transactions, and outcomes. In R. Barr, M. Kamil, P. Mosenthal, & D. Pearson (Eds.), *The handbook of reading research* (Vol. 2, pp. 246–280). New York: Longman.

Yarrow, F., & Topping, K. J. (2001). Collaborative writing: The effects of metacognitive prompting and structured peer interaction. *British Journal of Educational Psychology, 71*, 261–282.

Zimmerman, B., & Reisemberg, R. (1997). Becoming a self-regulated writer: A social cognitive perspective. *Contemporary Educational Psychology, 22*, 73–101.

Chapter 2

Writing Instruction in Preschool and Kindergarten

DAVID L. COKER, JR.

Writing may be one of the most difficult academic tasks for students. Years of instruction and practice are necessary to develop the knowledge, skill, and dispositions of a strong writer. However, including effective writing instruction when students begin preschool and kindergarten can strengthen students' writing achievement. To help readers interested in writing development and instruction in the early years, this chapter is organized around two goals. First, I hope that readers will appreciate the substantial challenges involved in young children's writing, particularly the confluence of skills and knowledge necessary to write well. The major writing challenges discussed in this chapter include understanding how we use writing to communicate; unlocking the conventions or concepts of print; discovering that the alphabet is used to represent speech sounds; deepening linguistic knowledge; developing knowledge of the world and of text genre; and writing or typing well enough to express ideas fluently. The second goal for this chapter is to present instructional approaches to address each of the challenges. The instructional methods were selected because they are appropriate for preschool and kindergarten classrooms, and they have been demonstrated to be effective. At the end of the chapter, I describe a writing lesson taught by Mrs. Nelson in her kindergarten classroom. In the context of a single lesson, Mrs. Nelson demonstrates how teachers can provide engaging instruction that addresses many of the writing challenges that students face when they write an opinion piece. The description of the writing challenges students face as well as the instructional suggestions that accompany them reflect the theoretical position that writing development is complex and can be attributed to the interplay of cognitive, social, linguistic, cultural, and instructional forces (Berninger & Chanquoy, 2012).

The Common Core State Standards and Writing

The recent landscape of writing instruction in the United States has begun what is likely to be a monumental change. The catalyst for this change is the widespread adoption of the Common Core State Standards (CCSS; National Governors Association & Council of Chief State School Officers, 2010). Every U.S. state except for five has elected to implement the CCSS. The CCSS have the potential to focus and transform writing instruction by providing teachers and schools with a set of expectations for the skills, processes, and products that will be expected of students from kindergarten through 12th grade. I suspect that in many preschools and kindergartens teachers will be examining the standards closely to determine how their instruction should evolve to address the standards.

The CCSS writing standards target three areas. The first is text types and purposes, which present progressively more sophisticated expectations for narrative, informative and opinion pieces from kindergarten through 12th grade. As most teachers know, young students have considerable difficulty writing connected text. Furthermore, students rarely have the kind of sophisticated genre knowledge that would allow them to write a complex story or a detailed informative text. The kindergarten standards recognize the limitations of young writers. To compensate for students' difficulties writing extended texts, the standards call for a range of compositional methods—including drawing and dictating. Furthermore, the expectations for each genre are somewhat limited. For example, the story standard requires that students describe an event (or several events) in chronological order with some kind of evaluation. Some of the more complex narrative elements, such as character development and conflict resolution, are not expected of kindergarteners. The second writing domain in the kindergarten standards is the production and distribution of writing. For this domain students are expected to improve their work by adding details and be involved with a range of methods for composing and publishing their writing. Once again, the expectations are made with the understanding that considerable help will be needed from adults. The final domain of the standards involves using research to inform writing. For this domain kindergarteners are expected to be involved in limited projects and to provide information from experiences or sources to pursue a question. The expectations are also made with the understanding that adults will be supporting students' work.

As teachers begin to study the standards, they will quickly notice some of their limitations. First, there are no writing standards (or any other standards) for preschoolers. The omission suggests several things. By beginning in kindergarten the CCSS make an implicit claim that meaningful writing does not begin until then. Additionally this perspective ignores the important work that teachers and students do, and need to do, in preschool to prepare for later writing challenges.

Similarly, the writing standards also neglect many of the skills and domains of knowledge that young students need in order to be strong writers. Some of these skills appear in the Common Core language standards, including alphabet and print knowledge as well as vocabulary development. However, by separating the standards, the authors of the CCSS suggest that the language and writing standards are less integrated than they really are.

Another critique of the kindergarten writing standards is that they ignore much of what is known about writing development. The developmental progression is widely recognized as more complicated than moving from early forms of a text type to more elaborated or sophisticated ones (Berninger & Chanquoy, 2012). Others have noted that the standards were designed by first identifying the writing forms and processes that students would need in college. The authors of the standards then worked backward to determine what would be reasonable standards for each grade level (Meisels, 2011). While this seems like a logical approach to prepare students for college-level work, it sacrifices what we know about the developmental process of writing.

The work of this chapter is to discuss how teachers in preschool and kindergarten can address the writing standards of the Common Core while also considering the important writing skills and processes that the CCSS do not target.

The Writing Challenge

Consider for a moment the task for a kindergarten student who has been asked to write an informational text about one thing she learned during a recent field trip to the science museum. To make sense of the assignment, she should be aware that writing serves as a tool for communicating ideas. Even in the highly regulated context of a classroom assignment, she needs to appreciate how people use writing to share information, and she must recognize that her teacher expects her to describe the experience well enough so that someone who did not join the class would understand.

The child sorts through her memory of the event, which could include everything from the demonstration of static electricity given by the guide to the argument she had with a friend on the bus to the miraculous water faucets in the bathroom that turn on when you put your hands in the sink. From the collection of memories of the field trip, she must decide which events are relevant to the task and which ones are not. To make the decision, she might be thinking about the expectations of her reader, who is probably her teacher. She also needs to choose how to organize her writing. By the end of kindergarten, her teacher will expect that she can identify the topic of her piece and provide some details. At this point in the year she may be unsure how to present her ideas. In her mind, she may debate whether she should follow the generic conventions of fairy tales and begin with the line "once upon a time," or adopt another frame such as a simple description. The decision will draw on her knowledge about how writers package and present their text.

Once she decides how to organize the piece, she must select the right words to represent her memories. The choices will depend on the breadth and depth of her vocabulary knowledge, particularly the technical words she may need to describe her visit to the science museum. The ideas she selects are then connected to each other through her understanding of syntax and planned at the sentence level. In order to write the words, she draws on her spelling knowledge. If she has difficulty spelling any of the words, which is likely, she might use a common spelling strategy such as segmenting the word into its individual sounds. When the sounds are isolated, she relies on her knowledge of the alphabetic principle to select the right letter or letters to represent each sound.

Even if she has quick access to a word's spelling, she needs to be able to write the letters. If her recall of the letter shapes or the motor plans for forming letters do not operate swiftly, she may labor just inscribing the words on the page. If her handwriting demands close attention, she runs the risk of forgetting her plans for words and sentence structure. As she writes, she must follow the conventions of English that dictate that she print in a row from left to right and use spaces to separate words. She also works to maintain her attention on the writing task and to try to ignore her best friend who has just slipped her a drawing on the way to the pencil sharpener.

The previous description was intended to demonstrate that writing is an immensely complex social, cognitive, and linguistic task. The challenges that children face as they develop into writers are substantial; however, thoughtful, responsive writing instruction can support young students and speed their growth as writers.

Challenge 1: Understanding How We Use Writing to Communicate

One essential lesson for young students is that writing is a way to share ideas and communicate. Although the CCSS do not target this lesson in a specific standard, it is impossible for students to meet the writing standards without understanding how writing can be used to communicate. This fundamental insight about writing must be learned through experience with writing and print (Tolchinsky, 2001). Very young children learn that oral language is a symbolic system used for communication. A crucial difference between speaking and writing is that young children have considerably more experience with oral forms than they do with written forms. Furthermore, evidence reveals that children's exposure to the uses and practices of writing and reading varies widely (Purcell-Gates, 1996). The amount and nature of exposure children have to writing and text-related practices may be related to how well they understand the way writing functions (Purcell-Gates, 1996). In one study of low-SES (socioeconomic status) students, Purcell-Gates and Dahl (1991) found that children entering first grade differed in how well they understood the uses and communicative nature of print. The differences in print understanding were related to the students' success in literacy instruction. Children who see the adults in their lives using writing in a variety of ways to express their ideas and to communicate may come to appreciate the utility of writing faster and better.

Children need to be introduced to the various ways in which we use writing to communicate in society and to gain practice using writing as a form of communication. As Wong and Berninger (2004) noted, an important instructional goal for developing writers is to learn that writing is similar to speaking because both offer ways to communicate with others. Children benefit from opportunities to see how adults use writing and to practice those forms.

In the classroom, teachers can create opportunities for students to observe and participate in authentic literacy activities through the use of thematic play areas. For example, by setting up a classroom post office where students can mail notes to each other and to others outside the classroom, teachers can create opportunities for students to use writing in a meaningful way. Other literacy-rich play areas might include a restaurant with menus and notebooks for servers to record patrons' orders. In a study of preschool literacy environments, Morrow (1990) created a veterinarian's office with a waiting room supplied with magazines and books. Students could take on the roles of doctors and nurses and record the condition of the imaginary animals who were treated. In this study, teachers modeled the writing and reading behaviors commonly found in the setting, and over time children incorporated the literacy behaviors into their play.

Another effective way to increase students' participation and exposure to writing activities is to supply classrooms with a range of writing materials. Morrow (1990) found that simply adding books, book-making materials, and various types of paper and pens resulted in children engaging in more writing behaviors in their classroom play. In another study, students in first-grade classrooms with access to writing materials were found to write longer descriptions in first through third grades (Coker, 2006).

The understanding that writing serves a communicative function is essential for young students to grasp. Teachers who create opportunities in their classrooms for students to write may be enhancing students' awareness of the instrumental use that writing plays in society.

Challenge 2: Unlocking the Conventions of Print

Experienced writers take their understanding of the rules of print for granted. As I revised this chapter, I did not have to remind myself that English is written in a horizontal line, that one writes along that line from left to right, and that words are bounded by spaces; however, children are not born knowing the conventions of print. A deep understanding of these conventions is foundational to both writing and reading. Some print conventions, such as the linear arrangement of writing and the insight that text does not directly represent its referent, are seen as universal writing features. Research with preschoolers has demonstrated that knowledge of the universal features typically emerges before children demonstrate skill with language-specific features, such as directionality and shapes of letters (or symbols) (Puranik & Lonigan, 2009). There is also evidence that preschoolers' print knowledge is associated with skill in writing letters, sentences, and even a student's own name (Puranik, Lonigan, & Kim, 2011). Furthermore, the National Early Literacy Panel's (NELP) review found that print knowledge was related to spelling skill (Lonigan, Schatschneider, & Westberg, 2008). Given the importance of print knowledge and the recognition that there may be a stable developmental sequence to the acquisition of these insights, it seems logical that young children would benefit from specific activities designed to expose them to print and to familiarize them with the rules of text. By interacting with text, children can learn the conventions of print. In this way, reading experience can benefit children's writing knowledge (see also Shanahan, Chapter 14, this volume). One effective approach for young children who are learning about print is to fill classrooms with books and to engage students in interactive book reading.

One crucial practice for classroom teachers is making sure that children are surrounded by many different kinds of books. Neuman (1999) demonstrated that giving child-care centers an abundance of books and training providers to engage in literacy activities can support children's engagement with print. The children who received the intervention developed their understanding of the concepts of print faster than the children who did not. Teachers also must engage in literacy activities to encourage students to interact with print.

One particularly effective practice is interactive book reading. During an interactive, or shared, book-reading lesson, the adult acts as a guide for the child. In one-on-one situations, the child and adult look at the text together, and the adult engages in a number of practices to draw attention to the content of the book and to the way that print operates. The book-reading practices involve drawing the child's attention to salient features of the text, including the print. As adults read, pointing with a finger helps illustrate the directionality of print and the way words are represented as isolated units. Good book-reading sessions involve discussion about how the illustrations contribute to the text's meaning and draw attention to new vocabulary or unusual syntax. Parent–child book reading has been identified as a powerful contributor to a range of skills, including emergent literacy skills such as name writing, letter identification, and sound blending and language skills such as vocabulary knowledge (Bus, van IJzendoorn, & Pellegrini, 1995).

Although book reading has been associated with a wide variety of literacy-related skills, not all book-reading practices are linked to student gains. Bus (2001) points out that the best book-reading practices involve drawing students into the text by making connections between the story and the children's experiences and interests.

One successful classroom adaptation of book-reading practices is dialogic reading (Whitehurst et al., 1999). The dialogic reading intervention aims to engage students in the reading process by having them assume the role of the storyteller. Teachers using dialogic reading follow the child's storytelling efforts closely and prompt the child with questions. For very young children, questions that teachers pose relate directly to the story, such as asking them to describe what a character is doing or to identify something in an illustration. For preschoolers, the questions are designed to be more complex, to encourage students to think about the overall story. The more challenging questions encourage children to make connections between the text and their lives. For example, a teacher might ask if a child has ever experienced something that happened in the book. Dialogic reading has been found to have a positive impact on children's knowledge of several print conventions including identification of the print, directionality of print, and the mechanics of writing (Whitehurst et al., 1999).

Another way that teachers modify the book-reading practice for the classroom is through the use of big books. These oversized books are typically propped on an easel or stand where all students can see them. During the session, the teacher models the reading practice by pointing to highlight the features of print such as directionality, spaces between words, and the relationship between words and the story. Big books have also been found to be effective when students can follow along in their own copies of the text. When teachers model reading behaviors with a big book as students follow along in their own copies, students have the opportunity to handle the book and track print themselves.

Modeling the writing process with young students also provides teachers with the opportunity to highlight important print conventions. As teachers compose on a large flip chart or chalkboard, children observe how writers do things like separate words with spaces and write from left to right. Wong and Berninger (2004) recommend daily teacher modeling of writing to underscore the relationship between sounds and letter patterns, to demonstrate how writing is used for communicative purposes, and to practice spelling. By engaging students in print and modeling writing behaviors, teachers can facilitate students' understanding of the conventions of written language.

Challenge 3: Discovering That the Alphabet Is Used to Represent Speech Sounds

An important insight that children make as their understanding of the writing system expands is that print represents the sounds of language. This insight and other forms of alphabet knowledge help children make sense of the written system and contribute to their success in spelling words (Lonigan et al., 2008). Understanding the alphabetic principle is not explicitly identified in the CCSS; however, in the language standards for kindergarten, students are expected to be able to print most of the letters.

In their work with Argentinean preschoolers, Ferreiro and Teberosky (1979) found that children frequently believed the length of a word was related to the size of the object it named. For example, they interviewed children who reported that the word for *bear* must be bigger than the word for *duck* because a bear is so much larger than a duck. As children's experience with print grows and they begin to understand that letters represent the sounds in words, they gradually abandon theories that do not successfully account for the way print operates.

In English, knowing the names of letters may provide children with an important source of knowledge about the relationship between oral language and the alphabet. Since many 4- and 5-year-olds can recite the alphabet and can match letters with their names, Treiman, Tincoff, and Richmond-Welty (1996) examined whether children use their letter-name knowledge in their spelling attempts. The relevance of letter names to children's spelling was assessed in a study that compared the spellings of words that begin with the same letter. Students spelled a series of word pairs. One word in each pair began with the sound that matched the letter name, and the other member of each pair began with a sound that did not match the letter name. For the letter *b* the words *beaver* and *bone* were contrasted. *Beaver* begins with a sound that matches the name of the letter, but *bone* does not. Words that began with sounds matching the letter were spelled more accurately. The results suggested that letter-name knowledge may offer children insight into the way the alphabet works. There are a variety of effective methods that teachers can use to enhance young children's letter knowledge.

Frequently, children learn their first letters through their own names. For many young children, their name is the earliest word they recognize, primarily because it is familiar and meaningful (Bloodgood, 1999; Clay, 1975). The importance of names to children often results in their learning to write their names before other words and learning the letters in their names before other letters. As children practice writing and spelling their names, they gain experience matching letters to sounds. Having a stable relationship between the graphic and phonological form of a name provides children with key insight into how writing works.

Writing instruction can capitalize on children's interest in their names by providing opportunities for children to print their names. Once children can write and spell their names fairly well, teachers can make connections between the initial sounds in the name and other words. For example, a teacher might ask 3-year-old Tobias how to spell *table*. If he were unsure, she could make the connection to his name explicit and encourage him to compare the initial sounds of *table* and *Tobias*. Knowing that his name begins with a *t*, he may listen to *table* and realize that it begins with the same sound.

Drawing on children's interest in and knowledge about their own names offers one instructional approach to the challenge of linking sounds to letters, which is known as the alphabetic principle. Many children learn some letters through the spontaneous analysis of their own names supported by their parents or teachers, but explicit instruction is also important to ensure that young children know all the letters in the alphabet.

In many preschool classes, teachers engage in a wide range of activities to teach children the alphabet, such as the alphabet song. Teachers also post the letters in the classroom and refer to them at meaningful moments. During book reading, teachers may draw students' attention to specific letters that are prominent in the text.

Another successful way to teach children the alphabet is through the use of mnemonic clues. Ehri and Roberts (2006) reviewed several approaches and concluded that pairing an illustrated mnemonic with letter sounds was effective. The technique involves having a character for each letter, such as Polly Parrot for the letter *p*. When the letter is taught, children are shown an illustration that integrates the shape of the letter with the character. This pairing is designed to boost children's memory of the letters and the sounds connected to the letters. Although teachers can create their own characters for each letter, there are commercial programs on the market that utilize this approach (Ehri & Roberts, 2006).

Another effective approach to learning the relationships between sounds and letters involves drawing students' attention to individual sounds in words (phonemes) and practicing writing letters (Berninger et al., 1998). One goal is to teach students that sound-to-letter relationships often involve more than one letter. Berninger and her colleagues (2002) have pointed out that when children receive phonics instruction in the context of learning to read, the lessons often target the relationship between single letters and sounds. Little attention is usually devoted to the role played by multiletter spelling units. When children attempt to spell words by applying phonics knowledge in the reverse direction, they tend to look for single letters to represent single sounds. For students operating with this assumption, spelling words with vowel teams or digraphs can be frustrating. In order to avoid this confusion, Wong and Berninger (2004) recommend explicit instruction on the relationship between phonemes and functional spelling units. Once children in prekindergarten and kindergarten are able to represent sounds with single letters, they may be ready to study consonant digraphs and blends (such as the *ch* in *chat* or the *fl* in *flat*). As children learn how functional spelling units represent sounds in words, their spelling skill has been shown to improve (Berninger et al., 1998). In addition, phonics instruction is recommended that proceeds from the phoneme to the grapheme so that it is directly transferable to the spelling process.

The approaches described above use a coordinated, systematic plan to introduce students to the alphabetic principle. Students also benefit from the opportunity to practice with the spelling system as they write on their own (Tolchinsky, 2001). Students' attempts at conventional spelling have been called *invented spelling*. Practice with invented spelling has been shown to promote spelling development because it allows children to test and refine their theories of how the writing system represents sounds (Tolchinsky, 2001).

Encouraging invented spelling can play an important role in fostering spelling knowledge. In fact, the linguist Charles Read, who first wrote about the importance of children's invented spelling, encouraged teachers and parents to foster a positive attitude toward invented spelling and writing in general (Read, 1986). In addition to remaining open to children's experiments with spelling, teachers also can use students' writing to gauge their level of spelling knowledge and to tailor instruction to fit their needs.

But before teachers can do either of these things successfully, they must understand the underlying logic behind invented spellings.

As Read (1986) pointed out, "children's beginning spelling is essentially phonetic" (p. 1). When children know enough about the writing system to map letters onto sounds, they frequently make spelling mistakes based on the sounds of words. This can be seen when kindergartner Michelle spells *wrecking* as RIKING. The silent *w* is absent and the short *e* is spelled with an *i*. Since the vowel sound in *wrecking* sounds more like *i* than it does *e*, Michelle's error is understandable.

Teachers will profit from an understanding that unconventional spelling patterns often reflect students' burgeoning knowledge of the alphabetic principle. One example of this is Michelle using an *i* to spell the short-*e* sound in *wrecking*. Once teachers can analyze spelling mistakes, they can design instruction that addresses the particular point of confusion. Spelling development for many students follows a sequence that begins with initial consonant sounds and moves through vowel sounds, consonant and vowel letter combinations, and spelling patterns based on word derivations (Bear, Invernizzi, Templeton, & Johnston, 2003). Spelling instruction, such as word study, that is sensitive to students' developmental levels and provides opportunities for students to work with orthographic patterns has been found to be effective (Bear et al., 2003; also see Schlagal, Chapter 11, this volume).

Challenge 4: Writing or Typing Well Enough to Express Ideas Fluently

In many kindergarten and first-grade classrooms, handwriting instruction is absent. On the basis of their experiences as students, many teachers believe that the sole function of handwriting lessons is to improve the appearance of printing or cursive. Furthermore, with personal computers widely available, very few important documents are handwritten any more. In some schools, primary-grade children receive instruction in keyboarding; however, these lessons are not widely offered.

Despite the assumption that handwriting does not affect writing quality, recent research contradicted that claim and found that when students receive handwriting instruction their writing is better, is longer, and is more fluent (Santangelo & Graham, 2012). In one study of handwriting, Graham, Berninger, Abbott, Abbott, and Whitaker (1997) examined the impact of handwriting on both the quality and the production of text. For students in the primary grades, handwriting measures were related to both the quality and the compositional fluency of their writing. As children write, they must manage several tasks at once. During the composition process, a number of things need to be considered, including the topic, the structure of the piece, and the words to be selected, as well as other concerns such as spelling. If handwriting is difficult and requires considerable effort, the child may not have enough resources to develop the ideas well, write in complete sentences, or determine the correct spelling of words. Children whose handwriting is fluid and automatic are able to transfer their ideas onto paper without experiencing an information bottleneck. From this perspective, handwriting is a low-level process that must be accomplished quickly and efficiently so that higher level tasks can receive attention.

Based on their research, Berninger and Richards (2002) made several recommendations for successful handwriting instruction. First, teachers should adopt explicit methods and limit lessons and practice to brief periods of only 5–10 minutes. They also recommended that opportunities to write connected text follow handwriting instruction. Opportunities to write after handwriting instruction are designed to help children transfer their handwriting to the authentic writing task. The sequence of instruction should begin with attention to the formation of the letters. Once letters can be produced with reasonable accuracy, instruction should target automatic production of letters (see Schlagal, Chapter 11, this volume, for a discussion of spelling).

Berninger's (1998) instructional method begins with attention to manuscript letters. The intervention combines attention to the physical formation of the letters with the higher order task of writing. Although cursive letters were traditionally taught sometime around third grade, Berninger and Richards (2002) suggest that instruction in keyboarding skills may be of greater value and should begin by first grade. It is not clear whether keyboarding instruction should be initiated *before* first grade.

Challenge 5: Deepening Linguistic Knowledge

By the time children enter preschool or kindergarten, they understand an enormous amount about how we use oral language to communicate. Even though nearly every preschooler knows that spoken words can serve a range of communicative functions, there are stark differences in children's language skills based on their experiences at home. One startling example of this was provided by Hart and Risley (1995), who have shown that children have vastly different early language experiences and that those experiences at home are closely related to the development of vocabulary knowledge. Although the CCSS for writing do not mention linguistic skills, the language standards provide targets for a limited number of skills related to grammatical, morphological, and vocabulary knowledge.

Some language skills, particularly vocabulary knowledge, have long been considered to be important for good writing. Evidence for this claim has been growing recently. For example, the NELP review found that oral language skills were predictive of spelling (Lonigan et al., 2008). Other researchers have investigated the links between various linguistic skills and writing quality. Preschool children's core language skill (knowledge of vocabulary, syntax, and morphology) was found to predict the quality of their writing years later in grades 3–5 (Hooper, Roberts, Nelson, Zeisel, & Kasambira Fannin, 2010). A similar relationship was also found in kindergarten where vocabulary and grammatical skills predicted writing quality (Kim et al., 2011). Many questions about how young writers leverage their linguistic knowledge to write remain, but we have a much clearer picture of the importance of linguistic knowledge for writing. Given our growing understanding of how language skills matter to writing, it is important to include classroom activities that facilitate children's vocabulary development and help them learn to use more complex grammatical forms.

One such approach, dialogic reading, engages children in discussions about a text during a read-aloud. As reviewed earlier in this chapter, dialogic reading has been found to strengthen children's print knowledge. In addition, it had a positive impact on language skills such as vocabulary (Whitehurst et al., 1999). The use of children's books, through practices such as dialogic reading, are an ideal approach to developing young children's linguistic knowledge. Books present children with vocabulary that they might not encounter any other way. For example, reading an informational book on mammals in the ocean could be used to introduce children to words such as *marine, habitat,* or *communication.* Pairing the reading of the text with activities like classroom discussions, written responses to the text, and word games can provide students with multiple opportunities to see, write, and think about new words.

The use of trade books in the preschool and kindergarten classroom can also provide students with models of sophisticated grammatical constructions. Even fairly simple children's books contain a range of syntactical forms such as modifying phrases, compound subjects and verbs, and even embedded clauses. The use of these constructions in spoken language is relatively rare, even for highly educated adults. As a result, children may depend on book reading to gain significant exposure to important grammatical forms. Engaging in interactive approaches designed to strengthen children's word knowledge as well as other types of linguistic skill will be an important component of a holistic writing curriculum.

Challenge 6: Developing Knowledge of the World and of Text Genres

In order for writing to be a meaningful activity for children, they must have something to say. Children come to school with personal experiences that can vary widely, from participating at a county fair to watching cartoons and talk shows on television to attending a ballet production. As teachers search for writing lessons that tap this vast range of experiences, they learn that few activities are equally engaging for all students. One solution to the problem of uneven background knowledge is the personal story. One reason many teachers focus on the personal narrative (sometimes called the *bed-to-bed story*) is that all children have relevant background knowledge. Teachers know that most children can write about some event or sequence of events in their lives, even if it is just the morning classroom routine. While the personal narrative offers many opportunities to practice a wide range of important writing skills, students also need practice with other kinds of writing. The Common Core writing standards place considerable emphasis on the genres, or text forms, that students produce. Traditionally instruction has focused on narrative forms such as the bed-to-bed story; however, the new standards place equal emphasis on narrative, opinion, and informative text. Initially teachers may consider the genre requirements to be too demanding, but evidence suggests that given opportunities and exposure to print and texts, children will explore their ideas and produce a broad range of texts spontaneously (Bissex, 1980). When children come to school without having experienced a wide range of ideas or kinds of writing, teachers can enhance their background knowledge by exposing them to different ideas and texts. Even students like Bissex's son, Paul, whose home offered many opportunities to engage with print, depend on teachers to broaden their understanding of the world and the world of text.

A time-honored method of introducing children to the ideas and language used in books is reading aloud. As discussed earlier, read-alouds can be instrumental in highlighting the conventions of print, although typically children are more attracted to the stories than to the instructional possibilities. The primary draw of hearing books is the delight experienced through entering a new and possibly unimagined world. As children delight in the text, they may experience contexts, learn new words, and expand their understanding of the world.

Although children's fiction has been the mainstay of preschool and elementary school classrooms, children also need to hear other kinds of books. For example, informational books that introduce children to scientific or historical topics can deepen background knowledge and stimulate interest in a wide range of topics. By choosing text that addresses topics related to classroom lessons, teachers can develop students' background knowledge in ways that will support their engagement in lessons as well as their ability to write about specific topics.

One way that teachers can pair book-reading activities with writing is to have students draw and write in response to their reading. As a first step, students need paper with room for a drawing and then wide lines for writing (the lines that contain a dotted midline are helpful). After reading and discussing a text, ask students to identify a favorite part. They can then draw the favorite part and write a description of it below the drawing. If the class read a book on whales, students might draw a picture of their favorite whale and then write as much as they could about it. This task provides students an opportunity to think about the ideas from the book and practice writing some of the words from the text. In addition, this activity can accommodate students who cannot write any words as well as those who are ready to respond in multiple sentences to their reading.

Children's genre knowledge can benefit from exposure to a wide variety of books. Early understandings of the conventions of stories, informational texts, and opinion essays draw heavily on oral language experiences. As early as kindergarten, children demonstrate an awareness that texts differ depending on their purpose (Donovan & Smolkin, 2006). Yet for most students in kindergarten or even the early primary grades, genre knowledge is nascent. In order to apply genre conventions to their own writing, students need more exposure to the varieties of texts that they will be expected to produce. Although the research on the impact of genre instruction is thin, there is support for surrounding students with a variety of different types of books. One study found a positive relationship between the range of text genres in the first-grade classroom library and students' writing growth through third grade (Coker, 2006).

Providing students with ready exposure to all types of print is important for their developing genre knowledge. Principals and teachers should work to stock classroom libraries with books of all types, especially the genres targeted by the CCSS. The inclusion of informational books into instruction may provide excellent models of how to structure a text that students are writing. Teachers should also look beyond informational books and incorporate children's books that take the form of a persuasive text (e.g., the amusing *Don't Let the Pigeon Drive the Bus* [Williams, 2003]). Teachers who integrate the books into their lessons may find that students are more motivated to explore new kinds of books.

The practice of reading a variety of books to children has been shown to support their acquisition of genre knowledge (Donovan & Smolkin, 2006). As genre knowledge grows, so does children's ability to apply that knowledge to their own writing.

An Illustration of Instruction

When writing instruction is most productive, it addresses a range of skills and practices relevant for good writing. With the adoption of the writing CCSS, teachers will want to use the standards to inform their lessons. Of course, not all lessons can target every important aspect of writing, but in many lessons teachers can address more than one facet of it. The following lesson from Mrs. Nelson's kindergarten classroom describes how she taught students a lesson on how to compose an opinion piece. The writing task drew on content they had researched together using informational books. Furthermore, the lesson illustrates how instruction can provide direction and practice in many of the important challenges that young writers face.

In her kindergarten classroom, Mrs. Nelson devotes 45 minutes to writing workshop nearly every day. Often the writing lessons and activities build on topics from other parts of the curriculum. Mrs. Nelson planned this lesson around the class's science unit that focused on endangered animals. She leveraged the students' interest in the material to engage her kindergarteners in multiple aspects of writing.

Mrs. Nelson began the lesson by calling the children to the carpet. When they were seated and quiet, she began the lesson.

MRS. NELSON: Today I want you to do something good writers do. Sometimes good writers use lots of detail, but sometimes it's done to make a quick point. Who's seen advertisements for McDonald's, or Coke? How many of you have seen them with a million words? (*Many students raise their hands.*) I haven't seen one. Could you read a Junie B. Jones book on a sign as you're going down the road?

STUDENT: Too quick.

MRS. NELSON: So you need something quick [for an advertisement]. You see "Drink Coke." The author's not saying it's a sweet brown liquid, it bubbles, and all those details. They want you to know "Drink Coke." How many of you have seen the commercials for milk with famous people? They say, "Got Milk?" What did the author want you to know?

STUDENTS: [Multiple responses.]

MRS. NELSON: All they needed to say was "Do you have milk?" Today, you're going to have some fun making a simple sign that's going to get to the point about saving the Earth. Think about what bothers you about the Earth. Who wants to give me an example of what bothers them?

STUDENT: [En]dangered animals.

MRS. NELSON: Give me an example.

STUDENT: Stop making animals endangered.

MRS. NELSON: Others?

STUDENT: Let animals cross the street?

MRS. NELSON: How about "Leave trees alone"? I'll give you a big piece of posterboard. First, write your message, and not in teeny-weeny letters. When you're going down the road and you see a sign (*writes in small letters on board*), is that going to catch your attention?

STUDENTS: No.

MRS. NELSON: You're going to write it to grab the attention of the kids in the hall. Watch this (*writes something very small*). Can you read that? Anyone having trouble reading that?

STUDENTS: [Various responses.]

MRS. NELSON: You're going to put big words on your poster, like this. (*Writes "Save animals" very large on the board.*)

STUDENT: As big as a school?

MRS. NELSON: Well, if it's as big as a school, it won't fit on the poster-board. Usually someone doing a commercial also uses an illustration or sometimes a fancy border to grab your eyes. I want you to make a sign that makes kids stop and think. Today, you're going to work on the floor because the poster is big. I want to see lots of detail in your drawing (not your writing), colors, and I want to see you make your point. I'm going to take the really good ones and hang them all over the school. If you're wearing red, get a coffee can and pick a spot. [Mrs. Nelson uses metal coffee cans to store pencils, pens, markers, and other writing materials for students.]

In the course of her brief lesson, Mrs. Nelson was able to highlight multiple characteristics of the writing system that are important to young writers. Her lesson referenced the communicative function of written language, the conventional arrangement of print, the relationship between speech sounds and written words, and the importance of background and genre knowledge. Even though she spent relatively little time on each point, her lesson was designed to draw students' attention to these challenges.

At the beginning of her discussion, Mrs. Nelson reminded students of their experience with the form of writing that was the focus of the lesson:

signs. She knew the students were familiar with advertising signs, so she led a discussion about the communicative function of signs. A unique feature of signs is that they are designed to communicate a single idea and to express the opinion of the sign's writer. As she explained to the class, "Sometimes good writers use a lot of detail, but sometimes it's done to make a quick point."

The discussion of signs also underscored the understanding that people write to communicate. Mrs. Nelson made this point particularly salient by referencing a written form that children have experienced outside of the classroom. For the students who have read and thought about roadside signs, Mrs. Nelson may be subtly signaling that writing has an important communicative function in their lives outside of school just as it does in school.

After a discussion of the conventions of signs, she encouraged students to create their own signs. The activity was designed to allow students to express their opinions about the importance of protecting the environment. From their science unit, the children understood that the natural world was threatened by humans, and they were making signs that would function like billboards. Messages such as "Save the animals" or "Stop wrecking habitats" were designed to convince people to change their behavior. Mrs. Nelson explained that she would post the signs around the school so that other students could read them. One implicit message in the lesson was that students could use written signs as a way to express their ideas. Furthermore, the ideas that students expressed would be displayed, just like signs are along the road. Not only will the kindergartners share their ideas through the signs, but they may also be able to change people's behavior. In this lesson, students experienced writing as a tool to share ideas and potentially influence behavior.

During her mini-lesson, Mrs. Nelson discussed the conventions of signs and modeled how to make one. After explaining that signs need to be brief so they can be read quickly, she also added that the letters should be big. She then wrote her message on the board in big letters, modeling for students the process of forming the letters and arranging the words. In this example, Mrs. Nelson did not discuss how she wrote from left to right and left spaces between words; she might have done so if she thought it would benefit the students. Instead she modeled the way to write words on a sign, giving students an opportunity to see how a writer composes text.

After her mini-lesson on signs, Mrs. Nelson walked around the room monitoring the children's progress and having brief conferences with them. When she asked Michelle what she was planning to write, the following exchange occurred:

MICHELLE: Stop wrecking.

MRS. NELSON: That's a good one. Maybe you can start right here. *(Points to a spot on the paper for Michelle to begin writing. Michelle writes* Stop *and then pauses.)*

MRS. NELSON: What vowel is it?

MICHELLE: *a?*

MRS. NELSON: Wr-e-cking. *(Stretches the word out for Michelle.)* Stop wr-e-cking, wr-e-cking. *(Says the word several more times, stretching out the vowel sound.)*

MICHELLE: *(Writes* riking.*)* Stop wrecking habitats.

MRS. NELSON: Habitats, that's even better.

In this exchange, Mrs. Nelson helped Michelle with a difficult vowel sound by stretching the word out. After Michelle produced a word that reflected the sounds in *wrecking,* Mrs. Nelson complimented her and moved on. The goal of the lesson had been met even though Michelle still has a lot to learn about conventional spelling.

In Mrs. Nelson's writing lesson, students composed signs expressing their opinion about how to respond to the problem of endangered animals. Their foray into sign making reflects elements of the CCSS and provides students opportunities to develop their writing skill. First, the signs could clearly be seen as an exercise composing an opinion piece, one of the central genres of the CCSS. For their signs to be persuasive, students also were taught how signs work. An understanding of the features of the sign genre coupled with background knowledge about the issues made it possible for them to write something that could be an effective opinion piece and change people's ideas about saving the Earth.

Another benefit of the sign-writing activity was the development of students' understanding about the kinds of information that writers need. First, writers need to have knowledge about the topic (in this case, endangered animals). Through their science lessons and read-alouds, the students had learned about animals, their habitats, and the wider ecological system. The students' research allowed them to build background knowledge about endangered animals and the reasons for the animals' declining numbers. Then as sign writers they could draw on that knowledge. In addition, the use of informational books in their research likely strengthened students' understanding of how those books are structured. Participating in research under Mrs. Nelson's guidance offers a rich example of how teachers can plan instruction to meet the CCSS writing standards related to using research to build and present knowledge.

Conclusion

For young children to develop into accomplished writers, they must learn to manage the substantial challenges of writing. The CCSS can provide direction for instruction as teachers work to meet the standards. At the same time, I hope that teachers recognize that the standards are but a starting point; they do not provide a comprehensive overview of all the skills and processes that students need to master to be strong writers. Many of the instructional methods described in the chapter detail ways to expose children to specific aspects of the writing system or process. Some of the recommendations have the potential to enhance more than one area of students' writing knowledge. For example, the use of book-reading interventions can enhance background knowledge, conventions of print, the understanding that writing is a communicative act, and linguistic knowledge.

It is also important to note that by themselves these approaches will only have a limited effect on children's writing development. Children also need to write on a daily basis. As Tolchinsky (2001) asserted, "it is by being exposed to writing and by using writing that children will learn to master it" (p. 95). The tasks of writing about a field trip to the science museum or of creating a sign about endangered animals have real value for young children. Challenges such as these offer opportunities for children to experiment with the writing system and to generate and refine their notions of how writing works.

References

Bear, D. R., Invernizzi, M., Templeton, S., & Johnston, F. (2003). *Words their way: Word study for phonics, vocabulary and spelling instruction.* Upper Saddle River, NJ: Prentice Hall.

Berninger, V. W. (1998). *Process assessment of the learner: Guides for reading and writing interventions.* San Antonio, TX: Psychological Corporation.

Berninger, V. W., & Chanquoy, L. (2012). What writing is and how it changes across early and middle childhood development: A multidisciplinary perspective. In E. L. Grigorenko, E. Mambrino, & D. D. Preiss (Eds.), *Writing: A mosaic of new perspectives.* (pp. 65–84). New York: Psychology Press.

Berninger, V. W., & Richards, T. L. (2002). *Brain literacy for educators and psychologists.* London: Academic Press.

Berninger, V. W., Vaughan, K., Abbott, R. D., Begay, K., Coleman, K. B., Curtin, G., et al. (2002). Teaching spelling and composition alone and together: Implications for the simple view of writing. *Journal of Educational Psychology, 94*(2), 291–304.

Berninger, V. W., Vaughan, K., Abbott, R. D., Brooks, A., Abbott, S. P., Rogan, L., et al. (1998). Early intervention for spelling problems: Teaching functional spelling units of varying size with a multiple-connections framework. *Journal of Educational Psychology, 90*(4), 587–605.

Bissex, G. L. (1980). *Gnys at wrk: A child learns to write and read.* Cambridge, MA: Harvard University Press.

Bloodgood, J. W. (1999). What's in a name?: Children's name writing and literacy acquisition. *Reading Research Quarterly, 34*(3), 342–367.

Bus, A. G. (2001). Joint caregiver–child storybook reading: A route to literacy development. In S. B. Neuman & D. K. Dickinson (Eds.), *Handbook of early literacy research* (Vol. 1, pp. 179–191). New York: Guilford Press.

Bus, A. G., van IJzendoorn, M. H., & Pellegrini, A. D. (1995). Joint book reading makes for success in learning to read: A meta-analysis on intergenerational transmission of literacy. *Review of Educational Research, 65*(1), 1–21.

Clay, M. M. (1975). *What did I write?* Auckland, New Zealand: Heinemann.

Coker, D. (2006). The impact of first-grade factors on the growth and outcomes of urban schoolchildren's primary-grade writing. *Journal of Educational Psychology, 98*, 471–488.

Donovan, C. A., & Smolkin, L. B. (2006). Children's understanding of genre and writing development. In C. A. MacArthur, S. Graham, & J. Fitzgerald (Eds.), *Handbook of writing research* (pp. 131–143). New York: Guilford Press.

Ehri, L. C., & Roberts, T. (2006). The roots of learning to read and write: Acquisition of letters and phonemic awareness. In D. K. Dickinson & S. B. Neuman (Eds.), *Handbook of early literacy research* (Vol. 2, pp. 113–131). New York: Guilford Press.

Ferreiro, E., & Teberosky, A. (1979). *Literacy before schooling* (K. G. Castro, Trans.). Portsmouth, NH: Heinemann.

Graham, S., Berninger, V. W., Abbott, R. D., Abbott, S. P., & Whitaker, D. (1997). Role of mechanics in composing of elementary school students: A new methodological approach. *Journal of Educational Psychology, 89*(1), 170–182.

Hart, B., & Risley, T. (1995). *Meaningful differences in the everyday experience of young American children.* Baltimore: Brookes.

Hooper, S. R., Roberts, J. E., Nelson, L., Zeisel, S., & Kasambira Fannin, D. (2010). Preschool predictors of narrative writing skills in elementary school children. *School Psychology Quarterly, 25*(1), 1–12.

Kim, Y.-S., Al Otaiba, S., Puranik, C., Sidler, J. F., Gruelich, L., & Wagner, R. K. (2011). Componential skills of beginning writing: An exploratory study at the end of kindergarten. *Learning and Individual Differences, 21*, 517–525.

Lonigan, C. J., Schatschneider, C., & Westberg, L. (2008). Identification of children's skills and abilities linked to later outcomes in reading, writing, and spelling. In *National Early Literacy Panel, developing early literacy: Report of the National Early Literacy Panel* (pp. 55–106). Washington, DC: National Institute for Literacy. Retrieved from: *www.nifl.gov/earlychildhood/NELP/ NELPreport.html.*

Meisels, S. J. (2011, November 29). Common Core standards pose dilemmas for early childhood. *Washington Post: The Answer Sheet.* Retrieved from *www. washingtonpost.com/blogs/answer-sheet/post/common-core-standards- pose-dilemmas-for-early-childhood/2011/11/28/gIQAPs1X6N_blog.html.*

Morrow, L. M. (1990). Preparing the classroom environment to promote literacy during play. *Early Childhood Research Quarterly, 5*, 537–554.

National Governors Association & Council of Chief State School Officers. (2010). *Common Core State Standards for English language arts & literacy in history/social studies, science, and technical subjects.* Retrieved from *www. corestandards.org.*

Neuman, S. B. (1999). Books make a difference: A study of access to literacy. *Reading Research Quarterly, 34*(3), 286–311.

Puranik, C. S., & Lonigan, C. J. (2009). From scribbles to Scrabble: Preschool children's developing knowledge of written language. *Reading and Writing, 24*(5), 567–589.

Puranik, C. S., Lonigan, C. J., & Kim, Y. S. (2011). Contributions of emergent literacy skills to name writing, letter writing, and spelling in preschool children. *Early Childhood Research Quarterly, 26*, 465–474.

Purcell-Gates, V. (1996). Stories, coupons, and the TV: Relationships between home literacy experiences and emergent literacy knowledge. *Reading Research Quarterly, 31*, 406–428.

Purcell-Gates, V., & Dahl, K. L. (1991). Low-SES children's success and failure at early literacy learning in a skills-based classroom. *Journal of Reading Behavior, 23*(1), 1–34.

Read, C. (1986). *Children's creative spelling.* London: Routledge & Kegan Paul.

Santangelo, T., & Graham, S. (2012, February). *Handwriting instruction: A meta-analysis.* Poster presented at the Pacific Coast Research Conference, Coronado, CA.

Tolchinsky, L. (2001). *The cradle of culture and what children know about writing and numbers before being taught.* Mahwah, NJ: Erlbaum.

Treiman, R., Tincoff, R., & Richmond-Welty, E. D. (1996). Letter names help children to connect print and speech. *Developmental Psychology, 32*(3), 505–514.

Whitehurst, G. J., Zevenbergen, A. A., Crone, D. A., Schultz, M. D., Velting, O. N., & Fischel, J. E. (1999). Outcomes of an emergent literacy intervention from Head Start through second grade. *Journal of Educational Psychology, 91*, 261–272.

Williams, M. (2003). *Don't let the pigeon drive the bus.* New York: Hyperion Press.

Wong, B. Y. L., & Berninger, V. W. (2004). Cognitive processes of teachers in implementing composition research in elementary, middle, and high school classrooms. In C. A. Stone, E. R. Silliman, B. J. Ehren, & K. Apel (Eds.), *Handbook of language and literacy: Development and disorders* (pp. 600–624). New York: Guilford Press.

Chapter 3

Best Practices in Teaching Writing for College and Career Readiness

DOLORES PERIN

Writing can be a satisfying and mind-expanding activity for the student who has acquired the necessary skills, but a frustrating and even aversive experience when these skills are lacking. By the middle and high school years, it is necessary for students to possess a level of writing skill that will allow them to express increasingly complex thoughts and take a critical stance toward information. These skills are represented in the Common Core State Standards (National Governors' Association [NGA] & Council of Chief State School Officers [CCSSO], 2010), which have been adopted by 46 U.S. states (Kober & Rentner, 2012).

Although middle and high school English language arts (ELA) teachers spend a great deal of effort teaching students how to express their ideas in writing, students may nevertheless not demonstrate strong writing skills when they enter college or the workplace, where writing is highly specialized. College instructors routinely assign writing not for the purpose of teaching writing skills but to promote students' development of knowledge and ideas. This situation illustrates the difference between learning to write and writing to learn (Graham & Perin, 2006). In jobs, employees write to communicate about issues that concern the specific setting, and workplace writing involves "adopting the discourse forms and methods of reasoning of that professional group" (Akdere & Azevedo, 2005, p. 1072).

Despite the best efforts of ELA teachers, students may face difficulties later because they do not transfer their skills to different settings, or because the emphasis and format of writing varies considerably in different environments (Shanahan & Shanahan, 2012). Beyond basic transcription skills of spelling and handwriting or keyboarding, different skills are needed to write a literary analysis, a science lab report, an essay comparing two historical documents, and a hospital patient report. Writing is not "a generalizable, elementary skill" that once taught can be applied in any setting (Russell, 2002, p. 6).

To prepare students for college and workplace writing, it is important for middle and high school teachers to teach "disciplinary writing," defined as writing in ways customary for subjects such as history and science (Grant & Fisher, 2010; Moje, 2007; Monte-Sano, 2010; Porter et al., 2010) and for workplace purposes (Couture & Rymer, 1993). The importance of disciplinary writing is highlighted in a section of the Common Core standards called "Writing Standards for Literacy in History/Social Studies, Science, and Technical Subjects 6–12" (NGA & CCSSO, 2010, pp. 64–66; Zygouris-Coe, 2012).

This chapter focuses on the writing skills of adolescents, defined as students in the 6th through 12th grades, and is addressed to secondary school teachers to familiarize them with the Common Core standards and instructional strategies that can be used to prepare students for writing in college and the workplace. The chapter seeks to answer two questions: (1) What adolescent writing skills are covered in the Common Core standards?; and (2) What approaches can middle and high school teachers use to prepare students for the writing demands of college and careers? To set the stage, the chapter begins with a theoretical framework for understanding writing activity. The two questions are then addressed, and recommendations are made for middle and high school writing instruction.

A Theoretical Context for Adolescent Writing Instruction

Writing is an extraordinarily complex activity that incorporates thought processes, feelings, and social interaction. When people write, their activity can be explained in terms of the *task environment* and the *individual* (Hayes, 1996, Fig. 3, p. 10). The task environment covers the social and physical environments in which writing takes place. The social environment refers to the audience, that is, the readership, for a student's writing, and other individuals with whom the writer may collaborate to produce a piece of writing. Peer collaboration and audience awareness contribute in important ways to the quality of a writing sample in both academic and workplace settings (Graham & Perin, 2006; Hart-Landsberg & Reder, 1995; Magnifico, 2010). The physical environment refers to the material a person has written so far, such as an organizational plan, a first draft of an essay, or a finished product that stimulates additional writing; and to the modality of writing. For example, e-portfolios, which create a physical environment for the submission and revision of written products, have been found beneficial to adolescent students (Acker, 2008). An example of a task environment of writing might be seen with a group of 10th-grade social studies students who are researching slavery in the United States in the 18th century using primary historical documents and are collaboratively using Google Docs to produce a persuasive essay addressed to their classmates arguing against the position that the United States was a true democracy at the time.

In the Hayes (1996) model, components of writing relating to the individual writer include cognitive processes by which students can reflect on their work during the planning of writing, the actual production of text, and the interpretation of their text in the course of revising what they have written. To produce written text, the student must be able both to generate ideas mentally and to transcribe those ideas using spelling knowledge, and handwriting or keyboarding, and applying correct grammar, punctuation, and capitalization. Another component of the individual aspect of writing concerns motivation and affect, which include the development and achievement of writing goals, predisposition to write, beliefs and attitudes about writing, and the writer's ability to weigh the advantages and disadvantages of engaging in a writing activity. The development and application of writing goals also has a cognitive dimension, as students need to self-regulate their writing process toward the end of expressing what they mean to say in a manner that is clear to the reader. Instruction in cognitive strategies for this purpose is best known in the form of self-regulated strategy development, which is important in the secondary grades for both typically developing students and students with learning disabilities (Graham & Perin, 2007; Harris, Graham, Mason, & Friedlander, 2008; Hoover, Kubina, & Mason, 2012; Mason & Graham, 2008). Finally, besides the cognitive and motivational aspects of writing, Hayes (1996) includes a category within the individual pertaining to different types of memory that are necessary in the act of writing. Thus, in this model, motivation and affect, memory, and cognitive processes work together as students engage in planning, drafting, and revising what they write.

While Hayes's (1996) model intended to characterize the writing processes of proficient writers, other work has described the development of writing (Bereiter, 1980). Development of writing ability is proposed to unfold in five overlapping phases, which combine cognitive and social processes. The first phase is *associative writing*, in which written messages are free associations that are hard for anyone but the writer to comprehend. The second phase is *performative writing*, in which the learner becomes able to adopt the conventions of style, punctuation, and capitalization. At this point, the writer is capable of producing full sentences, although, similar to the first phase, they are self-referential and may not have much meaning for another person. At the third phase, *communicative writing*, the writer is aware of an audience for what is being written. Thus, the writer understands that the reader has a need for certain information in order to understand the text. Writing becomes more sophisticated at the fourth phase, *unified writing*. Here, the writer can express opinions and otherwise evaluate information in logically flowing essays and reports. The fifth and last phase is the *epistemic* phase, in which writing is used as a means of developing knowledge and extending ideas. Through the act of writing in this phase, a person's thought process itself changes, a phenomenon referred to as *knowledge-transformation* (Bereiter & Scardamalia, 1987, p. 6). In the epistemic phase, students can write to deepen their understanding of subject matter (Klein & Samuels, 2010; Stewart, Myers, & Culley, 2010).

It is useful when planning instruction to locate the performance level of individual students within Bereiter's (1980) developmental progression. The phases do not imply any particular age or grade level, although children of average and above-average writing achievement will probably accomplish all phases by adolescence. Many adolescents, however, may be operating at the lower phases of writing development. For example, a low-achieving adolescent student may be "stuck" at the communicative phase of writing and have difficulty planning and producing written work that expresses a coherent point of view, which becomes possible at the higher unified phase. Furthermore, many adolescent students cannot effectively write to learn in the epistemic phase because of lower level difficulties with spelling, sentence construction, and basic strategies for planning and producing a piece of written text. Since adolescent students need to learn disciplinary writing, and some need to strengthen lower level skills, the need for writing instruction continues through the middle and high school grades.

What Adolescent Writing Skills Are Covered by the Common Core Standards?

Many middle and high school teachers observe writing difficulties in their students. The National Assessment of Educational Progress (NAEP) found that only 33% of the nation's 8th graders and 24% of 12th graders show proficient writing skills, and 56% of 8th graders and 57% of 12th graders write only at a basic level (Planty et al., 2008). The Common Core standards provide a detailed array of grade-level writing competencies that, when taught thoroughly, promise to result in high-quality writing by all students, whether gifted, typically developing, or initially low skilled. Adolescent writing standards appear in two places in the Common Core standards document. First is a set of writing standards for K–12 ELA, which appears alongside lists of standards for reading, speaking, and listening. Second is a set of writing standards for history/social studies, science, and technical subjects for grades 6–12. The latter set will be referred to as "disciplinary writing standards" in this chapter. The two sets of writing standards are organized slightly differently in terms of grade levels, with the ELA writing standards presented for grades 6, 7, 8, 9–10, and 11–12, and the disciplinary standards for grades 6–8, 7–9, and 10–12.

There is much overlap across the two sets of standards, the main difference being the mention of discipline-specific writing practices in the second set. For example, the standard for grade 11–12 ELA informational/explanatory writing is "write informative/explanatory texts to examine and convey complex ideas, concepts, and information clearly and accurately through the effective selection, organization, and analysis of content," while the subject-specific standard for the same type of writing at the same grade level is "write informative/ explanatory texts, including the narration of historical events, scientific procedures/experiments, or technical processes" (NGA & CCSSO, 2010, pp. 45, 65).

Both sets of standards consist of 10 "anchor" standards organized in four categories. The first category is Text Types and Purposes (Anchor Standards 1–3), which refers to competencies needed to write argumentative/persuasive, informational/explanatory, and narrative compositions. The second category, Production and Distribution of Writing (Anchor Standards 4–6), covers clarity; coherence; style; use of the writing process, including planning, writing, and revising; and use of technology to collaborate on writing with others and share written products. Third is the category of Research to Build and Present Knowledge (Anchor Standards 7–9), which refers to gathering and analyzing information to answer research questions. The use of text and other sources is emphasized in this category. Also included is the problem of plagiarism, not explicitly addressed in theories of writing but familiar to instructors (Elander, Pittam, Lusher, Fox, & Payne, 2010; Zeek, 2011). The fourth and last category, Range of Writing (Anchor Standard 10), refers to writing for short or longer periods of time for a variety of purposes. Subskills are listed for each anchor standard. As an example, Figure 3.1 shows the subskills a teacher should focus on when teaching informative/explanatory writing (Standard 2).

Most of the subskills in Standard 2 do not change appreciably from 6th to 12th grade, although at the later grades the subskills indicate that students should be aware of the audience when they develop their topic. In contrast, expectations are more clearly differentiated across successive grade levels for argumentative (persuasive) writing (Standard 1). According to this standard, students should be able to express a clear position on a controversy, state an opposing view, or "counterargument," and be able to

Core Writing Standard 2: Write informative/ explanatory texts to examine a topic and convey ideas, concepts, and information through the selection, organization, and analysis of relevant content.

Teach students to:

- Introduce a topic.
- Organize information.
- Develop a topic.
- Provide transitions to show relationships.
- Use appropriate language.
- Write in a formal style.
- Write a concluding statement that follows from information given in the paper.

FIGURE 3.1. Subskills to be taught for informative/explanatory writing (Core Standard 2).

rebut the counterargument in order to confirm and strengthen the initial position (De La Paz & Felton, 2010; Ferretti, Lewis, & Andrews-Weckerly, 2009). To make the argument convincing, the student needs to provide relevant evidence at each step, taking into account what the audience might be thinking. The Common Core standards indicate that by the 10th–12th grades, students should be able to write a fully developed persuasive essay.

The Common Core writing standards present a comprehensive overview of adolescent writing demands, and, importantly, draw attention to the importance of nonfiction writing. Nevertheless, the standards could be modified and expanded in five ways to make them more immediately useful to secondary education teachers. First, the grade-level presentation of the ELA and disciplinary writing standards could be reorganized so that the grade-level bands are the same. This would facilitate curricular alignment in writing instruction between ELA and content-area classrooms. Second, differences between general and disciplinary writing skills as described in the research literature (Shanahan & Shanahan, 2012) are not clear in the Common Core writing standards. Some ELA subskills seem disciplinary in nature, and it is not clear how the standards for science, history/social studies, and technical subjects really differ. The standards could be modified to show the differences more clearly.

Third, the standards do not specify the ways in which skills in informational/explanatory writing become more sophisticated with advancing grades, even though secondary teachers know that this type of writing is much more complex at the end of high school than at the beginning of middle school. Thus, it would be helpful to expand the standards by detailing the increasing expectations at each grade level. Fourth, although the use of sources in research-related writing is acknowledged in Standards 7, 8, and 9, the integration of writing and reading is not directly addressed. Much of academic writing in both secondary and postsecondary education is text-based (Carson, Chase, Gibson, & Hargrove, 1992; Graham & Hebert, 2010; Shanahan, 2009) and, moreover, students need to comprehend writing prompts, some of which require making inferences from background knowledge (de Oliveira, 2011). The standards could be expanded to indicate how reading and writing must be used in concert if students are to produce high-quality writing, especially for content-related purposes.

Fifth, several dimensions of the writing process that adolescents need to learn are not covered in the standards—self-regulation of writing, peer collaboration in producing a written text, and the development and maintenance of motivation to write. Since all of these dimensions can be taught or facilitated by teachers (Bruning & Horn, 2000; Graham & Perin, 2006), the writing standards could be expanded to include them.

What Approaches Can Teachers Use to Prepare Students for the Writing Demands of College and Careers?

Middle and high school teachers should prepare students for the writing demands of college and careers, and include disciplinary writing as part of the ELA or content-area curriculum. This section discusses characteristics of disciplinary writing and summarizes the types of writing found in college and in the workplace; describes current approaches to adolescent writing instruction; and gives examples of how middle and high school teachers can best teach writing to prepare adolescents for the writing demands of college and the workplace.

Disciplinary Writing

Writing demands increase with advancing grades, as students learn to organize their thoughts and, when writing about subject matter, start to approximate the writing styles of disciplinary experts such as historians and scientists (Shanahan & Shanahan, 2012). As described in Common Core writing standard 2, students need to "convey a knowledgeable stance in a style that responds to the discipline" (NGA & CCSSO, 2010, p. 65).

When teaching disciplinary writing, middle and high school teachers should orient students to the fact that writing goals vary by subject area. For example, based on research with middle and high school students

- Describe the steps in a process.
- Draw relationships between concepts, hypotheses, and theories.
- Evaluate the quality of an experiment.
- Provide evidence for claims.
- Argue why findings support one theory rather than another.
- Assess the replicability of a procedure.
- Relate findings to everyday life.
- Provide visual displays, such as illustrations, tables, and graphs, to accompany text.

FIGURE 3.2. Features of science writing.

(Keys, 2000; Klein & Samuels, 2010; Krajcik & Sutherland, 2010; Yore, Hand, & Prain, 2002), Figure 3.2 lists features in writing about science.

In contrast, writing about history has its own characteristic features (de Oliveira, 2011; Nokes, Dole, & Hacker, 2007; Wineburg, Martin, & Monte-Sano, 2011), which are quite different from those in science writing, and are listed in Figure 3.3.

Writing in any one discipline will require a particular knowledge base and vocabulary (Elton, 2010), although writing in all academic areas requires accuracy and clarity. The format of writing differs by discipline. Science lab reports are traditionally organized in terms of predetermined categories of purpose, methods, results, and conclusions (Keys, 2000), whereas writing in history tends to be structured in categories drawn from

- Use the language of history.
- Use multiple sources as the basis of writing about a historical event.
- Decide if a source is trustworthy.
- Assess a historical account for possible bias.
- Decide if information has been omitted from an account, and, if so, try to explain the omission.
- Present events in the context of their time.
- Construct and defend arguments, taking into account alternative viewpoints.
- Interpret carefully the question to be answered in the writing task.

FIGURE 3.3. Features of writing about history.

the specific content (de Oliveira, 2011). For example, de Oliveira (2011), who worked closely with secondary history teachers and analyzed the writing of their students, found that a writing prompt concerning the balance of power achieved by the framers of the U.S. Constitution resulted in essays structured around the three branches of government, while a prompt about the experiences of immigrants elicited essays organized according to description of various aspects of immigrants' lives and judgments as to whether their sacrifices were worth the effort.

Writing in the disciplines usually involves reading, but the difficulty of source text varies across subject areas. For example, Shanahan and Shanahan (2012) described differences in the types of vocabulary and the extent to which nominalization is used in science compared to history text. Science text tends to contain more low-frequency technical vocabulary and more use of nominalized words, that is, the expression of verbs and adjectives as nouns (e.g., water evaporates, scientists study evaporation). These text characteristics interact with prior knowledge of subject matter, directly affecting a student's ability to comprehend source text consulted when writing in the disciplines.

Although this chapter recommends the teaching of disciplinary writing skills, teachers might still consider it unnecessary, thinking that students who write well in one context would write well in any setting. For example, shouldn't students who write excellent essays in history also write excellent science lab reports? In fact, some educators have argued that instruction in general writing strategies is preferable to discipline-specific instruction (Faggella-Luby, Graner, Deshler, & Drew, 2012; Yancey, 2009). However, secondary education teachers have observed a discrepancy between the quality of writing in ELA and content-area classrooms. For example, high school science teachers have noted that students may not make inferences from data when attempting to write conclusions in a lab report, even if they are competent at writing compositions in social studies and ELA classes (Porter et al., 2010). According to research into writing instruction with secondary science students (Keys, 2000), and on self-regulation, metacognition, and problem-solving in literacy (Fox, 2009; Mason, Harris, & Graham, 2011; Mayer & Wittrock, 1996), the skills shown in Figure 3.4 need to be taught to prepare adolescent students to draw appropriate conclusions when writing a science lab report.

Writing in College

The release of the Common Core standards reminded secondary education teachers of the literacy skills that need to be taught to prepare students for college and careers. This section intends to familiarize teachers with the types of writing tasks typically assigned in college, so that they gear their writing instruction to college readiness.

- Teach self-regulation skills—instruct students to set goals for writing the science report and monitor their progress toward those goals.
- Build metacognition—teach students to make inferences from the science data they report in a science lab report.
- Teach students to clarify the meaning of the research question or hypothesis tested, the reasons for the tests or procedures used, and the relation of findings to the theory underlying the experiment.

FIGURE 3.4. Preparation to draw conclusions when writing a science lab report.

Writing skills are critically important in college, and an expert in college readiness has suggested that "writing may be the single overarching academic skill most closely associated with college success" (Conley, 2008, p. 4). Most writing at the postsecondary level is persuasive and informational (Common Core Writing Standards 1 and 2), with relatively little creative or narrative writing (Beaufort, 2004; Bridgeman & Carlson, 1984; Brockman, Taylor, Kreth, & Crawford, 2011; Melzer, 2009). Typical college writing tasks are listed in Figure 3.5. Even in college English composition courses, almost half of writing assignments involve argumentation (Yancey, 2009). Also, most writing at the college level, whatever the discipline, is based on reading, which emphasizes the close relation of reading and writing skills (Brockman et al., 2011).

College students are often required to enroll in one or more "writing-intensive" courses, which follow the conventional discipline-area curriculum except that there are more writing assignments (Boyd, 2010). Writing-intensive courses are examples of "writing across the curriculum," "writing to learn," and "writing in the disciplines" (Fallahi, 2012; Melzer, 2009, p. 244; Stewart et al., 2010, p. 46), which are all designed to help students deepen their knowledge of and think critically about course content, but sometimes also to improve basic literacy skills (Hansen, 1993; Robinson,

- Argumentative essays
- Position papers
- Critical analysis
- Literary interpretation
- Descriptions of new information

- Summaries of material learned
- Reviews of books and articles
- Lab reports
- Research, technical, and progress reports

FIGURE 3.5. Typical college writing tasks.

Stoller, Horn, & Grabe, 2009). Assignments vary across writing-intensive courses, but generally these courses require up to 6,000 words of writing per semester, at least 2,000 of which are graded, and at least half of which count toward the course grade (Boyd, 2010).

Workplace Writing

As in college, writing is of great importance in the workplace (Beaufort, 2009), so it is important for secondary teachers to be aware of the types of writing their students will be expected to do once in a job. Many high school graduates will simultaneously enroll in college and hold jobs, and each setting has its own unique writing demands (Beaufort, 2009). To help students become ready for college and careers, secondary teachers should teach the kinds of writing characteristic of both these settings.

There are two types of workplace writing, first, writing performed by people who write for a living ("career writers"), and second, routine writing tasks by other employees ("professionals who write") (Couture & Rymer, 1993, p. 9). Professionals who write are highly knowledgeable about job tasks, while career writers often do not have technical expertise in the jobs they are writing about, but excel in writing ability. The large majority of the writing of professionals who write involves memoranda, reports, and letters, while career writers often produce job manuals and bulletins. Both types of workplace writing involve the writing of job procedures, and both have the same variety of goals, including to persuade, to inform, to explain, or to instruct (Schriver, 2012). Persuasive writing in workplace and academic settings may be highly similar. For example, an environmental scientist who writes a report intended to present arguments for and against the use of insecticides (Whithaus, 2012) would need to present claims and evidence in the same way as shown in Common Core Writing Standard 1.

Whether employees are in clerical, service, or managerial positions, they must be adept at using the language and genres customary in the particular job domain (Beaufort, 2009; DeKay, 2010; Kaestle, Campbell, Finn, Johnson, & Mikulecky, 2001). This need indicates that workplace writing is a type of disciplinary literacy. What may distinguish disciplinary writing in the workplace from that in academic settings is the large amount of collaboration in the former. It is rare for a sole employee to plan, draft, and revise a written product; rather, several people typically work together in this process (Hart-Landsberg & Reder, 1995). Moreover, collaboration will often occur among employees who work in different disciplines in the same company. Middle and high school teachers have a number of strategies to choose from in teaching adolescents how to collaborate on writing (Graham & Perin, 2006). However, whereas collaboration is in-person in school settings, collaborative workplace writing tends to take place at a distance (Schriver, 2012).

Current Adolescent Writing Instruction

Three major sources of information about writing instruction in the secondary grades are a meta-analysis of effective adolescent writing interventions (Graham & Perin, 2006), discussed in Chapter 1 in this volume, a national survey of high school teachers (Kiuhara, Graham, & Hawken, 2009), and classroom observations and interviews with high school teachers in the New York City school system (Llosa, Beck, & Zhao, 2011). The meta-analysis provides information on effective writing interventions for both middle and high school students, but otherwise there is a shortage of research on writing instruction in middle school classrooms. The meta-analysis identified 11 effective approaches to writing instruction for students in grades 4–12, the most effective ones being cognitive strategies instruction, especially self-regulated strategy instruction, and the teaching of summarization skills. However, the meta-analysis focused on effective writing interventions conducted in controlled experimental conditions, and was not designed to assess whether writing instruction in secondary education was preparing students for college and the workplace.

More pertinent to this aim are findings from the national survey of Kiuhara et al. (2009), which provides information on high school writing assignments. The survey asked ELA, science, and social studies teachers how frequently they assigned 22 different writing tasks over time periods ranging from several times per week to once per year. The most frequent tasks, assigned at least once per week by a majority of respondents, were short-answer responses to homework, responses to material read, answers on worksheets, and summaries of materials read. Another two tasks, writing journal entries and lists, were assigned by a majority of teachers at least once per month. The authors pointed out that three of these six relatively frequently assigned tasks involved "writing without composing" (Kiuhara et al., 2009, p. 151), which suggests that current writing instruction is not preparing adolescents adequately for typical college writing tasks or for the writing-intensive courses that are often required for college graduation.

As mentioned earlier, the nature of writing differs across content areas, and, in fact, Kiuhara et al. (2009) found a few differences in writing tasks across the disciplines included in their survey. For example, 38% of ELA teachers, 26% of social studies teachers, and only 15% of science teachers asked their students to respond in writing to material read several times per week. There were large differences in the writing of persuasive essays, with 30% of social studies teachers, 19% of ELA teachers, and 5% of science teachers assigning this task once per month. However, writing practices in the three areas tended to be similar otherwise. For example, the frequency of summarization was similar across disciplines, with 16–20% of the teachers assigning this task several times per week and 24–29% of teachers in the three areas asking students to summarize text once per month. Further, the ELA teachers were more likely than the science or social studies teachers to provide direct instruction in writing skills; while the content teachers assigned writing tasks, the ELA teachers taught students procedures to prepare them to perform those tasks.

Although the Common Core standards do not explicitly specify length of writing products, the types of writing described for grades 6–12 imply that products would consist of at least several paragraphs, rather than short-answer responses. However, Kiuhara et al. (2009) reported that only eight of the 22 tasks involved writing more than one paragraph. In contrast, most of the college writing tasks identified by Melzer (2009) and Bridgeman and Carlson (1984) were multiparagraph assignments. The eight high school multiparagraph tasks were five-paragraph essay, persuasive essay, research paper, short story, book report, biography, autobiography, and dramatic play. Two-thirds of the ELA teachers assigned at least one multiparagraph writing assignment at least monthly, but only 29% of these teachers assigned at least one of these tasks weekly. Science teachers were less likely than the ELA and social studies teachers to assign multiparagraph writing. Among teachers from all three areas, 51% assigned them at least monthly but only 20% assigned them weekly.

Llosa et al. (2011) observed and interviewed 12 ELA teachers in seven schools selected equally from all four quartiles of state ELA writing scores. They observed many classroom writing tasks, including narratives, argumentative/analytical essays, informational reports, freewrites, short journal entries, summaries, and cohesive paragraphs on topics chosen by students. Argumentative/analytical writing (called "exposition" in this study) was the most frequently observed type of writing and usually took the form of literary analysis. When interviewed, 9 of the 12 teachers stated that exposition was their top priority in writing instruction. Connections between writing instruction and the content area were not a focus of the study, and none were mentioned.

Taken together, the high school and college studies suggest that there are three discrepancies between writing tasks at these two educational levels. First, college tasks require mostly multiparagraph products whereas short-answer tasks predominate in high school. Second, while writing tasks typically assigned in ELA and content courses tend to differ in college, the most frequently assigned high school writing tasks were similar in ELA, science, and social studies. A third difference between high school and college assignments that emerges from these studies is that much more creative and narrative writing, such as personal narratives, short stories, poems, book reports, autobiographies, and dramatic plays, is assigned in high school than in college.

Recommendations for Middle and High School Teachers

It is gratifying to teachers when students improve their writing skills. It is not only exciting to see students develop their ability to express their thoughts, but it is a relief to read pieces of writing that are coherent and creative and demonstrate knowledge about a topic. It is no easy task to teach writing but there are pointers from the research literature that teachers can follow. The following four recommendations, which emerge from research, are made to secondary teachers, in both ELA and the content areas, to promote the kinds of high-quality writing their students need to be ready for college and careers.

1. *Teach writing using extended rather than short-answer writing assignments.* Assign and teach students strategies for writing longer products, such as summaries of articles, research reports, informational and argumentative essays, and literary analyses.

2. *Provide explicit instruction in writing strategies.* It is important to distinguish between teaching writing and assigning writing—assigning a writing task is not the same as teaching students how to write. Explicit instruction involves teaching students strategies to produce a piece of writing. Although practice through writing assignments may improve writing to some extent, there is no substitute for explicit instruction. Unless students demonstrate proficiency with a type of writing assignment, teachers should follow the following four steps whenever writing is assigned:

- Introduce the writing strategy and explain its importance.
- Model the strategy—show students each step, talking them through the mental process at each point. Modeling needs to be carefully planned in advance.
- Provide guided practice with corrective feedback—ask students to work in small groups to practice the writing strategy, and circulate among groups to monitor progress and give feedback.
- Provide independent practice—when students are ready, ask them to employ the writing strategy on their own.

3. *Include disciplinary writing in the ELA and content-area classroom.* Secondary education teachers should be aware of current writing demands in college and workplace settings and utilize that information in the planning of writing instruction. Students may be able to gather this information through research projects, which could involve web searches

and field trips to college classrooms or workplaces. An increase in the amount of disciplinary writing instruction will orient students to how the structure of writing and the informational needs of the audience vary across disciplines.

Writing should be taught not only by ELA teachers but by content teachers. This may be somewhat challenging at first for content teachers. After all, their goal is to teach their subject matter, not literacy. However, students will learn the subject matter more completely if writing instruction is included (Carnine & Carnine, 2004). Some examples of how secondary content teachers can incorporate writing in their classrooms are as follows. The examples come from science, but can be adapted for other subject areas.

- A middle school science teacher, while teaching a unit on the immune system and causes of disease, teaches his students how to write an essay to answer the prompt, "Can good friends make me sick?" (Krajcik & Sutherland, 2010, p. 457).
- In a unit on plants, secondary science students learn to write a persuasive or informational/explanatory essay by taking the role of a root and writing a letter to an audience of stems, leaves, seeds, and flowers to persuade them of the importance of roots (Shanahan, 2012).
- In learning about health and nutrition, adolescents are taught how to answer the following prompt "write a story, essay, newspaper article, or poem about an issue or problem associated with health and nutritional practices. Describe potential solutions provided by others and also your own suggested potential solutions" (Misulis, 2009, p. 16).

4. *Teach disciplinary writing using contextualization.* Contextualization is an approach in which instruction is anchored in specific content and practices (Johnson, 2002). This approach takes two forms, "contextualized" and "integrated" instruction (Perin, 2011, p. 271), as summarized in Figure 3.6.

Examples of the Contextualization of Writing Instruction for ELA and Content-Area Teachers

Example 1: Contextualized Essay-Writing Instruction for the Secondary ELA Classroom Using Social Studies Content. In this example, self-regulated strategy development (SRSD) is used to teach students to write five-paragraph argumentative essays using documents from their social studies class (De La Paz, 2005). The teacher should do the following:

- Introduce the argumentative essay strategy (see STOP and DARE below) by having students write journal entries on how to persuade a parent or peer.
- Ask students to review a sample argumentative essay.
- Teach students to use mnemonics to plan and write the essay: STOP (Suspend judgment; Take a side, Organize ideas; Plan as you write), and DARE (Develop a topic sentence; Add supporting ideas; Reject an argument for the other side; End with a conclusion).
- Explain the nature of the five-paragraph essay, and show examples of essays on a social studies topic.
- Model the SRSD strategy, demonstrating the writing of the first and third paragraph.

Contextualized writing instruction

Taught by ELA teachers

Teach writing skills using content-area text. The primary focus is the writing skills. The content material is the backdrop.

- *Example:* Teach ELA students the steps in writing an argumentative essay using text on the Western expansion currently used in their social studies class (De La Paz, 2005).
- *General principle:* Provide explicit instruction in the skills in the writing curriculum using content-area materials rather than traditional all-purpose, generic text.

Integrated writing instruction

Taught by content-area teachers

Incorporate writing instruction into routine content-area teaching. The primary focus is the subject matter. Writing skills are taught to promote understanding of the content (Nieswandt & Bellomo, 2009).

- *Example:* Teach science students how to use a graphic organizer to plan an informational essay on ozone depletion (Bulgren, Marquis, Lenz, Schumaker, & Deshler, 2009).
- *General principle:* Follow the content-area curriculum, weaving in explicit, evidence-based writing instruction (Harris, Graham, Mason, & Friedlander, 2008; Mason, Reid, & Hagaman, 2012) for the purpose of knowledge development.

FIGURE 3.6. Contextualization to teach disciplinary writing to adolescents.

- Have students work in groups to plan their essays using the mnemonics.
- Have students write an essay on a social studies topic using a graphic organizer that lays out the content for each paragraph (introduction; first, second, and third body paragraph; and conclusion).

Example 2: Contextualized Written Summarization Instruction for the Secondary ELA Classroom Using Workplace Material. ELA teachers should consult with career and technical education (CTE) teachers or guidance counselors to identify text related to occupations that could be used as source text for argumentative or informational/explanatory writing. Since many adolescents are understandably not sure of their career paths, it would be appropriate to use career-exploration material. However, material gleaned from a field trip to a specific job site would also be valuable. Using the selected text, ELA teachers should teach summarization skills using the TRAP/IDEAS strategy (Mason, Reid, & Hagaman, 2012) as follows:

- Define summarization, introduce the TRAP/IDEAS strategy and tell students why it is important. Introduce the concept of mnemonics and spell out TRAP (Think before you read. Read a paragraph. Ask "What is the paragraph mostly about, what is the most important information?" Paraphrase the important information) and IDEAS (Identify important ideas to support the main idea, Delete trivial details, Eliminate redundant details, Add a term for a list of words or concepts, Summarize).
- Model the writing of a summary using a portion of the job text, talking aloud while modeling to illustrate mental processes involved in using the mnemonics.
- Provide graphic organizers to support the use of the mnemonics (provided in Mason et al., 2012).
- Ask students to work in small groups to practice writing a summary of a portion of the job text using the mnemonics, and provide corrective feedback to groups.
- When students are ready, assign independent writing of a summary based on a new portion of the job text.

Example 3: Integrated Essay-Writing Instruction for the Secondary Science Classroom. In this example, science students learn about ozone depletion following a "question exploration routine" (QER), which involves the use of a graphic organizer called a "question exploration guide" (QEG). The QEG is divided into sections on the critical question to be answered in the essay, key terms and explanations, supporting questions and answers, main idea answer, exploration and use of the main idea, and extension of the main idea to everyday life. The graphic organizer is used for note taking as students prepare to write an informational essay (Bulgren, Marquis, Lenz, Schumaker, & Deshler, 2009). The teacher should do the following:

- Show a video on ozone depletion.
- Introduce the QER and QEG and explain how the strategy will help students prepare to write an essay on the topic.
- Explain how note taking using the QEG will help students understand the subject matter.
- Guide the students in completing each section of the QEG, discussing the relevant subject matter.
- Review the information on students' completed QEGs, and discuss the process by which students arrived at the information they filled in.
- Ask students to write an essay using the completed QEG to answer the prompt "How do problems with the ozone layer teach us about human effects on our environment?" (Bulgren et al., 2009, p. 280).

Example 4: Integrated Instruction in Writing from Sources for the Secondary Social Studies Classroom. In this example, the secondary social studies teacher asks students to "write from a scenario" using multiple sources (McKenna & Robinson, 2009, p. 179) . This is a complex task involving summarization, comparison and synthesis of written sources, and elements of both informational/explanatory and argumentative writing. The teacher integrates writing instruction into the teaching of social studies by doing the following:

While teaching a unit on the U.S. presidency, ask the students to take the role of the current president and write a State of the Union address. Elements of writing should be taught explicitly, based on Standard 2 of the Core Standards for disciplinary writing (NGA & CCSSO, 2010, pp. 64–66). Using the text on the U.S. presidency taught in the social studies unit, and with the scenario assignment in mind, the teacher should provide explicit instruction, including modeling, to teach the students to:

- Introduce and support claims.
- Organize ideas.
- Develop the topic.
- Use transitions to create coherence of ideas.
- Use the concepts, language, and vocabulary of the social studies unit.
- Provide a concluding statement.

Conclusions

This chapter focused on the preparation of adolescents for writing practices in postsecondary education and careers. The Common Core writing standards for grades 6–12 were discussed, and several suggestions were made for how they might be revised. The nature of disciplinary writing was explored, and typical writing tasks in college and the workplace were described. Research with secondary teachers was discussed that suggested a need to reorient instruction in several ways to prepare students for these tasks. Recommendations and examples were offered to middle and high school ELA and content teachers toward the goal of preparing adolescents to write in college and career settings.

References

Acker, S. R. (2008). Preparing high school students for college-level writing: Using an e-portfolio to support a successful transition. *Journal of General Education, 57*, 1–15.

Akdere, M., & Azevedo, R. E. (2005). *Writing in the workplace: Implications for human resource development.* Education Resources Information Center (ERIC) Document No. ED492328. Minneapolis: University of Minnesota.

Beaufort, A. (2004). Developmental gains of a history major: A case for building a theory of disciplinary writing expertise. *Research in the Teaching of English, 39*, 136–185.

Beaufort, A. (2009). Preparing adolescents for the literacy demands of the 21st-century workplace. In L. Christenbury, R. Bomer, & P. Smagorinsky (Eds.), *Handbook of adolescent literacy research* (pp. 239–255). New York: Guilford Press.

Bereiter, C. (1980). Development in writing. In L. W. Gregg & E. R. Steinberg (Eds.), *Cognitive processes in writing* (pp. 73–93). Hillsdale, NJ: Erlbaum.

Bereiter, C., & Scardamalia, M. (1987). *The psychology of written composition.* Hillsdale, NJ: Erlbaum.

Boyd, J. (2010). The best of both worlds: The large lecture, writing-intensive course. *Communication Teacher, 24*, 229–237.

Bridgeman, B., & Carlson, S. B. (1984). Survey of academic writing tasks. *Written Communication, 1*, 247–280.

Brockman, E., Taylor, M., Kreth, M., & Crawford, M. K. (2011). What do professors really say about college writing? *English Journal, 100*, 75–81.

Bruning, R., & Horn, C. (2000). Developing motivation to write. *Educational Psychologist, 35*, 25–38.

Bulgren, J., Marquis, J., Lenz, B. K., Schumaker, J. B., & Deshler, D. D. (2009). Effectiveness of question exploration to enhance students' written expression of content knowledge and comprehension. *Reading and Writing Quarterly, 25*, 271–289.

Carnine, L., & Carnine, D. (2004). The interaction of reading skills and science content knowledge when teaching struggling secondary students. *Reading and Writing Quarterly, 20,* 203–218.

Carson, J. G., Chase, N. D., Gibson, S. U., & Hargrove, M. F. (1992). Literacy demands of the undergraduate curriculum. *Reading Research and Instruction, 31,* 25–50.

Conley, D. T. (2008). Rethinking college readiness. *New Directions for Higher Education, 144*(Winter), 3–13.

Couture, B., & Rymer, J. (1993). Situational exigence: Composing processes on the job by writer's role and task value. In R. Spilka (Ed.), *Writing in the workplace: New research perspectives* (pp. 4–20). Carbondale and Edwardsville: Southern Illinois University Press.

De La Paz, S. (2005). Effects of historical reasoning instruction and writing strategy mastery in culturally and academically diverse middle school classrooms. *Journal of Educational Psychology, 97,* 139–156.

De La Paz, S., & Felton, M. K. (2010). Reading and writing from multiple source documents in history: Effects of strategy instruction with low to average high school writers. *Contemporary Educational Psychology, 35,* 174–192.

de Oliveira, L. C. (2011). *Knowing and writing school history: The language of students' expository writing and teachers' expectations.* Charlotte, NC: Information Age.

DeKay, S. H. (2010). Designing email messages for corporate readers: A case study of effective and ineffective rhetorical strategies at a "Fortune" 100 company. *Business Communication Quarterly, 73,* 109–119.

Elander, J., Pittam, G., Lusher, J., Fox, P., & Payne, N. (2010). Evaluation of an intervention to help students avoid unintentional plagiarism by improving their authorial identity. *Assessment and Evaluation in Higher Education, 35,* 157–171.

Elton, L. (2010). Academic writing and tacit knowledge. *Teaching in Higher Education, 15,* 151–160.

Faggella-Luby, M. N., Graner, P. S., Deshler, D. D., & Drew, S. V. (2012). Building a house on sand: Why disciplinary literacy is not sufficient to replace general strategies for adolescent learners who struggle. *Topics in Language Disorders, 32,* 69–84.

Fallahi, C. R. (2012). Improving the writing skills of college students. In E. L. Grigorenko, E. Mambrino, & D. D. Preiss (Eds.), *Writing: A mosaic of new perspectives* (pp. 209–219). New York: Psychology Press.

Ferretti, R. P., Lewis, W. E., & Andrews-Weckerly, S. (2009). Do goals affect the structure of students' argumentative writing strategies? *Journal of Educational Psychology, 101,* 577–589.

Fox, E. (2009). The role of reader characteristics in processing and learning from informational text. *Review of Educational Research, 79,* 197–261.

Graham, S., & Hebert, M. (2010). *Writing to read: Evidence for how writing can improve reading: A report from Carnegie Corporation of New York.* Washington, DC: Alliance for Excellent Education. Retrieved from *http://carnegie. org/fileadmin/Media/Publications/WritingToRead_01.pdf.*

Graham, S., & Perin, D. (2006). *Writing next: Effective strategies to improve writing of adolescents in middle and high schools. A report to Carnegie*

Corporation of New York. Washington, DC: Alliance for Excellent Education. Retrieved from *www.all4ed.org/files/reports/writing_next.pdf.*

Graham, S., & Perin, D. (2007). What we know, what we still need to know: Teaching adolescents to write. *Scientific Studies of Reading, 11,* 313–335.

Grant, M. C., & Fisher, D. (2010). *Reading and writing in science: Tools to develop disciplinary literacy.* Thousand Oaks, CA: Corwin Press/SAGE.

Hansen, W. L. (1993). Teaching a writing intensive course in economics. *Journal of Economic Education, 24,* 213–218.

Harris, K. R., Graham, S., Mason, L. H., & Friedlander, B. (2008). *Powerful writing strategies for all students.* Baltimore: Brookes.

Hart-Landsberg, S., & Reder, S. (1995). Teamwork and literacy: Teaching and learning at Hardy Industries. *Reading Research Quarterly, 30,* 1016–1052.

Hayes, J. R. (1996). A new framework for understanding cognition and affect in writing. In C. M. Levy & S. Ransdell (Eds.), *The science of writing: Theories, methods, individual differences, and applications* (pp. 1–27). Mahwah, NJ: Erlbaum.

Hoover, T. M., Kubina, R. M., & Mason, L. H. (2012). Effects of self-regulated strategy development for POW + TREE on high school students with learning disabilities. *Exceptionality, 20,* 20–38.

Johnson, E. B. (2002). *Contextual teaching and learning: What it is and why it's here to stay.* Thousand Oaks, CA: Corwin Press.

Kaestle, C. F., Campbell, A., Finn, J. D., Johnson, S. T., & Mikulecky, L. J. (2001). *Adult literacy and education in America: Four studies based on the National Adult Literacy Survey* (NCES 2001-534). Education Resources Information Center (ERIC) No. ED461718. Washington, DC: National Center for Education Statistics, U.S. Department of Education.

Keys, C. W. (2000). Investigating the thinking processes of eighth grade writers during the composition of a scientific laboratory report. *Journal of Research in Science Teaching, 37,* 676–690.

Kiuhara, S. A., Graham, S., & Hawken, L. S. (2009). Teaching writing to high school students: A national survey. *Journal of Educational Psychology, 101,* 136–160.

Klein, P. D., & Samuels, B. (2010). Learning about plate tectonics through argument-writing. *Alberta Journal of Educational Research, 56,* 196–217.

Kober, N., & Rentner, D. S. (2012). *Year two of implementing the Common Core State Standards: States' progress and challenges.* Washington, DC: Center on Education Policy. Retrieved from *www.cep-dc.org/index. cfm?DocumentTopicID=1.*

Krajcik, J. S., & Sutherland, L. M. (2010). Supporting students in developing literacy in science. *Science, 328,* 456–459.

Llosa, L., Beck, S. W., & Zhao, C. G. (2011). An investigation of academic writing in secondary schools to inform the development of diagnostic classroom assessments. *Assessing Writing, 16,* 256–273.

Magnifico, A. M. (2010). Writing for whom?: Cognition, motivation, and a writer's audience. *Educational Psychologist, 45,* 167–184.

Mason, L. H., & Graham, S. (2008). Writing instruction for adolescents with learning disabilities: Programs of intervention research. *Learning Disabilities Research and Practice, 23*, 103–112.

Mason, L. H., Harris, K. R., & Graham, S. (2011). Self-regulated strategy development for students with writing difficulties. *Theory into Practice, 50*, 20–27.

Mason, L. H., Reid, R., & Hagaman, J. L. (2012). *Building comprehension in adolescents: Powerful strategies for improving reading and writing in content areas.* Baltimore: Brookes.

Mayer, R. E., & Wittrock, M. C. (1996). Problem-solving transfer. In D. C. Berliner & R. C. Calfee (Eds.), *Handbook of educational psychology* (pp. 47–62). New York: Macmillan.

McKenna, M. C., & Robinson, R. D. (2009). *Teaching through text: Reading and writing in the content areas* (5th ed.). Boston: Pearson Education.

Melzer, D. (2009). Writing assignments across the curriculum: A national study of college writing. *College Composition and Communication, 61*, W240–W261.

Misulis, K. E. (2009). Promoting learning through content literacy instruction. *American Secondary Education, 37*, 10–19.

Moje, E. B. (2007). Developing socially just subject-matter instruction: A review of the literature on disciplinary literacy teaching. *Review of Research in Education, 31*, 1–44.

Monte-Sano, C. (2010). Disciplinary literacy in history: An exploration of the historical nature of adolescents' writing. *Journal of the Learning Sciences, 19*, 539–568.

National Governors Association & Council of Chief State School Officers. (2010). *Common Core State Standards for English language arts & literacy in history/social studies, science, and technical subjects.* Washington, DC: Authors. Retrieved from *www.corestandards.org.*

Nieswandt, M., & Bellomo, K. (2009). Written extended-response questions as classroom assessment tools for meaningful understanding of evolutionary theory. *Journal of Research in Science Teaching, 46*, 333–356.

Nokes, J. D., Dole, J. A., & Hacker, D. J. (2007). Teaching high school students to use heuristics while reading historical texts. *Journal of Educational Psychology, 99*, 492–504.

Perin, D. (2011). Facilitating student learning through contextualization: A review of the evidence. *Community College Review, 39*, 268–295.

Planty, M., Hussar, W., Snyder, T., Provasnik, S., Kena, G., Dinkes, R., et al. (2008). *The condition of education 2008* (NCES 2008-031). Washington, DC: National Center for Education Statistics, Institute of Education Sciences, U.S. Department of Education. Retrieved from *http://nces.ed.gov/programs/coe/pdf/coe_wrt.pdf.*

Porter, R., Guarienti, K., Brydon, B., Robb, J., Royston, A., Painter, H., et al. (2010). Writing better lab reports. *The Science Teacher, 77*, 43–48.

Robinson, M. S., Stoller, F. L., Horn, B., & Grabe, W. (2009). Teaching and applying chemistry-specific writing skills using a simple, adaptable exercise. *Journal of Chemical Education, 86*, 45–49.

Russell, D. R. (2002). *Writing in the academic disciplines* (2nd ed.). Carbondale and Edwardsville: Southern Illinois University Press.

Schriver, K. (2012). What we know about expertise in professional communication. In V. W. Berninger (Ed.), *Past, present, and future contributions of cognitive writing research to cognitive psychology* (pp. 275–312). New York: Psychology Press.

Shanahan, C. (2012). Learning with text in science. In T. L. Jetton & C. Shanahan (Eds.), *Adolescent literacy in the academic disciplines: General principles and practical strategies* (pp. 154–171). New York: Guilford Press.

Shanahan, T. (2009). Connecting reading and writing instruction for struggling learners. In G. A. Troia (Ed.), *Instruction and assessment for struggling writers: Evidence-based practices* (pp. 113–131). New York: Guilford Press.

Shanahan, T., & Shanahan, C. (2012). What is disciplinary literacy and why does it matter? *Topics in Language Disorders, 32,* 7–18.

Stewart, T. L., Myers, A. C., & Culley, M. R. (2010). Enhanced learning and retention through "writing to learn" in the psychology classroom. *Teaching of Psychology, 37,* 46–49.

Whithaus, C. (2012). Claim–evidence structures in environmental science writing: Modifying Toulmin's model to account for multimodal arguments. *Technical Communication Quarterly, 21,* 105–128.

Wineburg, S., Martin, D., & Monte-Sano, C. (2011). *Reading like a historian: Teaching literacy in middle and high school history classrooms.* New York: Teachers College Press.

Yancey, K. B. (2009). The literacy demands of entering the university. In L. Christenbury, R. Bomer, & P. Smagorinsky (Eds.), *Handbook of adolescent literacy research* (pp. 265–270). New York: Guilford Press.

Yore, L. D., Hand, B. M., & Prain, V. (2002). Scientists as writers. *Science Education, 86,* 672–692.

Zeek, S. (2011). Teaching the research paper through inquiry-based instruction. *Inquiry, 16,* 75–85.

Zygouris-Coe, V. (2012). Disciplinary literacy and the Common Core State Standards. *Topics in Language Disorders, 32,* 35–50.

PART II

Types and Purposes of Writing

Chapter 4

A Developmental Approach to Teaching Narrative Composition

ANNE McKEOUGH

The Common Core State Standards (CCSS; National Governors Association [NGA] & Council for Chief State School Officers [CCSSO], 2010) for writing specify student competencies across the grades in four domains: text types and purposes, production and distribution, research to build and present knowledge, and range of writing. As such, they represent an important step toward educators' understanding of the knowledge and skills students must gain through the grades so that they will be well prepared for their college studies and career. According to the CCSS document (2010), "Students advancing through the grades are expected to meet each year's grade-specific standards and retain or further develop skills and understandings mastered in preceding grades." Thus, the CCSS for writing offer a developmental roadmap of competencies, as higher grade knowledge and skills build and expand on lower grade knowledge and skills. Although it was not designed as an instruction tool, such a roadmap can help teachers plan where to focus their teaching as well as help them to evaluate students' learning accomplishments. In general terms, because the CCSS for writing build developmentally, teachers can use them to assess the learning needs of typical, challenged, and advanced students by examining the expected competencies across several grade levels and then targeting areas for enrichment or remediation, as well as grade-appropriate instruction.

In spite of their general utility, the CCSS for writing have certain drawbacks that, if addressed, would make the document more helpful to teachers of writing. My overall aim in this chapter is twofold: (1) to discuss how teachers might use the current CCSS to determine if their students are meeting the competencies specified for grade levels and (2) to outline how the CCSS for writing can be improved so that they more exhaustively describe the knowledge and skills developing young story writers need to gain to ensure success in college and career. More specifically, in this chapter I

- Illustrate how the CCSS can be applied to students' story-writing samples across three levels of student proficiency in a fourth-grade class
- Outline important narrative writing competencies that are not specified in the CCSS and discuss how they develop from grades 1 to 12
- Discuss how these competencies can be supported in the classroom by identifying specific links between narrative reading and writing competencies

Analysis Using the CCSS for Writing: Text Type and Purpose

To illustrate how the CCSS can be applied to students' story writing, I present a story written by a fourth-grade student who was engaged in a trickster tale writing unit (see Jarvey, McKeough, & Pyryt, 2008 and McKeough, Palmer, Jarvey, & Bird, 2007 for a description of the unit and its outcomes). The story was written during class time, following a 3-week period of reading and discussing trickster tales, and in response to a request made to students to write their own trickster tale. The story represents an average level of performance for students attending this middle socioeconomic suburban public school. I initially analyze the story using the grade four writing standards specified for samples of narrative writing, namely, "Text Type and Purpose" (item W.4.3; see analysis following the story) and then reanalyze it using criteria related to important narrative writing knowledge and skills that are not included in the CCSS.

UNTITLED STORY BY JESSICA

One bright sunny school day, when all the kids in (city's name) were getting ready for school, Kelly was talking to her little sister Megan. She was telling her about school. "You should go to school because it is really fun and you'll get candy," she said. "Your teacher will take you to the movie theatre." There was nothing stopping Megan now. She was off to grade one.

They ate their breakfast really fast and off they went. But school wasn't what Megan expected. They did five pages of Math, read a chapter in Social, answered thirty questions in Science. Then they had lunch. After lunch they did silent reading. Next they cleaned their desks and went home. "That was the most boring time of my life," thought Megan.

The next day Megan didn't want to go to school because she thought school was not fun at all. "We don't play any games," she complained. But Kelly said, "There's going to be treats." "What kind of treats?" asked Megan suspiciously? "I'm not sure . . . it's a surprise," said Kelly, with a giggle. So Megan went to school. She was excited about the surprise. But at 2:00 there still weren't any treats. No cookies. No candy. No nothing. Just work. "This stinks," thought Megan. She scrunched up her nose and pouted.

But the next day, Kelly and Megan were arguing about going to school. "You should go to school," said Kelly. "Why?" said Megan with a really mad look on her face. Her face was really red, and getting redder by the minute. Finally Kelly said, "I will call the truant officer." "What's a truant officer?" said Megan. "A truant officer checks up on kids who are missing school." Really?" said Megan. "Let's go to school right now."

"OK. Let's go," said Kelly.

Again, school was very boring. "I wish we didn't have to go to school," grumbled Megan. "We read two 18 paged stories until lunch. Then we did writing practice until the bell. This is so boring. I need to make myself an adventure. Maybe I will make up a short cut home," thought Megan. Megan got great joy. She was having a ball making up a short cut. But after awhile it wasn't that much fun. She was lost. "Oh no!" Luckily there was a phone booth a few meters away. Megan ran to the phone booth. She looked up the number for the school. Finally at the school the secretary answered. "I'll be right over," said Mrs. Howard the secretary.

Megan learned that going to school can help you, and sometimes it can even save your life.

In what follows, the CCSS are quoted, and excerpts are taken from Jessica's writing sample to illustrate each element.

Write narratives to develop real or imagined experiences or events using effective technique, descriptive details, and clear event sequences.

a. Orient the reader by establishing a situation and introducing a narrator and/or characters

- One bright sunny school day, when all the kids in [city's name] were getting ready for school, Kelly was talking to her little sister Megan. She was telling her about school.

Organize an event sequence that unfolds naturally

- Kelly tells her little sister, Megan, she should go to school because it is fun and tricks her with promises of candy and a movie.
- But school is just hard work and Megan doesn't want to go back.
- Kelly persists in her ruse, telling Megan that she'll get surprise treats. Megan is enticed to go to school but she is disappointed again as no treats materialize.
- The next day the two sisters argue over school attendance and Kelly threatens to call a truant officer. Megan relents but school is just hard and boring.
- To raise her spirits, Megan decides to have an adventure, gets lost, and then calls the school for help.
- When she's rescued, Meagan realizes that "going to school can help you, and sometimes it can even save your life."

b. Use dialogue and description to develop experiences and events or show the responses of characters to situations.

- The next day Megan didn't want to go to school because she thought school was not fun at all. "We don't play any games," she complained. But Kelly said, "There's going to be treats." "What kind of treats?" asked Megan suspiciously? "I'm not sure . . . it's a surprise," said Kelly, with a giggle. So Megan went to school.

c. Use a variety of transitional words and phrases to manage the sequence of events.

- There was nothing stopping Megan now. She was off to grade one. They ate their breakfast really fast and off they went.
- The next day Megan didn't want to go to school because she thought school was not fun at all.

d. Use concrete words and phrases and sensory details to convey experiences and events precisely.

- "Why?" said Megan with a really mad look on her face. Her face was really red, and getting redder by the minute.

e. Provide a conclusion that follows from the narrated experiences or events.

- Megan learned that going to school can help you, and sometimes it can even save your life.

Critique of CCSS Analysis

The foregoing analysis demonstrates that Jessica has met the CCSS criteria for fourth-grade narrative writing. She has more knowledge and many more skills than this analysis reveals, however. To help uncover a more complete view of just what Jessica knows about stories, consider the features that Bruner (1991) asserted that all stories have in common:

- Sequentiality. Story events occur in a sequence, linked by connecting words such as *and, then, because,* and *but*).
- Particularity. Stories are about something in particular; extraneous events that do not relate to this particular something should not be included in the story.
- Intentional states. Story characters' actions are motivated by their intentions (i.e., goals, desires, wants, and needs).
- Canonicity and breach. In stories, the expected order of things (i.e., the canon or norm) is breached or violated, thus situating the story character in a dilemma or trouble.

Whereas the CCSS address sequentiality, particularity (both beginning in grade one), and intentional states (beginning in grade two), they do not focus on the essential narrative feature, canonicity and breach. According to the eminent educator Jerome Bruner, "Trouble is the engine of narrative" (Bruner, 1996, p. 99). "The trouble is a violation of the legitimate, the expectable, the appropriate. And the outcome of the story depends upon seeing legitimacy maintained, restored, or redefined" (Bruner & Lucariello, 1989, p. 77). In traditional European folktales, as with realistic fiction, trouble typically takes the form of something or someone thwarting the hero from achieving his or her goal. In the course of attempting to reach his or her goal, the hero typically faces obstacles or troubles (i.e., subproblems). Finally, he or she succeeds, wrong is made right, and normalcy is restored.

In trickster tales, a subgenre of folktales, trouble takes the form of a negative trickster who plagues the hero or a positive trickster who outwits the antihero and, as a result, trouble and character are an integrated package. Jessica's trickster, Kelly, is an example of a positive trickster; she is attempting to motivate her little sister to attend school. Trickster tales typically include a series of tricks (as did Jessica's) that are contrived by a trickster who is aware of the psychological vulnerabilities of the victim (i.e., what he or she is likely to fall for; Babcock-Abrahams, 1975). As such, trickster tales require the writer to understand that positive character traits (such as generosity) create vulnerability to a certain type of trickster (e.g., one who poses as needy), whereas negative character traits (e.g., pomposity) create vulnerability to a different type of trickster (e.g., one who flatters).

Thus, authors of trickster tales need to create characters with specific vulnerabilities that spell "trouble" and then put them alongside characters who will play to those vulnerabilities, thus creating "double trouble." In other words, trickster tale authors need to seamlessly integrate the psychological profile of the characters with the plot's breach (or trouble). Students accomplish this gradually, of course, beginning with stereotypic character types that they experience frequently in their daily lives and in books and movies. Jessica's Megan is such a stereotypic character—a child who is motivated to comply through the promise of treats and surprises. In Jessica's story, Kelly understands Megan's vulnerability and uses it to motivate her to go to school, thus managing to integrate the story's breach (i.e., a little sister who was less than enthusiastic about school) and the character's psychological profile (i.e., vulnerability to promises of treats) in a seamless fashion. However, although Kelly's tricks work in the short term, they eventually backfire. When in school, Megan is bored and decides to alleviate her boredom by creating an adventure of her own, only to get lost. Through this new problem or trouble, Jessica introduced a twist into her story that links back to the initial problem—Megan now realizes that school is worthwhile. This novel linkage nested the three trick episodes within a larger story, integrating the whole story and making it more cohesive (Jarvey et al., 2008).

What does this analysis add to the CCSS analysis? First, it highlights the role that breach plays in narrative plots of young writers. Second, it shows how character development is an integral component of plot when seamlessly linked to breach. Stories are, at their very core, about people and their problems (or trouble). Structuring events around this thematic content in an increasingly complex fashion is one of the major accomplishments of narrative writing during the elementary school years (Applebee, 1978; Bruner, 1986, 1990). Throughout the elementary school years, students learn to create increasingly complex characters that exist on both physical and mental dimensions (McKeough et al., 2007), moving toward creating characters who hold contrasting desires, which in turn create story tension and propels the story plot forward (Jarvey et al., 2008).

The foregoing analysis offers a snapshot of what one average-functioning fourth-grade student knows about creating complex characters and breach in stories. In what follows, I provide a roadmap of the developmental path leading up to this level of narrative competency (i.e., average fourth-grade proficiency), and then discuss how it continues to evolve. On this roadmap I have used grade levels as signposts. This does not mean that all or even most children perform as specified in the story sample on any given day. It does, however, mean that the majority of average-functioning students perform at this level much of the time. As teachers, you are well aware that in all children's lives there are days they perform at their optimal level and days they do not hit that mark. You also know that your students vary considerably from each other. In my view, our goal as teachers is to identify where, along the journey to writing competence, each child generally is situated and then to help him or her reach the next level of competence. Thus, this chapter does not specify a set of standards that all children at a given grade level should meet. Rather, it offers a map of how narrative composition changes and develops on two critical dimensions, namely, character and problem plot structure, and how teachers can use that map to help them evaluate each student's performance and plan accordingly.

Developmental Change in Character and Story Breach

Even before they enroll in the first grade, children have a considerable understanding of the narrative genre, especially as it pertains to the two narrative elements discussed in the foregoing analysis, trouble and character development, as the following three brief stories show. Of course, children at this age are unable to write stories but many are able to offer coherent accounts of imaginary and real-life events, if given support such as a story prompt or toys to enact the story.

ABBIE'S STORY
(told to her grandmother while explaining a picture she had drawn)

"There's a girl and her magic horse and they live in a magic castle and the horse can fly and . . . even with the girl and they flied over the fence and then the tree and the moon. And they like to fly high up. And then they flied home" (McKeough, Bird, Romaine, & Tourigny, 2008).

Trouble is not the engine of Abbie's story, nor is it in most 4-year-old's stories. Rather, she relies on a script, of sorts, for magical beings and little girls. She has, however, introduced her story characters, identified one explicit mental state for them (i.e., "like"), and created an appropriate sequence of actions. Such a "happy-ever-after" event sequence is a typical precursor to stories that include a problem, as is the case in Zoey's story.

ZOEY'S STORY
(composed during instruction that focused directly on supporting children's storytelling and modeled on a story that was told to the children)

Once a little girl was walking in the woods and she saw a sad lamb and he wanted a friend. And the girl said, "I can be your friend." And he says, "O.K." And then she built a little house in the woods for it and kept it there and brought food for her everyday.

Because it is modeled on a story Zoey had heard during class instruction, this story is considerably more complex than Abbie's story and is not typical of the original stories told by most 4-year-olds. Zoey not only has introduced her characters but has also attributed explicit mental state to her lamb character (i.e., a feeling: "sad"), which is integral to the trouble (i.e., his unfulfilled desire to have a friend). Thus, if supported through appropriate teaching, 4-year-olds appear to be capable of expressing characters' feelings and desires in relation to the story's "trouble" (McKeough & Sanderson, 1996). This finding calls into question the CCSS for narrative writing that introduce characters' thoughts, feelings, and desires only at the grade-two level.

By the first grade, many average-functioning children spontaneously include breach and characters' mental states in their stories (McCabe & Peterson, 1991; McKeough, 1992), as the following orally composed story demonstrates. In it, Sam creates a lamb character that is trapped inside a fence and is lonely. Although not cued to do so, he creates trouble (or a problem), which is resolved when a horse rescues him from the enclosure and befriends him. In the end, both characters are happy together.

SAM'S STORY
(composed in response to a prompt requesting a story about a kind old horse and a happy little lamb)

A horse was walking along in a field and he saw a little lamb in one of the places of the barn and it was a fence. And it was a nice little lamb and it—it was lonely. So the horse jumped in and then the lamb jumped onto the horse and then they—and then the lamb jumped onto the horse and then they got out. And then they went to a place where there was no one except them. And they picked some blueberries and they ate them. And the horse found some hay and he liked the hay better than the blueberries. And a lamb found some grass and he liked the grass better than the blueberries. And then they went and lived together. And they lived happily ever after.

By the third grade, further development typically occurs in how students structure their stories around breach and their characters' internal mental states. At this point we often see a complicating event or events that impede resolution in students' stories and the attribution of additional associated mental states to their characters. A sample of this type of story is presented in Figure 4.1. It was written by Bailey, an 8-year-old third-grade student, in response to a request to write a story about someone who has a problem.

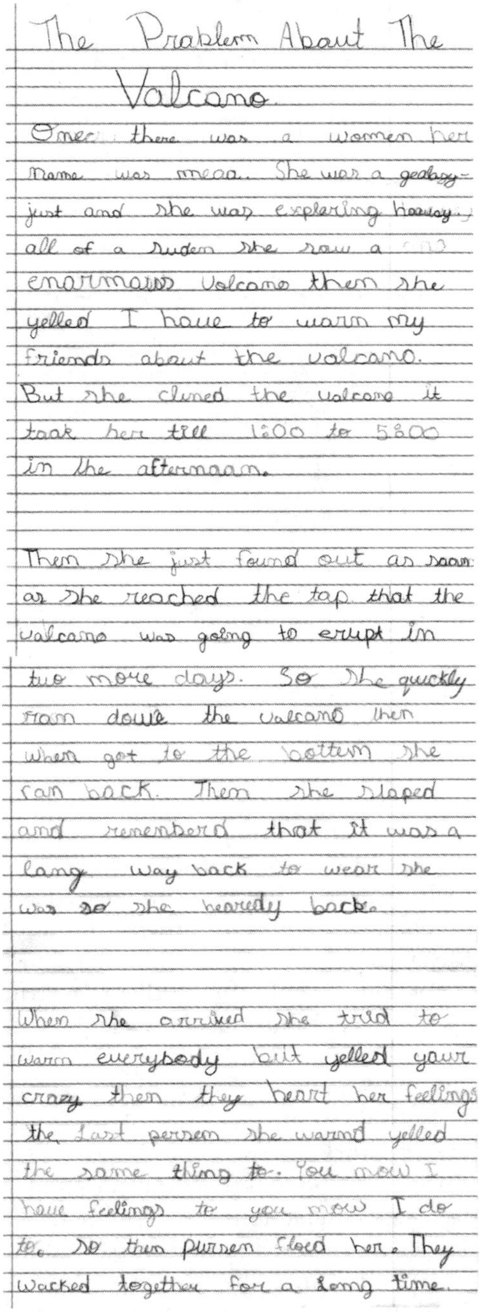

The Problem About The Volcano

Once there was a women her name was mega. She was a geology-just and she was exploring houswy. all of a suden she saw a enourmouss volcano then she yelled I have to warn my friends about the volcano. But she clmed the volcano it took her till 1:00 to 5:00 in the afternoon.

Then she just found out as soon as she reached the top that the volcano was going to erupt in two more days. So She quickly from down the volcano then when got to the bottom she ran back. Then she sloped and remembered that it was a long way back to wear she was so she heavely back.

When she arrived she tried to warn everybody but yelled your crazy then they heart her feelings the last person she warnd yelled the same thing to. You now I have feelings to you now I do to. so then purrson floed her. They wacked together for a long time.

(continued)

FIGURE 4.1. Bailey's story.

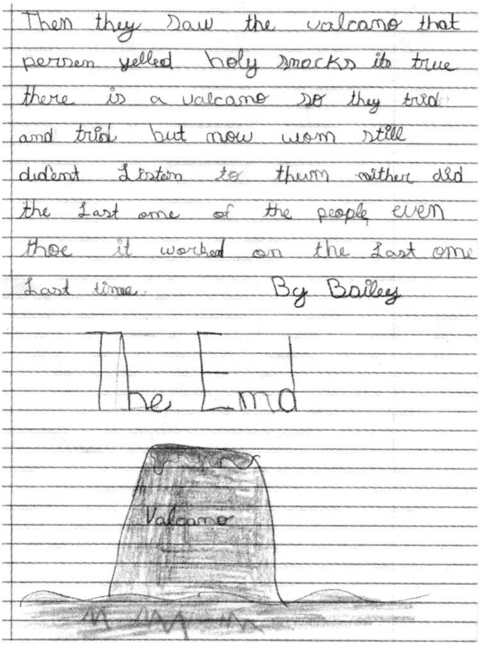

Then they saw the volcano that person yelled holy smocks its true there is a volcano so they tried and tried but now wom still dident listen to them neither did the last one of the people even thoe it worked on the last one last time. By Bailey

The End

Volcano

FIGURE 4.1. *(continued)*

As is evident, Bailey creates a problem or "trouble"—an enormous volcano that is going to erupt is discovered by a geologist, Meaa. Meaa's efforts to warn others of the imminent danger are not successful, however, because of their refusal to believe her. This creates a second problem for Bailey's protagonist, who now must prove that the volcano really exists. Although Meaa proves the volcano's existence to one other person, in the end they cannot convince all of the others. In structuring this more complex plot line, Bailey has also depicted characters with multiple mental states. Meaa moves from contentedly exploring, to alarm, to feeling hurt, and finally to determination; the other story character expresses feelings of surprise/alarm and determination.

Comparing Bailey's story to fourth-grade Jessica's trickster tale presented previously reveals that both authors include trouble, more trouble in the complicating events, and depictions of the characters' associated mental states. However, Jessica has created more complex characters than Bailey has (which is not surprising since she is a year older and has had more instruction in writing in general and related to the particular task). Specifically, Jessica's character, Kelly, tricks her little sister by anticipating her responses (i.e., she knows what she will fall for), which allows the tricks to work to a certain extent. In contrast, Bailey's main character, Meaa, does not show insight into other story characters. Rather, Bailey focuses on Meaa's mental/emotional responses to them and the story events.

By the fifth grade, many students include a resolution that fully addresses the problems and complications. As well, their characters' motivations are made clearer in relation to trouble they experience and they behave consistently unless there is a clear reason for them to change. As such, characters become increasingly plausible (see Kirkland & Davies, 1987, for a discussion of the principles of convincing characterization). These two features are evident in Emily's story (see Figure 4.2). Her resolution (i.e., telling her mother of the bullying she is experiencing and her mother's subsequent intervention) not only solved her problem but also solved the problem for the other children. Her main character's motivations and intentions are clear throughout the story, and when this "good" young girl lies to her mother, the reader can understand why. And, after a night of dreaming about her bullying experience, Sally tells her mother the truth. Thus, ultimately Sally is a consistent and plausible character, albeit a rather stereotypic one.

(continued)

FIGURE 4.2. Emily's story.

The Girl Who Solved Her Problem!

There's a little Girl her name is Sally. Sally just moved from Victora to New York. Sally now has a big house. Sally went upstairs to unpack. She was so excited to go to School in two more days. Finally it was time to go to School. Sally made her lunch, fixed her hair. Ate. Brushed her teeth. Washed her face and was off to school. Sally got to School. When she got to her class she stoped and looked around. Hellow said Sally. Teacher My name is Ms. Rose. My name is Sally. It's very nice to meat you Ms. Rose. Take your time and find a seat. Sally found somewhere to sit She picked a spot beside another little girl named Mia. She was a pretty girl. She had a nice long brown hair. She was a girl who's been at the school last year. Sally had learned a lot today. She learned how to Spell, do math like three digits by one digit. The recess bell just rang. Everybody ran outside Sally thought of Mia as a nice girl so she ran up to Mia and asked her it She would like to play tag. Mia Said Yes!

Two months came by. Everything was great except one thing it was another girl named Kacy. She was the bully of the school but of corse the Grades only went up to Grade Six Kacy bullyed everbody in the school even Mia. It was a couple of weeks later untill Kacy started bullying Sally. Sally did'nt Know what to do She asked Mia but she said just to ignore Kacy. So she did. Kacy did'nt like it So she went up to sally and toll her to meat her after school The Bell just rang. Ms. Rose said you are Dismissed Sally forgot ①

Everything what Kacy had said untill she saw Kacy. Sally Started running as fast as she could She saw her house it was just around the corner she ran faster but she could also her Kacys voice. She finally got to her house she stoped and turned around Kacy wasn't there. Sally walk'd up the stairs and opened the door her mom was there. She asked Sally how was her day she said it was good and she ran up to her room layed on her bed and thought about what she had did to her mom. Lieing to her mom was the worst thing she did to her mom. It was time to go to sleep. Sally fell asleep really quick. She was haveing a dream. It was about Kacy fighting her. This dream went on untill it was time to get up. Sally got up. She could hear Kacys voice repeating and repeating. Sally could not take it anymore She had to tell her mom. Her mom got upset she went to the school and pulled the Teacher out of class and talked to her and asked her if she knew anything about Kacy bullying Sally. Ms. Rose said No! Ms. Rose said She will watch Kacy and Sally see if anything goes on. Sallys mothe said ok! But I would like to talk with Kacys mom and you and me. OK Said Ms. Rose I'll see if I could get a whole of her. Since that day Kacy never bullyed anyone again.

Written by: Emily Bird
★
②

FIGURE 4.2. *(continued)*

Through our analyses of sixth- and seventh-grade students' writing samples, we have determined that a significant change occurs in the way characters and their troubles are depicted. Specifically, average-functioning students at these grade levels begin to lay out immediate experiences (i.e., mental and physical) that occurred at different times and in different situations and then interpret these experiences in terms of higher level characteristics such as personality traits or enduring mental states (McKeough & Genereux, 2003). For example, one 12-year-old student described several incidents in which her main character was nervous when trying to make new friends and then explained her nervousness as being due to long-term shyness caused by the family's history of moving from city to city. Thus story characters experience the "trouble" in their lives in a unique way, based on their psychological profile.

Throughout middle school, students develop the ability to create story trouble and characters that are more psychologically complex. By the eighth and ninth grades, average-functioning students typically include additional enduring states and traits, often in the form of contrary tendencies within the same character that create an internal psychological conflict in addition to conflict being experienced between the character and outer elements in her world. The following excerpts from a 14-year-old's story illustrate this structure. The teenage protagonist is not only in conflict with some of her friends (i.e., outer elements) she is also torn within (i.e., torn between wanting to be with them to gain popularity and wanting to break away from them so she can be herself).

That's the problem with some of my friends. Popularity is such an important thing to them. If your not popular you're definitely not one of them. I don't think they ever really accepted me. Sometimes I hate the way they criticize and make fun of people who don't live up to their standards. . . . You know when you think about it it's all very stupid. I mean it wasn't long ago when I would have done anything to get into their group, and now that I'm with them I'll do almost anything to get out. I've just got to break apart from them slowly and hopefully find people that know the meaning of friendship. I can't wait for the day to come. The day that I can be me and the day when someone will like me just for being myself.

During the high school years, students continue to add layers of psychological complexity within their stories. Students increasingly resolve the dialectic of the internal and external struggles of their protagonists in a coordinated and coherent fashion. They accomplish this by using several literary devices to a greater extent from the 10th to the 12th grade. These literary devices include but are not limited to the following:

- Psychological/social similes and metaphors (e.g., "So now it's like the whole world has closed up around me" and "The wall had started to build. Not a wall of concrete or stone but a mental wall that no one, except for Rachel herself, could move or tear down").
- Flashback and foreshadowing (e.g., " I thought about the first time I met her in grade one" and "That was one promise I wished I had kept").
- Paradoxical consequences or juxtaposed alternatives (e.g., "And poor Laurie. An innocent girl who got what she did not deserve . . . Things like this sometimes happen. Too often though").
- Perspective taking (e.g., " 'I am 16 and mature enough to handle the responsibility of a vacation alone.' No. That would be no good it sounded to superior").

The foregoing analysis has demonstrated how breach or "trouble" in stories (Bruner, 1991) develops across the elementary school years from kindergarten to 12th grade. The analysis has shown that even kindergarten students can, with teaching, include simple problems and that they begin to describe characters in terms of their physical and mental states. Through elementary school, students increasingly include characters mental states (i.e., thoughts, feelings, and desires) that are central to the story's trouble. Throughout the middle school and high school years, students develop the psychological profiles of the characters in ever more complex ways.

In the next section, I take up the issue of instruction by addressing the following question: How can teachers help to support their student's narrative composition knowledge and skills, specifically in the areas of the problem structure of plot and characterization?

Supporting the Development of Narrative Composition in the Classroom

From grade 4 through to grade 12, the "Research to Build and Present Knowledge" strand (i.e., item 9 in the CCSS for narrative writing) includes very limited, albeit useful, suggestions for encouraging students to model their writing on the literature they read. Before grade 4, however, the strand contains no information. This is problematic as teachers can do much to help their students learn how to write by reading narrative texts not just for an understanding and appreciation of the story but also for an understanding and appreciation of how the story was put together. In fact, what has often been referred to as "reading with a writer's eye" (e.g., Tiedt, 1988) has been the practice of many elementary teachers for many years.

What Is Reading with a Writer's Eye?

Reading with a writer's eye (RwWE) is noticing how expert writers write as one reads a selection so that one's own writing can be improved. It's paying attention to literary elements and techniques so that they can be used in one's own writing. When reading narrative selections with a writer's eye, students read to notice why and how the author created the setting and developed the characters and why he or she structured the text in a certain manner. They read with attention to why the author wrote in a particular way: why he or she said things in certain ways (i.e., why the author used certain words and phrases and why he or she used a particular style). When they RwWE, students also pay attention to what the author's purpose was and why he or she chose to use a particular subgenre (e.g., myth, realistic fiction, or folktale). RwWE means reading with curiosity about how the author created the whole literary experience.

Students approach text differently as readers and writers. When they approach a text as a reader they read for the sake of gaining new information, novel experiences, and interesting viewpoints. When they approach the text as a writer they turn the text inside-out to see how it is made, how it is held together, and what makes it work. RwWE occurs on the second (or later) reading of the selection. During a selection's first reading students are engaged with comprehension strategies. Understanding, appreciating, and learning from a text occur before students RwWE because readers need to take time to see what there is to see and feel what there is to feel. Students return to the text for a second view to look more closely at what an author has done to create this particular experience with words. It's important to read for understanding and enjoyment first and RwWE later because without the first part (experiencing the story), the second part (examining the author's craft) may well become dry, dull literary criticism. To illustrate, it's the tasting of a delicious dish that prompts one to wonder about the recipe. It's the experience of eloquent literature that motivates readers to figure out how it was done.

How does RwWE improve writing? RwWE supports students to take a metacognitive stance toward story. It gets children inside the process of story making so that they can better appreciate stories themselves and become better, more skilled, and more informed story writers. To benefit maximally from RwWE, though, students need excellent literature. Excellent literature provides models for building students' narrative writing resources. As students progress through the grades, story texts become increasingly complex and, hence, provide ever richer opportunities for understanding the writer's craft. Writing techniques and strategies that were once only recognized are gradually analyzed and evaluated.

To support teachers to undertake RwWE activities, we constructed developmentally based rubrics (McKeough & Jeary, 2007; see Appendix 4.1) that were based on the research literature (Fountas & Pinnell, 2001; Hansen, 2001; McCabe & Peterson, 1991; McKeough, 1992; Prose, 2006; Shanahan, 2006; Tiedt, 1988). Rubrics were constructed for various literary devices from grades 1–5 (see Appendix 4.1). We then worked with a group of master teachers to refine the rubrics in terms of content and teacher usefulness. Finally, we developed for grades 3–5 a student version of the rubrics for use in their analysis of the devices authors use when crafting stories (see Appendix 4.2). Students then were asked to apply the devices to their own writing efforts, as appropriate. Although we developed rubrics for six literary devices (i.e., setting, characterization, problem plot structure, language use, type of subgenre, and author's purpose), the current discussion will focus only on problem plot structure and characterization because these two elements are the focus of this chapter.

As can be seen from inspecting Appendix 4.1, for each grade, three levels are specified: low (Level 1), average (Level 2), and high (Level 3). Performance indicators across the grades overlap, with Level 1 representing typical performance at the previous grade (e.g., grade one), Level 2 representing typical performance at the target grade level (e.g., grade two), and level 3 representing typical performance at the next grade (e.g., grade three).

Using RwWE Rubrics in the Classroom

To illustrate how teachers can use the rubrics, I will use items from the first-grade and fourth-grade rubrics for character development and problem plot structure.

First-Grade Application of RwWE Rubric

To illustrate how teachers can use the rubrics, I present a lesson plan designed for the selection *The Kite*, excerpted from *Days with Frog and Toad* (Lobel, 1979). In the story Toad and Frog are trying to fly a kite. First, Toad tries to get the kite in the air by running quickly across the meadow, but he is unsuccessful. Three robins laugh at him and declare, "That kite will not fly!" Toad is discouraged and returns to Frog lamenting that the kite won't fly and that he gives up. Frog perseveres, however, and suggests a second try. The story continues in this vein, with the robins making disparaging remarks, Toad falling victim to them, and Frog suggesting alternate strategies for getting the kite in the air. Recall that RwWE occurs after students have read and understood the content of the story. The lesson plan follows [see similar work in *Imagine It!* (SRA/McGraw Hill, 2008)].

Character development item. Can recognize and understand the author's use of techniques to allow readers to understand who the story characters are: Characters with both physical and mental qualities (see Appendix 4.1, First Grade: Level 2).

After rereading the first episode of the story:

■ Remind students that there is a special word for the people and animals in stories. Ask them what it is. If necessary, explain that the people and animals in stories are called *story characters*. Ask students who the story characters are in *The Kite* (Frog, Toad, and the robins) and have them tell what the characters have done so far. Have students share what they think of what the robins did. Help them understand the robins are being rather mean when they laugh at Toad and tell him to give up. Discuss with students how authors often put a mean story character or a bad story character in their stories and ask students if they can think of other stories that have such characters (*The Three Little Pigs* and *Little Red Riding Hood*). Ask students why authors might do this.

■ Ask students to think about what is different about the two story characters, Frog and Toad (Toad gives up easily but Frog wants to keep trying). Next ask students how Frog and the robins are different (robins discourage Toad and Frog encourages him). Create a character chart containing words that describe the robins, Toad, and Frog. Discuss with students that authors often create story characters that are different and ask them why they think they do that.

■ Tell students that the story character you want them to think about is Toad. Ask them to describe what Toad is like. Record their responses on the character chart. Ensure that students understand that he is easily influenced by the robins to give up. Ask students how Arnold Lobel shows what Toad is like (he tells what he does and what he says). Have students locate sentences that show what Toad is like and ask them to read them aloud to each other. Have them tell if the sentence tells about what Toad does or what he says.

After reading the second story episode:

■ Ask students to describe what Frog is like. Record their responses on the character chart. Ensure that they understand that he is not easily influenced by the robins to give up. Ask students how Arnold Lobel shows what Frog is like (he tells what he does and what he says). Have students locate sentences that show what Frog is like and ask them to read them aloud to each other. Have them tell if the sentence tells about what Frog does or what he says.

After reading the entire story:

■ Follow the procedure outlined for Toad and Frog focusing on the robins.

Problem story plot item. Can recognize and understand that the author stipulates goals (or problems), complications (or failed attempts), and resolutions when building a story plot (see Appendix 4.1, First Grade: Level 3).

After reading the first story episode:

■ Discuss with students how stories often have a problem that a story character wants to solve or a goal he or she wants to reeach. Ask students if they know what Frog's and Toad's goal was and what problem they are having reaching it (their goal was to fly the kite but it wouldn't fly). Ask students if they have ever told or written stories that had a problem and allow them to share their thoughts.

After reading the second story episode:

■ Tell students that stories often have more than one problem. Ask them to recall the story problem they just discussed and ask them if they can think of another problem (The robins keep telling Toad that he shouldn't keep trying and that he should give up). Record both problems on a chart. Ask students if they have ever written or told stories that have more that one problem and allow them to share their thoughts.

After reading the entire story:

■ Ask students if they recall what the two story problems were. Ask them if they were both solved and how (The kite finally flew and the robins were shown to be wrong). Ensure that students understand that Arnold Lobel solved *both* story problems. Record the solutions on the problem chart.

Linking to students' writing:

■ Begin a group composition in which students model on the story *The Kite*, but use different characters. Start by having students think of names and descriptors for the characters and record the descriptors in columns. Draw students' attention to how the characters are different. Ask students to think of some problems that these characters might have and record them on a chart, along with how the problems might be solved. Beginning with a story starter frame (e.g., Once long ago when animals could talk . . .), have students introduce the characters and the first story problem. Continue through the story, with children generating content as you record the story on chart paper.

Fourth-Grade Application of RwWE Rubric

I have selected items from the fourth grade RwWE rubrics for both character development and problem plot structure that represent grade-appropriate proficiency to (1) focus the instruction on the author's craft and (2) support students in their own writing.

Character development item. Can recognize and understand the author's use of techniques to allow readers to understand who the story characters are by building believable characters by (a) integrating external factors (e.g., actions, speech, and appearance) and (b) integrating internal factors (e.g., thoughts, attitudes, dreams, and memories; see Appendix 4.1, Fourth Grade: Level 2).

In a previous instruction study (Jarvey et al., 2008) we encouraged students to focus on the characters' interior mental states by highlighting the contrast between what the trickster in *The Tale of Tricky Fox* (Aylesworth, 2000) said and meant (see Figure 4.3). We accomplished this in the following way:

■ The story was read aloud and each of the three trick sequences was discussed.

■ A large sheet of paper was divided into four sections to represent the sequence of events comprising the first trick in the story. On this grid, one character was drawn in each box, with the negative character in the top two sections, and the positive character in the bottom two sections.

■ As each character was drawn, the students were asked what he said, and the dialogue was added to speech bubbles.

■ Next, the students articulated what the character was thinking, and the teacher recorded these words in thought bubbles.

FIGURE 4.3. Trickster tale plot plan.

- The two subsequent trick sequences in the story were also discussed, and students worked with individual copies of the drawings, adding speech and thought bubbles as they thought appropriate.

- To bridge to story writing, students discussed how authors express characters thoughts in narrative format, examples were found throughout various trickster tales, and specific language samples were recorded so students could use them as models when writing their own stories.

As can be seen in Jessica's story, included previously in the chapter, there are multiple instances of students using this technique in their own writing, as follows:

- There was nothing stopping Megan now. She was off to grade 1. But school wasn't what Megan expected. They did five pages of Math, read a chapter in Social, answered 30 questions in Science. Then they had lunch. After lunch they did silent reading. Next they cleaned their desks and went home. "That was the most boring time of my life," thought Megan.

■ So Megan went to school. She was excited about the surprise. But at 2:00 there still weren't any treats. No cookies. No candy. No nothing. Just work. This stinks," thought Megan. She scrunched up her nose and pouted.

■ But the next day, Kelly and Megan were arguing about going to school. "You should go to school," said Kelly. "Why?" said Megan with a really mad look on her face. Her face was really red, and getting redder by the minute.

■ Maybe I will make up a short cut home," thought Megan. Megan got great joy. She was having a ball making up a short cut. But after awhile it wasn't that much fun. She was lost. "Oh no!"

Problem plot structure item. To illustrate how teachers can use the problem plot structure rubrics to (1) focus the instruction on the author's craft and (2) support students in their own writing I have selected the following item: Can recognize and understand the author's use of suspense to manipulate mood by building tension through thwarting a character's attempts (see Appendix 4.1, Fourth Grade: Level 2).

In the trickster tale unit discussed previously (Jarvey et al., 2008), we illustrated the notion of tension in a narrative plot by asking two students to demonstrate a tug-of-war with a blanket. One student pulled a little of the blanket over to her side in a sequence of three tugs. Then, following the third tug, the other student yanked the blanket back. This action was related to the tension in a trickster tale, as one character tries to get more than his or her fair share, but justice is restored in the end. A graphic scaffold was used to sequence events of the trickster tale *Anansi and the Moss-Covered Rock* (Kimmel, 1987) along a plot line as the story was read aloud. These events were placed either above or below a central line of equilibrium, depending on whether each had a negative or a positive effect (see Figure 4.4). As Figure 4.4 shows, Anansi tricks animals out of their food until finally Little Bush Deer sets things right by turning the tables on Anansi. A review of Jessica's story reveals that she was able to apply the graphic scaffold in her own writing by having Kelly trick Megan into attending school. Megan is not convinced by Kelly's efforts, but in the end equilibrium is restored when she realized school is worthwhile.

Instructing Students in Middle and High School

Throughout middle school and high school, instruction in narrative composition often receives considerably less focus and attention than instruction in expository writing. This is an unfortunate circumstance, although it

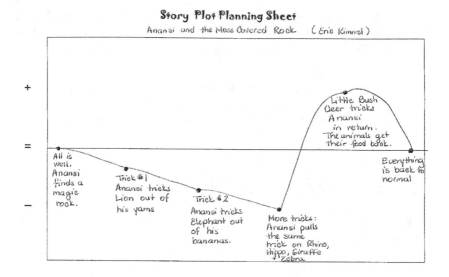

FIGURE 4.4. Trickster tales tension mnemonic.

is an understandable one. Teachers are faced with limited instruction time and many competing demands. Additionally, teachers are aware of the limited demand for narrative writing relative to expository writing in higher education contexts. Moreover, the study of literature involves analyses of literary devices and so students are offered opportunities to study how authors put stories together. In spite of these factors, however, I believe it is essential that teachers place a greater emphasis on narrative writing as it can improve students understanding and appreciation of literature. That is, the interaction between reading and writing is a two-way street, with experience in each bootstrapping performance in a mutually beneficial fashion.

When engaging middle school and high school students in story writing, it is important for teachers to analyze and understand students' capabilities first and then to build on those abilities. Briefly, then, our research (McKeough, Wigmore, & Genereux, 2003) has determined that by middle school, teachers can begin to encourage students to analyze story characters in terms of their long-standing personality traits, enduring psychological states, and personal history and to create similar story characters in their own writing efforts. By high school, a greater emphasis can be placed on developing more complex and multifaceted characters and on interpreting characters in terms of their social context.

Conclusions

- The CCSS offer a useful roadmap for teachers by highlighting competencies in narrative writing that should typically be reached at specific grade levels.
- The standards would be enhanced with an increased focus on character development and problem plot structure.
- Further development of items that target modeling student writing on good literature is essential.
- Teaching is a developmental enterprise wherein curriculum and teaching materials must be adapted to meet the needs of each child in an ongoing fashion.
- The grade-specific content outlined in this chapter is to be viewed as a description of what the average student typically is capable of accomplishing.
- Teachers are encouraged to (1) look across the grade levels to develop an understanding of how knowledge and skills build from less to more complex, then (2) determine where in the sequence each of their students lies, and finally (3) take up the suggestions made in this chapter as their students' needs dictate.
- As with any teaching tool or strategy, the suggestions outlined here work best when a teacher's professional judgment is applied.

Acknowledgments

I wish to express my appreciation for the work and cooperation of the students and teachers who participated in the research discussed in this chapter. I also wish to acknowledge the generous financial support provided by the Social Sciences and Humanities Research Council of Canada and the Alberta Teachers' Association. Finally, I am deeply grateful to my colleagues and graduate students for their significant contributions. Specifically, I wish to thank Drs. Randy Genereux, Joan Jeary, Jennifer Malcolm, Deborah Misfeldt, Jamie Palmer, Alex Sanderson, and Barb Wigmore-MacLeod, as well as Ms. Marya Jarvey, Erin Johnson, and Erin Tourigny.

References

Aylesworth, J. (2001). *The tale of Tricky Fox*. New York: Scholastic.

Applebee, A. N. (1978). *The child's concept of story: Ages two to seventeen*. Chicago: University of Chicago Press.

Babcock-Abrahams, B. (1975). "A tolerated margin of mess": The trickster and his tales reconsidered. *Journal of the Folklore Institute, 11,* 147–186.

Britton, J., Burgess, T., Martin, N., McLeod, A., & Rosen, H. (1975). *The development of writing abilities* (pp. 11–18). London: Macmillan Education.

Bruner, J. S. (1986). *Actual minds, possible worlds.* Cambridge, MA: Harvard University Press.

Bruner, J. S. (1990). *Acts of meaning.* Cambridge, MA: Harvard University Press.

Bruner, J. S. (1991). The narrative construction of reality. *Critical Inquiry, 18,* 1–21.

Bruner, J. S. (1996). *The culture of education.* Boston: Harvard University Press.

Bruner, J. S., & Lucariello, J. (1989) Monologue as narrative recreation of the world. In K. Nelson (Ed.), *Narratives from the crib* (pp. 73–97). Boston: Harvard University Press.

Fountas, I. C., & Pinnell, G. S. (2001). *Guiding readers and writers, grades 3–6: Teaching comprehension, genre, and content literacy.* Westport, CT: Heinemann.

Hansen, J. (2001). *When writers read* (2nd ed.). Westport, CT: Heinemann.

Jarvey, M., McKeough, A., & Pyryt, M. (2008). Teaching trickster tales. *Research in the Teaching of English, 42*(1), 42–73.

Kimmel, E. A. (1987). *Anansi and the moss-covered rock.* New York: Holiday House.

Kirkland, G., & Davies, R. (Eds.). (1987). *Inside stories I.* Toronto: Harcourt, Brace, Jovanovich.

Lobel, A. (1979). *Days with Frog and Toad.* New York: HarperCollins.

McCabe, A., & Peterson, C. (Eds.). (1991). *Developing narrative structure.* Hillsdale, NJ: Erlbaum.

McKeough, A. (1992). The structural foundations of children's narrative and its development. In R. Case (Ed.), *The mind's staircase: Stages in the development of human intelligence* (pp. 171–188). Hillsdale, NJ: Erlbaum.

McKeough, A., Bird, S., Romaine, A., & Tourigny, E. (2008). Parent/caregiver narrative development: 49–60 months. In L. M. Phillips (Ed.), *Handbook of language and literacy development: A roadmap from 0–60 months* (pp. 1–13). London, ON: Canadian Language and Literacy Research Network. Retrieved from *www.theroadmap.ualberta.ca.*

McKeough, A., & Genereux, R. (2003). Transformation in narrative thought during adolescence: The structure and content of story compositions. *Journal of Educational Psychology, 95*(3), 537–552.

McKeough, A., & Jeary, J. (2007, May). *Reading with a writers eye: Turning text inside out to see how it's made.* Paper presented at the annual meeting of the International Reading Association, Toronto, Canada.

McKeough, A., Palmer, J., Jarvey, M., & Bird, S. (2007). Best narrative writing practices when teaching from a developmental framework. In S. Graham, C. A. MacArthur, & J. Fitzgerald (Eds.), *Best practices in writing instruction* (pp. 50–73). New York: Guilford Press.

McKeough, A., & Sanderson, A. (1996). Teaching storytelling: A microgenetic analysis of developing narrative competency. *Journal of Narrative and Life History, 6*(2), 157–192.

McKeough, A., Wigmore-MacLeod, B., & Genereux, R. (2003). Narrative thought in childhood and adolescence: Hierarchical models of story composition and interpretation. In B. Apolloni, M. Marinaro, & R. Tagliaferri (Eds.), *Neural nets: Proceedings of the 14th Italian Workshop on Neural Networks* (pp. 325–338). New York: Springer-Verlag.

National Governors Association & Council of Chief State School Officers. (2010). *Common Core State Standards for English language arts & literacy in history/social studies, science, and technical subjects.* Washington, DC: Authors. Retrieved from *www.corestandards.org.*.

Prose, F. (2006). *Reading like a writer.* New York: HarperCollins.

Shanahan, T. (2006). Relations among oral language, reading, and writing. In C. A. MacArthur, S. Graham, & J. Fitzgerald.(Eds.), *Handbook or writing research* (pp. 171–183). New York: Guilford Press.

SRA/McGraw Hill. (2008). *Imagine It!* Worthington, OH: Author.

Tiedt, I. M. (1988). Reading with a writer's eye. *Learning, 16*(7), 66–68.

RwWE Rubrics for Teachers

Problem Plot Development RwWE: Grade 1				
Level	Illustrative examples	Often	Sometimes	Never
1 Can recognize and understand the author's use of:				
• Story plots that include a desire/goal that is attained or problem that is resolved	Can retell the gist of a problem/resolution story.			
• Story plots as a sequence of story events	The events that occur at a birthday party or other family event.			
• Chronological timelines in stories	The events that occur at a birthday party or other family event linked with connectives such as *and* and *then*.			
2 Can recognize and understand the author's use of:				
• Cause and effect when building story plots using connecting words such as *because* and *so*	A boy's desire for a dog causes him to get a job helping his uncle			
• Story plots in terms of event categories (e.g., problem and resolution)	Problem: A girl has no friends. Solution: Asks a new neighbor to be her friend.			
• Meaningful detail to flesh out story problems	New neighbor of a friendless girl, who she has asked to be her friend, uses walker because she has been in an accident and so lonely girl needs to help her.			
3 Can recognize and understand that the author stipulates:				
• Goals (or problems), complications (or failed attempts), and resolutions when building a story plot	A little girl wants a horse to ride. She asks her father to buy her one but he has no money. She then does chores for her neighbor who lets her ride his horse.			
• Two timelines that eventually come together when building a story plot	*The Elves and the Shoemaker* **Timeline 1:** Poor shoemaker and his wife struggle to make a living during the day. **Timeline 2:** Elves come to help at night.			
• Stories with multiple attempts to solve a problem	*The Great Big Enormous Turnip* A farmer elicits the help of all those around him to pull a huge turnip from the ground.			

Problem Plot Development RwWE :Grade 2				
Level	**Illustrative examples**	**Often**	**Sometimes**	**Never**
1 Can recognize and understand the author's use of:				
• Cause and effect when building story plots	A boy's desire for a dog causes him to get a job.			
• Story plots in terms of event categories (e.g., problem and resolution)	Problem: A girl has no friends. Solution: Asks a new neighbor to be her friend.			
• Meaningful detail to flesh out story problems	New neighbor of a friendless girl, who she has asked to be her friend, uses walker because she has been in an accident and so lonely girl needs to help her.			
2 Can recognize and understand the author's use of:				
• Goals (or problems), complications (or failed attempts), and resolutions when building a story plot	A little girl wants a horse to ride. She asks her father to buy her one but he has no money. She then does chores for her neighbor who lets her ride his horse.			
• Two timelines that eventually come together when building a story plot	*The Elves and the Shoemaker* **Timeline 1:** Poor shoemaker and his wife struggle to make a living during the day. **Timeline 2:** Elves come to help at night.			
• Stories with multiple attempts to solve a problem	*The Great Big Enormous Turnip* A farmer elicits the help of all those around him to pull a huge turnip from the ground.			
3 Can recognize and understand that the author:				
• Builds a more elaborate and complex story plot by expanding the complicating events to create a second goal (or problem) for the character	Girl's first goal was to get into a ballet company. Her goal is interrupted when she develops diabetes. Thus her goal becomes getting healthy.			
• Builds a more coherent and integrated story plot by dealing with both goals in the resolution	The story resolves when she realizes she will not join a competitive company but instead dances for her enjoyment while staying healthy.			
• Adds excitement or color to the story plot by adding descriptive detail.	She looked into the mirror and saw the disappointment in her eyes.			

Problem Plot Development RwWE: Grade 3				
Level	Illustrative examples	Often	Sometimes	Never
1 Can recognize and understand the author's use of:				
• Goals (or problems), complications (or failed attempts), and resolutions when building a story plot	A little girl wants a horse to ride. She asks her father to buy her one but he has no money. She then does chores for her neighbor who lets her ride his horse.			
• Two timelines that eventually come together when building a story plot	*The Elves and the Shoemaker* **Timeline 1:** Poor shoemaker and his wife struggle to make a living during the day. **Timeline 2:** Elves come to help at night.			
• Cause and effect when building story plots	A boy's desire for a dog causes him to get a job.			
2 Can recognize and understand that the author:				
• Builds a more elaborate and complex story plot by expanding the complicating events to create a second goal (or problem) for the character	Girl's first goal was to get into a ballet company. Her goal is interrupted when she develops diabetes. Thus her goal becomes getting healthy.			
• Builds a more coherent and integrated story plot by dealing with both goals in the resolution	The story resolves when she realizes she will not join a competitive company but instead dances for her enjoyment while staying healthy.			
• Adds excitement or color to the story plot by adding descriptive detail.	She looked into the mirror and saw the disappointment in her own eyes.			
3 Can recognize and understand the author's use of:				
• Surprise or trick endings when building a story plot	A Chinese emperor sends seeds to all the children in the country, telling them that whoever grows the most beautiful flowering plant will be the next emperor. All children except for one arrived on the appointed day with beautiful plants. The one child admitted that his seed did not grow. The emperor chooses him as king because of his honesty— all of the seeds had been roasted so that they would not germinate.			

		Often	Sometimes	Never
• Flashback to create more elaborate (complex) plots	A boy who is lost in the forest on a cold evening thinks back to a time when his grandfather taught him how to start a fire with two sticks. The events from the past are recounted as if the grandfather and boy are present.			
• Suspense to manipulate mood by building tension through thwarting a character's attempts	A girl who is on a raft at sea loses her sail, runs out of water, and is circled by sharks.			

Problem Plot Development RwWE: Grade 4				
Level	Illustrative examples	Often	Sometimes	Never
1 **Can recognize and understand that the author:**				
• Builds a more elaborate and complex story plot by expanding the complicating events to create a second goal (or problem) for the character	Girl's first goal was to get into a ballet company. Her goal is interrupted when she develops diabetes. Thus her goal becomes getting healthy.			
• Builds a more coherent and integrated story plot by dealing with both goals in the resolution	The story resolves when she realizes she will not join a competitive company but instead dances for her enjoyment while staying healthy.			
• Adds excitement or color to the story plot by adding descriptive detail	She looked into the mirror and saw the disappointment in her eyes.			
2 **Can recognize and understand the author's use of:**				
• Surprise or trick endings when building a story plot	A Chinese emperor sends seeds to all the children in the country, telling them that whoever grows the most beautiful flowering plant will be the next emperor. All children except for one arrived on the appointed day with beautiful plants. The one child admitted that his seed did not grow. The emperor chooses him as king because of his honesty—all of the seeds had been roasted so that they would not germinate.			
• Flashback to create more elaborate (complex) plots	A boy who is lost in the forest on a cold evening thinks back to a time when his grandfather taught him how to start a fire with two sticks. The events from the past are recounted as if the grandfather and boy are present.			

			Often	Sometimes	Never
	• Suspense to manipulate mood by building tension through thwarting a character's attempts	A girl who is on a raft at sea loses her sail, runs out of water, and is circled by sharks.			
3	**Can recognize and understand the author's use of:**				
	• Techniques to create a surprise or trick ending	Hiding a character's true intention (e.g., emperor); laying ambiguous or false clues; hiding character's true nature/personality; omitting crucial information			
	• Revised character goals	A girl's original goal is to join her people when she is mistakenly left behind on an island by following them on a raft. Because of multiple problems her revised goal is to return to the island and survive alone.			
	• Multiple character perspectives to create more elaborate (complex) plots	A boy's family, teachers, and friends see him as an accomplished athlete but he lives in fear that he will not measure up.			

Problem Plot Development RwWE: Grade 5					
Level	**Illustrative examples**		Often	Sometimes	Never
1 **Can recognize and understand the author's use of:**					
• Surprise or trick endings when building a story plot	A Chinese emperor sends seeds to all the children in the country, telling them that whoever grows the most beautiful flowering plant will be the next emperor. All children except for one arrived on the appointed day with beautiful plants. The one child admitted that his seed did not grow. The emperor chooses him as king because of his honesty— all of the seeds had been roasted so that they would not germinate.				
• Flashback to create more elaborate (complex) plots	A boy who is lost in the forest on a cold evening thinks back to a time when his grandfather taught him how to start a fire with two sticks. The events from the past are recounted as if the grandfather and boy are present.				
• Suspense to manipulate mood by building tension through thwarting a character's attempts	A girl who is on a raft at sea loses her sail, runs out of water, and is circled by sharks.				

2	**Can recognize and understand the author's use of:**		Never	Seldom	Often
	• Techniques to create a surprise or trick ending	Hiding a character's true intention (e.g., emperor); laying ambiguous or false clues; hiding character's true nature/personality; omitting crucial information.			
	• Revised character goals	A girl's original goal is to join her people when she is mistakenly left behind on an island by following them on a raft. Because of multiple problems her revised goal is to return to the island and survive alone.			
	• Multiple character perspectives to create more elaborate (complex) plots	A boy's family, teachers, and friends see him as an accomplished athlete but he lives in fear that he will not measure up.			
3	**Can recognize and understand the author's use of:**				
	• Character traits to build plot	A character's honesty, courage, dedication, or loyalty propels the story plot in a particular direction (e.g., friends' loyalty results in them laying their life on the line for each other).			
	• One story nested within another	A young boy's befriending of his misunderstood boarder reveals the triumphs and tragedies of the boarder's life while also telling the boy's story.			
	• A metaphoric setting to complement and support the story plot	Story of personal quest set in rugged mountains.			

Character Development RwWE: Grade 1					
Level		**Illustrative examples**	Never	Seldom	Often
1	**Can recognize and understand the author's use of techniques to allow readers to understand who the story characters are:**				
	• Characters with basic categorical affective descriptors	Good, bad, happy, sad			
	• By describing characters in terms of their physical features	Black shiny crow; snowy white lamb			
	• Representations of basic character types	Heroes, villains, and victims			

2	Can recognize and understand the author's use of techniques to allow readers to understand who the story characters are:				
	• Characters with both physical and mental qualities	Strong and kind; messy and sneaky			
	• Character names as they relate to basic character type	Rascal the fox			
	• Characters in whom physical and mental features connect	"He looks mean."			
3	Can recognize and understand the author's use of techniques to allow readers to understand who the story characters are:				
	• Characters' speech (i.e., dialect or particular expressions) to provide more information about the character	A young boy from rural Arkansas uses unique expressions (*Bridge to Terebithia* by Katherine Paterson)			
	• By creating flaws within the character, such as laziness or greed	A selfish raccoon looks for a child to live with for the winter knowing that he'll leave in the spring. (*Macaroon*, by Judith Cunningham)			
	• Characters who have contrasting traits	An aggressive schoolyard bully tries to make the daily bus ride difficult for a new boy, who chooses to ignore the daily taunts and sit at the front of the bus with a friend instead of fighting back.			

Character Development RwWE: Grade 2				
Level	Illustrative examples	Never	Seldom	Often
1	Can recognize and understand the author's use of techniques to allow readers to understand who the story characters are:			
	• Characters with both physical and mental qualities	Strong and kind; messy and sneaky			
	• Character names as they relate to basic character type	Rascal the fox			
	• Characters in whom physical and mental features connect	"He looks mean."			

2	**Can recognize and understand the author's use of techniques to allow readers to understand who the story characters are:**		Never	Seldom	Often
	• Characters' speech (i.e., dialect or particular expressions) to provide more information about the character	A young boy from rural Arkansas uses unique expressions (*Bridge to Terebithia* by Katherine Paterson).			
	• Characters have flaws such as laziness or greed	A selfish raccoon looks for a child to live with for the winter knowing that he'll leave in the spring (*Macaroon*, by Judith Cunningham).			
	• Characters who have contrasting traits	An aggressive schoolyard bully tries to make the daily bus ride difficult for a new boy, who chooses to ignore the daily taunts and sit at the front of the bus with a friend instead of fighting back.			
3	**Can recognize and understand the author's use of techniques to allow readers to understand who the story characters are:**				
	• Stereotypic characters such as tricksters, fools, and helpers	In *Mrs. Frisby and the Crow* (Robert O'Brien), the crow is foolishly attracted to shiny objects. Mrs. Frisby helps him even when it puts her life at risk.			
	• By presenting more than one perspective on a character or characters	In *The Pain and the Great One* (Judy Blume) a sister tells how horrid her brother is and how persecuted she is. But when the boy shares his story the reader sees the opposite perspective.			
	• By depicting characters' inner worlds by explicitly describing their thoughts, feelings, and desires	"Ramona remained silent. She felt mean and unhappy because she wanted to forgive her mother, but something in that dark, deep-down place inside her would not let her" (*Ramona Quimby, Age 8*, by Beverly Cleary).			

Character Development RwWE: Grade 3				
Level	**Illustrative examples**	Never	Seldom	Often
1 **Can recognize and understand the author's use of techniques to allow readers to understand who the story characters are:**				
• Characters' speech (i.e., dialect or particular expressions) to provide more information about the character	A young boy from rural Arkansas uses unique expressions (*Bridge to Terebithia* by Katherine Paterson).			

	• Characters have flaws such as laziness or greed	A selfish raccoon looks for a child to live with for the winter knowing that he'll leave in the spring (*Macaroon*, by Judith Cunningham).			
	• Characters who have contrasting traits	An aggressive schoolyard bully tries to make the daily bus ride difficult for a new boy, who chooses to ignore the daily taunts and sit at the front of the bus with a friend instead of fighting back.			
2	**Can recognize and understand the author's use of techniques to allow readers to understand who the story characters are:**				
	• Stereotypic characters such as tricksters, fools, and helpers	In *Mrs. Frisby and the Crow* (Robert O'Brien), the crow is foolishly attracted to shiny objects. Mrs. Frisby helps him even when it puts her life at risk.			
	• By presenting more than one perspective on a character or characters	In *The Pain and the Great One* (Judy Blume) a sister tells how horrid her brother is and how persecuted she is. But when the boy shares his story the reader sees the opposite perspective.			
	• By depicting characters' inner worlds by explicitly describing their thoughts, feelings, and desires	"Ramona remained silent. She felt mean and unhappy because she wanted to forgive her mother, but something in that dark, deep-down place inside her would not let her" (*Ramona Quimby, Age 8*, by Beverly Cleary).			
3	**Can recognize and understand the author's use of techniques to allow readers to understand who the story characters are:**				
	• By using first versus third person. First person: Limited to character's perspective, creates empathy. Third person: Overall perspective, explanatory	**First person:** "I wondered why he always made fun of me when we played on the same team." **Third person:** Billy was embarrassed that his twin brother couldn't keep up with the rest of the team.			
	• By building believable characters by integrating their physical factors (e.g., actions, speech, and appearance)	In *Bridge to Terabithia* by Katherine Paterson, Jess Aarons is an adolescent boy growing up in rural Arkansas. This is reflected in his dress and speech.			
	• By building believable characters by integrating internal factors (e.g., thoughts, attitudes, dreams, and memories)	Memories of a life of moving around and leaving friends behind as a young child causes the child of a serviceman to hesitate to reach out to make friends.			

Character Development RwWE: Grade 4				
Level	Illustrative examples	Often	Sometimes	Never
1 Can recognize and understand the author's use of techniques to allow readers to understand who the story characters are:				
• Stereotypic characters such as tricksters, fools, and helpers	In *Mrs. Frisby and the Crow* (Robert O'Brien), the crow is foolishly attracted to shiny objects. Mrs. Frisby helps him even when it puts her life at risk.			
• By presenting more than one perspective on a character or characters	In *The Pain and the Great One* (Judy Blume) a sister tells how horrid her brother is and how persecuted she is. But when the boy shares his story the reader sees the opposite perspective.			
• By depicting characters' inner worlds by explicitly describing their thoughts, feelings, and desires	"Ramona remained silent. She felt mean and unhappy because she wanted to forgive her mother, but something in that dark, deep-down place inside her would not let her" (*Ramona Quimby, Age 8*, by Beverly Cleary).			
2 Can recognize and understand the author's use of techniques to allow readers to understand who the story characters are:				
• By using first versus third person. First person: Limited to character's perspective, creates empathy. Third person: Overall perspective, explanatory	**First person:** "I wondered why he always made fun of me when we played on the same team." **Third person:** Billy was embarrassed that his twin brother couldn't keep up with the rest of the team.			
• By building believable characters by integrating external factors (e.g., actions, speech, and appearance)	In *Bridge to Terabithia* by Katherine Paterson, Jess Aarons is an adolescent boy growing up in rural Arkansas. This is reflected in his dress and speech.			
• By building believable characters by integrating internal factors (e.g., thoughts, attitudes, dreams, and memories)	Memories of a life of moving around and leaving friends behind as a young child causes the child of a serviceman to hesitate to reach out to make friends.			
3 Can recognize and understand the author's use of techniques to allow readers to understand who the story characters are:				
• Characters with enduring psychological traits	A mother's sadness about losing her newborn baby affects the way in which she interacts with her other children.			

		Often	Sometimes	Never
• By creating contrasting traits within the same character	A young girl loves her twin sister but feels jealousy toward her because she is so talented.			
• By creating story setting and events to impact and transform a character	If you are a child who is never told the truth, you begin to make up your own. After my father left, no one mentioned his name again, I simply made up things about him" (*But I'll Be Back Again*, by Cynthia Rylant).			

Character Development RwWE: Grade 5				
Level	Illustrative examples	Often	Sometimes	Never
1 Can recognize and understand the author's use of techniques to allow readers to understand who the story characters are:				
• By using first versus third person. First person: Limited to character's perspective, creates empathy Third person: Overall perspective, explanatory	**First person:** "I wondered why he always made fun of me when we played on the same team." **Third person:** Billy was embarrassed that his twin brother couldn't keep up with the rest of the team.			
• By building believable characters by making their actions, speech, and appearance hang together	In *Bridge to Terabithia* by Katherine Paterson, Jess Aarons is an adolescent boy growing up in rural Arkansas. This is reflected in his dress and speech.			
• By building believable characters by making internal factors hang together (thoughts, attitudes, dreams, and memories)	Memories of a life of moving around and leaving friends behind as a young child causes the child of a serviceman to hesitate to reach out to make friends.			
2 Can recognize and understand the author's use of techniques to allow readers to understand who the story characters are:				
• Characters with enduring psychological traits	A mother's sadness about losing her newborn baby affects the way in which she interacts with her other children.			
• By creating contrasting traits within the same character	A young girl loves her twin sister but feels jealousy toward her because she is so talented.			
• By creating story setting and events to impact and transform a character	"If you are a child who is never told the truth, you begin to make up your own. After my father left, no one mentioned his name again, I simply made up things about him" (But I'll Be Back Again, by Cynthia Rylant).			

3	Can recognize and understand the author's use of techniques to allow readers to understand who the story characters are:				
	• Characters who experience internal conflict or face dilemmas	A Thai boy who has survived a horrific tsunami wrestles with helping two orphaned American children or looking for his own missing father (*The Killing Sea* by Richard Lewis).			
	• Through change/transformation in character's point of view	*In Beethoven Lives Upstairs* (Barbara Nichol) a young boy comes to view L. V. Beethoven as a frustrated artist rather than a cranky old man.			
	• By depicting relationships to convey a character's psychology	An adolescent girl's memories of her father's strengths and her mother's constant criticisms cause her to reflect on how each of them has shaped who she is.			

APPENDIX 4.2

RwWE Analysis for Students

GRADE 3 STORY PLOT

Level 1
- What problem does the author create for the character(s)? Were their attempts to solve the problem(s) successful? How does the author finally resolve the problem?
- What are the timelines for the story? When does the author make the timelines meet or come together? What happens when the timelines meet?
- Does the author use cause and effect in the story? Where?

Level 2
- Does the author create more than one problem/goal in this story? What are they? Explain.
- Does the author resolve all of the problems/goals? How?
- Give examples of how the author used descriptive language to make the story exciting and interesting.

Level 3
- Does the author use surprise or trick ending? Explain.
- Does the author use flashback to tell the story? How?
- Does the author create tension? Where and how?

GRADE 3 STORY CHARACTERS

Level 1
- Does the author make the characters speak in a particular way? Do you understand more about the characters from the way they talk? Explain.
- Does the author give the characters faults or flaws? What are they? What problems do these flaws cause?
- Does author create characters that have different or contrasting behaviors and personalities? Explain some of the ways that the two main characters are different.

Level 2
- Does the author have stereotypic characters in this story? Who are they? What are stereotypes?
- Does the author provide more than one point of view on character(s)? How does this help to understand the characters?
- Does the author show the characters' personality by describing their thoughts, feelings, or desires? Give examples.

Level 3
- Does the author use first person or third person to tell the story? Why has the author done this?
- Does the author use action, speech, and appearance to create a believable character? How?
- Does the author use thoughts, attitudes, dreams, and memories to create a believable character? How?

GRADE 4 STORY PLOT

Level 1
- Does the author create more than one problem/goal in this story? What are they? Explain.
- Does the author resolve all of the problems/goals? How?
- Give examples of how the author used descriptive language to make the story exciting and interesting.

Level 2
- Does the author use surprise or trick ending? Explain.
- Does the author use flashback to tell the story? How?
- Does the author create tension? Where and how?

Level 3
- What techniques does the author use to create a surprise or trick ending?
- Does the author make the characters' goals change throughout the story? Why does the author make the characters' goals change?
- Does more than one characters tell this story? How many? Why does the author do this? How does this technique affect the plot?

GRADE 4 CHARACTER DEVELOPMENT

Level 1
- Does the author have stereotypic characters in this story? Who are they? What are stereotypes?
- Does the author provide more than one point of view on character(s)? How does this help to understand the characters?
- Does the author show the characters' personality by describing their thoughts, feelings, or desires? Give examples.

Level 2
- Does the author use first person or third person to tell the story? Why has the author done this?
- Does the author use action, speech, and appearance to create a believable character? How?
- Does the author use thoughts, attitudes, dreams, and memories to create a believable character? How?

Level 3
- What main personality trait does the author give the character that is present through his or her life and affects everything that the character does?
- Does the author create a character that has, within him or her, traits that contrast (that are very different)? Describe the conflict that occurs because of the contrasting traits. Why does the author show us the character in this way?
- Does the author use the setting/events to make the character change? How does the character change? What is it that affects or changes the character in this story?

GRADE 5 STORY PLOT

Level 1
- Does the author use surprise or trick ending? Explain.
- Does the author use flashback to tell the story? How?
- Does the author create tension? Where and how?

Level 2
- What techniques does the author use to create a surprise or trick ending?
- Does the author make the characters' goals change throughout the story? Why does the author make the characters' goals change?
- Does more than one characters tell this story? How many? Why does the author do this? How does this technique affect the plot?

Level 3
- What personality traits did the author create in the main character that make him or her act in a certain way. How does this character's traits affect the plot?
- Did the author tell this story by putting one story inside of another? What were these two stories? Why did the author do this?
- How is the setting important to the story plot? Is the setting metaphorical?

GRADE 5 CHARACTER DEVELOPMENT

Level 1
- Does the author use first person or third person to tell the story? Why has the author done this?
- How does the author use action, speech, and appearance to create a believable character?
- How does the author use thoughts, attitudes, dreams, and memories to create a believable character?

Level 2
- What main personality trait does the author give the character that is present through his or her life and affects everything that the character does?
- Does the author create a character who has within him or her traits that contrast (that are very different)? Describe the conflict that occurs because of the contrasting traits. Why does the author show us the character in this way?
- Does the author use the setting/events to make the character change? How does the character change? What is it that affects or changes the character in this story?

Level 3
- Has the author created a main character who faced an internal conflict or dilemma and had to make a difficult choice? What was this conflict or dilemma? What did the character's actions tell you about him or her?
- Has the author written about a character whose point of view changed? How did his point of view change? What caused it to change?
- Does the author describe relationships the character has? How do these relationships affect the main character's personality?

Chapter 5

Best Practices in Teaching Argumentative Writing

RALPH P. FERRETTI
WILLIAM E. LEWIS

From the beginning of speech, toddlers have a natural and intuitive understanding of the importance of argumentative discourse (Dunn, 1988). For those of us who are parents, a little reflection will recall heartfelt and sometimes disconcerting early interactions with our children concerning our differing perspectives about their behavior. Although sometimes vexing, these arguments are critical to our children's social understanding (Dunn, 1988). Some of the most valued developmental outcomes originate with the inevitable conflicts that arise from the pursuit of self-interested purposes. When resolved to the child's long-term interests, arguments contribute to the development of empathy and cooperation, language, perspective taking, and rule-governed behavior (Bruner, 1990; Dunn, 1988), and more broadly, to the intellectual, social, and cultural capacities on which democratic institutions depend (Dewey, 1916). Perhaps for this reason, the study of argument has a vibrant history (e.g., Aristotle, trans. 1991; Walton, Reed, & Macagno, 2008).

Everyday experience shows that youngsters have some skill in argumentation. Unfortunately, children (and adults!) often ignore relevant information that is inconsistent with their perspective (Perkins, Farady, & Bushey, 1991), are insensitive to potential criticisms of their opinion (Kuhn, 1991), lack standards for evaluating their arguments (Ferretti, Lewis, & Andrews-Weckerly, 2009), and fail to adapt their strategies to the communicative context (Felton & Kuhn, 2001). As a result, people's arguments are often poorly developed and insensitive to alternative perspectives. These qualities are also evident in students' written arguments, which are usually shorter and less well developed compared to narrative and expository writing (Applebee, Langer, Mullis, Latham, & Gentile, 1994). The National Assessment of Educational Progress (NAEP) Writing Report Card (Persky, Daane, & Jin, 2003) showed that only 17% of 4th graders, 18% of 8th graders, and 31% of 12th-graders wrote argumentative essays that were judged to be "skillful" or better. Skillful essays generally offered a thesis and some supporting reasons and examples, but lacked clear transitions among arguments and may not have considered alternative perspectives. The 2007 NAEP assessment showed that only 27% of 12th graders' argumentative essays were skillful (The Nation's Report Card: Writing 2007, 2007). Students' argumentative essays rarely acknowledge opposing positions, consider the merits of different views, or attempt to systematically integrate or rebut alternative perspectives (Ferretti et al., 2009; Ferretti, MacArthur, & Doudy, 2000). Perhaps for these reasons, the new K–12 Common Core State Standards (National Governors Association [NGA] & Council of Chief State School Officers [CCSSO], 2010) mandate that students become proficient in "logical arguments based on substantive claims, sound reasoning, and relevant evidence."

The purpose of this chapter is to distill principles from the best available evidence about effective instructional practices for argumentative writing. Before discussing and illustrating these principles, we begin by defining the concept of argumentation. We then highlight the importance of dialogue in argumentation because an argument is a communicative act that depends on the actual or imagined involvement of other people. For this reason, dialogic support is essential for the development of reflective argumentative writing. We next present argumentative writing as a problem-solving activity, and explain the importance of supporting the development of self-regulatory skills for students' argumentative capacities. Finally, we discuss content-area arguments because they become increasingly important as students progress through the academic curriculum. After briefly summarizing these core themes, we further elaborate them with examples from the literature that illustrate their contributions to effective instructional practices.

Defining Argumentation

Arguments typically occur in the context of a discussion and are used to persuade, defeat, negotiate, consult, debate, and resolve differences of opinion. In the interest of clarity, we offer the following definition of argument:

> Argumentation is a verbal and social activity of reason aimed at increasing (or decreasing) the acceptability of a controversial standpoint for the listener or reader, by putting forward *a constellation of propositions* intended to justify (or refute) the standpoint before a rational judge. (van Eemeren, Grootendorst, & Henkemans, 1996, p. 5)

This definition highlights three important aspects of argumentation that will be taken up in our recommendations for improving argumentative writing. First, argumentation is an inherently social activity involving dialogue among people who may hold different perspectives about a controversial issue. Second, the presentation of a *constellation of propositions* implies that arguments possess a structure and organization that in their totality affect the acceptability of a standpoint. Third, arguments are acts of reason, and reasonable people use *critical standards* to judge the acceptability of a standpoint. These critical standards may include criteria such as the inclusion of argumentative discourse elements, the writer's sensitivity to audience considerations, or perhaps more importantly the relevance of their argumentative strategies for accomplishing their purposes. With respect to the latter criterion, there is general agreement that people can best defend their arguments by answering *critical questions* about the relevance of their argumentative strategies (Walton et al., 2008).

Argument as Dialogue

Argumentation is an inherently dialogic activity between people who may have a difference of opinion about a controversial issue. This means that in everyday arguments, people actually interact for the purpose of resolving their differences of opinion. The quality of that interaction and the successful resolution of these differences depend upon people's willingness to faithfully fulfill their communicative obligations (van Eemeren & Grootendorst, 2004). When these obligations are met, people learn about the strengths and weaknesses of their respective opinions, and are more likely to satisfactorily resolve their differences.

For these reasons, dialogic approaches provide a framework for supporting the development of students' argumentative thinking and writing. These approaches help promote students' understanding of other perspectives, as well as the limitations of their own perspective, by engaging them in planning, composing, and revising argumentative discourse within groups (Reznitskaya & Anderson, 2002), conversational partners (Kuhn, Shaw, & Felton, 1997) or in online argumentative conversations (Newell, Beach, Smith, & VanDerHeide, 2011). Dialogic interactions afford instructional opportunities that challenge writers to consider competing perspectives (Kuhn & Crowell, 2011). Interactions such as these should provide greater access to the "relevant and sufficient evidence" that the Common Core standards demand (NGA & CCSSO, 2010).

Proponents of dialogic approaches view argumentative writing as woven into the literacy practices of specific communities (Newell et al., 2011). Therefore, unlike the argumentative writing that is often assigned in schools that conforms to its own genre-specific writing conventions (e.g., the five-paragraph essay), proponents of dialogic approaches see argumentative writing as a flexible tool for gaining, elaborating on, and communicating knowledge through meaningful and motivating writing tasks (Boscolo & Gelati, 2007). According to Newell et al. (2011), the goal of those with a dialogic perspective is to "envision the types of classrooms where students are interested in what teachers teach, and in reading and writing arguments that are of significance to them and the culture at large" (p. 274).

Strategic Support for Self-Regulated Writing

Dialogic support for effective argumentation is important because argumentation usually involves interactions among people who have different perspectives. However, it is also useful to understand argumentative writing as a problem-solving process (Bereiter & Scardamalia, 1987) that requires the writer to use goal-directed self-regulatory processes (Graham & Harris, 1997). Like all problem solving, writing is constrained by the writer's available cognitive capacities. As a consequence, the writer must manage all aspects of the writing process, including setting goals, planning, composing, and revising his or her essay. If the writer's self-regulatory capacities are exceeded by the task requirements, performance usually suffers.

Faced with the goal of resolving a difference of opinion, writers draw on their knowledge of argumentative discourse, the topic, and critical standards to write effectively (Ferretti & De La Paz, 2011; Ferretti, Andrews-Weckerly, & Lewis, 2007). In contrast to expert writers, who usually set relevant and specific goals to guide the writing process, novices often write down only topically relevant information and then use this information to generate related information (Page-Voth & Graham, 1999). Furthermore, young and less able writers are often unable to devise strategies for managing the demands associated with planning and revising their essays (Graham, Harris, & McKeown, 2013). As a result of these self-regulatory problems, young and less able writers often produce argumentative essays that lack critical components and are of inferior quality (Ferretti et al., 2009; Graham et al., 2013). In these cases, explicit instructional support for self-regulation of the writing process may be needed (Graham & Perin, 2007).

Content-Area Arguments

People routinely argue about commonplace issues for which no specialized expertise is needed. In fact, many tasks that are used to instruct students about argumentative writing draw on common knowledge that is usually acquired in everyday experience. Commonplace topics are sometimes used to avoid the potential influence of background knowledge on students' argumentative writing (e.g., Ferretti et al., 2009). In other cases, these tasks can facilitate instruction because they enable young and less able writers to draw on accessible knowledge to construct an argument. However, as students progress through the curriculum, literacy and content-area learning become inextricably interlinked, so academic progress increasingly depends upon the acquisition of highly specialized knowledge and skills that are specific to the discipline (Heller & Greenleaf, 2007). In short, students are increasingly expected to read, write, and argue like disciplinary experts (Ferretti & De La Paz, 2011). This expectation is echoed in the College and Career Readiness Standards for Writing (NGA & CCSSO, 2010), which requires that students write arguments in response to content texts across the disciplines.

Research shows how experts think and argue in a number of disciplines, including literary studies (Fahnestock & Secor, 1991; Wilder, 2005) and history (Wineburg, 1991a, 1991b). We will review some of this work later, but for now suffice it to say that experts engage in arguments that are highly dependent on their disciplinary knowledge and skills. To promote acquisition of disciplinary argumentation, we must design instructional activities that promote the acquisition of disciplinary knowledge and skills, including the disciplinary standards used to evaluate arguments.

Summary

Argumentation involves dialogic communication among people who hold differing views about controversial issues. These differences should be addressed by presenting a constellation of propositions that is relevant and well structured. In addition, people should address alternative perspectives and anticipate potential criticisms of their views, and attempt to systematically respond to them. A reasonable response is not possible without applying critical standards of evaluation. Furthermore, the knowledge that people bring to bear on the resolution of their disagreements is influenced by the knowledge they have about the topic. As students' progress through the curriculum, this knowledge becomes increasingly specific, domain-dependent, and intellectually demanding. Clearly, argumentative writing is a challenging problem-solving activity that requires strategic self-regulation of the writer's resources and instructional support for its development. These challenges are magnified for young and less able students. As a result, explicit support for self-regulated argumentative writing will be needed for many writers.

Dialogic Approaches to Supporting Argumentative Writing

Earlier we explained that argumentation is inherently dialogic. Whether the writer is having an actual or an imagined exchange of views, he or she must consider other people's perspectives about the controversy. For this and other reasons, it would be wise to incorporate dialogic approaches into classroom instruction. Unfortunately, teachers are often apprehensive about introducing argumentative activities that might breed conflict and competition among students (Johnson & Johnson, 2009; Newell et al., 2011). This apprehension can lead to instruction that avoids substantive arguments to keep peace in the classroom (Newell et al., 2011). Additionally, the inauthentic nature of many school writing assignments—which are written without real purposes and for no real audience beside the teacher—potentially undermines students' abilities to anticipate other people's perspectives and potential criticisms of their own (Coker & Lewis, 2012). Andrews (1995) believes there is little point in engaging in argumentative discourse without a clear understanding of its audience and their perspective, a meaningless act that he calls "whistling in the wind" (p. 53). For Andrews and others who advance dialogic instructional frameworks, argument depends upon contrasting different perspectives.

The inherently dialogic nature of argumentation has some important implications for the teaching of argumentative writing. First, it suggests that teachers should find ways to incorporate writing tasks into their instruction that have a real audience and topics for which students are invested. Research shows that providing students with real-world social contexts for argumentative writing can have positive effects on the quality of their writing, and help them produce clearer and more precise arguments (Avery & Avery, 1995). In addition, authentic writing tasks encourage freedom to think more broadly about evidence as students focus on a real audience instead of just the teacher's possible reaction. Many researchers have addressed this challenge for school-like writing (Boscolo & Gelati, 2007).

More important, dialogic approaches encourage teachers to design collaborative writing activities that allow their students to entertain other students' perspectives. As Felton and Herko (2004) point out, adolescents are able to engage in effective and elaborate face-to-face argumentation, adjusting strategies to fit their audiences, and taking into account, and sometimes rebutting, alternative perspectives. However, these authors also stress that written arguments are less effective when the dialogic support is absent and face-to-face interactions do not occur. Therefore, teachers should provide collaborative experiences that help their students "bridge the gap" between written and face-to-face argument (Felton & Herko, 2004). This would help students gain access to alternative perspectives (Newell et al., 2011) in ways that support democratic discourse in the classroom (Emmel, Resch, & Tenney, 1996). To return to the definition of argument we mentioned earlier, these interactions can help writers to evaluate the *constellation of propositions* needed to support their standpoints (van Eemeren et al., 1996) by receiving critical feedback from a partner about the argument's reasonableness and its potential persuasiveness to other people.

Wagner's (1999) study of role playing demonstrates the positive effects of dialogic partnerships on the argumentative writing of fourth and eighth graders. Wagner sought to determine the degree to which dramatic role playing increased students' ability to take into account another person's perspective in their written arguments. Students were assigned to a role-playing condition, a direct instruction condition, or a no-instruction condition. In the role-playing condition, students worked in pairs to role-play a persuasive situation between a student and the school principal, each student having the opportunity to play both the student's and the principal's role before writing to the principal about controversial topics. In the direct instruction condition, students received a list of eight rules of effective persuasion, and practiced analyzing and discussing one exemplary and one poor model of persuasive writing on a topic similar to the one on which they would write. In the no-instruction condition, students were shown the topic just before they wrote. Wagner (1999) found that the students who participated in the role-playing activities wrote argumentative letters that were better adapted to the audience's needs than those in the direct instruction condition. This finding shows the value of including prewriting supports into instruction that involve dialogic interactions, for example, role playing. These activities can scaffold the argumentative writing process for students (Morgan & Beaumont, 2003; Felton & Herko, 2004).

A more recent study by Kuhn and Crowell (2011) used a dialogic debate format that has been used successfully in other interventions (see Felton & Herko, 2004), but added an electronic chat room component to the debate phase of the intervention. In this 3-year study, the researchers created topic cycles during which they introduced an argumentative topic, and then guided students through a series of three dialogic activities that were designed to promote the development of argumentative thinking (see Table 5.1). In the "pregame" phase of the intervention, students worked with small same-side groups facilitated by an adult, during which they generated reasons for their side and evaluated and ranked those reasons. At the end of year 1, students were also provided researcher-generated questions

TABLE 5.1. Example of Dialogic Support for Argument: Using Debate and Technology to Support Student Argumentation

Pregame phase

1. Students are provided with an argumentative topic
2. Students work in "same side" groups to generate and rank the reasons for their side's opinion on the topic
3. Students are provided questions—and answers for those questions—about their opinion, or students generate their own questions about their opinion with coaches providing answers
4. "Same side" groups generate reasons for the alternative perspective and "comebacks" (rebuttals) for those reasons

Game phase

5. Pairs of students from the same side compete via Google Chat with a pair from the opposing side
6. Students complete a reflection sheet between turns to reflect on their arguments and their opponents' arguments, including possible counterarguments and rebuttals that could be generated for their opponents' arguments

Endgame phase

7. Students return to their pregame groups to review their reasons, counterarguments, and rebuttals
8. Students participate in a 3-minute "hot seat" debate in which each team member debates a member from the other team with points awarded for effective argumentative moves

Writing phase

9. Students write essays on their opinion using what they have learned from the debate to support their point of view and address the alternative perspective.

Note. Based on Kuhn and Crowell (2011).

and answers to those questions for their topics. In years 2 and 3, students began asking their own questions with coaches supplying answers to the questions. At the end of the pregame phase, these same-side groups would then focus on generating reasons for the alternative perspective and generate "comebacks" (rebuttals) for these alternative perspectives.

During the "game" phase of the intervention, pairs of students competed electronically against opposing-side students via Google Chat. The students debated each other and completed a reflection sheet between turns. These sheets guided students to identify and reflect on their arguments and their opponents' arguments, including possible counterarguments and rebuttals, in order to improve them. This was followed by the "endgame" phase of the intervention, during which students returned to their "pregame" groups; reviewed their arguments, counterarguments, and rebuttals; and participated in a "hot seat" debate during which each team member had 3 minutes to debate a team member from the opposing side. Students were then debriefed, given points for effective argumentative moves, and stripped of points for ineffective argumentative moves, with a winning side declared at the end of the activity. This phase finished with students writing individual argumentative essays on the topic.

Kuhn and Crowell (2011) analyzed the essays for the type and number of arguments that students produced, and whether the arguments addressed both sides of the issue. They also analyzed the number and types of questions that students asked during the pregame phase of the intervention. Although students in the control condition engaged in teacher-led discussions of similar topics and wrote significantly more essays on the topics over the course of the year than students in the instructional condition, students who received the dialogic intervention wrote essays that contained significantly more arguments that addressed both sides of the controversy. In fact, few students in the control condition wrote essays that addressed both sides. Additionally, students who received instruction generated significantly more questions related to the topics than those in the control group.

Earlier we mentioned that teaching students to apply critical standards to their written arguments is important, and that the evaluation and defense of their arguments is best accomplished by answering *critical questions* about the relevance of their argumentative strategies (Walton et al., 2008). Students are often assigned the task of writing arguments about questions such as "Should teachers assign more homework?" Questions like this invite the use of the *argument from consequences* strategy in which the proponent argues in favor of or against the policy on the basis of the consequences that may result from its enactment. The proponent might argue that homework (1) enables students to practice what they learned in school, (2) allows students to develop the habit of working without the constant presence of the teacher or other people, and (3) helps students make more rapid progress in learning skills. Skeptics of this policy might ask a series of *critical questions* about the purported advantages of homework. For example, they could ask: (1) How sure are you that the good consequences will actually happen?; (2) Do you have evidence that these consequences are likely to happen?; (3) Are there potentially bad consequences that might happen if we implement the policy? In turn, the policy's proponent could ask these same questions about the reasons for the skeptic's perspective. In other words, critical questions can help establish the relevance of an argumentation strategy by encouraging consideration of the alternative perspective (Ferretti et al., 2007, 2009; Song & Ferretti, 2013; Nussbaum & Edwards, 2011).

Nussbaum and Edwards (2011) explored the effects of teaching seventh-grade social studies students to ask critical questions during dialogic interactions about controversial issues. The controversies were drawn from current events presented in *Newsweek* magazine. Eight different controversies were discussed over the course of 20 weeks, and two additional controversies, for which there was no discussion, were used to assess the effects of the intervention. Three classrooms were involved in this study. In two of the classrooms, students were taught to use critical questions along with a graphic organizer (called an *argumentation vee diagram*) to represent contrasting arguments about the controversies and to evaluate the strength of the arguments. For example, students in the critical questions condition were told to ask questions such as "Are any of these arguments unlikely?" about the arguments that were represented on the graphic organizer. In the third classroom, students were taught to use the graphic organizer to represent different arguments but they were not taught to ask the critical questions. The researchers were interested to see if the inclusion of critical questions led students to write more integrated arguments, that is, arguments that consider alternative perspectives and potential objections to their own perspective.

The researchers found that that the inclusion of the critical questions, which were introduced during the fifth discussion session, seemed to be associated with an increase in the number of arguments that weighed different perspectives about the controversy. However, this effect did not always occur when the class discussions and the critical questions were unavailable. Furthermore, students in the critical questions condition did not seem to produce more arguments that explained how a solution to a controversy should be designed to address different perspectives. The researchers expected to see greater use of design arguments by students in the critical questions condition because these arguments are inherently integrative. Finally, the researchers included a case study that illustrated how dialogic support with critical questions and the graphic organizer might impact one student's argumentative development. In total, the findings provide some evidence about the potential benefits of including critical questions in instruction for argumentative writing. We note, however, that explicit instruction about using critical questions to evaluate the relevance of students' argumentative strategies was not provided by the researchers. In fact, the argumentation strategies about which the critical questions could have been asked were not taught at all. In the absence of explicit instructional support, students may not have mastered the application of these challenging skills (see Song & Ferretti, 2013).

In conclusion, the evidence shows that dialogic support of argumentative writing can positively impact the quality of students' argumentative thinking and writing as well as their ability to address alternative perspectives (Wagner, 1999; Felton & Herko, 2004; Kuhn & Crowell, 2011). Furthermore, students can experience the positive motivational effects of using writing as an expressive and communicative tool through active engagement with others in the classroom community (Boscolo & Gelati, 2007). In this way, writing becomes a "first moment" (Boscolo & Gelati, 2007) for building other substantive classroom interactions and engaging content-area material. Furthermore, if students are given multiple chances to consider others' viewpoints, they can begin to internalize this perspective-taking process. This will enable students to understand how to represent different viewpoints, set more effective argumentative goals related to different perspectives (Flower & Hayes, 1980), and craft the constellation of propositions needed to increase the acceptability of their arguments (van Eemeren et al., 1996).

Supporting Self-Regulated Strategies for Argumentative Writing

Many young and unskilled writers, including students with learning disabilities (LD), are challenged to regulate the many demands of writing argumentative essays. Difficulties with self-regulation are seen in all aspects of their problem solving, including goal setting, planning, writing, and revising their essays (Graham et al., 2013). As a result, these students may need explicit strategic support and scaffolding while planning, writing, and revising their essays. Luckily, research shows that strategy instruction, which involves the explicit and systematic teaching of the writing process, has a dramatic and positive effect on the quality of students' writing (Graham & Perin, 2007; Graham et al., 2013).

The self-regulated strategy development (SRSD) model is one demonstrably effective approach to teaching argumentative writing (Graham & Perin, 2007; Graham et al., 2013). The key concept of SRSD is to use explicit instruction to scaffold the process of acquiring and independently applying writing strategies. Strategy instruction provides explicit and intensive support, which is especially important for struggling writers (Graham & Harris, 2005). Through six phases of instruction, students learn to regulate their behavior in the writing processes, set goals, and find appropriate ways to achieve their goals (see Figure 5.1). The teacher first provides explicit instruction about the strategy's purposes and potential benefits ("Develop Background Knowledge" Phase), and then explicitly supports learning specific strategies through instructional mnemonics ("Discuss It" Phase), including modeling their use ("Model It" Phase). Over time, the student memorizes the mnemonic through practice ("Memorize It" Phase) and the teacher cedes control to the student, who assumes greater responsibility

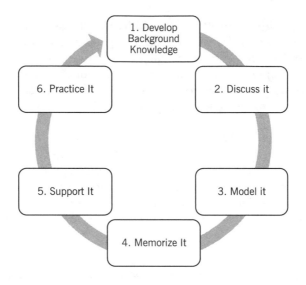

FIGURE 5.1. Phases of SRSD instruction.

for monitoring the strategy's application ("Support It" Phase), and provides experiences designed to ensure the strategy's internalization, maintenance, and generalization ("Practice It" Phase) (Graham & Harris, 2005; Graham et al., 2013). Table 5.2 illustrates how specific steps of SRSD instruction are used to teach two argumentative writing strategies.

A number of SRSD argumentative writing strategies have been developed to support the planning process (Graham & Harris, 1989; Sexton, Harris, & Graham, 1998). Graham and Harris (1989) conducted the earliest study of the effects of SRSD instruction on the argumentative writing of three sixth-grade students, who were taught to write using a multistep planning strategy. The TREE strategy prompted students to provide a *Topic* sentence, provide *Reasons* for their opinion, *Examine* the reason from the audience's perspective, and provide an *Ending*. The strategy elements were based on a general framework for arguments that includes a premise, supporting reasons and data, and a conclusion. Children were also encouraged to consider the audience's response to their argument, although specific guidance for doing so was not provided. The TREE strategy instruction had a positive effect on students' argumentative writing and self-efficacy as writers. Prior to instruction, few of the students' essays contained elements of argumentative discourse and most of it served no discernable rhetorical purpose. After instruction, nearly all of the essays included the basic elements of argumentative discourse, and were of a higher quality than before instruction.

TABLE 5.2. Cognitive Support for Writing: POW and TREE and STOP and DARE

Steps in SRSD instruction	TREE: An argumentative strategy for younger children	STOP and DARE: An argumentative strategy for older children
1. *Build background knowledge:* Providing students a rationale for the instructional strategy	Teacher explains the importance of argumentative writing, its connection to state and national standards, the role it plays in school and society, and how this strategy will help them write better arguments.	
2. *Discuss it:* Introducing the strategic mnemonic to the students, and how the mnemonic can be used to set manageable goals for their writing	Teacher presents students the mnemonic. When they write an argument it should include: **T:** A clear Topic sentence. **R:** Reasons (three or more). **E:** Explanations where they say more about the reasons. **E:** An Ending where they wrap it up right.	Teacher presents students the mnemonic. When they *plan* their argument they should: **S:** Suspend judgment by listing reasons for both sides of an issue. **T:** Take a side by deciding which side has the strongest support. **O:** Organize ideas for their chosen side by numbering how they will appear in the composition. **P:** Plan more as you write. When students *write* their argumentative essay they should remember to: Develop their topic sentence. Add supporting details. Reject at least one argument for the other side. End with a conclusion that wraps it up right.
3. *Model it:* Modeling how the strategy works by thinking aloud through the writing process, and demonstrating how to use the mnemonic to plan and write text.	Teacher models writing an argumentative paragraph or essay by "thinking aloud" in front of the students. She will use a topic sentence (T) and three or more reasons (R) for her opinion, and then show students how to write more about each reason	Teacher models planning for an argumentative essay while thinking aloud and using a t-chart graphic organizer where she stops (S) to list reasons for both sides of an argumentative topic, evaluates the strength of both sides and takes a side (T) and then organizes (O) her plan by numbering the arguments she will use in her composition. She will remind herself to continue to plan (P) throughout the writing process.

(continued)

TABLE 5.2. *(continued)*

Steps in SRSD instruction	TREE: An argumentative strategy for younger children	STOP and DARE: An argumentative strategy for older children
3. *Model it (continued)*	(E) by providing elaborations or examples, and demonstrate how to write an ending (E) that reinforces her point of view.	Teacher then models writing using her plan by developing a topic sentence (D), adding (A) supporting details from the numbered list of reasons from her t-chart plan sheet, addressing the alternative perspective and rejecting (R) one of the reasons for that perspective that would be found on the t-chart, and then end (E) the essay by reinforcing her point of view.
4. *Memorize it:* Encouraging students to memorize the mnemonic in order to internalize the planning and writing process	Teacher provides students with the opportunity to commit the strategy to memory. This can be done through a game format or through additional collaborative practice using the mnemonic to plan or write arguments.	
5. *Support it:* Using scaffolding to support students' independent acquisition of the strategy	Teacher provides additional collaborative experiences through peer interactions or shared writing experiences to reinforce the use of the strategy with other argumentative topics.	Teacher provides additional collaborative experiences through peer interactions, to reinforce the strategy use with other argumentative topics. This would be a particularly good time to reinforce how students can address the alternative perspective and reject arguments for that perspective.
6. *Independent performance:* Independent use of the strategy for a variety of argumentative tasks	Teacher provides students the opportunity to use the strategy to independently produce argumentative texts for a variety of purposes, in compositions of various lengths, and addressing both policy issues and analytic and evaluative questions based on content-area material.	

Sexton et al. (1998) taught three fifth graders and three sixth graders to use the TREE strategy to write argumentative essays and encouraged these students, who lacked academic motivation, to attribute their success to effort and the use of the TREE strategy. Prior to instruction, the students spent little time planning and included few discourse elements in their essays, which were judged to be of poor quality. Furthermore, the students believed that effort and strategy use were not especially important to writing success compared to extraneous factors. After instruction, students used the TREE strategy to plan their essays, which resulted in a dramatic increase in the number of discourse elements and in essay quality. Furthermore, students made stronger attributions about the relative importance of effort and strategy use as influences on writing performance.

Graham, MacArthur, Schwartz, and Page-Voth (1992) taught four fifth-grade students with LD to use a planning and writing strategy to improve their argumentative writing. The PLANS strategy (Pick goals, List ways to meet goals, And make Notes, Sequence notes) included process and product goals that were meant to guide students' writing. The product goals helped to define the purpose of writing, the structure of the essay, and the essay's length; the process goals broke the steps of the writing process into manageable subproblems. In brief, the PLANS strategy was designed to help students regulate the planning process. Prior to instruction, the students averaged very few argumentative elements per essay; after instruction, they averaged more elements per essay and the gains were maintained for several weeks. Furthermore, less than a quarter of students' essays contained all of the elements of argumentative discourse before instruction, but almost all included these elements after instruction. Essays written after instruction were also longer, more coherent, and of higher quality. Finally, students planned little before instruction, but after instruction they systematically used the planning strategy before attempting to write.

De La Paz and Graham (1997a) taught three fifth-grade students with LD to use a planning and writing strategy to improve their argumentative writing. This strategy required students to generate ideas on both sides of an issue during planning and examine these ideas from multiple perspectives before writing. The STOP and DARE strategy was designed to ensure that students stopped, reflected, and planned before writing (Suspend judgment, Take a side, Organize their ideas, and Plan as they wrote more) and then included the four essential elements in their argumentative essays (Develop a topic sentence, Add supporting ideas, Reject possible arguments for the other side, and End with a conclusion). Prior to instruction, students spent little time in planning or writing their essays; consequently, their essays included few reasons or elaborations for their standpoint. After instruction, students wrote longer essays that included many more argumentative elements. Interestingly, the researchers reported that 70% of the posttreatment essays contained refutations of the alternative standpoint. However, they neither described the nature of students' refutations nor the evaluative standards for refutation that were taught during instruction.

Kiuhara, O'Neill, Hawken, and Graham (2012) taught six tenth-grade students with disabilities to use the STOP, AIMS, and DARE strategy to plan and write persuasive essays. The STOP and DARE components were modified slightly for high school students, but the most significant change to this strategy involved the inclusion of AIMS. The AIMS strategy was designed to help students construct an introduction to their essays that would help the audience understand the context for information provided about the topic (Attract the reader's attention, Identify the problem of the topic so the reader understands the issues, Map the context of the problem or provide background needed to understand the problem, and State the thesis so the premise is clear). Prior to instruction, the students spent little time planning and writing their essays, so the quality of their essays was poor and they were relatively impoverished, that is, they usually included a premise and an unelaborated supporting reason. After instruction, students spent much more time planning and writing their essays, which were of much higher quality. In addition to elaborating the reasons for their position and attempting to refute the alternative perspective, their postinstruction essays usually contextualized the topic about which they wrote and provided relevant background information about it.

As we previously mentioned, SRSD strategies have been developed for planning and composing written arguments (Graham & Harris, 1989; Sexton et al., 1998). In addition, strategies have been designed to support the revision of argumentative essays (Graham & MacArthur, 1988; Song & Ferretti, 2013). These strategies are potentially important because the revision process enables students to reflect on their ideas, develop and apply critical standards of evaluation, and improve their writing skills (Scardamalia & Bereiter, 1986). Research shows that expert writers revise their work to improve its overall quality and to clarify important ideas, while novices revise to correct grammar, spelling, diction, and punctuation (MacArthur, Schwartz, & Graham, 1991). Revising skills clearly develops over time (Fitzgerald & Markman, 1987), but unfortunately, even many college students are unable to revise effectively (Kinsler, 1990).

Graham and MacArthur (1988) taught three fifth- and sixth-grade students with LD the SCAN strategy for revising argumentative essays on a word processor. The SCAN strategy teaches a procedure for reflecting on the following questions: Does it make Sense? Is it Connected to my belief? Can I Add more? Note Errors. Instruction in the use of the SCAN strategy positively impacted students' revising behavior. Prior to instruction, only a third of the students' revisions involved the addition of reasons for the writer's standpoint. In contrast, nearly two-thirds of the revisions involved the addition of reasons after instruction, and their postinstruction essays were longer and of higher quality. The criteria for revising argumentative essays embedded in the SCAN strategy included presenting a clear belief, providing reasons to support this belief, and removing mechanical errors. These criteria are appropriate for younger students and students with LD, but do not focus attention on the critical standards that older students should use to evaluate their argumentation strategies.

As we mentioned earlier, critical standards of argumentation are important because they provide the criteria that students should use to evaluate the relevance of their argumentation strategies. Earlier we discussed how Nussbaum and Edwards (2011) used dialogic discussions to teach adolescents about the use of critical standards in their argumentation. We mentioned that the effects of their instruction were somewhat unclear, perhaps because the researchers did not include explicit instruction about the use of critical questions to evaluate the relevance of students' argumentation strategies. Song and Ferretti (2013) conducted the only SRSD study of which we are aware that was specifically designed to teach critical standards of argumentation to college students. Although the study included college students, this work is applicable to the instruction of middle and high school students, who must also learn how to evaluate their arguments. In Song and Ferretti's (2013) study, college students were assigned to one of three conditions: the *Ask and Answer Critical Questions* (ASCQ) condition, the *Argumentation Schemes* (AS) condition, and an uninstructed control condition. In the ASCQ condition, students were taught to revise their essays by asking and answering critical questions about two argumentation strategies that are commonly used to address controversial policies (Ferretti et al., 2007, 2009). The *argument from consequences strategy* justifies a policy based on the potential positive or negative consequences that may result from its enactment. The *argument from example strategy* uses particular cases or instances to illustrate a generalized claim. In contrast, students in the AS condition were taught to revise their essays by using the above-mentioned argumentation strategies to justify their standpoint, but did not learn to apply the critical questions. Finally, students in the uninstructed control condition received no instruction about either the argumentation schemes or the critical questions.

Song and Ferretti (2013) expected that the ASCQ strategy would not only improve the quality of students' essays, but also increase their responsiveness to alternative perspectives in comparison to the other conditions. This is because students who learned the ASCQ strategy were taught to ask and answer questions that could be used to evaluate the reasons for their standpoint (i.e., counterarguments), and they were also taught to ask and answer those critical questions for the reasons for the alternative standpoint (i.e., rebuttals). The researchers also expected that students in the AS condition would use their knowledge of the argumentation schemes to further elaborate the reasons for their standpoint. In fact, students in the ASCQ condition wrote essays that were of higher quality, and included more counterarguments, alternative standpoints, and rebuttals than those in the other conditions. Furthermore, the students who learned the AS strategy produced more reasons for their standpoints than those in the other conditions. Interestingly, the effects of these revision strategies were evident for students' revised drafts, but they were also apparent in their first drafts. This is an educationally desirable outcome because standards for good writing acquired during the revising process should positively impact the quality of students' writing (MacArthur, 2012). In conclusion, these findings indicate that that strategy instruction that includes critical standards for argumentation increases college students' sensitivity to alternative perspectives.

The evidence clearly shows that SRSD instruction can improve the planning and revision processes of young and less able students, and those with LD. There is, however, less evidence about the efficacy of SRSD instruction for older and more able students (see Graham et al., 2013). Furthermore, SRSD instruction is usually implemented in a small-group or individually (De La Paz & Graham, 2002) because students are usually taught until they can perform independently. Consequently, there is less evidence about the efficacy of the classroom-wide implementation of SRSD instruction. However, De La Paz and Graham (2002) demonstrated the efficacy of SRSD instruction in normalized classroom settings. They examined the effects of a teacher-delivered SRSD planning, drafting, and revision framework on seventh- and eighth-grade students' expository and argumentative writing.

Students in De La Paz and Graham's (2002) experimental condition learned about the characteristics of five-paragraph expository essays, and were then taught to use the SRSD PLAN and WRITE mnemonic to plan and draft their essays. This mnemonic encouraged students to PLAN (Pay attention to prompt; List main ideas; Add supporting ideas; Number your ideas) before drafting, and then to WRITE (Work from you plan to develop your thesis statement; Remember your goals; Include transition words for each paragraph; Try to use different kinds of sentences; add Exciting, interesting words). Students used these writing goals during the revision process to evaluate the effectiveness of their essays in peer-revising conferences. Students in the control condition were provided with the same general instruction in the characteristics of five-paragraph expository essays, and wrote about the same topics as those in the experimental condition, but their instruction focused on mechanics, idea generation, and organization. Students receiving the SRSD PLAN and WRITE intervention created better developed writing plans, and wrote essays that were significantly longer and of overall higher quality than those students in the control condition. Additionally, PLAN and WRITE students wrote essays with a greater variety of 7+ letter words than those in the control condition. All effects were maintained 1 month after instruction.

SRSD instruction clearly improves students' argumentative writing, and the benefits are especially clear for younger students and those with LD. After instruction, students write longer essays that include a greater number of elements of argumentative discourse. Furthermore, they are able to use strategies that allow them to manage the planning and revising processes. There is less evidence about the effects of SRSD instruction on the writing of college students (see Graham et al., 2013), but at least one study (Song & Ferretti, 2013) shows the benefits of strategy instruction, including the use of critical standards to evaluate their own and other people's perspectives.

Summary of Dialogic and Strategy Supports for Student Argumentation

There is often a robust discussion between those who either see argument as grounded in people's social practices or in their cognition (Coker & Lewis, 2012; Graham & Perin, 2007). Dichotomies such as these are almost always unproductive and often misleading. Our discussion makes clear that dialogic and strategic instructional practices are complementary supporting frameworks for effective argumentative thinking and writing. As we stated earlier, argumentative writing is a challenging activity that few American students do well (Nation's Report Card: Writing 2007). Among other things, students are expected to meet structural and organizational expectations for their work, apply critical standards of evaluation (van Eemeren et al., 1996), anticipate opposing perspectives, and systematically address those perspectives (Ferretti et al., 2009; Song & Ferretti, 2013). Teachers can provide powerful integrated writing instruction by using both conversational supports that scaffold students' representation of alternative perspectives and the cognitive strategic supports that scaffold the planning, drafting, and revising of argumentative writing processes. Furthermore, by combining these two approaches, teachers are better able to meet the Common Core standards, which call for instruction that integrates reading, writing, speaking, and listening skills across the K–12 curriculum (NGA

& CCSSO, 2010). Only by combining these approaches can we empower students to meet these rigorous standards.

Instructional Support for Content-Area Arguments

As children progress through the curriculum, their academic progress depends on the development of literacy skills that become increasingly specific and dependent on disciplinary knowledge and skills (Ferretti & De La Paz, 2011; Heller & Greenleaf, 2007). Expert writers draw on their general world knowledge, knowledge of text structure (RAND Reading Study Group, 2002), and their disciplinary expertise to write effective content-area arguments (De La Paz, 2005; Lewis & Ferretti, 2009; Shanahan & Shanahan, 2008). In what follows, we review some evidence about how disciplinary experts think and reason in literary studies (Fahnestock & Secor, 1991; Lewis & Ferretti, 2009, 2011) and history (De La Paz, 2005). This work will illustrate how we can design instructional activities that empower students to write disciplinary arguments.

Literary Arguments

The skills involved in analyzing and interpreting literary text are an important focus of the English curriculum for high school students (Lewis & Ferretti, 2009). Despite the significance of these skills, students are rarely able to construct arguments about interpretations of literature (Marshall, 2000) or go beyond basic plot summary to engage in substantive thematic issues of a text (Persky, Daane, & Jin, 2003). Unfortunately, little instructional time is devoted to interpretative or analytic writing (Applebee & Langer, 2006; Kiuhara, Graham, & Hawken, 2009).

Students must be able to analyze and interpret literature before they are able to write analytic arguments about it. The analysis and interpretation of literature depends on two interdependent processes (Lewis & Ferretti, 2009, 2011). First, students must be able to recognize the patterns of language created by the author that enable them to comprehend the text and interpret it. Second, students must translate these interpretations into a written argument that supports their interpretations. According to Fahnestock and Secor (1991), disciplinary experts use very specific critical approaches when interpreting literature and writing literary arguments. A full description of these approaches is outside the scope of this chapter. However, it is enough to say that literary experts justify their interpretations of literature on the basis of "repetitions" and "oppositions" that appear in text (Scholes, 1985). The repetitions are similar repeated patterns of imagery, symbolism, or syntactic elements, and the oppositions are repeated patterns that stand in opposition to one another (Lewis & Ferretti, 2009, 2011). These patterns are what Scholes (1985, pp. 31–32) calls "an interpretive code" for "thematizing" and interpreting literary text. When these interpretations are then translated into literary arguments, literary analysts are expected to bolster their arguments with quotations, textual references, and explanations that warrant the use of these sources as evidence (Lewis & Ferretti, 2009, 2011).

Lewis and Ferretti (2009, 2011) demonstrated the instructional implications of these ideas. High school students who were poor writers learned about figurative language and pattern recognition skills. Students were also taught THE READER strategy, which was designed to help them plan and write interpretative arguments about literature using pattern recognition skills to develop robust literary interpretations. Six lessons, based on the principles of SRSD instruction (Graham et al., 2013), were used to teach THE READER strategy and the disciplinary knowledge needed to use it effectively. In brief, students were taught to develop a *THE*sis, back up the thesis with *REA*sons, include *D*etails as illustrations of those reasons (direct quotes or references to the text), *E*xplain how those quotes and references are related to their reasons or thesis (warrant), and *R*eview their main points in a conclusion. Students also learned to use a graphic organizer to help plan their essay.

Before instruction, students wrote literary arguments that were of poor quality, and did not invoke the patterns, include textual citations, or warrant the connection between textual citations and their interpretative claims. Together these elements are the discourse-specific constellation of propositions (van Eemeren et al., 1996) that are at the heart of critical literary discourse (Fahnestock & Secor, 1991). At the completion of instruction, students were able to invoke the patterns, use textual citations to support their interpretations, and warrant the relationship between the textual evidence and their point of view. In general, the quality of students' literary arguments improved as a result of instruction, and furthermore, they showed a rudimentary understanding of literary analysis and argument (Lewis & Ferretti, 2009, 2011). In addition, Lewis and Ferretti (2011) found that experienced English teachers favorably evaluated their instructional protocol. However, like most SRSD interventions, the study was not conducted under the conditions of everyday classroom instruction. Individual students were provided explicit instruction about the background knowledge and skills needed to write interpretative arguments about literature. Evidence about how the intervention might be adapted to the complexities of the everyday classroom was not provided. Nevertheless, Lewis and Ferretti's (2009, 2011) findings show that strategy instruction grounded in the disciplinary knowledge used in literary analysis produced marked improvements in students' written arguments.

Historical Arguments

There is general agreement that history instruction should promote the acquisition of disciplinary knowledge and critical habits of mind that are needed to participate in democratic decision making (Ferretti & Okolo, 1996; Ferretti, MacArthur, & Okolo, 2001). Historical thinking requires that students puzzle about sources (artifacts and accounts of the past) to construct an interpretation of an event (Ferretti et al., 2001). These sources are a representation of the past, so students must analyze evidence to determine how the sources came into being, who constructed them and for what purposes, what other accounts exist, and which of these accounts are trustworthy (Seixas, 1996). In judging and evaluating evidence, historians use strategies and standards that are shared by members of their discourse community. Wineburg's (1991a, 1991b) research shows that historians use the strategies of corroboration, contextualization, and sourcing to judge the trustworthiness of the evidence. They compare the details of one source against those of another (*corroboration*), situate the event in its historical context (*contextualization*), and check the document's source to determine the purposes for which it was created (*sourcing*). Unfortunately, the evidence shows that students' understanding of historical perspective and their ability to conduct historical analysis are limited (Lee & Weiss, 2007).

De La Paz (2005) demonstrated how instruction about argumentative writing and historical interpretation could be combined in middle school classroom classrooms. Students of wide-ranging abilities (including talented students and students with LD) were taught to apply Wineburg's strategies for interpreting primary source documents, and were also taught the *STOP and DARE* strategy (De La Paz & Graham, 1997a, 1997b) for writing argumentative essays based on these sources. The sources, which focused on the period of Westward Expansion, included information about different perspectives concerning controversies that arose during this historical period. Students read and took notes about primary sources, and were taught to use their notes to prepare for writing argumentative essays. The *STOP and DARE* strategy, the components of which we previously described, was modified to address historical elements of the argumentative writing task, including the use of source material as evidence to support a historical argument. In contrast, students in a comparison condition read these sources but were not taught either the historical reasoning or argumentative writing strategies.

De La Paz's (2005) three-step historical reasoning strategy, which was based on Weinburg's (1991a, 1991b) seminal work, included two self-questioning routines. The first routine prompted students to consider the text's source and then analyze it for potential inaccuracies. Students answered three questions: (1) What was the author's purpose? (2) Do the reasons make sense? And (3) Do you find evidence of bias? To detect bias students were guided to examine the author's *word choice* and whether there was *only one point of view* in the document. The second routine prompted students to ask five questions that focused on conflicting perspectives or information. Students asked: (1) Is an author inconsistent? (2) Is a person described differently? (3) Is an event described differently? (4) What is missing from the author's argument? (5) What can you infer from reading *across* sources? These questions helped students to recognize and ignore untrustworthy information, and to attend to information that could be corroborated, that is, consistent across sources.

The findings showed that students who learned the historical reasoning and argumentative writing strategies wrote higher quality essays that contained more argumentative elements and more accurate historical content than students in the comparison condition. Furthermore, the length and quality of the argumentative essays written by students with LD after instruction were comparable to the pretest papers written by talented writers. De La Paz's (2005) findings suggest that strategy instruction that includes relevant disciplinary knowledge and skills has a salutary effect on students' written arguments about historical controversies.

Conclusions

We began by describing the importance of argumentative discourse and identifying some persistent constraints on its development. These constraints, which include both the privileging of one's perspective to the negligence of others and ignorance of genre-specific and discipline-relevant knowledge, are also seen in students' argumentative writing. While these are formidable obstacles to the development of students' argumentative writing, they can be overcome by instructional practices that provide carefully structured opportunities for dialogic interactions, strategic support for effective self-regulation, and the acquisition of specialized expertise (including evaluative standards) needed to argue effectively. Equipped with this knowledge, our students will be better prepared to participate in the institutions of democratic life.

References

Andrews, R. (1995). *Teaching and learning argument.* New York: Cassell.
Applebee, A. N., & Langer, J. (2006). *The state of writing instruction: What existing data tell us.* Albany, NY: Center on English Learning and Achievement.

Applebee, A. N., Langer, J. A., Mullis, I. V. S., Latham, A. S., & Gentile, C. A. (1994). *NAEP 1992: Writing report card.* Washington, DC: U. S. Government Printing Office.

Aristotle (1991). *The art of rhetoric* (H. Lawson-Tancred, Trans.). London: Penguin Classics.

Avery, C. W., & Avery, K. B. (1995). Real audiences, real issues transform high school students into real writers. *Journal of Adolescent and Adult Literacy, 39,* 235–237.

Bereiter, C., & Scardamalia, M. (1987). *The psychology of written composition.* Hillsdale, NJ: Erlbaum.

Boscolo, P., & Gelati, C. (2007). Best practices in promoting motivation in writing. In S. Graham, C. A. MacArthur, & J. Fitzgerald (Eds.), *Best practices in writing instruction* (pp. 202–221). New York: Guilford Press.

Bruner, J. (1990). *Acts of meaning.* Cambridge, MA: Harvard University Press.

Coker, D. L., & Lewis, W. (2012). Beyond *Writing Next*: A discussion of writing research and instructional uncertainty. In J. Ippolito, J. L. Steele, & J. F. Samson (Eds.), *Adolescent literacy* (pp. 231–251). Cambridge, MA: Harvard Educational Review.

De La Paz, S. (2005). Effects on historical reasoning instruction and writing strategy mastery in culturally and academically diverse middle school classrooms. *Journal of Educational Psychology, 97,* 139–156.

De La Paz, S., & Graham, S. (1997a). Strategy instruction in planning: Effects on the writing performance and behavior of students with learning difficulties. *Exceptional Children, 63,* 167–181.

De La Paz, S., & Graham, S. (1997b). The effects of dictation and advanced planning instruction on the composing of students with writing and learning problems. *Journal of Educational Psychology, 89,* 203–222.

De La Paz, S., & Graham, S. (2002). Explicitly teaching strategies, skills and knowledge: Writing instruction in middle school classrooms. *Journal of Educational Psychology, 94,* 687–698.

Dewey, J. (1916). *Democracy and education.* New York: Macmillan.

Dunn, J. (1988). *The beginnings of social understanding.* Cambridge, MA: Harvard University Press.

Emmel, B., Resch, P., & Tenney, D. (1996). *Argument revisited; argument redefined.* Thousand Oaks, CA: Sage.

Fahnestock, J., & Secor, M. (1991). The rhetoric of literary criticism. In C. Bazerman & J. Paradis (Eds.), *Textual dynamics of the professions: Historical and contemporary studies of writing in professional communities* (pp. 77–96). Madison: University of Wisconsin Press.

Felton, M. K., & Herko, S. (2004). From dialogue to two-sided argument: Scaffolding adolescents' persuasive writing. *Journal of Adolescent and Adult Literacy, 27,* 672–683.

Felton, M. K., & Kuhn, D. (2001). The development of argumentative discourse skill. *Discourse Processes, 32,* 135–153.

Ferretti, R. P., Andrews-Weckerly, S., & Lewis, W. E. (2007). Improving the argumentative writing of students with learning disabilities: Descriptive and normative considerations. *Reading and Writing Quarterly, 23,* 267–285.

Ferretti, R. P., & De La Paz, S. (2011). On the comprehension and production of written texts: Instructional activities that support content-area literacy. In R. E. O'Connor & P. F. Vadasy (Eds.), *Handbook of reading interventions* (pp. 326–355). New York: Guilford Press.

Ferretti, R. P., Lewis, W. E., & Andrews-Weckerly, S. (2009). Do goals affect the structure of students' argumentative writing strategies? *Journal of Educational Psychology, 101,* 577–589.

Ferretti, R. P., MacArthur, C. A., & Dowdy, N. S. (2000). The effects of an elaborated goal on the persuasive writing of students with learning disabilities and their normally achieving peers. *Journal of Educational Psychology, 92,* 694–702.

Ferretti, R. P., MacArthur, C. A., & Okolo, C. M. (2001). Teaching for historical understanding in inclusive classrooms. *Learning Disability Quarterly, 24,* 59–71.

Ferretti, R. P., & Okolo, C. M. (1996). Authenticity in learning: Multimedia design projects in the social studies for students with disabilities. *Journal of Learning Disabilities, 29,* 450–460.

Fitzgerald, J., & Markman, L. (1987). Teaching children about revision in writing. *Cognition and Instruction, 4,* 3–24.

Flower, L., & Hayes, R. H. (1980). The cognition of discovery: Defining a rhetorical problem. *College Composition and Communication, 31,* 21–32.

Graham, S., & Harris, K. R. (1989). Improving learning disabled students' skills at composing essays: Self-instructional strategy training. *Exceptional Children, 56,* 201–214.

Graham, S., & Harris, K. R. (1997). It can be taught, but it doesn't develop naturally: Myths and realities in writing instruction. *School Psychology Review, 26,* 414–424.

Graham, S., & Harris, K. J. (2005). *Writing better: Effective strategies for teaching students with learning difficulties.* New York: Brooks.

Graham, S., Harris, K. R., & McKeown, D. (2013). The writing of students with learning disabilities, meta-analysis of self-regulated strategy development writing intervention studies, and future directions: Redux. In H. L. Swanson, K. R. Harris, & S. Graham (Eds.), *Handbook of learning disabilities* (2nd ed., pp. 405–438). New York: Guilford Press.

Graham, S., & MacArthur, C. (1988). Improving learning disabled students' skills at revising essays produced on a word processor: Self-instruction strategy training. *Journal of Special Education, 22,* 133–152.

Graham, S., MacArthur, C. A., Schwartz, S., & Page-Voth, V. (1992). Improving learning disabled students' compositions using a strategy involving product and process goal setting. *Exceptional Children, 58,* 322–334.

Graham, S., & Perin, D. (2007). *Writing next: Effective strategies to improve writing of adolescents in middle and high schools.* New York: Carnegie Corporation.

Heller, R., & Greenleaf, C. (2007). *Literacy instruction in the content areas: Getting to the core of middle and high school improvement.* Washington, DC: Alliance for Excellent Education.

Johnson, D. W., & Johnson, R. T. (2009). Energizing learning: The instructional power of conflict. *Educational Researcher, 38,* 37–51.

Kinsler, K. (1990). Structured peer collaboration: Teaching essay revision to college students needing writing remediation. *Cognition and Instruction, 7*(4), 303–321.

Kiuhara, S. A., Graham, S., & Hawken, L. S. (2009). Teaching writing to high school students: A national survey. *Journal of Educational Psychology, 101*, 136–160.

Kiuhara, S. A., O'Neil, R. E., Hawken, L. S., & Graham, S. (2012). The effectiveness of teaching 10th-grade students *STOP, AIMS*, and *DARE* for planning and drafting persuasive text. *Exceptional Children, 78*, 335–355.

Kuhn, D. (1991). *The skills of argument*. New York: Cambridge University Press.

Kuhn, D., & Crowell, A. (2011). Dialogic argumentation as a vehicle for developing young adolescents' thinking. *Psychological Science, 22*, 545–552.

Kuhn, D., Shaw, V., & Felton, M. (1997). Effects of dyadic interaction on argumentative reasoning, *Cognition and Instruction, 15*, 287–315.

Lee, J., & Weiss, A. (2007). *The Nation's Report Card: U.S. History 2006* (No. NCES 2007-474). Washington, DC: U.S. Department of Education, National Center for Education Statistics.

Lewis, W. E., & Ferretti, R. P. (2009). Defending interpretations of literary texts: The effects of topoi instruction on the literary arguments of high school students. *Reading and Writing Quarterly, 25*, 250–270.

Lewis, W. E., & Ferretti, R. P. (2011). Topoi and literary interpretation: The effects of a critical reading and writing intervention on high school students' analytic literary essays. *Contemporay Educational Psychology, 36*, 334–354.

MacArthur, C. A. (2012). Evaluation and revision processes in writing. In V. W. Berninger (Ed.), *Past, present, and future contributions of cognitive writing research to cognitive psychology* (pp. 461–483). London: Psychology Press.

MacArthur, C. A., Schwartz, S., & Graham, S. (1991). Effects of a reciprocal peer revision strategy in special education classrooms. *Learning Disabilities Research and Practice, 6*, 201–210.

Marshall, J. (2000). Research on response to literature. In R. Barr, M. L. Kamil, P. Mosenthal, & P. D. Pearson (Eds.), *Handbook of reading research* (Vol. 3, pp. 381–402). Mahwah, NJ: Erlbaum.

Morgan, W., & Beaumont, G. (2003). A dialogic approach to argumentation: Using a chat room to develop early adolescent students' argumentative writing. *Journal of Adolescent and Adult Literacy, 47*, 146–157.

National Governors Association & Council of Chief State School Officers. (2010). *Common Core State Standards for English language arts & literacy in history/social studies, science, and technical subjects*. Washington, DC: Authors. Retrieved from *www. corestandards.org*.

Nation's Report Card: Writing 2007. (2007). Retrieved February 25, 2011, from *http://nces.ed.gov/nationsreportcard/pdf/main2007/2008468.pdf*.

Newell, G. E., Beach, R., Smith, J., & VanDerHeide, J. (2011). Teaching and learning argumentative reading and writing: A review of research. *Reading Research Quarterly, 46*, 273–304.

Nussbaum, E. M., & Edwards, O. V. (2011). Critical questions and argument stratagems: A framework for enhancing and analyzing students' reasoning practices. *Journal of the Learning Sciences, 20,* 443–488.

Page-Voth, V., & Graham, S. (1999). Effects of goal-setting and strategy use on the writing performance and self-efficacy of students with writing and learning problems. *Journal of Educational Psychology, 91,* 230–240.

Perkins, D. N., Faraday, M., & Bushey, B. (1991). Everyday reasoning and the roots of intelligence. In J. F. Voss, D. N. Perkins, & J. W. Segal (Eds.), *Informal reasoning and education* (pp. 83–105). Hillsdale, NJ: Erlbaum.

Persky, H. R., Daane, M. C., & Jin, Y. (2003). *The nation's report card: Writing 2002* (U. S. Department of Education Publication No. NCES 2003-529). Washington, DC: U.S. Government Printing Office.

RAND Reading Study Group. (2002). *Reading for understanding.* Santa Monica, CA: RAND.

Reznitskaya, A., & Anderson, R. C. (2002). The argument schema and learning to reason. In C. C. Block & M. Pressley (Eds.), *Comprehension instruction: Research-based best practices* (pp. 319–334). New York: Guilford Press.

Scardamalia, M., & Bereiter, C. (1986). Research on written composition. In M. C. Wittrock (Ed.), *Handbook of research on teaching* (pp. 778–803). New York: Macmillan.

Scholes, R. (1985). *Textual power: Literary theory and the teaching of English.* New Haven, CT: Yale University Press.

Seixas, P. (1996). Conceptualizing the growth of historical thinking. In D. R. Olson & N. Torrance (Eds.), *The handbook of education and human development* (pp. 765–783). Oxford, UK: Blackwell.

Sexton, M., Harris, K. R., & Graham, S. (1998). Self-regulated strategy development and the writing process: Effects on essay writing and attributions. *Exceptional Children, 64,* 295–311.

Shanahan, T., & Shanahan, C. (2008). Teaching disciplinary literacy to adolescents: Rethinking content-area literacy. *Harvard Educational Review, 78,* 40–59.

Song, Y., & Ferretti, R. P. (2013). Teaching critical questions about argumentation through the revising process: Effects of strategy instruction on college students' argumentative essays. *Reading and Writing: An Interdisciplinary Journal, 26,* 67–90.

van Eemeren, F. H., & Grootendorst, R. (2004). *A systematic theory of argumentation: The pragma-dialectical approach.* Cambridge, UK: Cambridge University Press.

van Eemeren, F. H., Grootendorst, R., & Henkemans, F. S. (1996). *Fundamentals of argumentation theory: A handbook of historical backgrounds and contemporary developments.* Mahwah, NJ: Erlbaum.

Wagner, B. J. (1999). *Building moral communities through educational drama.* Stamford, CT: Ablex.

Walton, D., Reed, C., & Macagno, F. (2008). *Argumentation schemes.* New York: Cambridge University Press.

Wilder, L. (2005). "The rhetoric of literary criticism" revisited: Mistaken critics, complex contexts, and social justice. *Written Communication, 22,* 76–119.

Wineburg, S. (1991a). Historical problem solving: A study of the cognitive processes used in the evaluation of documentary and pictorial evidence. *Journal of Educational Psychology, 83,* 73–87.

Wineburg, S. (1991b). On the reading of historical texts: Notes on the breach between school and the academy. *American Educational Research Journal, 28,* 495–519.

Chapter 6

Best Practices in Teaching Informative Writing from Sources

GEORGE E. NEWELL
JENNIFER VanDerHEIDE
MELISSA WILSON

The Need for Teaching Informative Writing from Sources

What are some of the challenges teachers encounter when they teach informative writing from sources to their students, and why is this writing an important part of a K–12 literacy curriculum? One way to understand some of the challenges is to consider the role of writing education in the contexts of American schooling. Over the last 30 years of efforts to reform writing instruction, two major themes have emerged: the significance of teachers' conceptions of writing and the role of writing in learning and critical thinking. Across subject areas, teachers now voice an understanding of the ways in which writing can contribute to learning, see writing as a valuable tool for assessing students' understandings, and in many cases see unique and particular roles that writing could play within various subject areas. At the same time, the actual writing that goes on in typical classrooms across the United States continues to be dominated by tasks in which the teacher does all the composing and students are left only to fill in missing information, whether copying directly from a teacher's presentation, completing worksheets and chapter summaries, replicating highly formulaic essay structures keyed to the high-stakes tests they will be taking, or writing the particular information the teacher is seeking (Applebee & Langer, 2011). In particular, Applebee and Langer (2011) report that "[given] the constraints imposed by high-stakes tests, writing as a way to study, learn, and go beyond—as a way to construct knowledge or generate new networks of understandings . . . is rare" (p. 26).

Without denying the importance of preparing students for standardized writing tests or for assigning writing to recall relevant knowledge and experience in preparing for new activities, we also believe that asking students to create their own texts from other texts is a hallmark of what some educators have called "high literacy" (Langer, 2002). This concept includes not just basic literacy but a "deeper knowledge of the ways in which reading, writing, language, and content work together" (Langer, 2002, p. 3), and in the case of writing from sources, the ability to analyze, synthesize, and integrate others' ideas with one's own writing. This is the kind of literacy that we believe should dominate schooling in all subject areas. Of course, English language arts teachers play a particularly significant role as "writing teachers" who are expected to teach their students the skills and strategies associated with process-oriented approaches designed to help students think through and organize their ideas before writing and to rethink and revise initial drafts. Process-oriented approaches to writing and high literacy both require and foster two key skills: the ability to engage in thoughtful reading and writing and the ability to perform well across a wide range of reading and writing tasks whether exploring new ideas and experiences or responding to the demands of high-stakes assessments. We think that writing from sources is at the heart of informative writing in that high literacy assumes that students are able to make sense of different and often conflicting voices in conversations both within and outside schooling. Although recent education reform movements, including the development of the Common Core State Standards (CCSS; National Governors Association [NGA] & Council of Chief State Officers [CCSO], 2010), have called for high literacy in all curricular areas and at all grade levels, we have found few good instructional models to support writing teachers.

In this chapter, after commenting on the place of informative writing in the CCSS, we define informative writing according to Britton et al.'s (1975) and Applebee's (1981, 1984, 2000) notions of discourse use or language function that has been taken up in K–12 schooling as well as in college writing (Melzer, 2009). We also offer a vision of teaching informative writing from sources as a way to foster student authorship from elementary school to high school. We then present portraits of two teachers' approaches to informative writing from sources in order to illustrate ways of not only enacting but also extending the CCSS's notions of such writing.

The Role of Informative Writing in the CCSS

One of the more significant shifts in the writing standards for the CCSS is an assumed progression through grade levels from the dominance of narrative writing to a focus on informative and argumentative writing. The reason for such a shift is a concern for academic standards that might prepare students for the world of work and college-level writing. The CCSS's authors assume that once students reach college and then begin careers they will need to write from sources as they present information or make arguments, and this is a form of literacy that should receive attention in early childhood as well. Although such a view of literacy has its critics (e.g., Bomer & Maloch, 2011), we believe there is much potential in asking K–12 literacy and English language arts teachers to support their students' efforts to "mine" texts in order to become more authoritative in their writing.

What is the progression assumed in the CCSS's standards for informative writing from early childhood, through middle childhood, to high school? While we do not have space here to offer a complete analysis, we offer three observations. First, there is a gradual yet distinct shift from narration in the early grades to a dominance of informative and argumentative writing by high school. Second, informative writing from sources has a place in the CCSS from the early grades through high school due to concerns that students not only show that they can analyze and synthesize sources but also "present careful analysis, well-defended claims, and clear information through their writing" (Coleman & Pimentel, 2011, p. 11). Third, the balance of writing students are asked to do should parallel the balance assessed on the National Assessment of Educational Progress (NAEP). For example, in elementary school 35% of the writing teachers assign should be to explain/inform, while 40% of the writing assigned to high school students should be to explain/inform.

Informative Writing from Sources as Language in Use

Although writing has been conceptualized in a wide range of ways, our framework for defining, teaching, and learning informative writing is grounded in the genre system of James Britton (1975) that has been adapted for use in American schools by Applebee (1981, 1984, 2000) and in studies of college writing (e.g., Melzer, 2009). Rather than focusing on the derivation of rules and conventions for various written genres, Britton constructed a way of studying school writing around the question of how students learn to use forms of writing to carry out particular kinds of messages. Britton and his colleagues offered a taxonomy whose internal structure suggests a way to think about the relationships among different kinds of writing, that is, a model of learning to write as a process of learning an increasing diverse array of uses of writing.

For Britton, writing within a particular function (e.g., to tell a story, to report an event, to argue for a stance) enables writers to organize meaning around intention and language use rather than around the structure of a completed product. Beginning with a continuum (see Figure 6.1) that places informational uses of writing at one end, personal (expressive) use in the middle, and literary or imaginative uses at the other end the system, Britton's taxonomy includes three main categories: informational, personal, and literary.

Informational uses of writing include the more typical variety of purposes such as informative (or expository) and persuasive writing used by the NAEP but also a range of subcategories. Based on Moffett (1968), these subcategories constitute an abstractive scale, moving from reporting to summarizing, analyzing, and finally theorizing. The *expressive* function or use of writing is best understood as corresponding to informal talk among friends, where rules of use are relaxed. The *imaginative* function, rather than relying on logical or analytic techniques, is essentially the language of literary genres (poetry, story, drama, etc.) used to represent the writer's experiences and, in turn, to represent a virtual experience for a reader. Since in this chapter we focus on informational or informative writing, we go into some depth about how, why, and when it is typically taken up in school settings.

Britton argues that other uses of language develop as differentiations from the personal or expressive and are characterized by formal structures that allow writers to communicate with increasingly distant audiences with whom they share few initial understandings. This means that as writers learn increasingly more formal conventions they are able to take up new purposes—to inform, to persuade, to entertain. For example, writers use the informational function to record or to convey information or ideas but the categories of this function grow more abstract (further away from immediate experience) as they go from recording to analyzing and theorizing. Because school writing assignments make minimal uses of theorizing (Applebee & Langer 2011), we do not discuss it in this chapter. Table 6.1 presents the writing functions with definitions and examples of each.

| Informational | Personal/Expressive | Imaginative |

FIGURE 6.1. Britton's (1975) functions of writing (as adapted by Applebee, 1984).

TABLE 6.1. Writing Functions with Definitions and Examples

Writing function and definition	Example
Record: The writer records what is immediately present.	"Suddenly the top of the tree starts to break and fall . . . "
Report: The writer retells one incident that occurred in the past and deals with events and situations in the virtual worlds of literary texts as well as the world of our experiences.	"*Great Expectations* begins on Christmas Eve, around 1812, when Pip encounters an escaped convict in the village churchyard while visiting his family's graves. The convict scares Pip into stealing food for him and a file to grind away his leg shackles."
Summary: When writing a summary, the writer is retelling recurrent events or noting the steps in a procedure. The writer generalizes from a number of events, procedures, or situations to tell how things are done or how they occur or what they are like.	"First, figure out where you'll run. If you're going outside, try to find roads made of dirt or asphalt rather than concrete, which is hard on the body. Remember to wear reflective clothing when running at night and to run towards traffic so you don't get nailed by a car."
Analysis: Informational writing that moves beyond concrete or specific experiences to classify and categorize ideas and experiences is analytic. Whenever students are asked to explain the reasons for an idea or emotion, to consider the parts of an idea to explain or to critique them, or to argue (from evidence) for a stance on an issue, the teacher requires them to write analytically. Analytic writing orders ideas and makes a case for them, makes logical or hierarchical connections between generalizations. Put simply, when students write analytically they are explaining causality, motivation, arguable positions, or relationships between people (or literary characters) or events.	"Is rap a form of literature or just a kind of noise as some people say? I see this question both asking for a defense of popular music and asking for a consideration of what is literature and what people value about it. I believe rap is literature in terms of what counts as literature, which is about how we live and what we believe. Even though rap is not in the books that we read in school I think it should be. And since rap or hip hop is about the everyday experiences of black people typically from the cities, I think it is literature and should be taught in schools if students are interested. But rather than starting with the question 'is it literature' I want to first look at the real issue which is who is writing rap and why do they write (and perform) rap."

Informative writing from sources includes all four of these functions in that there are times when writing focuses on particular events during (report) or after (record) they have occurred or on the development of generalizations (summary) or analysis of ideas or events based on ideas gleaned from a source text. We also assume that "sources" include both print sources as well as other semiotic sources such as images, paintings, and audio recordings. The instructional value of these distinctions in terms of purpose or use is that each function represents a different level of task complexity and challenge. For example, if a teacher asks her students to write an analytic essay using sources that are also analytic in content and structure, then it is likely that students will need to learn new strategies that support their efforts to develop reasons for why something occurred or to understand how and why an author explains the relationships between causes and effects. On the other hand, if students are asked to write a report on what they noticed as significant during a trip to a museum, they may simply need to be reminded to organize their reports by time and space and then to add their own ruminations within the narrative structure.

Writing from Sources as Authorship

In this section we describe a particular approach to writing instruction that captures the principles and practices that are the basis for our framework for teaching informative writing from sources. The portraits of writing instruction that follow this section are then used to exemplify what we have found to be particularly robust approaches. We begin by interpreting writing from sources as learning to author one's own ideas. We then describe what we mean by "from sources" as one way to teach authorship. Finally, we articulate the principles and practices of what we consider effective writing instruction using Applebee's (1986) "structured process approach" that entails Hillocks' (1995) notion of inquiry. (See also Smagorinsky, Johannessen, Kahn, and McCann [2010] for a more recent approach to writing instruction in grades 6–12 based on Hillocks's [1995] notion of a process-oriented approach.)

For writing teachers to establish authorship as an instructional goal for their students is now a kind of truism in writing education. In some classrooms this may mean learning to write for different audiences or taking pride in one's work or "publishing" a story to be read by a parent. Recent work in writing research and theory, however, moves beyond simple notions of audience to a broader consideration of the social contexts within which writing occurs and develops. In these contexts, writers negotiate their place within the many communities of which they are a part, with a variety of resources and competing demands. Dyson (1989, 1993, 2000), for example, in her ethnographies of primary-grade children learning to write, has described the complicated interplay among previous experiences, the uses of writing, the uses of other symbol systems, peer relationships, and the goals and orientation of the teacher. Children in different classrooms learn to write in different ways, and children in the same classroom show great variations in the strategies they use and the genres they prefer as they negotiate their roles with their teacher and their peers. In such contexts, children develop a sense of the many different purposes that writing can serve and a growing repertoire of strategies for orchestrating what they write.

Writing from sources poses particular challenges and opportunities for students as authors. Creating a text from other texts requires students to make sense of different and sometimes conflicting voices from different sources of information. Greene (1995) has described this process as one of learning how to assume the role of authorship within a new context, a role that a writer can only assume by learning how to speak with authority within disciplinary traditions such as literary studies, science, history, or the arts or within local domains such as the home or community (Applebee, 1996). This notion of writing as taking social action within situated contexts such as classrooms strikes us as a particularly apt way to understand the value, the challenges, and practices associated with writing from sources. Greene (1995) has conducted case studies on how college freshman use a range of sources requiring a synthesis of sources to construct something new, that is, newly authored:

> To synthesize information in advancing one's argument [or explanation] marks an important intellectual step in which an author represents a community of writers and their abiding interests, not simply a single author. The sources writers use provide the basis for their work in the form of support and elaboration, particularly as they begin to assimilate ideas of other writers and find a way to say something new. (Greene, 1995, p. 187)

Creating new texts in this way is a complex and recursive process in which context (task, social setting, prior experience, etc.), one's expertise as a reader, and one's ability to use strategies play important roles. However, in this chapter we are concerned with the classroom and with how teachers and students take up informative writing from sources.

Structured Process as a Mode of Instruction

We include two scenarios for teaching informative writing from sources in this chapter. While varying in terms of classroom context, reading and writing tasks, and sources, the scenarios share a set of principles grounded in what Hillocks (1986, 1995) referred to as "environmental" teaching. We prefer Applebee's (1986) renaming of this approach since the term "structured-process" retains the notion of process-oriented approaches while including the powerful instructional principles that Hillocks argues for: the writing teacher organizes instructional activities in a structured manner to support student writers in accomplishing new and more complex tasks. This approach to teaching students how to write from sources is particularly important in that students have to learn how to do a new task as well as how to think about doing the task so that it can be done in the future in different contexts and with different materials. Such an approach can be described as a "social constructivist view of learning to write," that is, as an active construction built up by the individual student acting in a social context through interaction with a teacher and peers that shapes but does not determine his or her learning to write. Below is a set of principles for a structured-process approach to teaching writing from sources (as well as other types of writing).

Ownership

This is a principle that is easily overlooked, especially when the task of using sources for informative writing is foregrounded rather than the purposefulness of the project. Students must feel that there is something of value in the assignment beyond simply completing a series of tasks. It is a sense of purposefulness for the task that allows students to integrate the various parts of the writing assignment. For example, rather than requiring that students include quotations from a literary text to demonstrate the skills necessary to do so, a more authentic purpose may be to ask students to use the quotations to clarify their negative responses to a relationship between two characters.

Structured Activities

Beginning with clear and specific goals, students are asked to consider an audience of peers as they develop plans for their writing. The teacher must develop activities that move students along a trajectory from an open-ended exploration to a sense of direction and consolidation of what needs to be researched and written. Recently, one of us (George E. Newell) observed an 11th-grade English language arts teacher who began the school year by asking students to write about issues for which they held strong opinions. Across the school year, as the students began to write for audiences beyond their classroom and their peers, they had to develop positions using sources quite new to them. As they did so, the teacher taught new skills such as interviewing and accessing online documents from the local government. Since each student wrote for a different audience, the teacher introduced new styles of language appropriate, and at times necessary, for their audiences.

Collaboration

As is the case with any type of composing, writing from sources is as much a social act as it is the work of individual students. Not only must writers realize the needs of an audience but their ability (and willingness) to makes sense out of complex materials is grounded in the situatedness of the classroom with its own social processes. In practice this requires the use of considerable peer interaction throughout the process of sharing work. Perhaps most significantly, evaluation and critical judgment are delayed to ensure confidence as well as to give students time to develop ideas and the discourse structures for presenting ideas.

Appropriate Tasks and Materials

"Appropriateness" refers to two key components of a structured process approach. First, the tasks and materials must be selected according to what students are prepared to do, that is, the kinds of contributions teachers expect must be appropriate for students' levels of skill and knowledge. Put another way, the teacher must seek the contributions students could not make on their own but can make with the help of others. Second, instruction must allow students to develop strategies that are appropriate for particular tasks such as arguing, explaining, and narrating. For example, in a study of writing from sources Greene (1994) describes how college-age students engaged in "mining" sources while authoring their own argumentative texts. Mining was fueled by three strategies: reconstructing context (rethinking the audience for and purpose of the writing), inferring or imposing structure (fitting source information into the structure of an argument), and seeing choices in language (why certain words or phrases might be appropriate or not). Such strategies need to be taught explicitly and directly through demonstration and example before students can be expected to employ them for their own rhetorical purposes.

Transfer of Control

Too often, as teachers, we keep doing what seems to work well without considering whether students still need the kind of support the activity was initially meant to provide. An example of this approach is requiring students to fill out a worksheet to ensure that they are employing process strategies (drafting, revising, etc.) whether the students find the worksheet useful or not. When teachers transfer control over to their students, on the other hand, process and skill become integrated as writers learn to look for and work with strategies for managing writing and achieving their rhetorical goals. Instruction then takes on a different look that requires new uses of materials and new ways of assessing whether learning has occurred. Although the teacher retains the role of planner and orchestrator, the activities provide students with tools to develop their own ideas and purposes rather than providing responses to fit into the teacher's predetermined framework.

Informative Writing from Sources in First Grade: A Research Report on Pond Animals

In the present section we provide two portraits of teaching informative writing from sources from each end of the developmental spectrum and from two different content areas: a 1st-grade teacher supporting her children's efforts to write science reports and a 12th-grade teacher orchestrating a series of lessons to support her students' efforts to write analytically about literary works. These writing teachers' practices share two key features: the uses of inquiry approaches to writing instruction and significant attention to the role of social processes in developing ideas that the students are expected to "authorize" with audiences of interested teachers and peers.

During the course of a school year in a suburban school district Ms. Jones (all teachers and students names are pseudonyms) and her first-grade students wrote in a range of genres using a structured process approach to writing. Specifically, Ms. Jones included four distinctly separate writing units associated with nonfiction: a poster, a "Did You Know" bubble (Corgill, 2008), a research report, and a family history inquiry project. The writing across the units ranged from shorter to more sustained informative writing based on questions students chose to investigate. Students routinely gathered information from a variety of texts and other sources and used their research, along with features of nonfiction texts, to produce writing that was appropriate to their purpose and audience.

Ms. Jones was in her 18th year of her teaching career; this scenario includes events that occurred in her second year of teaching first grade. One of us (Melissa Wilson), a retired teacher and doctoral student at the time, spent part of the 2009–2010 school year in Ms. Jones's first-grade classroom. Across this period of time I videotaped the teaching lessons at the beginning of writing workshop time, videotaped the individual conferences that occurred between Ms. Jones and her students during writing workshop time, and videotaped some sharing sessions at the conclusion of writing workshop time. The following scenario was developed from my observations from the third of four nonfiction writing units, that is, the research report on pond animals that occurred from late March to mid-April.

Daily Writing Workshop

Daily writing instruction varied from 30 to 60 minutes and was generally divided into three distinct segments: a mini-lesson, sustained writing, adult–teacher conferences, and sharing time. This chain of instructional events is suggestive of the principle of "structured activities" that provide a coherent trajectory beginning with generating ideas and shifting to knowledge building through interaction with interested audiences. Typically, these sessions began with a mini-lesson that included reading or talking about a book or books to support and enlighten writers as authors and, in the case of informative writing, researchers as authors. Ms. Jones used the mini-lessons as a series of interrelated discussions to build on and extend information from the previous day, and the cumulative information was usually collected on a large chart. This was the case, for instance, when she was teaching about the differences between fiction and nonfiction and later when she was introducing visual and print text features commonly found in the nonfiction texts that students might use in their writing.

The bulk of the writing workshop time was spent reviewing books to generate questions and collecting information regarding topics of interest (in the case of the research report, the pond animal each student was writing about) or writing and illustrating text. There was a constant buzz of collaborative talk and activity in the room during this time as students read aloud and showed each other illustrations from books or their own writing. Students also read or were read to by the adults in the room from the many nonfiction books in the classroom library; and students and adults worked together using conferences to discuss the writing, getting help with composition and spelling, receiving encouragement as needed, and generally checking in on where they were with their work. The final part of writing workshop was sharing time during which Ms. Jones selected students to read and talk about their writing and sketching or to describe what they had discovered during their writing time. At times everyone in the class shared something but more often just a few students shared. This is also the part of the writing workshop omitted because of time constraints. These instructional moves illustrate the principles of transfer of control and collaboration as the students' gradual appropriation of new ways of thinking and writing is supported initially by social activities but then shifts to activities, such as time for reading and writing, requiring more independent efforts.

An Illustration: Pond Animal Research Reports

During one of the workshops, Kali, a student in the class, talked with me about the ongoing research for her pond animal report on the swan. On this particular day in April, she began by explaining her question:

> "I don't think I wrote it down [in the Discovery Journal used to record questions, information to answer the question or other items of interest, and sketches], but did you know that swans are the biggest water birds? And, um, but I really want to know, like, how big they are?"

Skimming through several books together to see if we could find information to answer this question, Kali explained her process for looking through sources for information relevant to answering her research questions.

> "I haven't been reading very carefully, like, whenever I see a cool picture that I really want to read I start reading it. Like when the . . . when, when the swan has its wings out. I read that page because it looked pretty interesting. Well, at least I tried reading it because my book's kind of hard, but I tried reading it."

Using the illustrations and texts in nonfiction books as a source for generating both the questions and answers for nonfiction writing had been part of the work of this classroom since September. Note that Kali also expresses the frustration she was experiencing using text sources for her research and writing. She indicates that it was sometimes hard to find the exact information she wanted; she then explains that some of her books were difficult for her to read. Later she expressed further dissatisfaction about the use of the Internet as a source. After I suggested the Internet as a tool for locating information about the size of swans, Kali reported that there was no "white paper" (term for a school-approved Internet site) available for her. She then said, "Because I'm not getting very much research done, because I can't find any good information in my books that I really want to know about." For Kali, then, her sources were letting her down. She was specifically interested in the size of swans; yet she was unable to locate this information in any of the text sources available to her.

In Kali's classroom, as in other elementary classrooms described in research (Jenkins & Earle, 2006; Many, Fyfe, Lewis, & Mitchell, 1996), written texts, especially books, were the most authoritative source for writing. During this research report unit, in particular, books (and limited Internet searches) functioned as the primary source for the nonfiction research report writers. The school librarian had gathered most of the library's elementary-level books on pond animals, put them together categorized by animal or insect name, and placed them on a library cart that was wheeled from classroom to classroom as teachers needed them for this project. On the first day of the project, Ms. Jones announced that "the librarian has the books in order and since all the first graders are using the books we will have to keep them in order. So I will take them off and put them back on the shelves." These books, then, were the primary sources for students as they decided what pond animal to choose for research and then conducted research for their reports.

In the discussion that follows, it became clear that Kali, despite her reliance on and frustration with these books, had found ways to incorporate and transform her use of them as part of her informative writing. Kali and I collaborate during a conference to collect more information for Kali's report on swans. In this conversation, Kali begins by posing the question, "Do swans have life cycles?" It is important to note here that the convention of using a circle with arrows as a diagram of a life cycle was one that had been introduced much earlier in the school year during Ms. Jones's mini-lessons that focused on the visual and text features of the nonfiction genre.

KALI: Do you know if swans have life cycles?

MELISSA: I didn't know that. Swans have life cycles?

KALI: No, I don't know. But I was wondering if they do, but I wanted to know because I wanted to do the life cycle of swans if they had those.

MELISSA: Do you have a book that you could look at?

KALI: Mm-hmm.

[Kali returns with a book; portion of transcript omitted.]

MELISSA: All right. So your question is . .

KALI: Do swans have a life cycle?

MELISSA: What, what do you think a life cycle is?

KALI: Well, like, first, well, like, it's how, they're like, it's like first, maybe they hatch out of an egg, and then, they're, um, a chicken; they grow up into a swan. Or, who knows if they even have a life cycle?

MELISSA: Do you have a life cycle?

KALI: *(Nods slightly.)*

MELISSA: Do human beings have a life cycle?

KALI: We're born, and then, um, we, um, about, we're babies and then we grow up.

MELISSA: And then we die, right? That's our life cycle?

KALI: *(Nods.)*

MELISSA: If you found some, it sounds like you've already said what the life cycle was.

KALI: Yeah, but, I was just making a guess, but I . .

MELISSA: Making a guess? So if we look in the book what would we look for to see if your guess was right?

KALI: We'd look for the life cycle.

MELISSA: Do we have . . . You're saying we actually have to see, like, the circle.

KALI: Well, maybe we could just find it in words like this *(pointing to text on page)* or we could find it in a circle.

MELISSA: So if we could, we might see it in words?

KALI: We might see it like in this word or in a circle.

MELISSA: Huh.

KALI: I haven't seen any circle pages.

MELISSA: So there are no circle pages.

MELISSA: All right, we're looking for, all right, I kinda see a life cycle right here because, look, what's under her *(pointing to picture)*?

KALI: Eggs.

MELISSA: And what's here?

KALI: Chicks.

MELISSA: Cygnets, is that what they call them, cygnets? And then we know the cygnets grow up to be.

KALI: The swan.

MELISSA: So could that be a life cycle?

KALI: Mm-hmm. But then they, um, grow up to be a swan and then they have babies and it keeps going on like there *(making circular motion with hand on page of book)*.

MELISSA: Exactly. So that's the circle part. *(Returns to Kali after some time and looks at her illustration.)* So you have the egg, number 1.

KALI: Mhmm *(erasing)*.

MELISSA: The cygnets are number 2.

KALI: Mhmm.

MELISSA: The grown up is number 3.

KALI: Hmm. *(Finishes erasing.)* And then it goes back onto an egg and then . .

MELISSA: Oh, are you *(pointing to space in life cycle)*. . . . Were you gonna draw the picture of the one making an egg or sitting on the nest? You could do that.

KALI: Hmm.

KALI: *(Showing Melissa her finished sketch some time later)* I did a cutaway to show that she was sitting on an egg.

MELISSA: Oh, nice. All right. That's great, Kali.

This sequence of events beginning in Ms. Jones's classroom and shifting to the collaboration of Kali and I illustrates many of the instructional principles introduced earlier in this chapter: ownership; collaborative, structured activities; appropriate tasks and materials; and transfer of control. My observations of and participation with Kali's research report strikes us as exemplary of what might be desired for disciplinary-based instruction (conceptualizing life cycles and the accompanying visual representation) that is well integrated with personal meaning construction (representing a life cycle with the support of an adult collaborator) —two approaches that are often presented as at odds with one another (cf. Hicks, 1997). Although this is only one of many forms that instructional scaffolding can take, it is a clear example of how well-staged questions can help the student think through the problems that are part of a complex writing task while also serving as a structure that reflects what the student needs to go through to complete the tasks. Presented in this way, students, such as Kali, learn to develop explanations on their own. But the tasks also must be appropriate for the learner. With tasks such as understanding (and representing) the life cycle of a swan both through writing and visual representations, the teacher must be ready to step forward to provide support or step back to allow for independent work. This, we think, illustrates how transfer of control occurs—it is orchestrated in instructional interaction when the student is trying to make sense out of new ideas and information. To be instructional tasks must be appropriate to the skills and knowledge students bring with them but must also challenge the student to move beyond known strategies and given knowledge.

With my support, Kali's co-constructed process provides insight into the complex ways in which a child develops her various understandings of writing from sources as she takes up and transforms the traditional as well as the alternative sources available to her. As Dyson has so often argued, "the social relationships—the dyadic and interactive events—realized through talk allow writers a sense of direction and purpose, as well as the supportive other who help them on their way" (2000, p. 60). Using books, information collected on classroom charts, and talk with me, Kali made use of a variety of sources to author the research notes that would eventually form the basis of her research report.

How, then, did Kali learn to integrate source material into her research report on pond animals over time? Kali was able to integrate her understanding of life cycles with source materials during her collaborative conference with me largely because of the instruction Kali had experienced previously. Using her Discovery Journal, Kali wondered out loud, recorded her questions in writing, and then researched to discover the answer that was, in turn, written down and sketched in a way that was consistent with the genre of nonfiction. This question–answer routine had been in place since September and refined over time to include such activities as note taking, multiple questions on the same topic, and extended writing. Likewise, the understanding of a report as a genre and the visual text features associated with it had been introduced, modeled, and shared throughout the year with additions made as the teacher or students discovered new and interesting features. Subsequently, Kali was able to make use of the life cycle, a text and visual feature common to nonfiction, in order to communicate information and details through her drawing that were not necessarily captured in her writing. (Note that while Kali's use of illustrations is typical of young children's writing [Graves, 1987; Rowe, 2010], it also reflects the conventions of illustration found in nonfiction texts and suggests Kali's constructed understanding of a convention of scientific explanation.)

The teacher and students in this classroom had constructed, over time, an understanding of what it meant to be a writer of nonfiction. While the structured process principles for teaching writing from sources were not part of Ms. Jones's explanation of her teaching, nevertheless my observations of her teaching over time revealed that the model of nonfiction writing constructed with and by the students and teacher in this classroom included many of the principles. In the story of Kali and the swans, then, one student took up and transformed the constructed understanding of writing from sources within the social context of the classroom and the structured writing principles of instruction. Further, we also get a brief hint of how these understandings had become more complex and sophisticated during the course of the school year as the teacher and students discovered new ways of writing from sources.

Analytic Writing about Literature in a 12th-Grade Advanced Placement Classroom: Text, Teacher, and Peers as Sources

One of us (Jennifer VanDerHeide) had the opportunity to study the teaching and learning of analytic writing in Ms. Hamilton's 12th-grade advanced placement literature and composition class, observing instruction at least once a week from October through April of one school year. Ms. Hamilton has been teaching English at her school for over 15 years, and she is locally regarded as an expert teacher of literature and composition. Ms. Hamilton's teaching illustrates how a teacher uses a structured process approach to writing instruction to encourage students to use sources, in this case literature, to develop authorship.

Ms. Hamilton's 12th-grade advanced placement literature and composition course culminated in the students taking the advanced placement exam on which they wrote analytic essays about literature, some of which they had not read and some that they had read previously. Because of this, Ms. Hamilton structured the course to encourage authorship—in which students could mediate and make sense of literature independently—and ownership—in which students could write about their own personal, original ideas about the literature. As she explained, "I think it's important that they have that burden of coming up with original [analyses] and supporting them and explaining them. For me, it's a pretty basic thing that they just need a lot of practice with in discussion and in writing."

The Unit Plan: Writing Analytic Argument about a Short Story

Throughout the school year, Ms. Hamilton's instructional units focused on different genres of literature, and each unit followed a similar pattern utilizing many key features of the structured process approach. The first part of the unit focused on reading the sources the students would later write with, in this case, literature. For the particular unit that is the focus of this chapter, the students read six different short stories over a 2-week period. After reading the short stories, Ms. Hamilton assigned an essay that was to be an original analytic argument about one of the short stories using at least one literary device (characterization, plot, etc.). She organized the unit to prepare the students for writing this essay; she provided spaces for them to develop ideas about original arguments; and she taught them the strategies they would need to read and write analytically about the literature. Using a structured process approach model of instruction, the beginning of the unit allowed for open-ended exploration of ideas with greater teacher involvement moving toward individual authorship of particular ideas. Figure 6.2 is a visual overview of the structure of the unit.

During each class session prior to analytic writing, the students read and annotated—underlined key passages and jotted notes in the margins—the assigned short story before coming to class, and the story was paired with a literary element, such as characterization, setting, or theme, for which they also read a chapter about in a literature anthology. Typically, as they were reading short stories, Ms. Hamilton taught strategies that were

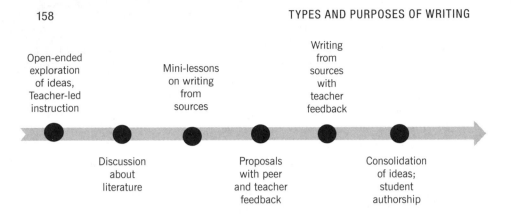

FIGURE 6.2. Visual representation of instructional unit on writing about a short story.

appropriate for the task of reading literature and later writing about it. She explicitly taught the students about the literary element, led them in discussions about it, and modeled on the Smart Board how to identify and analyze that particular literary element within the context of the story. For example, early in the unit, they discussed characterization, and Ms. Hamilton led the students through the first page of the story, underlining on the Smart Board words and phrases the author used to develop the characters. Each day, she transferred control of this process to the students, so a few days into the unit when they focused on the literary element of theme, she had the students meet in groups to choose one theme of the story and then present it to the class. In this way, she gradually released control of the strategy use from herself to the students.

The reading portion of the unit also allowed for open-ended exploration of ideas through the classroom discussion, a chance for students to explore the texts, the ideas in the texts, and their own ideas about the texts in a nonthreatening setting. These discussions accomplished two purposes in Ms. Hamilton's writing instruction: practicing strategies appropriate for the task and building a bank of ideas that students could draw from when it was time to write their essays. Over time, she had come to understand that students need to be explicitly taught the skills necessary for literary analysis: identifying textual evidence that supports an analysis, explaining the evidence for the reader, and connecting the evidence to the analysis. Ms. Hamilton used these classroom discussions as an opportunity to model these skills, to frame discussion in a way to push the students to practice these skills verbally, and to allow students who are struggling to hear how other students are using these skills as they read and interpret the literary text. As she explained, "I feel like discussion is important to help kids try on ideas and to understand how you support claims, to be able to dig more deeply into whatever we're reading and to come to new understandings."

Using Textual Evidence during a Literary Discussion: The Role of Annotation

To illustrate, consider a brief segment of one of these classroom discussions. Ms. Hamilton's students sat in a semicircle of desks, discussing the main character from "Say Yes" by Tobias Wolffe (1996). Ms. Hamilton sat at a table in the front middle of the semicircle, orchestrating the conversation yet allowing the students' ideas to determine the topics and direction of the conversation. They were discussing whether they sympathized with the main character (and the narrator), a husband who is having an argument with his wife. The students had been sharing their opinions, and the teacher next moved them to look to the text to support those opinions.

> TEACHER: Anything you annotated that you thought was important?
>
> CHLOE: Going back to the magazine scene, I marked that paragraph that was like, "she was demonstrating her indifference to him, and it had the effect she intended, it hurt him" [Wolffe, 1996, p. 3]. Um, I don't know, I think that might spark some sympathy, but at the same time, he's trying to explain her every move, and he might not be right. I think she might just be upset, and she might not be trying to hurt him with the way she's flipping the pages. I think he might be part to blame.
>
> TEACHER: Okay.
>
> SAMANTHA: And then later at the end he says he's ashamed for letting her get him in a fight, and so, I don't know—I don't know if that should make me have more sympathy, but it doesn't because if you can be that calculated about someone and you know they're trying to get you in a fight, and I don't know.

Looking closely at the students' responses, they offered ideas and opinions about the story but did so by sharing specific textual evidence. Chloe pointed to a particular quotation and then explained what it meant, why it was significant, and why it supported her opinion. Samantha made a similar move by referencing a specific example from the story and her interpretation of that example. The teacher's words did not lead the students toward any particular ideas, but they did act to frame the type of talk that she wanted them to use, in this case pointing them to their annotations so that they used textual evidence to support their ideas.

In this classroom, discussions about the literature were an integral part of Ms. Hamilton's writing instruction. The acts of reading and writing were intertwined and recursive: close reading provided students with ideas for writing, and writing was a means to better understand the reading and usually prompted more close reading. The class discussions were a place to try out ideas and practice the skills of interpretation and providing evidence from the literature, both skills necessary for successful writing from sources in an advanced placement literature class. These discussions were social in nature because students had the opportunity to share their ideas with each other, opening up other possible interpretations and providing a real audience in which to share ideas.

Writing Analytic Arguments: Beginning with Textual Evidence

When Ms. Hamilton finished the primary reading portion of the unit, she moved through the structured process to a planning phase in which the students chose a short story to focus on and an analysis to present in their writing. Again, Ms. Hamilton explicitly taught strategies appropriate to the task. To do so she drew on Hillocks's (2010) work to teach the students to consider the evidence in the story before writing a thesis statement. Hillocks argues that rather than write a thesis statement and then find textual evidence to support that statement, instead teachers and students should follow an inquiry model: reading and rereading the texts to discover what they say and crafting the ideas and analysis from the sources. Hillocks describes the process: "At its beginning is the examination of data, not the invention of a thesis statement in a vacuum" (2010, p. 26). In a mini-lesson, she suggested the following reading/writing process based on this inquiry model:

1. Choose a favorite story—reread and annotate further.
2. Develop analytic questions based on the data about literary elements in the story.
3. Use a question as the lens for further close reading.
4. Use the data to develop an interpretive argument.

By focusing first on the source and then on an analysis, Ms. Hamilton pushed the students to carefully consider the source itself rather than coming up with an analysis and making the source fit.

Ms. Hamilton's next step in the structured process was to ask the students to write a proposal. The proposal is similar to an outline, but she did not expect any particular format. She asked the students to present their analysis in written form and to do the "intellectual heavy lifting" of rereading, analysis, and interpretation prior to actually writing the essay.

The students worked on these proposals outside of class and then pre-sented them to their peers in groups of four. This allowed for collaboration and was another way Ms. Hamilton transferred control to the students. For many students, presenting the proposal to the group was a key site of knowledge construction, where they socially constructed what counted as analysis of a source. For example, as one student talked with his group, he realized that his proposal was more of a summary than an analysis, and the other students helped him move his thesis statement from what he called a "summarizing sentence" to a cohesive analytic argument for which he drew from textual evidence to build his own idea about the story. By struc-turing time for this collaboration, Ms. Hamilton allowed the students to build knowledge together and fostered individual authorship of ideas and writing.

After sharing their proposals in a group, the students revised their proposals and turned them in to Ms. Hamilton for feedback. Ms. Ham-ilton described the next step as the teacher's "intellectual heavy lifting." She took several days to pore over their proposals and write comments on the proposals to provide individual instruction for each student. Her feedback was detailed and specific to each student's ideas and included questions, comments, and an endnote. Her questions raised concerns that she had as both a teacher and a reader, such as "How does this relate to the allusion?" or "What gives it this power?" Her comments were more directive, indicating weak areas of the students' analysis to prompt further reading and thinking: "Be more clear about how this relates to the story of the Prodigal Son" and "You need to be able to show how this is developed in the story." She ended each proposal with a long endnote, pointing out areas of strength and weakness and summarizing next steps for the stu-dent. Although this type of feedback was hard, time-consuming work for Ms. Hamilton, she saw it as a key point of writing instruction. She could offer individual instruction to students early in their writing process and push them to reread their sources, think critically about those sources, and develop original ideas in response to their reading.

Ms. Hamilton's timing for this feedback is critical: *early* in the writing process. One worry writing teachers often have about providing feedback is that the students pay no attention to it. Because she provided individual feedback early in the writing process, the students considered her ques-tions and comments seriously and used them as an additional source as they revised what they wrote. In an interview at the end of the unit, a stu-dent explained, "I read through Ms. H.'s notes almost as though as I read through the story itself. That was just equally as important to me." After receiving his proposal back with her comments, his first reaction was to reread the story three times in response to her comment that he had, in his words, "contradictory arguments all over the proposal." Ms. Hamilton's written remarks reveal that she only mentioned contradictory arguments twice, once in response to his character argument when she wrote, "Seems contradictory of what you have just said about the influence of WWII on Trevor" and once as an endnote: "You have some contradictory points that you need to think about." These two comments prompted the student to go back to the text for several close readings, an important practice when writing from sources.

The students worked on their essays at home for about 2 weeks; although they were working on a new unit during class, Ms. Hamilton provided time in and out of class to meet individually with students if they chose. This type of writing required significant intellectual work from the students. They had to integrate what is written in the literature with their own ideas and interpretations in order to come up with an original analysis. To do so, they drew on all of the instruction Ms. Hamilton led them through throughout the unit: they reread the short story several times using the analytical strategies they had practiced in class, they referred to notes from class discussions to draw on their own and others' ideas, they responded to their peers' suggestions in the proposal meetings, and they responded to Ms. Hamilton's comments on their proposals. Every part of the instructional process came together in the writing of the essay.

Conclusion

As our arguments in this chapter and in other chapters in this book make plain, literacy theory and research have provided a strong empirical foundation for social constructivist approaches to literacy instruction in general and writing instruction in particular. But challenges remain: teachers must possess a great deal of pedagogical knowledge and be able to respond quickly to partially predictable moments during instructional conversations whether they are working with whole classes or one-on-one during a writing conference. And, as a high school English teacher mentioned to one of us (George E. Newell) recently during an interview for a research project, "It is easy to forget that students also have to take some risks when I teach this way." In an age of accountability that includes the use of test scores to measure teachers' effectiveness, a scripted and mandated curriculum, and harsh public criticism for failure to meet standards, it is unfair to blame teachers who may be reluctant to create classrooms with moments of uncertain (though intellectually stimulating) rather than consistently predictable (and possibly tedious) instructional conversations.

To move forward, then, literacy educators will need to enact the vision of the "new" classroom grounded in social constructivism that has been the focus of educational reform over the last 20 years—our chapter is one small effort to develop the principled practice necessary for deep and lasting reform. Consider, for example, the two classrooms we described. A thread that binds them together is the nature of the social interaction that took place. The two teachers played a central role in their respective classrooms by choosing the source materials to be introduced, providing the structure that ensured learning could took place, and supporting their students with the informative writing tasks they undertook. As they did so, the teachers encouraged their students to take a more central role in the classroom dialogue: finding their own sources and constructing their own interpretations, defending their ideas against alternatives raised by the teachers and peers, and checking them against their own experiences and the clarity and logic of sources and evidence.

Most teachers will likely point out that these two classrooms are more complicated and less predictable than classrooms based on transmission of basic knowledge and skills. To run smoothly and effectively, they will require the guidance of teachers with the pedagogical knowledge of Ms. Jones and Ms. Hamilton who are clearly empowered to shape and support classroom dialogue that emerges in ways that will help their students progress and develop over time. Until schools vest teachers with the authority to implement such approaches in their own classrooms, no amount of research, Common Core standards, testing mandates, or curriculum planning is likely to make a significant difference in the teaching and learning of writing.

Acknowledgments

Some of the research reported here was supported by the Institute of Education Sciences, U.S. Department of Education, through Grant No. 305A100786 to The Ohio State University. The opinions expressed are those of the authors and do not represent views of the Institute of Education Science or the U.S. Department of Education.

References

Applebee, A. N. (1981). *Writing in the secondary school*. Urbana, IL: National Council of Teachers of English.

Applebee, A. N. (1984). *Contexts for learning to write*. Norwood, NJ: Ablex.

Applebee, A. N. (1986). Problems in process approaches: Towards a reconceptualization of process instruction. In D. Bartholomae & A. R. Petrosky (Eds.), *The teaching of writing: The eighty-fifth yearbook of the National Society for the Study of Education*. Chicago: National Society for the Study of Education and University of Chicago Press.

Applebee, A. N. (1996). *Curriculum as conversation: Transforming traditions of teaching and learning.* Chicago: University of Chicago Press.

Applebee, A. N. (2000). Alternative models of writing development. In R. Indrisiano & J. R. Squire (Eds.), *Perspectives on writing: Research, theory, and practice* (pp. 90–110). Newark, DE: International Reading Association.

Applebee, A. N., & Langer, J. A. (2011). A snapshot of writing instruction in middle schools and high schools. *English Journal, 100*(6), 14–27.

Bomer, R., & Maloch, B. (2011). Relating policy to research and practice: The common core standards. *Language Arts, 89*(1), 38–43.

Britton, J.. Burgess, T., Martin, N., McLeod, A., & Rosen, H. (1975). *The development of writing abilities* (pp. 11–18). London: Macmillan Education.

Coleman, D., & Pimentel, S. (2011, June 3). *Publisher's criteria for the Common Core State Standards in ELA & literacy, grades 3–12.* n.p. Available at *www.corestandards.org/assets/Publishers_Criteria_for_3–12.pdf.*

Corgill, A. M. (2008). *Of primary importance: What's essential in teaching young writers.* Portland, ME: Stenhouse.

Dyson, A. H. (1989). *Multiple worlds of children writers: Friends learning to write.* New York: Teachers College Press.

Dyson, A. H. (1993). *Social worlds of children learning to write in a primary school.* New York: Teachers College Press.

Dyson, A. H. (2000). Writing and the sea of voices: Oral language in, around and about writing. In R. Indrisano & J. R. Squire (Eds.), *Perspectives on writing* (pp. 45–65). Newark, DE: International Reading Association,

Graves, D. (1983). *Writing: Teachers and children at work.* Portsmouth, NH: Heinemann.

Greene, S. (1994). Constructing a voice from other voices: A sociocognitive perspective on the development of authorship in a beginning writing classroom. In K. H. Pogner (Ed.), *Odense working papers in language and communication* (pp. 11–40). Odense, Denmark: Institute of Language and Communication, Odense University.

Greene, S. (1995). Making sense of my own ideas: The problems of authorship in a beginning writing classroom. *Written Communication, 12*(2), 186–218.

Hicks, D. (1997). Working *through* discourse genres in school. *Research in the Teaching of English. 31*(4), 459–485.

Hillocks, G. Jr. (1986). *Research on written composition.* Urbana, IL: National Conference on Research in English.

Hillocks, G. Jr. (1995). *Teaching writing as reflective practice.* New York: Teachers College Press.

Hillocks, G. Jr. (2010). Teaching writing for critical thinking and writing: An introduction. *English Journal, 99*(6), 24–32.

Jenkins, C. B., & Earle, A. A. (2006). *Once upon a fact: Helping children write nonfiction.* New York: Teachers College Press.

Langer, J. A. (2002). *Effective literacy instruction: Building successful reading and writing programs.* Urbana, IL: National Council of Teachers of English.

Many, J. E., Fyfe, R., Lewis, G., & Mitchell, E. (1996). Traversing the topical landscape: Exploring students' self-directed reading–writing–reading processes. *Reading Research Quarterly, 31*(1), 12–35.

Melzer, D. (2009). Writing assignments across the curriculum: A national study of college writing. *College, Composition, and Communication, 61*(2), 240–261.

Moffett, J. (1968). *Teaching the universe of discourse.* Boston: Houghton Mifflin.

Rowe, D. (2011). Directions for studying early literacy as social practice. *Language Arts, 88*(2), 134–143.

Smagorinsky, P., Johannessen, L. R., Kahn, E., & McCann, T. (2010). *The dynamics of writing instruction: A structured process approach for middle and high school.* Portsmouth, NH: Boynton/Cook.

Wolffe, T. (1996). Say yes. In *Back in the world: Stories.* New York: Vintage Press.

Chapter 7

Best Practices in Writing to Learn

PERRY D. KLEIN
AMY MEICHI YU

We take it for granted that reading contributes to learning. A search of Google Scholar turns up thousands of research studies on reading comprehension; curriculum guidelines in many districts require the teaching of reading comprehension strategies; and it is the topic of scores of teacher resources. But what about writing? In disciplines such as social studies, science, and English, teachers regularly ask students to complete essays and other kinds of texts; this suggests that they believe that writing is a useful tool for learning. And yet, writing to learn has been given much less attention than reading to learn. Only a handful of studies investigate the topic each year (Bangert-Drowns, Hurley, & Wilkinson, 2004; Graham & Perin, 2007). In our experience, writing to learn is not a common topic in teacher education, and few resources address it directly. The purpose of this chapter is to change that situation.

Writing to learn is an educational practice in which teachers assign students writing with the intention of helping them to understand subject matter in disciplines such as science, social studies, history, English, and mathematics. It can take a variety of forms, from informal learning journals to extensive end-of-unit reports. The goal of writing to learn is most often to help students better understand concepts and theories in a subject (Bangert-Drowns et al., 2004; Klein, 1999). Additionally, writing can also help students to commit facts to memory, to learn modes of reasoning such as literacy criticism (Kieft, Riujlaarsdam, & van den Bergh, 2008), or to learn about how inquiry is carried out in a subject area (Boscolo & Mason, 2001).

A consideration of best practices is particularly important because writing does not lead automatically to learning. For several decades the amount of research on writing to learn was limited, and the effects of writing on learning were found to be variable and, on average, small (Bangert-Drowns et al., 2004; Klein, 1999). During the past two decades, the quantity and variety of research has increased, allowing us to identify writing activities that make medium or large contributions to learning (e.g., Bangert-Drowns et al., 2004; De La Paz & Felton, 2010; Graham & Perin, 2007; Hand, Wallace, & Yang, 2004; Hübner, Nückles, & Renkl, 2010).

What do "best practices" mean in writing to learn? For some topics in education, a single set of best practices can be identified; however, the situation in writing to learn is more complex. Different kinds of writing activities have been created to serve different kinds of learning goals and different roles within classroom programs. Consequently, this chapter takes a pluralistic approach to best practices; it is divided into three sections, each focusing on how to improve the effectiveness of one type of approach. The first approach, which we call *reflective writing to learn*, involves brief writing activities that can be added to any discipline; they contribute to learning, as well as allowing teachers and students to monitor their progress formatively. The second approach to writing to learn, which we call *writing to learn in informational genres*, involves students in writing nonfiction texts of specific kinds (e.g., arguments) to support corresponding kinds of thinking and learning (e.g., critical thinking). The third approach, which we call *writing to learn in the disciplines*, involves students writing a type of text specific to a given discipline, such as a history essay based on primary sources; this approach contributes to conceptual understanding, and also introduces students to the forms of writing and inquiry particular to that discipline.

Reflective Writing to Learn

In reflective writing to learn, students write journals, often called "learning logs," about their thinking and learning in a subject. The logs contribute to conceptual learning and provide evidence of students' progress, but because they are brief and informal, they can be completed by young students, and can be carried out regularly without compromising other learning activities (Bangert-Drowns et al., 2004).

An Example: KWL Journals in Social Studies

A study by Cantrell, Fusaro, and Dougherty (2000) illustrates several features that contribute to reflective writing to learn. This project was carried out by a team consisting of researchers and a social studies teacher with students in four seventh-grade classrooms. Reflection was encouraged using journal entries based on the KWL reading comprehension strategy. First, the researcher modeled for students how to complete a journal using this strategy. Each entry was formatted in three parts labeled K (what we Know), W (what we Want to know), and L (what we Learned). Before beginning to read a given chapter, students viewed the title and headings; then in the "K" section of the journal, students wrote about what they knew about the topic. Then, also before reading, students wrote in the "W" section about what they wanted to know about the topic of the chapter. Next, they read the chapter. Finally, in the "L" part of the entry, they responded to their earlier questions by writing about what they had learned. The teacher used journal writing with students twice a week in the fall term and three times a week in the spring term. Students who wrote these reflective journal entries learned more from the unit than students who simply wrote summaries of the same material.

Research on Effective Reflective Writing to Learn Activities

Based on a review of 39 previous studies of writing-intensive curriculum units, Bangert-Drowns and colleagues (2004) identified several features that made the difference between units that were effective and those that were ineffective. Several of these are illustrated by the Cantrell et al. (2000) study described above.

Metacognitive Prompts

Writing prompts that required students to reflect on "their current level of comprehension in a content area, comprehension failures and successes, or affective and motivational responses to content that might facilitate or debilitate learning" (p. 38) were significantly more effective than other kinds of writing prompts.

Brief Writing Activities

Surprisingly, students learned more from brief writing tasks than from longer ones. Writing tasks less than 10 minutes in length were most effective, followed by those 10 to 15 minutes in length; those over 15 minutes were ineffective. Why? The authors suggested that longer assignments might seem onerous to students and reduced the time available for other discipline-specific activities.

Not Middle School

Writing to learn was effective for students in first through fifth grade, secondary school, and college. Surprisingly, writing intensive units were not more effective than ordinary units of study for students in sixth through eighth grade. The authors suggested several possible explanations, such as the challenge of subject-specific writing in late elementary education. They also pointed out that this null finding does not mean that writing to learn can never be effective for middle school students (see later projects in this chapter), but suggests the need for more research on effective activities for this age group.

Sustained Programs

Students learned more when writing intensive units of study were sustained for one full semester or longer than if they were less than one semester in length.

Marginally Important Characteristics

Some practices appeared to contribute to learning, but did not have a statistically significant effect: *Frequent writing* (three to four times per week) was marginally more effective than less frequent writing; and projects in which teachers provided *feedback* to students were marginally more effective than those in which they did not.

Designing Reflective Writing Activities

Input

Just as the KWL learning log activity (Cantrell et al., 2000) discussed previously was based on textbook readings, learning logs typically "piggyback" on some other activity, which provides the content about which students can reflect and write. Examples of activities that students write about can include science experiments, trade book readings, field trips, class discussions, simulation games, guest speakers, audiovisual presentations, and problem sets in mathematics.

Writing Prompts

Writing prompts designed to encourage metacognition include the following:

■ What did you learn from this activity? How did you learn it?
■ What have you learned about _____ that you did not already know?
■ For me, the most important ideas in today's lesson were . . .
■ What was the most difficult part of this reading/activity?
■ What I want to learn next is . . .
■ Something that I still find confusing is . . .
■ What do you think is the importance of [this topic]?
■ In math: Did you use any learning/problem-solving strategies? What made you use them?
■ In math: I missed question # ____ because . . .

Responding to Journal Writing

As we saw, feedback has a marginal positive effect on students' writing. However, writing is likely to make more sense to students if it has some kind of readership. Here are some options:

■ The teacher reads the learning log entries, writes responses to the ideas, but does not grade them.
■ Students can exchange learning logs with a partner and write a response.
■ The teacher can ask a few students, selected to represent a range of insights and questions, to share their journal entries with the class.
■ Young students can take home learning logs to communicate with parents about what they are learning.

Teaching Students How to Write More Reflectively

Recently a group of German researchers has been extending the study of learning logs, also known as "learning protocols," with significant positive effects (e.g., Hübner, Nückles, & Renkl, 2010; Nückles, Hübner, & Renkl, 2009). They have identified three kinds of strategies that contribute to learning; each kind of strategy is encouraged by a different kind of writing prompt. *Organizational strategies* are used by students to make connections between ideas within a topic; teachers can elicit them with prompts such as "What are the main ideas in this reading?" *Elaboration strategies* are used by students to make connections between new information and their previous knowledge; they are prompted by questions such as "Can you think of examples of the main idea?" *Metacognitive strategies* are used by students to monitor their learning; they are encouraged by prompts such as "Which main ideas haven't I understood yet?" Metacognitive prompts also include prompts that help students to remediate their understanding, for example "What could I do to understand this better?" (We have paraphrased the prompts from the original research report, using expressions familiar to English-speaking students.)

However, these researchers realized that when teachers provide these prompts, students do not always respond strategically; this is particularly true for younger students. Consequently, in a recent study (Hübner et al., 2010), they used two techniques to teach secondary students to respond more deeply to writing prompts. The research took place as students were learning about topics in psychology. First, the researchers presented students with a videotape about social pressure and conformity. Second, the students viewed a PowerPoint presentation about learning logs, which emphasized that the purpose of these logs is to support learning. Third, some students received *informed prompting* that explained how the writing prompts could contribute to their learning; for example, they were taught that writing about examples of a concept could help them to make a bridge between their previous knowledge and the new information, so that they could remember it more effectively. Additionally, some students in the study received a *learning journal example*. This was a journal entry that the students were asked to study and identify where the writer had responded to various kinds of writing prompts (organization, elaborative, or metacognitive). Fourth, the researchers asked the students to practice what they had learned by providing them with an additional reading on the conformity topic, and encouraging them to revise their journal entries. In a subsequent journal writing activity, the students who had experienced informed prompting or studied the learning journal example, or both, learned more about the topic than students who had not. This suggests that teachers can increase the impact of learning logs in three ways:

- Provide students with writing prompts for organizing ideas, elaborating ideas, monitoring their understanding, and remediating their understanding.
- Teach students about why these kinds of prompts are useful for learning.
- Present students with a model learning log entry and ask them to find places where the writer has organized (related ideas from readings to one another); elaborated (related ideas in the reading to their prior knowledge); monitored his or her own understanding; or remediated his or her understanding.

Writing to Learn in Informational Genres

Some texts present information in a way that foregrounds specific kinds of relationships among ideas. These include texts such as arguments and explanations, which are important in disciplines such as science and history (Christie & Derewianka, 2008). Writing such texts provides students with the opportunity to think analytically about ideas and issues, to understand relationships among concepts, and to remember them (e.g., Klein & Rose, 2010; Newell & Winograd, 1989; Wiley & Voss, 1999; Zohar & Nemet, 2002). At the same time, teachers may use writing assignments in the content areas to teach students how to write various types of informational texts (Klein & Rose, 2010). The Common Core State Standards initiative identifies three main types of texts that students should learn to write, two of which are the focus of this section: "arguments" and "informative/explanatory texts" (National Governors Association [NGA] & Council of Chief State School Officers [CCSSO], 2010, pp. 19, 42).

On Argument Texts

Argument writing can be an opportunity for students to understand ideas and theories (Klein & Ehrhardt, 2012; Wiley & Voss, 1999; Zohar & Nemet, 2002). It also presents an opportunity for students to think critically about subject matter, exploring the social aspects of issues such as the genetic revolution (Zohar & Nemet, 2002).

A Classroom Example of Persuasive Writing to Learn

Ms. F's fifth-grade class was studying a science unit about space. One of the expectations of the curriculum was that students would learn about meteors, asteroids, and comets. To engage students in thinking about this topic, she created a persuasive writing activity about the "Tunguska Mystery," an enormous explosion that took place in Siberia in 1908. It flattened trees for thousands of square miles, but its cause remains unknown. Ms. F had been teaching her class a strategy for persuasive writing, encouraging them to include a claim (opinion), several pieces of evidence, a competing opinion (counterclaim) and reasons for it, a rebuttal of the competing opinion, and a conclusion.

To support their writing, Ms. F provided students with a brief portfolio of information; it contained several short documents from the Internet, including a map of Siberia, an eyewitness account of the explosion, a newspaper article, photographs of the scene, and an information sheet on meteors, comets, and asteroids. On the folder was a writing prompt, asking students to review the information, decide what caused the explosion, and write an argument to persuade their classmates. The information in the portfolio allowed more than one reasonable conclusion, so that each student could create a unique text.

Here are some excerpts from one students' paper [dots represent text omitted for conciseness]:

The Tunguska event was an explosion that occurred at 7:17 am on June 30, 1908. . . . Whether it was a comet or an asteroid, no one knows for sure, but I think it was caused by a comet. . . . My first piece of evidence is that there wasn't a crater in the area, so it couldn't have been a meteor or meteorite. . . . Those who think it was an asteroid have their reasons. They could say that asteroids are closer to the earth than comets, but many comets have entered the earth's atmosphere. . . . My last piece of evidence is that comet-like material was found at the site. . . . Comets are made of water, methane, and ammonia ices mixed with silicates and a little metal dust.

As this piece illustrates, the Tunguska Mystery intrigued the students. All of them considered at least two possible explanations, and wrote an argument that took into account the characteristics of meteors, asteroids, and comets such as their size, composition, and origins.

Creating Effective Argument Activities for Writing to Learn

Possible Topics, Sources, and Writing Prompts

Previous studies of writing to learn have included the following kinds of assignments:

- Tenth-grade students were taught how to write arguments in the context of a series of writing activities concerning literary interpretation. They wrote on questions such as "Is this story too old-fashioned for today's students?" and "Tell a classmate what the story is about, and what your opinion about the story is" (Kieft et al., 2008, p. 384).

- Fifth-grade students learned about the role of nutrients in a healthy diet. They received a portfolio about a student named Michael that included information about his daily diet and weekly activities, as well as general information about nutrition (food groups, etc.). They wrote on the question "Should Michael's parents make him eat more nutritious snacks?" (Klein & Rose, 2010).

■ Eighth-grade students were studying a unit on fluids, which included the topic of buoyancy. They received a portfolio that included definitions of the concepts of weight, volume, and density; and illustrations of objects that float or sink, with data related to these concepts. Students were asked to give their opinion on what makes objects float or sink; to persuade the reader with as many reasons as they could; to write about an opinion different from their own and the reasons for it; and to persuade the reader that the reasons for the opposing opinion were not good ones (Klein & Ehrhardt, 2012).

Multiple Sources of Information

Many writing to learn activities, such as the Tunguska Mystery, ask students to draw information from several sources. Some research indicates that students learn more if they use multiple sources rather than a single source (Wiley & Voss, 1999), and if they draw information from each source (Klein & Samuels, 2010). It should be noted, however, that writing from multiple sources is a demanding activity for which many students lack appropriate strategies (Mateos, Martín, Villalón, & Luna, 2008). In one recent study, writing arguments from multiple sources produced significantly greater text comprehension than writing summaries for high-knowledge participants, but not for low-knowledge participants (Gil, Bråten, Vidal-Abarca, & & Strømsø, 2010; cf. Klein & Ehrhardt, 2012). Furthermore, some research indicates that it is the effort to find relationships among sources, rather than the effort to form an opinion, that is important for learning from multiple sources (Kobayashi, 2009).

Using Talk as a Prewriting Activity

The research literature on learning through argumentative talk is substantially larger than the literature on learning through argumentative writing (e.g., Kuhn, 2010). Several studies described here have included talk as a prewriting activity or complementary activity (Zohar & Nemet, 2002; cf. Kieft et al., 2008). For example, in one study, 11th-grade students learned about the genetic revolution. The researcher provided case studies, which included background information on genetics, information about a specific genetic disease, a vignette describing a fictitious person with a dilemma about a genetic disease, questions for individual consideration and group discussion concerning this dilemma, and questions to guide the writing of an argument (Zohar & Nemet, 2002). This combination of activities contributed significantly to learning.

Looking for Effective Argument Elements

Students appear to learn more during argument writing, and their texts are rated higher in holistic quality if they include several of the following elements: several pieces of evidence; elaboration of evidence (describing the evidence or telling why it supports the claim); presentation of both sides of an issue (counterclaims); evidence for the counterclaim; rebuttal of the counterclaim; and a conclusion (Klein & Samuels, 2010). The inclusion of these elements is highly consistent with the Common Core State Standards; for example, the standard for writing grades 11–12, 1a (p. 45) indicates that students should be able to "write arguments to support claims in an analysis of substantive topics or texts, using valid reasoning and relevant and sufficient evidence. . . . Introduce precise, knowledgeable claim(s), establish the significance of the claim(s), distinguish the claim(s) from alternate or opposing claims, and create an organization that logically sequences claim(s), counterclaims, reasons, and evidence" (NGA & CCSSO, 2010, p. 45).

Teaching Argumentation to Boost Learning

Of the studies just described, some showed that students who have been taught to write arguments learn more than those who have not (Kieft et al., 2008; Zohar & Nemet, 2002; but cf. Klein & Samuels, 2010).

Explanation: A Neglected Genre

An *explanation* is a kind of text that makes an idea understandable to a reader (Rowan, 1988). In this chapter, we focus on explanations that answer "how" or "why" questions by focusing on the causal relationships that lead to some natural or social phenomenon (Christie & Derewianka, 2008; Coffin, 2006; Unsworth, 2001). Explanations are central to learning in content-area subjects such as science, in which students learn about topics such as "What causes eclipses?" and "How does a hydroelectric plant generate electricity?" Explanations are also critically important in history and social studies, in which students learn about topics such as "Why do people who live in different regions grow different crops?" and "How did World War II change the role of women in American society?"

Most studies of explanations have focused on the linguistics of the texts that students read or write (e.g., Christie & Derewianka, 2008; Coffin, 2004). These studies have shown that across the years of school, explanations evolve (Veel, 1998). Those written for younger students explain concrete events, often with reference to the visible actions of individuals and objects (e.g., how a newspaper is produced). In contrast, many explanations for older students invoke both causes and effects comprising abstract objects and processes (e.g., how organisms evolve, the causes of the Great Depression).

Explanations may be developed through a series of stages, each of which serves a specific purpose. These vary from text to text, but often include the elements shown in Table 7.1, which is illustrated by the explanation of a Cartesian diver by Devika, a fifth-grade student (Chambliss, Christenson, & Parker, 2003; Raison et al., 2004; Unsworth, 2001).

In the Common Core standards, the "informational/explanatory" strand (W 1.2–W 12.2) is one of three major categories of writing that runs through the elementary and secondary grades; for example, for grade six: "Write informative/explanatory texts to examine a topic and convey ideas, concepts, and information through the selection, organization, and analysis of relevant content" (NGA & CCSSO, 2010, p. 42). Some promising professional resources for teaching explanations writing are available (e.g.,

TABLE 7.1. Example of Explanation Stages

The Cartesian diver is filled with water. Inside the bottle is a medicine dropper. The medicine dropper also known as the diver dives when you squeeze the bottle . . .	*Introduction.* Orients the reader; defines the topic; states importance; provides overview.
The parts of a Cartesian diver are: a 2-liter bottle filled with water 2 centimeters from the top and a medicine dropper mostly filled with water. The medicine dropper represents the diver.	*Participants.* Describes the objects, components, or abstractions involved in the explanation.
When someone squeezes the bottle the pressure forces the medicine [dropper] to get filled with water which makes the diver heavy. The weight of the medicine dropper causes the dropper to sink.	*Subexplanation:* A sequence of cause-and-effect relationships that bring about a phenomenon. An explanation may contain several subexplanations.
As soon as you let go of the bottle there's no more pressure. Now the medicine dropper lets some water out. The medicine dropper rises because there isn't as much weight. There isn't as much weight because there isn't as much water in the medicine dropper.	*Subexplanation.* A second series of cause-and-effect relationships.
The medicine dropper can be fun to play. If you're mad you can squeeze the bottle to calm yourself down. . . . In science the Cartesian diver shows what pressure can do. . . .	*Conclusion.* States the importance or application; identifies other examples or applications covered by the explanation.

Raison et al., 1994). However, to date, very little research has addressed the teaching of explanation writing or the role of explanations in writing to learn. If students read several sources, writing an explanation can prompt students to integrate information across sources and increase their understanding (Cerdán & Vidal-Abarca, 2008). Some evidence suggests that teaching students to write explanations allows them to integrate information across sources and produce quality texts (Chambliss et al., 2004; Klein & Kirkpatrick, 2010). Teaching students to write explanations may increase their ability to use this genre as a learning tool (Klein & Rose, 2010; however, cf. Klein & Kirkpatrick, 2010).

A Classroom Example: Writing about the Cartesian Diver

Students in Ms. R's class participated in a strand of study on explanation writing that was woven through several content-area curriculum units (Klein & Rose, 2010). Throughout the term, the students read explanations, compared and evaluated them, reconstructed explanations that had been cut into pieces and discussed the purpose of each part, learned a brief strategy for composing explanations, completed shared writing with the teacher, and collaborated on writing explanations with partners.

For this final activity, the students chose one of six kinds of kits made from "found" materials that related to one topic in the elementary science curriculum. One type of kit was the Cartesian diver. Students had learned in earlier grades about air and water; this activity would allow them to apply these principles to explain a novel piece of technology. First, the students worked together as partners to build their projects; Devika and her partner chose the Cartesian diver and built it together. They experimented with the diver to examine how it worked.

Each pair of partners outlined an explanation of their project. For this, they used a template from the *First Steps Writing Resource* (Raison et al., 1994). It presented the following prompts: The Topic (title); Definition; Components/Parts; Operations; Applications; and Interesting features/Special features/Evaluation (p. 123). Devika and her partner also drew a diagram of their Cartesian diver and labeled it.

The most challenging part of the outline for students was the "Operations" section, which included the cause-and-effect relationships that comprised the heart of the explanation. The students had been taught the following strategy for this section:

1. Get informed (Observe or research the process).
2. Include each step.
3. Tell *why* each step happens.

After outlining their ideas, students who worked on the same kind of technology project (e.g., Cartesian divers) met in groups with the teacher. Each student read his or her explanation to the group. The teacher scaffolded the discussion of the operation section using the three strategy prompts listed above. At this point, most students needed to experiment with their projects further, observe them carefully, and pool their ideas with their groupmates. On the basis of this discussion, each student revised her or his outline.

Based on the outline, the students wrote rough drafts and then conferenced with their partners to edit them. The teacher read the drafts and marked them up with feedback on content and mechanics. Finally, the students produced the final versions of their texts using the computer; Devika's text appears in Table 7.1. On open house night, friends and family visited the classroom. The students displayed their written explanations, and talked with the guests about them. Materials were provided so that the guests could try making the same projects "from scratch." Overall, the effect of this unit of study was to improve students' knowledge of explanation texts, quality of explanation writing, and ability to use writing as a tool for learning about a new topic (Klein & Rose, 2010; but cf. Klein & Kirkpatrick, 2010).

Teaching Students to Write Explanations

To date, only a few studies have focused on teaching students to write explanations or to use them for writing to learn. In a study by Chambliss et al. (2003), the teacher, Mr. T, worked with researchers to teach fourth-grade students about explanation writing in the context of a unit on ecosystems. Early in the unit, students created ecosystems in aquariums. They read about the effects of pollutants on ecosystems, and Mr. T modeled strategies for comprehending explanations. A key idea was that an explanation may contain several smaller "subexplanations." The students then worked in groups to read explanations and summarize them using graphic organizers.

Mr. T then told the students that they would be writing explanations for the third graders in their school, so that the latter would have a good introduction to the topic of ecosystems. The students researched the topic using print materials. Mr. T modeled for the students how to write an explanation, and then students worked in various groupings to plan their own explanations. They used graphic organizers in which they could record their questions, possible subexplanations, and rationales discussing why they had chosen each subexplanation. The students drafted their texts, and then shared them with a peer for feedback using guidelines that reminded them to look for guiding questions, more than one kind of subexplanation, and a logical order in the text.

A Framework for Teaching Writing to Learn, Using Explanation

Klein and Rose (2010) used the following framework to guide one semester of learning about explanation writing, which was woven into a series of science units. The purpose was to prepare students to use explanation writing as a tool for learning.

- *Content-area literacy with a writing focus.* Students wrote two to three times per week, often briefly; reading and talk were used to support writing activities. Typically, students completed one brief explanation each week.
- *Conception of writing as learning.* The teacher and researcher discussed with students the idea that writing is an opportunity to think and learn.
- *Analytic genres as heuristics for thinking and learning.* Students wrote arguments to think critically about issues, and wrote explanations to understand processes, in science and social studies.
- *Inquiry writing as a preferred lesson type.* Many writing lessons were built around hands-on experiences, such as the Cartesian diver project described above. Students then used writing to reflect on and interpret these activities.
- *Cognitive strategy approach to instruction.* Students were explicitly taught strategies for writing arguments and explanations (cf. Graham & Harris, 2005, for information on strategy instruction).
- *Assessment to scaffold self-monitoring.* Students were explicitly taught to monitor their writing, checking that the elements of explanations or argumentation were present, and revising their text to include these elements.
- *Building intrinsic motivation.* Activities included interesting topics, hands-on experiences, and peer collaboration.

Following this unit of study, students made gains in knowledge about explanation texts, quality of explanation texts, and learning during writing (Klein & Rose, 2010; but cf. Klein & Kirkpatrick, 2010).

Writing to Learn in the Disciplines

In the previous section, we saw that approaches to writing to learn can be differentiated according to the genre of text written; in this section, we will see that approaches have also been differentiated by discipline. There is a growing awareness that for each discipline learning to read with understanding, learning to write, and learning how inquiry is conducted are all intertwined (e.g., Shanahan & Shanahan, 2008). To date, two discipline-specific forms of writing to learn have been created. One is the Science Writing Heuristic, a sequence of activities that begins with a science experiment or other experience, and invites students to reason critically about it (e.g., Keys, Hand, Prain, & Collins, 1999; Hand, Hohenshell, & Prain, 2007). The second discipline-specific sequence is writing arguments from primary historical sources (De La Paz & Felton, 2010). Both of these approaches are consistent with the Common Core State Standards, particularly the Writing Standards for Literacy in History/Social Studies, Science, and Technical Subjects, in that they directly address writing arguments (1), text organization (4), planning and revision (5), conducting research projects (7), use of multiple sources in various media (8), the use of evidence from texts (9), and a range of kinds of writing (10).

The Science Writing Heuristic

The Science Writing Heuristic (SWH) incorporates practical laboratory work with peer group reading, discussion, and writing. It is particularly effective for low-achieving students, who benefit from integrating writing with talk (Akkus, Gunel, & Hand, 2007; Rivard, 2004). The SWH is

---

1. Exploration of preinstruction understanding through individual or group concept mapping.

2. Prelaboratory activities, including informal writing, making observations, brainstorming, and posing questions.

3. Participation in laboratory activity.

4. Negotiation phase I—writing personal meanings for laboratory activity (e.g., writing journals).

5. Negotiation phase II—sharing and comparing data interpretations in small groups (e.g., making a group chart).

6. Negotiation phase III—comparing science ideas to textbooks or other printed resources (e.g., writing group notes in response to focus questions).

7. Negotiation phase IV—individual reflection and writing (e.g., writing a report or textbook explanation).

8. Exploration of postinstruction understanding through concept mapping.

FIGURE 7.1. Teacher template for the science writing heuristic. From Hand, Wallace, and Yang (2004, p. 132). Reprinted with permission from Taylor & Francis Ltd. *www.informaworld.com*.

summarized by a template for teachers in Figure 7.1 (from Hand, Wallace, & Yang, 2004, p. 132). This can be modified for various kinds of science topics and activities, and for students at different grade levels.

The SWH in the Classroom: Cell Biology in Seventh Grade

A study of a seventh-grade biology unit on cells illustrates the key features of the SWH (Hand, Wallace, & Yang, 2004). The teaching was carried out over the course of 8 weeks in four classes. The SWH begins by exploring students' initial understanding, often using a method such as concept mapping. For this study, the students initially completed a pretest that included multiple-choice questions, as well as constructed responses that required them to write an analogy, an argument, and an explanation of a diagram.

The students then began the instructional component. Throughout this process, students were guide by the following template (p. 132).

1. Beginning Ideas—What are my questions?
2. Tests—What did I do?
3. Observations—What did I see?
4. Claims—What can I claim?
5. Evidence—How do I know? Why am I making these claims?
6. Reading—How do my ideas compare with other ideas?
7. Reflection—How have my ideas changed?

The students began the instructional phase by participating in group discussions, during which they initiated their own questions for a lab activity. For this first lab, the teacher led these discussions to guide students to develop reasonable research questions. These included the following: "What is the function of a cell membrane? What is the structure of a cell membrane? What are the relationships between organelles, cells, organs, and organ systems?"

These research questions then guided the development of lab activities. The teacher provided various materials appropriate to each topic (e.g., microscopes, glass slides, beakers, vegetable oil, pieces of leaf), but did not provide step-by-step instructions. Instead, the students designed their own investigations, using the materials and equipment provided. This included deciding on observations and methods of collecting appropriate evidence in order to answer their particular research question. For this first activity, the teacher also organized class and small-group discussions that focused on the relationships between students' evidence and their claims. The students wrote a report on each activity. Each student shared this report with a peer; they evaluated one another's writing and gave appropriate feedback.

Finally, the students completed a research paper requiring individual reflection and writing. In this case, they summarized the ideas that they had learned across the several activities of the unit. The instructor provided questions to guide their writing, such as "How do substances move in and out of cells?"

Variations That Increase the Effectiveness of SWH Activities

In a series of studies, researchers have investigated the ways in which variations on the SWH affect students' learning:

- Teachers who *comprehensively implement* the SWH increase student achievement relative to those who partially implement it (Akkus et al., 2007).
- Students who complete *multiple writing experiences* during a SWH (e.g., laboratory report *and* textbook explanation) learn more than those who complete only one writing activity (Hand, Hohenshell, & Prain, 2004, 2007).
- Students who *write for real, younger audiences* learn more than those who write for the teacher as audience (Gunel, Hand, & McDermott, 2009; Hand, Wallace, & Yang, 2004).
- Students who *receive feedback* from a real audience learn more than those that do not, although the effects of feedback have not yet been separated from the effects of having a real audience; feedback can be assisted by templates (Hand et al., 2007; Hand, Wallace, & Yang, 2004).

Writing to Learn in History Using Argumentation from Primary Sources

The last two decades have seen a growing interest in students writing arguments from historical sources (e.g., De La Paz & Felton, 2010; VanSledright, 2002). These activities support several kinds of learning goals: they improve students' understanding of history; they introduce students to the ways in which historians carry out research; and they teach students strategies for writing arguments. Because these activities teach argumentation, they overlap with those described in the previous section (e.g., Wiley & Voss, 1999); however, studies described here additionally include instruction in reasoning about historical sources. Recent research has shown that this approach is effective for students from the midelementary grades through the secondary grades, and for students with learning disabilities, as well as those who are gifted (De La Paz, 2005; De La Paz & Felton, 2010; MacArthur, Ferretti, & Okolo, 2002).

This section focuses on a recent study by De La Paz and Felton (2010), in which students learned both a strategy for reading historical sources critically and a strategy for writing arguments. First, the social studies teachers of five 11th-grade classes in 20th-century American history chose a series of six topics, from Prohibition to the cold war. The students in the classes completed a pretest in which they read primary sources, and then wrote an argument concerning the Spanish–American War. The teachers then began instructing students in a strategy for reasoning critically about sources that included four main components in an attempt to have students engage in sourcing, corroboration and contextualization: consider the author, understand the source, critique the source, and create a more focused understanding (see Figure 7.2). They used an approach to teaching that was based

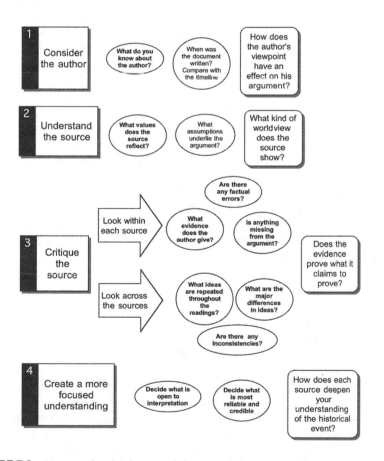

FIGURE 7.2. Strategy for thinking with historical documents. From De La Paz and Felton (2010, p. 181). Reprinted with permission from Elsevier.

on self-regulated strategy development (Harris & Graham, 1996), which included five phases (develop background knowledge, describe it, model it, support it, and independent performance), with one or two lessons per phase.

First, the teachers helped students *develop background knowledge* by presenting them with two arguments based on the same topic as the pretest (the Spanish–American War), using the same sources, but expressing different conclusions, to teach students that the same historical sources could be used to argue for different positions. The teachers then introduced the topic of Prohibition, which became the context for most of the instruction in the strategy for reading sources, as well as the strategy for writing arguments. They engaged the students by asking them to write briefly on the topic of alcohol in contemporary society, and then discussing as a class whether alcohol should be made legal or illegal. Then, for the main focus of the lesson, the teachers provided students with several brief primary source documents related to Prohibition, including cartoons and 1926 testimony in the U.S. Senate. They asked students to read the source documents and determine whether each author was for or against Prohibition, and they showed students how to mark up the evidence in the document.

The teachers then *described* and *modeled* the historical reasoning strategy by applying each of the four steps to the documents about the Prohibition topic. They discussed the subquestions associated with each phase of the strategy; for example, for *understanding the author*, they focused on what was known about the author, when the document was written, whether the writer had a particular motivation, and how these considerations could affect the author's credibility.

At this point, the teachers switched from teaching the source strategy to teaching the prewriting strategy because the students would need to use both strategies together to write a historical argument. The prewriting strategy, called STOP (De La Paz & Graham, 1997), focused on critically considering both sides of an issue (or in this case, both sources).

- Suspend judgment.
- Take a side.
- Organize (select and number) ideas.
- Plan more as you write.

First, the teachers *described* the writing strategy by presenting an overview of it. They provided students with the structure for writing an essay, as well as providing two sample essays (one for each argument), and a set of possible transition words that they could use to connect ideas in text. They then *modeled* the strategy by beginning with a completed essay by one of the teachers, and showing students how he had created a plan that had used the sources, selecting and organizing material for the text. Later, the teachers also shared essays from students, discussing how they had used or omitted the various steps.

For the final phases of instruction, the teachers helped students apply both the reasoning strategy and the prewriting strategy. They introduced the New Deal topic, providing students with a timeline of events, a two-page backgrounder, and several primary sources. In this *support it* phase of instruction, the teachers began to move the students toward some independence by having them work in small groups to apply the historical reading and writing strategies with the materials. The teachers also provided a rubric that combined text features based on the historical reasoning strategy with features based on the writing strategy.

Finally, in the *independent* phase of instruction, the students worked on two tasks: one brief activity focused on the American debate on isolationism versus entry into World War II and the other based on the Cuban Missile Crisis. Teachers provided important assistance to students by introducing them to the historical background, reviewing the context with engaging presentations, and discussing the need to cite evidence. In the Cuban Missile Crisis example, students were prompted to identify the position of the sources tangibly, by writing "For Blockade" or "For Airstrike" on each. Most interestingly, one of the teachers actually asked students to create a plan for an argument on each side of the issue before choosing to develop one of the two plans.

Conclusion

We have described how teachers and researchers have implemented three different approaches to writing to learn in the classroom. With respect to the first of these approaches, *reflective writing to learn*, a substantial amount of research has differentiated between more and less effective practices. With respect to the second approach, *writing to learn in informational genres*, several studies have indicated that argumentation contributes to learning, but investigations of explanation writing have only recently begun, so further studies are needed to identify best practices. With respect to the third approach, *writing to learn in the disciplines*, the SWH and writing arguments from primary sources in history are both supported by growing bodies of research.

We have suggested that the choice among the three approaches to writing to learn depends on the goals that the teacher has for a particular learning activity and the way in which the activity fits into the larger classroom program. An additional consideration is the educational level of learners: reflective writing to learn can be relatively brief and informal, so it is appropriate in early elementary school, as well as secondary school and college. Writing to learn in informational genres and disciplinary writing to learn are more challenging and so are appropriate in upper-elementary school, secondary school, and college. Finally, an important practice that has recently emerged across all three approaches to writing to learn is the teaching of writing strategies. Early research on writing to learn depended almost entirely on students' existing writing skills (see Klein, 1999, for a review); however, several studies have now supported the important principle that if students are taught writing strategies, they will be able to use writing more effectively as a learning tool (e.g., De La Paz & Felton, 2010; Hübner et al., 2010; Kieft et al., 2008; Reynolds & Perin, 2009).

Acknowledgments

We wish to thank Charles A. MacArthur, Brian Hand, and Susan De La Paz for their helpful comments on an earlier draft of this chapter.

References

Akkus, R., Gunel, M., & Hand, B. (2007). Comparing an inquiry-based approach known as the Science Writing Heuristic to traditional science teaching practices: Are there differences? *International Journal of Science Education, 29,* 1745–1765.

Bangert-Drowns, R. L., Hurley, M. M., & Wilkinson, B. (2004). The effects of school-based writing-to-learn interventions on academic achievement: A meta-analysis. *Review of Educational Research, 74,* 29–58.

Boscolo, P., & Mason, L. (2001). Writing to learn, writing to transfer. In G. Rijlaarsdam (Series Ed.), & P. Tynjälä, L. Mason, & K. Lonka (Vol. Eds.), *Studies in writing, Vol. 7: Writing as a learning tool: Integrating theory and practice* (pp. 83–104). Dordrecht, The Netherlands: Kluwer Academic Press.

Cantrell, R. J., Fusaro, J. A., & Dougherty, E. A. (2000). Exploring the effectiveness of journal writing on learning social studies: A comparative study. *Reading Psychology, 21,* 1–11.

Cerdán, R., & Vidal-Abarca, E. (2008). The effects of tasks on integrating information from multiple documents. *Journal of Educational Psychology, 100,* 209–222.

Chambliss, M. J., Christenson, L. A., & Parker, C. (2003). Fourth graders composing scientific explanations about the effects of pollutants. *Written Communication, 20,* 426–454.

Christie, F., & Derewianka, B. (2008). *School discourse: Learning to write across the years of schooling.* London: Continuum.

Coffin, C. (2006). Learning the language of school history: The role of linguistics in mapping the writing demands of the secondary curriculum. *Journal of Curriculum Studies, 38,* 413–429.

De La Paz, S. (2005). Effects of historical reasoning instruction and writing strategy mastery in culturally and academically diverse middle school classrooms. *Journal of Educational Psychology, 97,* 139–156.

De La Paz, S., & Felton, M. K. (2010). Reading and writing from multiple source documents in history: Effects of strategy instruction with low to average high school writers. *Contemporary Educational Psychology, 35,* 174–192.

De La Paz, S., & Graham, S. (1997). Effects of dictation and advanced planning instruction on the composing of students with writing and learning problems. *Journal of Educational Psychology, 89,* 203–222.

Gil, L., Bråten, I., Vidal-Abarca, E., & Strømsø, H. I. (2010). Summary versus argument tasks when working from multiple documents: Which is better for whom? *Contemporary Educational Psychology, 35,* 157–173.

Graham, S., & Harris, K. R. (2005). *Writing better: Effective strategies for teaching students with learnung difficulties.* Baltimore: Brookes.

Graham, S., & Perin, D. (2007). A meta-analysis of writing instruction for adolescent students. *Journal of Educational Psychology, 99,* 445–476.

Gunel, M., Hand, B., & McDermott, M. A. (2009). Writing for different audiences: Effects on high-school students' conceptual understandıng of biology. *Learning and Instruction, 19,* 354–367.

Hand, B., Hohenshell, L., & Prain, V. (2004). Exploring students' responses to conceptual questions when engaged with planned writing experiences: A study with year 10 science students. *Journal of Research in Science Teaching, 41,* 186–210.

Hand, B., Hohenshell, L., & Prain, V. (2007). Examining the effects of multiple writing tasks on year 10 biology students' understandings of cell and molecular biology concepts. *Instructional Science, 35, 343–373.*

Hand, B., Wallace, C., & Yang, E. (2004). Using the science writing heuristic to enhance learning outcomes from laboratory activities in seventh grade science: Quantitative and qualitative aspects. *International Journal of Science Education, 26,* 131–149.

Harris, K. R., & Graham, S. (1996). *Making the writing process work: Strategies for composition and self-regulation.* Cambridge, MA: Brookline.

Hübner, S., Nückles, M., & Renkl, A. (2010). Writing learning journals: Instructional support to overcome learning-strategy deficits. *Learning and Instruction, 20,* 18–29.

Keys, C. W., Hand, B., Prain, V., & Collins, S. (1999). Using the Science Writing Heuristic as a tool for learning from laboratory investigations in secondary science. *Journal of Research in Science Teaching, 36,* 1065–1084.

Kieft, M., Riujlaarsdam, G., & van den Bergh, H. (2008). An aptitude–treatment interaction approach to writing-to-learn. *Learning and Instruction,18,* 379–390.

Klein, P. D. (1999). Reopening inquiry into cognitive processes in writing to learn. *Educational Psychology Review, 11,* 203–270.

Klein, P. D., & Ehrhardt, J. (2012). Effects of writing goals and previous writing achievement on cognitive load and science learning. Manuscript submitted for publication.

Klein, P. D., & Kirkpatrick, L. C. (2010). A framework for content-area writing: Mediators and moderators. *Journal of Writing Research, 2,* 1–46.

Klein, P. D., & Rose, M. A. (2010).Teaching argument and explanation to prepare junior students for writing to learn. *Reading Research Quarterly, 45,* 433–461.

Klein, P. D., & Samuels, B. (2010). Learning about plate tectonics through argument writing. *Alberta Journal of Educational Research, 56,* 196–217.

Kobayashi, K. (2009). Comprehension of relations among controversial texts: Effects of external strategy use. *Instructional Science, 37,* 311–324.

Kuhn, D. (2010). Teaching and learning science as argument. *Science Education, 94,* 810–824.

MacArthur, C. A., & Ferretti, R. P., & Okolo, C. M. (2002). On defending controversial viewpoints: Debates of sixth graders about the desirability of early 20th-century American immigration. *Learning Disabilities Research and Practice, 17,* 160–172.

Mateos, M., Martín, E., Villalón, R., & Luna, M. (2008). Reading and writing to learn in secondary education: Online processing activity and written products in summarizing and synthesizing tasks. *Reading and Writing, 21,* 675–697.

National Governors Association Center for Best Practices, Council of Chief State School Officers (2010). *Common Core State Standards for English language arts & literacy in history/social studies, science, and technical subjects.* Washington, DC: Authors. Retrieved from *www.corestandards.org.*

Newell, G. E., & Winograd, P. (1989). The effects of writing on learning from expository texts. *Written Communication, 6,* 196–217.

Nückles, M., Hübner, S., & Renkl, A. (2009). Enhancing self-regulated learning by writing learning protocols. *Learning and Instruction, 19,* 259–271.

Raison, G., Rivalland, J., Derewianka, B., Johnson, T. D., Sloan, P., Latham, R., et al. (1994). *First steps: Writing resource book.* Portsmouth, NH: Heinemann.

Reynolds, G. A., & Perin, D. (2009). A comparison of text structure and self-regulated writing strategies for composing from sources by middle school students. *Reading Psychology, 30,* 265–300.

Rivard, L. P. (2004). Are language-based activities in science effective for all students, including low achievers? *Science Education, 88,* 420–442.

Rowan, K. E. (1988). A contemporary theory of explanatory writing. *Written Communication, 5,* 23–56.

Shanahan, T., & Shanahan, C. (2008). Teaching disciplinary literacy to adolescents: Rethinking content area literacy. *Harvard Educational Review, 78,* 40–59.

Unsworth, L. (2001). Evaluating the language of different types of explanations in junior high school science texts. *International Journal of Science Education, 23,* 585–609.

VanSledright, B. A. (2002). Fifth graders investigating history in the classroom: Results from a researcher-practitioner design experiment. *Elementary School Journal, 103,* 131–160.

Veel, R. (1998). Learning how to mean—scientifically speaking: Apprenticeship into scientific discourse in the secondary school. In F. Christie & J. R. Martin (Eds.), *Genre and institutions: Social processes in the workplace and school* (pp. 161–195). London: Cassell.

Wiley J., & Voss, J. F. (1999). Constructing arguments from multiple sources: Tasks that promote understanding and not just memory for text. *Journal of Educational Psychology, 91,* 301–311.

Zohar, A., & Nemet, F. (2002). Fostering students' knowledge and argumentation skills through dilemmas in human genetics. *Journal of Research in Science Teaching, 39,* 35–62.

PART III

Strategies for Teaching and Learning in Writing

Chapter 8

Best Practices in Teaching Planning for Writing

CINDY LASSONDE
JANET C. RICHARDS

Scholars and teachers of writing understand that planning is the initial stage of the writing process in which writers invent and expand their ideas. We know planning involves contemplating the task, activating one's prior knowledge about the topic and task, considering vocabulary and language use, and organizing ideas. Have you ever considered, though, that a writer plans her writing as she continues drafting, revising, and editing her work? From this perspective, planning overarches *all* of the stages of the writing process. That's why planning is such an important part of the writing process and why learning how to teach planning effectively will improve students' self-regulated writing. This chapter offers innovative ways to think about and teach planning. The ideas presented are well grounded in what research tells us about writing theory and practice.

We begin this chapter by providing a succinct overview of two broad and well-documented approaches to the planning process: a top-down approach (advance planning through concept maps, outlining, etc.) and a bottom-up approach (discovery as one writes freely followed by extensive revision) (Alamargot & Chanquoy, 2001; Deane et al., 2008; Elbow, 1973, 1981). To clarify these two planning approaches, which reflect cognitive models of writing, we connect top-down and bottom-up planning to the personal planning we engaged in as we contemplated and developed initial ideas for this chapter. Next, we discuss the differences among the planning processes of younger children, students in middle and high school, students who struggle with writing, and experienced writers. Then we look at what research has to say about the benefits of planning writing.

Studies indicate significant positive effects when teachers demonstrate and explain planning strategies to students (Graham, 2006). Therefore, we conclude this chapter by providing an array of "advance planning strategies" (i.e., a top-down approach where writers plan prior to writing) and "discovery planning strategies" (i.e., a bottom-up approach in which writers discover new and important ideas as they write) that can be used prior to and also while writing (Deane et al., 2008). Classroom teachers and we have successfully helped students use all of the self-regulating planning strategies we include in this chapter.

Advance Planning and Discovery Planning

Effective writing teachers recognize that "even skilled writers can be limited by working-memory capacity so that they cannot handle all aspects of the writing task simultaneously" (Deane et al., 2008, p. 36). Therefore, they help students understand that strategic advance planning minimizes working memory overload (Hayes, 1996). Good teachers of writing also recognize that writers discover new ideas as they write; so, planning can take place at any time in the writing process.

Effective writing teachers support students as they practice advance and discovery planning strategies and learn how to self-regulate and monitor their planning. Furthermore, they help students learn how to choose appropriate planning strategies based on the writing task, the audience for the completed text, and students' personal planning styles and preferences.

It is revealing and interesting to see how each of us, Cindy and Janet (two experienced, published authors who have written together for several years) tackled the planning phase of writing this chapter. Some experienced writers plan by formulating "goals for their texts (e.g., to reach a given audience, to present a particular persona) and then develop plans to achieve those goals" (McCutchen, 2006, p. 116). For example, Cindy, a linear thinker, initiated her planning of this chapter by first creating an outline of ideas that reflected her goals for the chapter. She based the outline on concerns and questions she knew her graduate teacher-education students had about teaching planning and also about other planning issues she wanted her students to recognize. She forwarded the outline to Janet and one of the editors of this text, Charles (Skip) MacArthur, and they initially approved the outline's contents. Skip cleverly and glibly responded, "How appropriate that the authors of the chapter on planning are getting an early start on their plan!"

Then Cindy started a rough draft, basically following the outline but reorganizing, synthesizing some subheadings together, and introducing new headings as she wrote. She found that as she wrote and researched planning further, additional questions and deeper insights caused revision of the initial outlined plan. The outlined plan evolved.

However, some writers minimally plan prior to writing. They discover as they write. This was (and is always) the case for Janet. Janet first attempted a draft of this chapter by writing in a sketchy, rough kind of way what she believed and knew about planning writing and how she recognized that planning has the potential to enrich students' writing processes, regardless of their grade level, writing experiences, developmental stage, or composing ability. Through her writing, she learned what she knew, didn't know, and needed to know about planning. As Janet wrote, she discovered. The bottom line is, writers plan differently. There is no one best way to get ready to write (Richards & Miller, 2010).

Additional research helps us situate these two approaches to planning. Much research indicates skilled writers plan their writing carefully like Cindy and may spend 70% of their writing time planning (Murray, 1992). Cindy's planning involved writing down and reorganizing ideas to satisfy the goals of what the final piece should include. Organizing the ideas in a linear format allowed her to conceptualize how all of the pieces of her understandings of planning writing fit together. As she placed the headings and the subheadings into outline format, she configured her understandings into a structure that would guide her drafting.

On the other hand, the work of noted British writing scholar David Galbraith (1996, 2009) helps explain Janet's diverse planning approaches. Janet's planning involved "dispositional spelling out" (2009, p. 140), which is not to be confused with the spelling of words. This style of planning involves spontaneously articulating thoughts as they emerge through text production and is associated with "the development of the writer's personal understanding of the topic" (2009, p. 140). This type of "real-time" planning, (i.e., planning as one writes) requires connecting planning to text generation and transcription that can place a considerable cognitive burden on the writer's working memory (Deane et al., 2008).

As we continued to cowrite, passing drafts back and forth electronically, we inquired, reflected, and wondered more about planning issues. We concurred that useful, implicit planning is not only connected to a writer's age, developmental cognitive stage, and writing experiences, but is often specific to the writing task. For example, a writer may approach composing fiction, poetry, or a memoir differently from how he or she approaches a persuasive writing task. Not only does genre influence planning, but the selected complexity of the language or word choices and expectations of the intended audience or purpose for writing can influence planning. One writer may use a bottom-up approach for creating poetry but prefer a top-down, more structured, "planful" approach for composing a persuasive piece. Or a writer may decide when writing a lengthy manuscript to engage in top-down thinking and prepare an outline to be sure all of the components of the piece are accounted for within the draft. Then, when composing, the author will have more space in her working memory to focus on the task at hand.

Despite the benefits of planning, research shows many developing writers are simply unable to plan because of the complexity of the demands of the cognitive processing tasks involved (Torrance & Galbraith, 2006). Yet these students are the same ones who need to engage in explicit, organized planning to help them construct cohesive texts.

These conclusions helped to solidify our thinking that developing writers and writers who struggle should be supported by teachers to employ diverse, self-regulated strategies to plan their writing. That is, rather than teaching and expecting all students to use a particular graphic organizer for an assigned task, we should teach students to think like writers who connect their composing task to their planning strategy and utilize the planning strategy that will most effectively and efficiently fit their purposes.

How Do Writers Plan?

Young students typically engage in little prior planning (Berninger, Whitaker, Feng, Swanson, & Abbott, 1996). They take a natural "tell-all" approach to composing, with one statement or thought cuing the next sentence they write. In addition, research indicates that as a rule children with learning disabilities plan less than their peers (MacArthur & Graham, 1987).

Our observations indicate that a significant number of students from the middle grades to graduate school also do not plan before they write. In fact, many resist planning. To conduct some simple research on this topic, Janet asked her 13-year-old grandson, Noah, how he plans his writing. He responded, "Planning??? Let's see—planning. Well, one way is if I have to write five pages, I write two and then I stick in things to make it longer." (Actually that sounds like a plan, although not a well-thought-through plan). Her 11-year-old grandson, Joshua, who is a gifted student and a discovery writer, explained, "I just begin writing and it comes to me. Planning takes too long. It takes about 2 days. That's a really long time." Even Janet's 18-year-old granddaughter, Maddie, concurred that planning was not worth the effort. She said, "Planning takes too long. I have no time to plan my writing. I have too much I have to write in college."

Next, Janet questioned her graduate students in a Writers and Writing course. Their first assignment was to write a two-or-more-page turning-point memoir. After Janet collected their papers she asked how many of her students did any planning prior to writing. Only 2 out of 11 said they engaged in planning. One had made considerable handwritten notes and the other had jotted down short phrases.

Apparently, Janet's grandchildren and most of her writing students had not learned to value planning as part of the necessary steps in the writing process. They consider writing a one-shot deal, wherein the writer sits down, writes or types the paper, reads it over, edits for any grammatical problems, such as spelling and punctuation, and turns in the paper to her teacher. Like many students, they consider prior planning time-consuming, and nonessential to writing a well-structured paper. Of course, annual standardized writing assessments influence students and teachers to disregard the planning process. In many states students have 45 minutes to write in response to a prompt. Time constraints prohibit prior planning and, in fact, influence students to discredit and doubt the value of planning their writing.

Benefits of Planning Writing

Research shows the process of planning, as is typical of all phases of writing, requires significant cognitive effort (Piolat, Roussey, Olive, & Farioli, 1996). How might we, as teachers, model ways to plan writing for students in grades K–12? How might we help students understand planning and the benefits of planning writing? One approach we have found useful for students in the primary and elementary grades is to compare planning and the planning of writing to formally planning and building a house. We say:

> "We want to build a house and because we're in a hurry we could start nailing everything together. [We model building in a haphazard way.] Can you imagine what we'd end up with if we didn't plan ahead? We might forget to put doorways in rooms, or we might make the bedrooms too small to fit our beds! Or we could not be able to walk outside to our nice backyard because we had forgotten to put doors in our house. But what if we drew up a building plan for our house before we started to build it? We could draw a picture or blueprint of the house. [We show students a house blueprint.] We could even change the blueprint of the house if we thought of something else we needed later, like a front porch. We could follow and revise our plan as needed to construct our house. When we were finished building, our house would be exactly the way we wanted it."

Of course, we model different planning strategies for older students. They have usually developed sufficient information-processing skills and acquired generalized knowledge to think abstractly. They also have adequate semantic (i.e., meaning) memory necessary to understand, retain, and recall information about planning writing. Writing tasks involve management of a complex array of skills over the course of a writing project, including language and literacy skills, document-creation and document-management skills, and critical-thinking skills (e.g., see Bereiter & Scardamalia, 1987; Inhelder & Piaget, 1958; Richards & Lassonde, 2011). Therefore, when we work with middle- and high-school students, we model an array of planning strategies that fall under both a top-down and a bottom-up approach, are specific for planning different types of writing tasks, and suit the individual planning styles and aptitudes of students (e.g., sketching ideas is helpful for students who prefer to learn through the visual modality and for those who are talented in the visual arts).

What Some Writing Scholars and Popular Writers Think about Planning

In addition to students who see no use for planning, some writing scholars and well-known writers discount the benefits of planning one's writing. For example, Fletcher (2000) cautions against devoting too much time and energy to prewriting because he thinks you may become "absolutely sick of the topic" (2000, p. 30). Quintilian, the great Roman rhetorician, also expected his students not to waste time with invention and first drafts. He wanted his students to write "quickly and with abandon" (Golden, 1969, in Bloodgood, 2002, p. 35). On the other hand, Judson of the Minnesota Writing Project (2001) thinks planning one's writing is crucial. She notes that through planning writers take control and ownership of their writing because this process "encourages experimentation while giving the first draft organization and purpose" (p. 1). Indeed, research shows that for the most part experienced writers spend more time planning than inexperienced writers (McCutchen, 2006). We, too, believe there is a strong likelihood that planning before writing and as needed within the recursive processes of writing allows students to take control of their composing initiatives. Planning helps organize and structure students' thinking. Planning makes visible all of the shadowy, obscure writing notions that float around in all writers' heads (Richards & Miller, 2005). Students who plan their writing and consciously recognize they are engaging in planning have opportunities to compose independently, purposefully, and confidently.

Teaching Planning and Connections to the Common Core Standards

Knowledgeable writing teachers know planning writing is addressed most directly in the Production and Distribution of Writing section of the

Common Core State Standards (CCSS; National Governors Association [NGA] & Council of Chief State School Officers [CCSSO], 2010). However, for prekindergartners, kindergartners, and students in grades 1 and 2, planning is not directly addressed. Thus, teachers may interpret this omission to mean planning for young students is confined to "responding to questions and suggestions from peers" during writing experiences and to "add details to strengthen writing as needed" (NGA & CCSSO, 2010, p. 19) with help from adults. These expectations certainly require students to plan their writing before or during writing. Responding to questions requires students to analyze the task, and adding details entails making plans to improve writing. Both are components of the planning process. Once students are in third grade, however, planning is mentioned specifically in the CCSS when students are expected to "develop and strengthen writing as needed by planning, revising, and editing" (p. 21) through grade 12.

As in all areas of instruction mentioned by the CCSS (e.g., disciplines such as mathematics and reading), the standards merely state what students should be able to do. For example, students should know how to plan their writing. The CCSS also imply teachers should increase their expectations and scaffolding of instruction for planning from grades 3 through 12.

We think it is fortunate the CCSS does not mandate how teachers should instruct students in planning their writing, although by omitting explicit directions for lessons on planning they might lead teachers to think planning for students in grade 3 looks the same as that for students in grade 12. However, this is not the case. It might be more helpful if authors of the CCSS had supplied a chart that portrayed progressive skills in writing similar to that provided in the CCSS for language progressive skills, by grade. In such a chart planning could be scaffolded, for example, with teachers helping kindergarten and first-grade students to plan their writing through drawing and sharing their ideas verbally with peers. As students mature, teachers might model planning strategies that help students self-regulate their planning.

Planning Strategies

Most writing in classrooms involves creating connected discourse, whether the author is a first-grade student who writes a story about her pet during writers' workshop or a 12th-grade student who composes a persuasive piece for the school newspaper. There are many different writing genres and approaches. In the process approach, students choose the topics and the teacher acts as the audience. In a teacher-based approach, the teacher assigns writing tasks. With an environmental approach, the teacher provides structured materials and activities as students engage in the process approach to generate text and write with students.

Regardless of what type of writing approach a school or teacher uses, writers have to translate their ideas into language and transcribe the words onto paper or a keyboard (Hillocks, 1986). Between or during the idea-transcribing phase, typically, student authors initiate a plan for their writing in one form or another regardless of the writing instructional approach that usually is required by the school district.

Some students' plans—as we noted earlier in our examples of writers in this chapter—may be to just start writing and add or delete as needed later. They may think they do not need to actually design a concrete plan because it takes too long or it isn't necessary because they know already what they want to write. The main difference between developing writers' and experts' planning is the type of planning in which they engage. Some students participate in minimal conceptual planning because they think they don't need to plan, because they are being resistant to doing the extra writing or taking the extra time planning takes, or because they are unaware of the advantages of planning. They plan by retrieving relevant content information from their schema and consider that sufficient planning (McCutchen, 2006).

Other students' plans are more calculated and strategic. They put a great deal of thought into their story or informational text before and as they write. They might incorporate a graphic organizer, a semantic map (for expository text), or an outline, or do some free or quick writing on the topic before they begin the draft. They may do extensive reading on the topic or talk with others as they construct their plans. Either way, whether they dedicate a great deal or very little time to a planning strategy, students begin writing with a plan in place.

Planning doesn't stop once a text is drafted either. A student continually plans her writing because of the recursive nature of the writing process. In the back of her writer's mind she continuously translates her ideas into words, phrases, and sentences and makes decisions about how to organize her thoughts. Original writing plans are revised as new ideas arise or are revealed through peer conferring, additional reflection, and reading. Sometimes all it takes is for a writer to reread what she has already written to decide that a writing plan needs to be revised (Litt, 2011). For some students, this recursive planning process happens automatically as they shift thoughts around, visualize, and reenvision the structure and content of a written composition. However, for many students thoughts become jumbled and their vision becomes blurry. They need guidance to learn how to self-regulate their use of strategies to help them come to clarity (Graham & Harris, 2005). English language learners and students with learning disabilities in particular will benefit from explicit planning strategies that help them put their ideas into concrete sentences.

Depending on what writing approach or program a school uses, planning may look different. Many programs rely on graphic organizers while others teach students how to expand on ideas previously noted in a writer's notebook, conceived through reflective thinking, or created through collaboration with peers. As others have argued (Boscolo, 2008), "the dynamics of prewriting . . . are appropriate for some writing tasks but not for others" (p. 300). To avoid students developing a perception of planning and process writing as formulaic and boring, teachers must make the link between a writing task or goal and the process clear. Teachers who model planning as a solution to achieving the end goal—a polished piece of writing that is coherent and meaningful to the student and others—help to motivate students to participate in purposeful planning (Applebee, 1986; Langer & Applebeee, 2007).

Students Plan Differently

Some students do not do enough planning. Others plan in ways teachers don't expect (i.e., by writing out or drawing their ideas). What made Cindy adjust her thinking about requiring her students to graphically display and plan out their writing was a conversation she had at the end of one school year when she was teaching sixth-grade language arts. Within writing workshop, she required students to use a standard graphic organizer, semantic map, or create their own planning outline or display of some kind. The writing center housed a binder full of different types of organizers from which students could choose the most appropriate one for their current project. Standard operational procedure was that they would complete a graphic organizer and confer with a peer and Cindy about their ideas for writing prior to starting their rough draft. Within content-area writing projects, such as social studies reports, she always handed out a graphic organizer for her students to complete and have approved before they started their report. She'd assign due dates to various parts of the report to keep them on schedule. She'd talk with them about their completed graphic organizer and "approve" it, which allowed them to move on to composing the first draft. Cindy thought this procedure allowed her to check that students were prepared and organized before beginning their first draft. After following this procedure the whole school year, a student who we'll call Katie admitted to Cindy that she didn't plan her writing using the numerous graphic organizers Cindy had handed out throughout the year. Cindy had always thought of Katie as her best writer. Imagine her shock when Katie told Cindy that all year she had been writing the full first draft, *then* filling in the graphic organizer just to meet the teacher's requirement. Katie said, "I don't like to use graphic organizers. I have to think out the whole story first as I write it. I plan as I write the draft. I can't feel or see what's going to happen or what I want to say by putting words into an organizer. I can't think that way. I have to tell the whole story through my writing. Then when you tell us we have to hand in a graphic organizer, I follow my first draft to fill in the organizer. I know it's backward, but it's the only way I can do those graphic organizers!"

Cindy came to realize that Katie was planning, but not in the ways Cindy taught her to plan. Cindy saw planning in a linear way because that's how she plans. Katie planned by talking with her mother and friends about her writing to expand and clarify her thinking. She took random notes and then started to draft to think through her writing goals.

Similarly, Janet recently reacted to required, overt planning in the only way that made sense to her. An editor asked her to turn in an outline of her chapter. So Janet wrote the chapter and then created the outline that she sent forward to the editor. When Janet's editor accepted the outline, Janet's chapter was already written!

And then, there's Xixi, a high-school earth science student, who combined methods for planning. Xixi's teacher asked her to write an essay to describe the difference between the relative temperature conditions and the relative depth under which diamonds typically form. Her first step in planning her response was to analyze the question to determine exactly what it was asking. Xixi evaluated the concepts and the expected outcome of the task. She then reflected on her purposes for writing. She recognized that the teacher basically just wanted to know if she understood the process. The piece would be a short description—an expository text—of what she knew about the effects of temperature and depth on diamond formation. She would have to accurately use the correct scientific vocabulary to describe the differences too. To clarify the process in her mind, she sketched these notes to plan her writing:

> Relative temperature:
> —hotter
> —higher temperature
>
> Relative depth:
> —deeper
> —greater depth

Pulling this structure from her thinking to a concrete structure on paper allowed her to turn her thinking from the abstract to concrete. For her writing purposes, this degree of planning was all she needed to move forward with her thinking and her writing. These bullet points clarified and organized her understandings. After this written phase of planning, she took a moment to mentally plan what she would write. She talked her way through the planning notes as a rehearsal of what she would write. Because this was a homework assignment, she was also able to verify the connections she had made with her earth science textbook to confirm her understandings. Finally, she reflected on how she would put what she wanted to say into words and began to write. This combination of planning steps facilitated her ability to write a clear, cohesive response to the complex question.

Why Don't Students Plan Their Writing?

When students say they do not plan their writing it is because either (1) they do not know how, (2) they do not recognize what they do is planning, (3) they do not find planning helpful because they have not discovered a planning approach that fits or suits their thinking style, or (4) they think it is too time-consuming. In short, they have not experienced the value or benefits of planning for various reasons or because they are planning in ways other than in ways they have been taught and recognize as viable planning strategies.

Yet we know that most effective writers plan considerably before, during, and after they write. And we know that writers plan their writing in many different ways that suit their cognitive styles. Therefore, we have to help students not only to see but also to experience the benefits and value of planning.

Best Practices in Planning Writing

To help students prepare for writing and see the benefits and value in planning, we need to set the stage. There should be a creative atmosphere in the room that invites students to share their ideas openly and provide constructive criticism to their peers. The environment should reflect a risk-free zone in which both convergent and divergent thinking are encouraged and collaboration and consultation are integral. All writers are seen as experts in generating ideas and planning the contents and structure of written pieces. The teacher models and encourages purposeful planning. He introduces various approaches for planning and offers various resources, tools, and opportunities to extend planning through peer collaboration. He is open and welcoming to diverse methods of planning that students find helpful.

The teacher who values and promotes planning knows that the level of a student's transcription skills will influence it. He knows that when a student's transcription skills are automatic, the student will be able to dedicate her working and short-term memory to planning and higher level composing (Wong & Berninger, 2004). When a student's efforts are focused on transforming sounds into orthographic symbols, she has less brain capacity to think about the content and structure of her writing. Therefore, teachers working with students who are developmentally contributing much of their writing efforts to cognitively working on phonics and spelling will want to provide concrete planning opportunities for students so less of the planning of writing is left to abstract thinking. This holds true for English language learners as well. Teachers will work with these students to graphically, visually, and perhaps orally through sound recording represent writing plans that can be referred to frequently while undergoing the hard work of the process of transcribing ideas.

Planning processes vary depending on the genre and situational factors, such as the amount of time allowed and the familiarity the student may have with a topic or assignment. When a student writes from personal experience, details may come to mind more automatically than when the student has to research a topic about which she is less familiar. The same is true when a student works with more and less familiar genres. For example, if a student is writing to persuade her readers, she may need to research multiple perspectives on a topic to build an argument. She will need to become knowledgeable about the components of a persuasive argument, including the level of formality of the language and the tone of expertise to use. A writer's plan for persuasive writing will reflect which arguments and counterarguments and supporting details and examples will be used to strengthen her writing. A writer who is new to writing persuasively will need to spend time planning the structure of her writing and then will insert her arguments into the structure. We can see how less familiar genres would require writers to invest additional time planning.

Components of the Planning Process

While planning is frequently seen as a prewriting activity that ends when a graphic organizer or semantic map is constructed, we see it as an ongoing thought process. Planning continues from the writer's initial thinking about the topic through the presentation of a final draft. The following steps reflect possible components of the planning process based on cognitive models of writing, research on writing instruction, and our collective experiences in working with kindergarten through college writers (Alamargot & Chanquoy, 2001; Bereiter & Scardamalia, 1987; Deane et al., 2008; Elbow, 1973, 1981; Lassonde, 2009a, 2009b; Richards & Lassonde, 2011). These steps are not linear, occurring one after the other in a one-way sequence. We see them, rather, as recursive, meaning a writer might move among the steps in a forward or backward progression based on the ebb and flow of the writing.

Step 1: Contemplating the Task and the Writing

Students—especially those at higher grade levels—are frequently expected to respond to prompts to construct or demonstrate their knowledge and understandings, such as Xixi was by her earth science teacher. Xixi realized task analysis was a necessary step to planning her response, including details such as:

- What is the question or assignment asking me to demonstrate or do?
- What concepts, vocabulary, and language will I incorporate?
- Is there a particular structure to my response, such as showing a cause-and-effect relationship?
- Is there a scoring rubric that will guide my writing?
- Is the piece to be objective or subjective, critically reflective or report-like?
- Is there a specified required page length?

As writers we have to contemplate and make decisions not only about what but how we will write. For example, to shape our writing we need to know the audience and purpose. Will the piece be read aloud to others, posted on a blog, sent to the reader, or shared with others at all? Are we trying to persuade, inform, or entertain readers? Our writing purpose and the audience will influence the writing genre and the structure of our writing. What will be the mood and style of the piece? Based on who the readers will be, is it more appropriate to use formal or informal language in our writing? What type of background knowledge will readers need to comprehend our writing? These are all decisions writers will make as they are planning their writing.

Step 2: Activating Prior Knowledge about the Topic

Whether a student is responding to a writing task or creating an original text, she will have to begin by thinking about what she knows and how she feels about the topic. She will activate her prior knowledge about the topic by reflecting on everything she knows about it and concepts that relate to it (Richards & Lassonde, 2011). She will make connections between the topic and what she knows and feels. When thinking about her feelings in relation to the topic, she will have to be honest with herself and will want to think about how her feelings might influence how and what she writes.

The student will also want to think deeply about what she does not know about the topic. Will it be necessary or helpful to do some research—through reading or field work—to fill in any gaps in her knowledge? How much of an expert on the topic will she need to be to write well?

Step 3: Considering Vocabulary and Language Use

The vocabulary choices we make in our writing will reveal our knowledge of the topic. Often writers who are just learning the vocabulary or jargon used in talking about a particular field of study will "use but abuse" the words they choose. They are newly acquainted with some of the terminology and use it inappropriately. When writers plan their writing, they will want to explore the terms and concepts that are acquainted with a topic and learn to use them accurately in their writing. Furthermore, what level of vocabulary should be used based on the reading level or expertise of readers? And, which is more appropriate, formal or informal language?

Step 4: Organizing Ideas

Once the writer has generated some ideas and has begun to explore the concepts and words to incorporate into her writing, she will begin to put these ideas into words. In organizing her thoughts, she will make connections and contemplate the relationships among various ideas. In this way, she will plan how to organize her writing in a meaningful way. At this point she not only has to think about what makes sense to her but also what will help her readers understand the topic and her ideas about the topic. Writers organize ideas so readers can understand the message. There are various strategies for organizing writing, such as using graphic organizers and outlines, and selecting the appropriate genre to fit the structure and demands of a topic and purpose. Organizing might also involve synthesizing them. As a writer reflects on the relationships and connections among her ideas, she will note that in some places she needs to "tighten up" her thinking. This task will involve doing some replanning to smooth over rough areas that don't connect well or are perhaps redundant (Lassonde, 2008). This step involves "planning on the go," as the writer clarifies and confirms the organization of a piece based on the purpose and audience.

Step 5: Ongoing Planning

As the writing progresses, the planning continues. The writer may discover she needs more information to fill gaps, or she wants to omit a section or go in a different direction. This back-and-forth motion between planning and writing continues throughout the whole process. As we reflect on our writing, we may discover we need to go back to a previous step in planning to look up the meanings of content-specific words we want to add. Through peer conferring, we may see that our readers cannot understand part of our piece because we left something out. It will take further planning to determine what is missing and where it should be explained.

Planning Strategies

Once young students know the basic structure of stories and older students know the structure of various types of informational text we believe they need to learn about different ways to plan their work. Then they won't think planning is boring, time-consuming, and worthless because they can determine what invention strategies best suit their diverse ways of thinking and perhaps the writing task. There is no one-size-fits-all prewriting plan (Richards & Miller, 2005). We saw this reality in the opening section in the description of how Cindy and Janet collaborated through the initial planning of this chapter. Cindy worked through a linear outline and Janet began by writing. They found talking through their drafting helped them co-construct their philosophy of planning.

One thing we are sure of is that planning a writing task does not have to be tiresome and unexciting. If we model various ways of planning writing for students that take into account and connect to students' preferred ways of thinking, they will discover not only the benefits of planning writing, but also learn that planning writing can be interesting, beneficial, and even fun. Here are some of our favorite planning approaches. We model these strategies for young students, older students, and even our graduate education majors. All of the strategies have been classroom-tested and proven effective

Simply Think

One way to plan writing is to simply think about the writing topic. E. B. White (1995) and Donald Murray (1982) refer to this thinking as an "essential delay." Teachers might model for their students how to think about a writing task and then provide time for students to "think" about how they will form their writing according to content and writing goals. At the end of each "thinking time" students can jot down all of the ideas that popped into their head. Then, at the end of a week, students might organize all of these thoughts into a cohesive structure that fits the writing genre (Richards & Miller, 2005).

Inquiry

Another planning strategy is inquiry (Lassonde, 2009b). Students can write down all of the questions they have about a topic. They also might interview others to find out what questions they have about the topic. These questions, when ordered according to superordinate and subordinate information can serve as a writing plan.

Sketch Journals

Sketch journals in which writers draw pictures of characters, places, processes, sequences, and so forth offer another way to plan writing. When developing a character, for example, a writer might sketch what the character looks like and the setting, or the problem and solution, to spark creative story ideas and descriptive vocabulary (Richards & Miller, 2005).

Various Types of Graphic Organizers

A number of authors use visual representations to help them see connections and relationships. "Drawing slows us down and helps us notice – important skills for writers" (Ernst da Silva, 2001, p. 4). Of course, teachers are familiar with concept maps and webs. Graphic displays, such as genre organizers that help writers sequence or structure a piece and content maps that allow writers to illustrate connections among ideas, help to represent an author's knowledge by visually representing relationships. "Like exemplary writing, good concept maps are usually the product of several drafts. Therefore, it is important that authors continue to refine and revise their concept maps as they extend and enhance their thinking" (Richards & Miller, 2005, p. 74).

Free Writing and Quick Writes

Many well-known writers including Elbow (2000) just sit down and engage in free writing or quick writes as a type of invention. Engaging in a free write allows students to write nonstop without worrying about spelling or punctuation. They just write to get their ideas on paper and then see what they know and still need to know about a topic. Of course, to free write, a writer has to have a large amount of schema about the writing topic, or she cannot generate ideas.

Talking into a Tape Recorder

Some writers plan by thinking aloud and talking into a tape recorder. Then they transcribe their ideas and discover where and how they need to rearrange their piece. This strategy is especially helpful to students who struggle with transcription or language production. English language learners can record the story in their native language so they don't forget their ideas. As they listen to the recording of their story, they can create a graphic organizer or draft from which they can begin writing (Richards & Miller, 2005).

Three-by-Five Note Cards

Another way to plan writing is to place information about a topic on separate index cards. Then students can rearrange the cards, placing those with related ideas together. Kinesthetic learners like this index card planning because they can move the cards around, which accommodates their learning style (Richards & Miller, 2005).

Outlining

The tried-and-true method of constructing an outline to organize one's ideas still helps many students plan their writing. This strategy is helpful particularly to writers who think in a linear fashion. Fulwiler (2002) calls outlines "organized lists" (p. 39). Outlining can be combined with other strategies, such as the inquiry or index-card approaches, to help bring order and sequence to groups of ideas or goals.

Technology

There is no doubt that technology enhances students' abilities to plan their writing. The ease of deleting, moving, and expanding a sentence or paragraph as a writer composes on a computer is helpful to many reluctant planners. Technology has transformed all stages of the writing process (Berninger & Winn, 2006). Students, for example, can be taught how to use the Outline feature in Microsoft Word to plan their writing during and after drafting. They only have to click on View and Outline to create an outline of a word-processed report.

Frequently, students compose not only in word-processing programs but also in other programs, such as PowerPoint and MovieMaker. Planning for digital and visual representations of one's ideas opens a whole new world of planning for students. Cindy has used storyboards—comic strip-like boxed sketches of scenes and sequences—with developing writers to help them plan their digital presentations (Lassonde, 2009a). Even the planning stage can be displayed digitally rather than with pencil and paper.

Combining Planning Strategies

Another idea to encourage learners to plan their writing is to offer mini-lessons that help them consider and combine planning strategies (Richards & Miller, 2005). For example, Janet's grandson, Noah, now uses a word-processing system to jot down the questions he and his peers have devised about his chosen writing topic. Joshua who loves to draw now draws and labels his ideas on 3"-by-5" notecards. Then he arranges and rearranges the cards until he is satisfied he has placed related ideas together. He can also recognize gaps in the notecards, which indicates where he needs to do some more necessary research on a topic. Maddie, who is always stressed because of lack of time, now employs "thinking time" to plan her writing. She keeps her writer's journal nearby to jot down random ideas so she can get into "thinking time mode" anytime about a piece she plans to write.

Adaptations

An unparalleled level of transnational migration has changed the face of our nation's schools. The numbers of students with limited English proficiency is quickly growing, doubling to over 5 million school-age students in just one decade (Hawkins, 2004). Writing teachers are responsible for and legally mandated to meet the literacy and learning needs of this increasing number of language-diverse students (Individuals with Disabilities Education Improvement Act, 2004) along with all of the students in their classes (Elementary and Secondary Education Act, 2004).

The beginning stages of writing development for English language learners are similar to those of first-language students (Araujo, 2011). For older students, complex writing requirements, especially involving writing in the content areas, can make writing to communicate and to learn very difficult tasks. "It will be [hard] for students to utilize strategies to write . . . if they are not fluent in the lower-level skills" (Graham & Perin, 2007, p. 24).

Teaching planning strategies can help students write to communicate, to express their understandings, and to learn. English language learners and other writers who struggle frequently benefit from strategies that encourage them to activate their prior knowledge of a topic and the vocabulary that goes along with it, talk with peers to broaden their understandings, and organize their ideas before beginning to put their ideas down on paper. Several classroom-tested planning strategies help English language learners and other writers succeed in generating and forming ideas, words, and sentence structure as they plan their writing (Matthews-Somerville & Garin, 2011; Richards & Lassonde, 2011). Here are several suggestions:

- *Peer collaborative planning.* Encourage peers to talk about their planning. Pair up partners who can complement each other's skills and assist each other in generating language and ideas, and transcribing words to construct a writing plan.
- *Technology aids.* Facilitate the use of electronic graphic organizers, outlining tools, and other technological resources. Allow students to tape-record and rehearse their stories to assist in planning.

- *Link the writing to shared experiences.* Talk individually with the student to help her to generate ideas and a plan for drafting.
- *Engage writers.* Use sensory perception and creative dramatic exercises to think about how they relate to the topic.

Concluding Comments

Whether we teach elementary, middle school, high school, or graduate students, we are all writing teachers. And, whether we teach language arts, English, earth science, or physics, we still are all writing teachers. We all seek to quantifiably improve students' writing skills. Teaching and modeling planning strategies will help students develop as writers if we teach them strategies that fit their learning and writing styles. As we see in this chapter, authors—even the coauthors of this chapter—go about planning their writing in different ways. Therefore, the planning approach writing teachers use must corral writers' enthusiasm and directly connect with the ways they understand planning and writing for an audience or readers.

The topics and issues described and explored in this chapter expand upon what current research has to say about planning. As writing teachers we have combined our teaching experiences with what we know about planning and writing from current literature to present a symphony of planning that causes readers to pause their thinking about planning and begin to recognize its vast importance in teaching and motivating our students to write.

Planning. It isn't *just* a prewriting strategy. Planning encompasses, shows, and shapes who we are as writers.

References

Alamargot, D., & Chanquoy, L. (2001). *Through the models of writing.* Dortrech, The Netherlands: Kluwer Academic.

Applebee, A. N. (1986). Problems in process approaches: Toward a reconceptualization of process instruction. In A. R. Petrosky & D. Bartholomae (Eds.), *The teaching of writing: Eighty-fifth yearbook of the National Society for the Study of Education* (Part 2, pp. 95–113). Chicago: National Society for Studies in Education.

Araujo, L. (2011). The writing development of English language learners. In J. F. Christie, E. J. Enz, & C. Vukelich (Eds.), *Teaching language and literacy: Preschool through the elementary grades, fourth edition* (pp. 337–339). New York: Pearson Education.

Bereiter, C., & Scardamalia, M. (1987). *The psychology of written composition.* Hillsdale, NJ: Erlbaum.

Berninger, V., & Winn, W. (2006). Implications of advancements in brain research and technology for writing development, writing instruction, and educational evolution. In C. MacArthur, S. Graham, & J. Fitzgerald (Eds.), *Handbook of writing research* (pp. 96–114). New York: Guilford Press.

Berninger, V., Whitaker, D., Feng, Y., Swanson, H., & Abbott, R. (1996). Assessment of planning, translating, and revising in junior high writers. *Journal of School Psychology, 34*(1), 23–52.

Bloodgood, J. (2002). Quintilian: A classical educator speaks to the writing process. *Reading Research and Instruction, 42*(1), 30–43.

Boscolo, P. (2008). Writing in primary school. In C. Bazerman (Ed.), *Handbook of research on writing: History, society, school, individual, text* (pp. 293–310). New York: Erlbaum.

Deane, P., Odendahl, N., Quinlan, T., Fowles, M., Welsh., C., & Bivens-Taum, J. (2008, October). *Cognitive models of writing: Writing proficiency as a complex integrated skill.* Princeton, NJ: Educational Testing Service.

Elbow, P. (1973). *Writing without teachers.* New York: Oxford University Press.

Elbow, P. (1981). *Writing with power: Techniques for mastering the writing process.* New York: Oxford University Press.

Elbow, P. (2000). *Everyone can write: Essays toward a hopeful theory of writing and teaching writing.* New York: Oxford University Press.

Elementary and Secondary Education Act. (2004). Public Law 107-110. Retrieved November 21, 2011, from *www2.ed.gov/policy/elsec/leg/esea02/107–110. pdf.*

Ernst da Silva, K. (2001). Drawing on experience: Connecting art and language. *Primary Voices K–6, 10*(2), 2–8.

Fletcher, R. (2000). *How writers work: Finding a process that works for you.* New York: Avon.

Fulwiler, T. (2002). *College writing: A personal approach to academic writing* (3rd ed.). Portsmouth, NH: Boynton/Cook Heinemann.

Galbraith, D. (1996). Self-monitoring, discovery through writing, and individual differences in drafting strategy. In. G. Rijlaarsdam, H. van den Bergh, & M. Couzijn (Eds.), *Theories, models and methodology in writing research* (pp. 121–141). Amsterdam: Amsterdam University Press.

Galbraith, D. (2009). Writing as discovery. *British Journal of Educational Psychology Monograph Series II, (6),* 1–27.

Graham, S. (2006). Strategy instruction and the teaching of writing: A meta-analysis. In C. A. MacArthur, S. Graham, & J. Fitzgerald (Eds.), *Handbook of writing research* (pp. 187–207). New York: Guilford Press.

Graham, S., & Harris, K. R. (2005). *Writing better: Teaching writing processes and self-regulation to students with learning problems.* Baltimore: Brookes.

Graham, S., & Perin, D. (2007). *Writing next: Effective strategies to improve writing of adolescents in middle and high schools—A report to Carnegie Corporation of New York.* Washington, DC: Alliance for Excellent Education.

Hawkins, M. R. (2004). Researching English language and literacy development in schools. *Educational Researcher, 33,* 14–25.

Hayes, J. R. (1996). A new framework for understanding cognition and affect in writing. In C. M. Levy & S. Ransdell (Eds.), *The science of writing: Theories, methods, individual differences and applications* (pp. 1–27). Hillsdale, NJ: Erlbaum.

Hillocks, G. Jr. (1986). *Research on written composition*. Urbana, IL: National Council on Rehabilitation Education.

Individuals with Disabilities Education Improvement Act. (2004). Public Law 108-446. Retrieved November 21, 2011, from *www.copyright.gov/legislation/pl108-446.pdf*.

Inhelder, B., & Piaget, J. (1958). *The growth of logical thinking from childhood to adolescence*. New York: Basic Books.

Judson, P. (2001). *Action research: How will direct instruction in prewriting strategies affect the quality of written products and student attitude toward their writing?* Minnesota Writing Project. Retrieved from *http://writing.umn.edu/mwp/summer/2001/judson.html*.

Langer, J. A., & Applebee, A. N. (2007). *How writing shapes thinking: A study of teaching and learning*. Retrieved online from WAC Clearinghouse Landmark Publications in Writing Studies at *http://wac.colostate.edu/books/langer_applebee*. [Originally published in print, 1987, by National Council of Teachers of English, Urbana, IL]

Lassonde, C. (2008). *New York State grade 6 English language arts test*. Hauppauge, NY: Barron's.

Lassonde, C. (2009a). Recognizing a "different drum." *Networks: An Online Journal for Teacher Research, 11*(1). Available online at *http://journals.library.wisc.edu/index.php/networks*.

Lassonde, C. (2009b). Transforming philosophy and pedagogy through critical inquiry. *New England Reading Association Journal, 44*(2), 41–50.

Litt, D. (2011). Reread so you know what to write next. In J. Richards & C. Lassonde (Eds.), *Writing strategies for all primary students: Scaffolding independent writing with differentiated mini-lessons* (pp. 117–122). San Francisco: Jossey-Bass.

Matthews-Somerville, R., & Garin, E. (2011). Writing strategy instruction for struggling writers. In J. Richards & C. Lassonde (Eds.), *Writing strategies for all primary students: Scaffolding independent writing with differentiated mini-lessons* (pp. 55–72). San Francisco: Jossey-Bass.

MacArthur, C., & Graham, S. (1987). Learning disabled students composing under three methods of text production: Handwriting, word processing, and dictation. *Journal of Special Education, 21*(3), 22–42.

McCutchen, D. (2006). Cognitive factors in the development of children's writing. In C. A. MacArthur, S. Graham, & J. Fitzgerald (Eds.), *Handbook of writing research* (pp. 115–130). New York: Guilford Press.

Murray, D. (1992). Teach writing as a process not a product. In D. Murray (Ed.), *Learning by teaching: Selected articles on writing and teaching* (pp. 14–17). Portsmouth, NH: Boynton/Cook Heinemann.

National Governors Association & Council of Chief State School Officers. *Common Core State Standards for English language arts & literacy in history/social studies, science, and technical subjects*. Washington, DC: Authors. Retrieved from *www.corestandards.org*.

Piolat, A., Roussey, J. Y., Olive, T., & Farioli, F. (1996). Mental load and mobilization of editorial processes: Review of the procedure of Kellogg. *French Psychology, 41,* 339–354.

Richards, J. R., & Lassonde, C. A. (2011). *Writing strategies for all primary students: Scaffolding independent writing with differentiated mini-lessons.* San Francisco: Jossey-Bass.

Richards, J. R., & Miller, S. (2005). *Doing academic writing: Connecting the personal and the professional.* Mahwah, NJ: Lawrence Erlbaum.

Richards, J. R., & Miller, S. (2010). *Doing academic writing: Connecting the personal and the professional.* Mahwah, NJ: Erlbaum (in e-book format).

Torrence, M., & Galbraith, D. (2006). The processing demands of writing. In C. A. MacArthur, S. Graham, & J. Fitzgerald (Eds.), *Handbook of writing research.* (pp. 67–80). New York: Guilford Press.

White, E. B. (1995). Sootfalls and fallout. In C. Anderson & L. Runciman (Eds.), *A forest of voices* (pp. 492–500). Mountain View, CA: Mayfield.

Wong, B. Y. L., & Berninger, V. W. (2004). Cognitive processes of teachers in implementing composition research in elementary, middle, and high school classrooms. In C. A. Stone, E. R. Silliman, B. J. Ehren, & K. Apel (Eds.), *Handbook of language and literacy: Development and disorders* (pp. 600–624). New York: Guilford Press.

Chapter 9

Best Practices in Teaching Evaluation and Revision

CHARLES A. MacARTHUR

Preservationists at the Library of Congress studying early drafts of the Declaration of Independence using the latest visualization technology recently discovered that Jefferson had changed "our fellow *subjects*" to "our fellow *citizens*" (Kaufman, 2010). This revision from "subjects" of a distant king to "citizens" of a new country symbolizes the revolutionary change to a democratic government. It also illustrates the importance of revision for accomplished writers trying to match their meaning and style to their rhetorical purposes.

Proficient adult writers revise frequently both during writing and after completing a draft. They evaluate their writing in terms of their goals and audience and make changes in overall organization and content as well as smaller changes in language and conventions (Hayes, 2004; MacArthur, 2012). In contrast, students at the elementary and secondary school levels generally do little substantive revising (Fitzgerald, 1987). Teachers often find it difficult to get students to engage in meaningful revision that goes beyond editing for errors or adding minor details.

Revision is an important aspect of the composing process, mentioned in the Common Core State Standards (National Governors Association & Council of Chief State School Officers, 2010), and included in some form in nearly all approaches to writing instruction. From an instructional perspective, revision is important for two reasons. First, as already noted, revising is an important aspect of the composing process that is used extensively by proficient writers. When writers revise, they have an opportunity to think about whether their text communicates effectively to an audience, to improve the quality of their prose, and even to reconsider their content and perspective, and, potentially, to transform their own understanding. To become proficient writers, students must learn to revise effectively.

Second, in an instructional context, revising provides an opportunity for teachers to guide students in learning about the characteristics of effective writing in ways that will not only improve the current piece, but that will also carry over to future writing (MacArthur, 2012). In learning to revise, students get feedback from readers on their work, learn to evaluate their writing, and discover new ways to solve common writing problems. Thus, revising is a way to learn about the craft of writing.

The purpose of this chapter is to provide guidance to teachers on ways to help their students develop revision skills and to teach revising in a way that improves overall writing ability. The information in the chapter is based on research on revising processes and on instructional methods. The chapter has three sections. First, I describe cognitive models of revising to provide a framework for understanding what students need to develop. Second, I review research on instructional methods for revising. Third, I provide classroom examples of revising instruction that incorporate approaches to teaching and supporting revision based on the research.

Cognitive Models of Revising

What do proficient writers do when they revise? Answers to this question can help us understand what less proficient writers need to learn and can inform the design of instruction. The most prominent models of the cognitive processes involved in writing have been developed (and revised) by Hayes and his colleagues (Hayes, Flower, Schriver, Stratman, & Carey, 1987; Hayes, 2004) and Bereiter and Scardamalia (1987). The discussion here is based on those models with an emphasis on the most instructionally relevant aspects. I would like to make several points about revising processes.

First, theoretical models of revising use a broad definition of revising that includes "changes made at any point in the writing process" (Fitzgerald, 1987, p. 484). Thus, revision includes mental evaluation and revision of sentences before writing them, changes in text during writing, and even changes in plans, as well as evaluation and revision of completed drafts. In contrast, in practice, teachers and even researchers view revision more narrowly as changes to text already written. Teachers have the greatest opportunity to teach students about good writing when students evaluate and change what they have already written. However, it is worthwhile keeping in mind that what students learn while revising can be applied during writing in ways that are not visible to the teacher.

Second, proficient writers have relatively sophisticated conceptions of and goals for revising. They see revising as a matter of evaluating all aspects of their writing that affect whether they have achieved their goals and purposes. They keep their overall purposes and audience in mind as they evaluate the organization and content of their paper as well as the language and errors. They look not only for problems in their writing, but also for opportunities to expand their ideas and communicate more clearly. Some expert writers make revision even more central to their composing processes (Galbraith & Torrance, 2004). Instead of planning extensively, they write quickly to explore their ideas and then evaluate what they have written to identify useful ideas to explore in future drafts (see Lassonde & Richards, Chapter 8, this volume, for further discussion of this approach to planning and revising). This approach to writing is what Murray (1991) had in mind when he wrote that "writing *is* revising, and the writer's craft is largely a matter of knowing how to discover what you have to say, develop, and clarify it, each requiring the craft of revision" (p. 2).

In contrast, struggling writers have limited conceptions of revising and unclear goals and purposes for writing. They have narrow conceptions of revising as correcting errors and making a neat copy (MacArthur, Graham, & Schwartz, 1991; McCutchen, Francis, & Kerr, 1997). In addition, they may not have clear goals and purposes for their writing as a whole. It is possible to get students to make more substantive revisions simply by giving them specific goals for revising. For example, in one study (Graham, MacArthur, & Schwartz, 1995) students made more substantive revisions and improved their papers when given a simple goal of adding ideas to make their papers more interesting. In another study (Midgette, Haria, & MacArthur, 2008) students produced better persuasive essays when given a goal to revise with a specific audience in mind who would disagree with their position.

Third, revising requires all the skills involved in good reading comprehension (Hayes, 2004). The writer must distance him- or herself from the writing and critically evaluate the text. To make changes in the text as a whole, for example, the writer must construct the gist of the text by attending to the main ideas and organization. Or, to identify problems of clarity, he or she must read as a reader and evaluate whether the content is clear with reasonable inferences. Without good reading skills, writers may read into the text their intended meanings and fail to see problems with the text as it actually exists. Reading comprehension skills parallel revision skills at all levels of text from overall organization to the sentence level. The difference is just the purpose for reading—to understand versus to identify problems and improve the text.

Fourth, proficient writers have extensive knowledge about criteria for good writing and about typical writing problems. Like English teachers,

they know to look for an interesting lead, a clear thesis, and good paragraph structure. They may automatically detect some kinds of problems
in grammar and clarity. Their knowledge includes general criteria as well
as criteria specific to particular kinds of texts. For exampler, in revising
a persuasive essay, they know that a good essay should consider opposing positions in a respectful way and marshal arguments against them.
(See Ferretti & Lewis, Chapter 5, this volume, for discussion of critical
questions for argumentative writing.) This knowledge of evaluation criteria and typical problems helps them to detect and diagnose specific problems in their texts. In contrast, younger and less proficient writers know
little about evaluating writing. Typical upper elementary school students,
when asked why they like one paper more than another, cite length, spelling, topic, and general characteristics, such as "It's funny" (MacArthur,
Graham, & Schwartz, 1991). When they do detect problems, they often
decide to rewrite the sentence rather than diagnose and fix the greater
problem.

Finally, proficient writers have solid metacognitive, self-regulation
skills. They can switch flexibly to evaluation and revision during writing when they notice problems or have a new idea. When revising a draft,
they can manage the multiple processes involved—keeping audience and
purpose in mind while critically reading the text and considering possible
changes. In contrast, less proficient writers have difficulty managing the
complexity of the writing process. Thus, they may restrict their revising to
problems at the sentence level. De La Paz, Swanson, and Graham (1998)
found that struggling writers could make revisions at the overall organizational level if they were provided with procedural support in the form of
prompts to consider the text as a whole before evaluating sentences.

These cognitive aspects of revising—goals and concepts of revising, critical reading skills, knowledge of evaluation criteria, and self-
regulation—are connected to the types of revising instruction that research
has found to be effective.

Research on Revising Instruction

In this section, I review the existing research on several instructional
approaches or methods. Further research is needed, but the findings are
generally consistent across instructional studies and consistent with cognitive models of revising.

Teacher Feedback

The most common approach to teaching writing, whether in high school
and college composition courses or in elementary school writing workshops,

is to provide feedback to students and ask them to revise. Feedback can be provided by teachers, peers, or more recently by computers. A recent review of research on formative assessment confirmed that feedback, in general, had positive effects on student writing (Graham, Harris, & Hebert, 2011). Int particular, verbal feedback from teachers or feedback on learning skills and strategies had positive effects. An earlier review by Hillocks (1986) found that written feedback from teachers was generally ineffective. From a practical perspective, the effects probably depend on the nature of the feedback. Feedback that is supportive, that explains problems and makes specific suggestions, and that helps students reflect on the rhetorical purpose of the writing is more effective (Beach & Friedrich, 2006). Teacher feedback provided in conferences may be more effective. Frequent teacher conferences are a key component of process approaches to writing instruction, which generally have positive effects when teachers receive professional development (Graham & Perin, 2007).

Peer Review

Peer review is a common feature of writing process classrooms, and it is often recommended as a way of providing student writers with an audience of readers who can respond to their writing, identify strengths and weaknesses, and recommend improvements. Peers can provide feedback that is more frequent and immediate than teachers' feedback. However, peer review also presents difficulties. When peers are asked to engage in peer review without specific guidance, they often are reluctant to criticize each other or are unable to provide significant help because their own evaluation and revision skills are limited.

However, when peer revising is integrated with instruction in evaluation and revision, peer interaction can be effective. Two recent reviews of writing research (Graham et al., 2011; Graham & Perin, 2007) found positive effects for peer review. For example, Boscolo and Ascorti (2004), in a study of elementary and middle school students, focused on the issue of clarity or comprehensibility, that is, understanding what readers might find difficult to understand. Students wrote personal narratives and worked in pairs to evaluate and revise them using the following procedure: the student serving as editor read until he or she found an unclear point, asked the author for clarification, and then discussed with the author how to fix the text until a change was agreed upon and made. The students improved their ability to identify comprehension problems in text and their own ability to write text without such problems.

Peer review is a reciprocal process, so students may learn as much from giving feedback as from receiving it. Giving feedback requires students to read critically and apply evaluation criteria. Two studies with college students (Cho & MacArthur, 2011; Lundstrom & Baker, 2009) found that experience giving feedback helped students to improve the quality of their own papers. A recent study has extended these findings to upper elementary students (Philippakos, 2012). In this study, all students were given a rubric for evaluating persuasive writing and shown how to apply it to evaluate strong and weak papers. Then one group used the rubric to evaluate papers written by unknown peers and to make suggestions for improvement. Another group read the same papers, and a control group read unrelated material. The reviewers improved the quality of their own writing compared to both other groups. This study has practical instructional implications. It is easy and time-efficient to give students the opportunity to apply evaluation rubrics to papers written by unknown peers, and it helps them to improve their own papers. This experience could be an effective way to train students for actual peer review.

Evaluation Criteria and Self-Evaluation

At the center of skill in revision is knowledge of evaluation criteria and the ability to apply them to one's own writing. Some research has directly taught students to apply specific criteria, or rubrics, to evaluate and revise their papers. Hillocks, in his meta-analysis of writing instruction studies (1986), reported that six studies using this approach found moderately strong effects on revision and writing quality. The recent review by Graham and colleagues (2011) confirmed the positive effects of self-evaluation. These studies are related to the study of giving feedback just discussed. In addition, teaching self-evaluation is a key part of the strategy instruction methods described below.

Two factors seem to be important in designing instruction in evaluation and revising. First, specific evaluation criteria seem to be more effective than general criteria such as content and organization. One way to make criteria specific is to teach them within particular genres. For example, in teaching about narratives, one might make content and organization more specific by using evaluation criteria such as "Are all the story elements included?," "Are the characters clearly described?," and "Does it show how characters feel?" Specific criteria are easier for students to learn and easier to use in making revisions. Then as students learn about various genres, they will come to understand that organization and content are always important criteria, but that they are applied differently depending on the type of writing. Specific evaluation criteria are not always genre-related. For example, criteria of clarity (Is there anything difficult to understand?) and detail (Where could I add information to make it more interesting?) are also specific enough to teach.

Second, it's important not only to teach students to evaluate their papers but also to give support and practice in applying the criteria in making specific revisions. One way to practice such application is to display papers with particular kinds of problems on a chart or overhead projector and then model and discuss how to apply a particular evaluation criterion and revise the paper to improve it. For example, in teaching the criteria of clarity, the teacher might display papers with missing information or unclear referents and guide students to find the problems by asking questions about the content. Then the teacher and students could collaboratively generate sentences that would clarify the content. Students may need extensive practice to learn to apply the criteria and to make revisions to solve problems.

Critical Reading

A few studies have improved revising skills by asking students to read texts critically and identify comprehension problems. For example, Holliway and McCutchen (2004) had students write descriptions of tangram figures (i.e., shapes of people, animals, etc. made from geometric blocks). Then one group received feedback on the accuracy of their descriptions, while a second group read other students' descriptions and tried to use them to identify one tangram figure from a group of four similar figures. Students who had the reading experience were better able to revise their own descriptions and to write better first-draft descriptions as well. This study demonstrated the importance of critical reading, but it used a rather artificial writing task.

Another study investigated the effects of being a reader on the more common task of writing a persuasive letter (Moore & MacArthur, 2012). Students met in small groups to discuss a set of three persuasive letters that varied in quality. Their task was to discuss the letters and evaluate whether they were persuasive and why; the discussion was structured with a few questions about audience and purpose. Compared to a control group that spent the same amount of time practicing writing additional persuasive letters, this group of collaborative readers made more substantive revisions to their writing, resulting in improved overall quality.

Word Processing

Computers are powerful and flexible writing tools that can support writing in many ways, particularly for struggling writers (for a review, see MacArthur, 2006). They can ease the physical process of writing, enable students to produce error-free final copies, support publication, and make revision possible without tedious recopying. However, using a word processor by itself has not been shown to result in more or better revision. Word processing in combination with writing instruction does appear to have modest positive effects on writing quality, especially for struggling writers. Furthermore, research that has focused specifically on teaching revising strategies in combination with use of a word processor has found improvements in revising and writing quality. It is easier to teach revising strategies if students can do the revisions on a word processor because students are less reluctant to apply revising strategies they have learned.

Strategy Instruction

One of the most extensively studied and effective approaches to teaching revising is cognitive strategy instruction. Graham (2006) reviewed six studies that taught revising strategies and another five that taught a combination of planning and revising. He reported large and consistent positive effects on the amount of revision and the quality of writing. Most of the studies included teaching students to self-evaluate their writing using specific criteria, often criteria related to genre or text structure. For example, in one study (Graham & MacArthur, 1988), fifth- and sixth-grade students with learning disabilities (LD) learned a strategy for revising persuasive essays. The steps in the strategy guided them to (1) read the essay; (2) find the sentence that tells what you believe and ask whether it is clear; (3) add two reasons why you believe it; (4) SCAN each sentence (Does it make *sense*? Is it *connected* to my opinion? Can I *add* more? *Note* errors.); (5) make changes; and (6) reread and make final changes. The strategy included evaluation criteria related to persuasive writing as well as nongenre criteria for comprehensibility, elaboration, and errors. Students increased the number of substantive revisions and improved the quality of their papers following instruction.

Most studies of instruction in strategies for revision include multiple components. They include instruction in specific evaluation criteria, often criteria based on genre or text structure. Many of them involve interaction with peers or teachers in peer response groups or teacher conferencing. Some involve word processing. Some involve teaching strategies for both planning and revising. Programs that have been implemented for a full year are especially likely to include multiple components. In this section, I describe two intervention studies that illustrate strategy instruction in combination with other elements.

The Cognitive Strategy Instruction in Writing (CSIW) program (Englert, Raphael, Anderson, Anthony, & Stevens, 1991) was designed to teach expository writing to upper elementary school students in inclusive classrooms that included students with LD. Students learned planning and revising strategies for writing different types of expository texts (e.g., explanation and compare/contrast). In the planning strategy, students identified the topic, audience, and purpose; brainstormed content; and organized the content using a graphic organizer appropriate for the particular text structure. In the editing and revising steps, students evaluated their text alone and with a peer using a set of evaluation questions that included criteria related to the specific text structure. For example, for compare/contrast writing, evaluation questions asked whether the paper told how the two things were the same and how they were different. "Think sheets" were used to scaffold the planning and revising strategies until students internalized them. The strategies were taught over the course of a year in classroom settings that emphasized peer collaboration, teacher scaffolding, and extensive dialogue about writing processes. Teachers modeled the strategies, and peers discussed their writing and applied the revising strategy in peer review. Students with and without LD made gains in the quality of their expository writing.

Along with some colleagues, I (MacArthur, Schwartz, & Graham, 1991; Stoddard & MacArthur, 1993) studied a reciprocal peer revising strategy that included strategy instruction, peer interaction, instruction in specific evaluation criteria, and word processing. The peer review strategy included five steps, described as directions to the student serving as editor: listen as the author reads the paper; tell what you liked best; read the paper and apply the evaluation questions; discuss suggestions; and author makes changes. The evaluation questions could vary depending on the students and the type of text.

In preparation for engaging in the peer revising, students learned specific evaluation criteria and how to apply them to make revisions. For example, teachers presented the criterion of clarity as a question, "Is there anything difficult to understand?" They used the overhead projector to display examples of papers that were clear and others that had various kinds of obstacles to comprehension, such as missing information or unclear referents. They modeled evaluating and revising the papers, and students practiced applying the evaluation questions to papers by unknown peers and revising them. Finally, they engaged in the peer revising strategy using the criteria they had practiced and applying them to their own writing. Both studies demonstrated that the instruction led to more substantive revision and improved quality of writing.

Summary of the Instructional Research

In planning methods for teaching revision, teachers can choose from several approaches that are supported by research on revising processes and by instructional studies. Research on cognitive processes describes revising as a complex set of processes that depends on a writer's goals and purposes for writing, critical reading ability, knowledge of evaluation criteria and typical writing problems, and self-regulation ability. The instructional approaches discussed make sense in terms of these underlying cognitive and social processes. Peer collaboration makes sense because a major consideration in revising is whether the writing communicates effectively to an audience. In addition, peer review gives students opportunities as editors to practice critical reading and evaluation. Teaching evaluation criteria and self-evaluation processes makes sense because proficient writers use their knowledge of criteria for good writing. Teaching critical reading makes sense because rereading to revise involves all the same skills as reading comprehension, from comprehending complex sentences, to getting the gist, to making inferences. Strategy instruction makes sense because revising, like planning, is a complex process requiring writers to coordinate multiple skills and attend to multiple considerations.

Teachers should not adopt specific instructional plans directly from research studies. Rather, they need to integrate instruction in revising with the rest of their writing and reading instruction, selecting elements of evidence-based practices that work and using them in ways that maintain their effectiveness. In the next section, I describe examples of teaching revision as part of an integrated writing curriculum.

Instructional Examples

In this section, I give two examples of how revision can be taught as part of instruction. The first example describes instruction in a fourth-grade class that is learning to write narratives. The second example focuses on a unit on persuasive writing in a middle school classroom. Both examples are composites of instruction from research projects and other examples of instruction that my colleagues and I have worked on. Both examples illustrate instruction that is organized around particular genres of writing. Knowledge about common genres is an important part of students' developing understanding of writing, and genre helps to organize writing around purposes as well as making both planning and revising instruction more specific. As students learn about basic genres, they develop the ability to generalize their knowledge to new purposes and forms for writing.

Revision in a Fourth-Grade Unit on Narrative Writing

It is early November in Ms. A's fourth-grade classroom and the students are accustomed to the schedule of writing workshop three times a week. The class includes a range of abilities from a few students who are fluent and imaginative writers to a couple of students with LD who struggle with reading and writing. The writing routine includes mini-lessons, time for independent writing, sharing with peers in small groups and in whole-class readings, and teacher conferences. Students engage in prewriting and revising activities. They display their work in the classroom and publish selected pieces in a classroom magazine that is sent home to parents. They write on a wide range of self-selected and teacher-assigned topics, including personal narratives and reports on issues and content they are learning. Ms. A believes that arranging for students to share and publish their work enhances motivation and helps them see writing as a meaningful activity.

Mindful of the curriculum, which includes narrative, informative, and persuasive writing, Ms. A decides to initiate a unit on narrative writing. She teaches the class a strategy for planning and writing stories. Students learn the elements of stories—character, setting, problem or goal, actions, and resolution—and use that knowledge to plan stories before writing them (Graham & Harris, 2005). She differentiates instruction by expecting all students to plan and write papers that include all the story elements, while expecting her better writers to produce more elaborate plans and stories.

As students develop mastery in planning and writing complete stories, she introduces instruction in evaluation and revision. She sees this instruction as a way for students to focus on the quality of their stories and learn how to write stories that are more interesting and effective.

Ms. A decides to teach a peer revising strategy that combines use of evaluation criteria with the peer revising that fits with her workshop approach. Students will work in pairs taking turns as editor and author to discuss both their papers. Pairs work better than small groups because it takes too long to focus on more than two papers; in addition, in pairs, each student has a clear responsibility. The steps in the strategy, written as directions to the editor, are as follows:

1. Listen while the author reads the paper.
2. Tell what the paper was about and what you liked best about it.
3. Read the story (or listen to it again) and ask the evaluation questions: [Evaluation questions go here.]
4. Discuss the evaluation and ways to make the paper better.
5. Author makes changes.

First, she has to select evaluation criteria that are worth teaching. She decides to begin with characters because characters' personalities and the way they approach problems are central to narratives. In particular, she wants students to describe characters' personalities, feelings, and motivations. She translates these ideas into the following evaluation questions: Are the characters described clearly? Does the author show how the characters feel? Can you tell why the characters act like they do?

She begins her instruction by integrating reading and writing. She explains to her students that they can learn how to write better stories by paying attention to how other authors write. She discusses how important characters are in stories—that stories are all about characters and their problems and that we enjoy stories because we get to know the characters and see how they deal with problems. She reads the first chapter of Louis Sachar's *Dogs Don't Tell Jokes* (1991), which begins with an engaging description of Gary, the class clown. She discusses what the author tells us about the character and what the reader can predict about the problems he will have. Then she introduces the evaluation questions and asks students to discuss how the author achieved these things.

This discussion of characters in stories is presented here as an introduction to teaching students to evaluate and revise their own stories. But note that this focus on characters also makes sense as reading comprehension instruction. Thinking about the personalities and motivations of characters is an important aspect of reading comprehension. Talking about characters is a good way to begin teaching students to make inferences when they read. As noted in the beginning of this chapter, critical reading and reading to revise have much in common. In this case, the teacher chose books that used fairly direct ways of conveying character so that students would be more likely to be able to use the techniques in their own stories.

The next part of instruction is one of the key elements: teaching students to evaluate writing and to revise based on the evaluation. Ms. A explains to the students that they can use these evaluation questions to revise their own stories and those of other students. She posts the evaluation questions on a bulletin board for easy reference. Then she models the process. She begins by using stories from students in other classes so that students will feel free to criticize and revise the stories. Later, students will practice evaluating and revising their own papers with peer support. She chooses stories that have all the basic story elements but that are lacking in character development. Here is a sample story and modeling script:

One Christmas, two brothers, Jim and Thomas, went up to New Hampshire with their family. When they got there, there was a lot of snow on the ground and it was really cold out. The very next day they both went skiing. They raced each other down the hill. Jim went over a small jump and went flying in the air. He crash landed. When Thomas skied over to him, he found he had broken a leg. There was no one around because they had skied off the course. Thomas didn't know whether to stay with Jim or go for help. Finally, he skied down the hill and found the ski patrol. The ski patrol came and rescued Jim. The ambulance took him to the hospital. Luckily he was okay after his leg healed.

Ms. A: *(Reads the story and then thinks aloud.)* Okay, this story has characters, setting, a problem, and a resolution. The problem is that one of the brothers breaks a leg, and the solution is that the other one finds the ski patrol who rescue him.

Now I want to use the evaluation questions to see if I can revise the story to make it more interesting. The questions are all about characters. I'll ask all the questions and then try to revise the story. The first question is, "Are the characters described clearly?" Well, it tells me their names and that they are brothers. And they can ski. That's about all. I'd like to know more about them. I'd like to know how old they were and whether they were good skiers.

The second question is, "Does the author show how the characters feel?" It's important to know how the characters feel in a story, and it's better if the author shows us through their actions instead of just saying it. This story doesn't say anything about their feelings. How do you think they felt when Jim broke his leg?

STUDENT: Scared!

Ms. A: I bet they were scared, especially because there was no one around.

The third question is, "Can you tell why the characters do what they do?" Let's see. What did the characters do? They had a skiing accident. Is there some reason why these boys had an accident? It sounds like they went off the regular ski trails which wasn't very smart. Why did they do that? Maybe they were racing against each other. Do you have any ideas?

STUDENT: Maybe one of them dared the other to do it.

Ms. A: That's a good idea. That would explain why they did it, and make the story more interesting.

Okay. Now let's see if I can revise it. I'll add information about the characters. I think I'll make them very competitive with each other which would explain why they were racing and got into trouble. Okay. "One Christmas, two brothers, Jim and Thomas, went up to New Hampshire with their family." I'll add some information here. "They were 12 years old and they were looking forward to skiing, which was their favorite sport." There, that tells us that they knew how to ski. "They were twins and were always trying to beat each other." Okay, that gives them a reason to be racing.

(reading) "When they got there, there was a lot of snow on the ground and it was really cold out. The very next day they both went skiing. They raced each other down the hill." Okay, I'm

going to add something here about the dare. Let's see. "They both wanted to be the first one down the hill. Jim yelled to Thomas, 'I'm taking a shortcut through the woods. Bet you can't follow me. Jim turned into the woods and Thomas raced after him."

Ms. A continues the revising, adding information about Jim's pain from the broken leg and how scared they both were. When she is done, she reads the story and discusses how much better it is now because you can tell more about the characters and why they acted like they did.

After this initial modeling, Ms. A provides ample practice with the whole class and in collaborative groups. She displays stories of varying quality on the overhead projector and engages students in applying the evaluation questions and, when they identify weaknesses, in revising the story. She begins with whole-class practice, which gives the students a chance to see other students applying the strategy and gives her a chance to prompt and guide students. However, whole-class practice doesn't engage enough students actively. Therefore, she also has students work on papers in small groups. Working together, each group evaluates a paper and makes revisions. Ms. A visits with the groups and gives feedback on their use of the evaluation and revising process. All groups work on the same papers so that they can discuss their evaluations and revisions in whole-class discussion.

When Ms. A thinks that the students have some understanding of the evaluation criteria, she introduces the full peer revising strategy. She posts the strategy with the evaluation questions on the board. Then she models the strategy with the help of her teaching aide. The aide reads a paper she has written, and the teacher thinks aloud to model how she applies the evaluation questions. Then the two have a discussion about how to revise the paper to improve on those criteria.

After this point, students begin using the strategy in pairs to evaluate and revise their own papers. Ms. A requires the students to take notes on the evaluations and suggestions made by the editor to compare to the actual revisions. She conducts conferences with the pairs asking them to show her how they applied the strategy. This gives her an opportunity to see whether students are using the strategy successfully and to give appropriate support. If she sees that a number of students are having trouble with one of the evaluation criteria, she can provide more modeling and practice in the whole-class group.

One of the challenges of strategy instruction in general is to get students to see the value of the strategy so they will be motivated to continue to use and improve it. Ms. A does several things to promote this sense of the value of the strategy. First, when she conferences with pairs of students, she gives feedback to students both on how well they used the strategy and on the quality of their papers. This combined feedback encourages the students to see how the strategy helps their writing. Second, when students share their papers in the class, they acknowledge the assistance of their editor. The teacher often asks them to describe some way the editor helped them. Third, she emphasizes that expert writers have editors, too. She asks students to help edit her papers and talks about how her colleagues read and edit her papers before she turns them in for her college classes.

Finally, when Ms. A collects the final drafts and grades them, she uses the evaluation criteria as an important part of her grading. This alignment between students' self-evaluations and the teacher's grading encourages students to see the self-evaluations as important.

As the students master these particular evaluation questions, the teacher goes on to teach new criteria. More likely than not, the class will by then be involved in learning a new type of writing with a new planning strategy and evaluation criteria appropriate to that form of writing.

Revision in an Eighth-Grade Unit on Persuasive Writing

Mr. B takes a somewhat different approach to teaching evaluation and revising in a unit on persuasive writing in his middle school English class. He works closely with the rest of his teaching team, and they have planned together to work on persuasive writing across the curriculum. Mr. B will take the lead to introduce persuasive writing in English class, and then other teachers will build on what the students learn. For example, the social studies teacher plans to engage the students in debates about immigration in American history followed by persuasive writing on various aspects of this broad issue. This close connection between writing and content-area instruction is consistent with the emphasis of the new Common Core State Standards.

Like Ms. A, Mr. B plans to teach both a planning and a revising strategy, but he plans to connect the elements of the two strategies more closely and teach them together. The connection between the planning and revising strategies will be text structure, or the elements of a type of text. Students will learn a strategy for planning persuasive essays that is based on an argumentative text structure. An argumentative essay includes a thesis or position, reasons, elaborations on those reasons including supportive examples and evidence, and a conclusion. In addition, by eighth grade, students are expected to consider opposing positions and reasons and refute those positions. Although even elementary students have a basic understanding of persuasion, persuasive writing is quite difficult for middle and high school students. It requires careful analytical thinking to generate reasons, connect reasons and evidence, and refute opposing positions.

Because of the difficulty of the task, Mr. B plans to use the evaluation strategy to directly support students in using the elements of argument that are in the planning strategy. Thus, the evaluation criteria will focus on the elements of an argument: position, reasons, elaborations, opposing positions, and refutations. He develops a self-evaluation scale for the students to use in evaluating their own papers and when working in peer revising (see Figure 9.1). He will use this same rating scale in grading and commenting on students' papers.

Before any instruction in persuasive writing, Mr. B has the students write two persuasive essays, one on an assigned topic and one on an issue of their choice. He will ask students to revise these essays later so they can see how much they have learned about persuasive writing. They also provide a pool of writing samples that he can use in other classes to teach the evaluation and revision strategy.

Instruction begins with critical reading and analysis of persuasive texts. Critical reading is an important aspect of Mr. B's instruction for

Score each question:	1	Needs revision			
	2	Okay			
	3	Well done			
Did I state my position clearly?			1	2	3
Are my reasons clear and well supported?					
First reason?			1	2	3
Second reason?			1	2	3
Did I consider the opposing position?			1	2	3
Did I refute the opposing position?			1	2	3
Did I use good transition words?			1	2	3
Did I conclude by summarizing my reasons?			1	2	3
Is the tone appropriate?			1	2	3
Is my essay persuasive?			1	2	3

Total points _____

What could I change to make my argument more persuasive? _____

_____

FIGURE 9.1. Evaluation of a persuasive essay.

three reasons. First, his ultimate goal is for students to be able to read and listen to other people's perspectives and to respond by explaining and supporting their own views, not just to give their own opinions. He believes that his students will be engaged by a discussion of controversial issues and that such discussion will help them to understand the purpose of persuasive writing and something about what it takes to be persuasive. Second, reading and analyzing texts is a way to show students the essential elements of persuasive writing that are used in the planning and revising strategies. Third, critical reading is very similar to the kind of rereading and evaluation required to revise their own writing. In both cases, students must read to identify reasons, evidence, and other elements and think about whether those reasons are convincing.

For one critical reading activity, Mr. B brings in copies of a newspaper editorial and several letters to the editor on a locally important issue: prohibiting smoking in restaurants and other public places. He is careful to choose an editorial that includes several reasons and directly addresses opposing positions. After a brief discussion of what one has to do to support an argument—give reasons and evidence and consider opposing arguments—he models analyzing the argument in the editorial. As he thinks aloud, he highlights the position, reasons, and refutations of opposing arguments in different colors. As he highlights the reasons, he thinks aloud about whether the reasons are really separate reasons or all part of the same reason. He also thinks aloud about whether the evidence is good and whether he agrees. As he highlights the refutations, he thinks aloud about who might have those opposing positions and whether the author has answered them effectively. The process of highlighting the elements gets students to focus on the structure of the argument and consider each reason and its evidence. Then Mr. B asks students, working in small groups, to analyze the letters to the editor in the same way. Students then write brief letters to the editor of their own.

Next, Mr. B introduces the evaluation scale for students and models using it to evaluate and revise essays written by students unknown to his class. Middle school students are particularly reluctant to criticize their peers on any task assigned and graded by a teacher. Using papers from unknown students makes it easier for students to evaluate and criticize the work. Mr. B focuses attention on the criteria about a clear position and reasons. As he models, he uses think-alouds to show his reasoning, but he also involves the students in the discussion. This sort of collaborative modeling allows the teacher to direct the overall process of applying the criteria but encourages student participation. Here is an example of collaborative modeling:

Student text displayed on overhead projector:

I think smoking should be banned in some public places.

Some people can't handle other people smoking around them. They could either get sick or really choked up. Secondhand smoke can also be a problem. A child could be around someone smoking and inhel smoke and can become very sick.

Smoking can also be very rude. It can be very disgusting when your eating something and someone's cigarette smoke blows into your food. Lots of pollutants can get into the air.

People might disapprove because it is free country and they can smoke if they want to. But they probably don't know how much it is harmful to other people and the earth.

MR. B: *(Reads the whole essay.)* Okay. Now I need to use the evaluation questions to help me figure out how to improve this essay. Let's see, is the position clear? It says smoking should be banned in some public places. So I know which side the author is on, but I'm not sure about *some* public places. Does it mean *all* public places? Does anyone have an idea about how to fix that?

STUDENT A: We could just say *all* public places.

STUDENT B: We could say restaurants. It mentions them later.

MR. B: How could we say that?

STUDENT B: "I think smoking should be banned in all public places including restaurants and stores."

MR. B: *(Crosses out and inserts the needed words.)* Okay. That's better. I think I'm going to rate this a 2 now. It's okay but not great because it isn't elaborated at all. The next evaluation question is whether the reasons are clear and supported. Let's find the reasons and underline them. There are two paragraphs here so each one should have a separate reason. This one starts *"Some people can't handle other people smoking around them."* Do you think that is clear?

STUDENT C: I don't think so. *Handle* could mean a lot of things. I think the author is talking about people getting sick. That's what the rest of the paragraph is about.

MR. B: I agree. How can we revise that first sentence to make it clearer?

STUDENT C: "Secondhand smoke can make other people sick."

STUDENT D: "If people smoke in public places, other people can get sick from the smoke."

MR. B: Both of those are good ideas. I like using the term *secondhand smoke*. And I also like referring back to the idea about public places. Let's try, "If people smoke in public places, other people can get sick from the secondhand smoke." *(Writes.)* That's better. The rest of the paragraph still needs some work, but let's get the rest of the reasons fixed before we do that.

MR. B: Let's look at the next paragraph. "Smoking can also be very rude." Again, I'm not sure what that really means. Why is it rude? The next sentence says it's disgusting when you are eating. I think the author means that the smoke is unpleasant. Is that a different reason from the first paragraph?

STUDENT A: I think so. The first paragraph was about the smoke making people sick. Disgusting is something else. They just don't like the smoke.

MR. B: I think you're right. So this paragraph should be about other people not liking the smoke. Let me think how to say that. "When other people are eating, smoke can be very disgusting." I'm not sure I like that word *disgusting*. Any other ideas?

STUDENT: "When other people are eating, smoke can be very unpleasant."

STUDENT: "When people are eating, they shouldn't have to smell cigarette smoke."

MR. B: Both of those ideas are good. *(Writes.)*

The discussion continues for a while longer. Mr. B considers how the support for the two reasons could be improved and evaluates how the author considered the opposing position. In the end, he reads the revised paper and comments that it is much better although it could be better with more content.

Over the next few days, Mr. B has students work in pairs to evaluate and revise more essays written by students unknown to them. They use the evaluation scale to support their evaluations. Mr. B also continues to evaluate and revise papers as a whole-class activity. The papers range widely in quality and include some essays that are well written and need little revision. Mr. B, however, always manages to find some way to improve the paper by strengthening the support for the reasons or the way the paper responds to the opposing position. As part of the discussion, students talk about whether they agree with the positions taken and whether they think the evidence is convincing. Persuasive writing is not just about whether writers follow the form; the content of the reasons and evidence is critical, and it is part of what they evaluate.

When students are consistently able to evaluate essays and revise them, Mr. B introduces a planning strategy for persuasive essays. Students already have a clear idea of what is required for an effective essay. The planning strategy helps students to generate and organize their ideas before writing. It asks them to list reasons and evidence on both sides of the issue so that they are prepared to defend their position and respond to potential opposing positions.

Students then begin writing persuasive essays and applying the evaluation scale to revise them. Mr. B has them work in pairs to evaluate and revise their papers. Students now are able to help each other because they have learned how to analyze and evaluate persuasive essays. Their natural reluctance to criticize each other is tempered somewhat by the knowledge that the teacher will be grading their papers on the same criteria that they are using. He also asks them to evaluate and revise the essays they wrote before instruction to show them how much they have learned.

The students write on a range of persuasive topics. They write on policy issues that are meaningful to middle school students, like whether students should have after-school jobs. They also write about the literature they are reading; Mr. B raises challenging questions about whether characters should have taken the actions they did, and the students respond, drawing evidence from the book as well as their own experience. Students also start to use the planning and revising strategies for assignments in other classes. Mr. B has worked together with the team of teachers so that they are all familiar with the strategy. Using the strategies in multiple classes addresses the common problem of maintenance and generalization.

Mr. B's instruction included several of the components that research has shown are important to learning to revise. He provided meaningful writing tasks with a clear goal to persuade some audience. Sometimes the audience was peers; other times it was an imagined audience but one within students' experience. He taught critical reading of persuasive essays as well as teaching evaluation criteria and how to use those criteria to revise their papers. He engaged students in whole-class and peer dialogue about evaluation and revision. Finally, he arranged with his colleagues to use the strategies across content areas.

Concluding Remarks

In closing, I would like to summarize a few principles for teaching revision in ways that help students develop their overall writing skills. First, it is important to provide a classroom context in which writing has meaningful goals. One of most common and best ways to make writing meaningful is to arrange authentic writing tasks that are read by peers and other audiences. However, authentic audiences are not the only way to provide meaningful goals. Students can also be engaged in writing tasks with clear goals based on learning specific objectives, for example, the task of describing tangrams mentioned above (Holliway & McCutchen, 2004). Revision is a process of comparing the actual text to the intended text; thus, it depends on the goals for the writing task.

Second, peer interaction and teacher–student dialogue are essential to learning to evaluate texts. Peers and teachers are first readers for students' writing, and students learn from serving as editors as well as from hearing the responses of others to their writing. Peer collaboration is also highly motivating, and it reflects the reality that most writing tasks outside of school are surrounded by rich oral communication.

Third, revision begins with evaluation, and the primary reason that students have difficulty revising is that they do not know how to evaluate their writing. Thus, it is important to teach students specific criteria for evaluation and how to revise based on those criteria. Most effective approaches to teaching revising involve instruction in evaluation.

Fourth, it is valuable to integrate reading comprehension instruction with instruction in evaluation and revision. Critical reading is similar in many ways to reading for revision; the main difference is in the purpose— reading to understand versus reading to identify problems and revise.

Fifth, word processing is a helpful tool in learning to revise. It simplifies the physical processes of revising and thus removes an important disincentive to revision: recopying. It also motivates students to produce final copies for publication, which is one of the main motivations for revising.

Finally, strategy instruction is a highly effective way to improve students' revising skills and the overall quality of their writing. Most strategy instruction in revision pulls together elements of evaluation criteria, peer interaction, and self-regulation. Much of the research combines instruction in strategies for planning and revising.

References

Beach, R., & Friedrich, T. (2006). Response to writing. In C. A. MacArthur, S. Graham, & J. Fitzgerald (Eds.), *Handbook of writing research* (pp. 222–234). New York: Guilford Press.

Bereiter, C., & Scardamalia, M. (1987). *The psychology of written composition.* Hillsdale, NJ: Erlbaum.

Boscolo, P., & Ascorti, K. (2004). Effects of collaborative revision on children's ability to write understandable narrative texts. In L. Allal, L. Chanqouy, & P. Largy (Eds.), *Revision: Cognitive and instructional processes* (Vol. 13, pp. 157–170). Boston: Kluwer.

Cho, K., & MacArthur, C. A. (2011). Learning by reviewing. *Journal of Educational Psychology, 103,* 73–84.

De La Paz, S., Swanson, P. N., & Graham, S. (1998). The contribution of executive control to the revising of students with writing and learning difficulties. *Journal of Educational Psychology, 90*, 448–460.

Englert, C. S., Raphael, T. E., Anderson, L. M., Anthony, H. M., & Stevens, D. D. (1991). Making writing strategies and self-talk visible: Cognitive strategy instruction in writing in regular and special education classrooms. *American Educational Research Journal, 28*, 337–372.

Fitzgerald, J. (1987). Research on revision in writing. *Review of Educational Research, 57*, 481–506.

Galbraith, D., & Torrance, M. (2004). Revision in the context of different drafting strategies. In L. Allal, L. Chanqouy, & P. Largy (Eds.), *Revision: Cognitive and instructional processes* (Vol. 13, pp. 63–85). Boston: Kluwer.

Graham, S. (2006). Strategy instruction and the teaching of writing: A meta-analysis. In C. A. MacArthur, S. Graham, & J. Fitzgerald (Eds.), *Handbook of writing research* (pp. 187–207). New York: Guilford Press.

Graham, S., & Harris, K. R. (2005). *Writing better: Teaching writing processes and self-regulation to students with learning problems.* Baltimore: Brookes.

Graham, S., Harris, K. R., & Hebert, M. (2011). *Informing writing: The benefits of formative assessment.* Washington, DC: Alliance for Excellent Education.

Graham, S., & MacArthur, C. A. (1988). Improving learning disabled students' skills at revising essays produced on a word processor: Self-instructional strategy training. *Journal of Special Education, 22*, 133–152.

Graham, S., MacArthur, C. A., & Schwartz, S. S. (1995). The effects of goal setting and procedural facilitation on the revising behavior and writing performance of students with writing and learning problems. *Journal of Educational Psychology, 87*, 230–240.

Graham, S., & Perin, D. (2007). A meta-analysis of writing instruction for adolescent students. *Journal of Educational Psychology, 99*, 445–476.

Hayes, J. (2004). What triggers revision? In L. Allal, L. Chanqouy, & P. Largy (Eds.), *Revision: Cognitive and instructional processes* (Vol. 13, pp. 9–20). Boston: Kluwer.

Hayes, J. R., Flower, L., Schriver, K. A., Stratman, J. F., & Carey, L. (1987). Cognitive processes in revision. In S. Rosenberg (Ed.), *Advances in applied psycholinguistics: Vol. 2. Reading, writing, and language learning* (pp. 176–240). New York: Cambridge University Press.

Hillocks, G. (1986). *Research on written composition: New directions for teaching.* Urbana, IL: ERIC Clearinghouse on Reading and Communication Skills.

Holliway, D. R., & McCutchen, D. (2004). Audience perspective in young writers' composing and revising. In L. Allal, L. Chanqouy, & P. Largy (Eds.), *Revision: Cognitive and instructional processes* (Vol. 13, pp. 87–101). Boston: Kluwer.

Kaufman, M. (2010, July 3). With the stroke of a pen, "subjects" no more. *Washington Post*, pp. A1, A12.

Lundstrom, K., & Baker, W. (2009). To give is better than to receive: The benefits of peer review to the reviewer's own writing. *Journal of Second Language Writing, 18*, 30–43.

MacArthur, C. A. (2006). The effects of new technologies on writing and writing processes. In C. A. MacArthur, S. Graham, & J. Fitzgerald (Eds.), *Handbook of writing research* (pp. 248–262). New York: Guilford Press.

MacArthur, C. A. (2012). Evaluation and revision processes in writing. In V. W. Berninger (Ed.), *Past, present, and future contributions of cognitive writing research to cognitive psychology* (pp. 461–483). London: Psychology Press.

MacArthur, C. A., Graham, S., & Schwartz, S. (1991). Knowledge of revision and revising behavior among learning disabled students. *Learning Disability Quarterly, 14,* 61–73.

MacArthur, C. A., Schwartz, S. S., & Graham, S. (1991). Effects of a reciprocal peer revision strategy in special education classrooms. *Learning Disabilities Research and Practice, 6,* 201–210.

McCutchen, D., Francis, M., & Kerr, S. (1997). Revising for meaning: Effects of knowledge and strategy. *Journal of Educational Psychology, 89,* 667–676.

Midgette, E., Haria, P., & MacArthur, C. A. (2008). The effects of content and audience awareness goals for revision on the persuasive essays of fifth- and eighth-grade students. *Reading and Writing, 21,* 131–151.

Moore, N., & MacArthur, C. A. (2012). The effects of being a reader and of observing readers on fifth-grade students' argumentative writing and revising. *Reading and Writing, 25,* 1449–1478.

Murray, D. (1991). *The craft of revision.* Austin, TX: Holt, Rinehart, & Winston.

National Governors Association & Council of Chief State School Officers. (2010). *Common Core State Standards for English language arts & literacy in history/social studies, science, and technical subjects.* Washington, DC: Authors. Retrieved from *corestandards.org.*

Philippakos, Z. A. (2012). *Effects of reviewing on fourth and fifth-grade students' persuasive writing and revising.* PhD Dissertation, University of Delaware.

Sachar, L. (1991). *Dogs don't tell jokes.* New York: Knopf.

Stoddard, B., & MacArthur, C. A. (1993). A peer editor strategy: Guiding learning disabled students in response and revision. *Research in the Teaching of English, 27,* 76–103.

Chapter 10

Best Practices in Sentence Construction Skills

BRUCE SADDLER

Children acquire many academic competencies during their school experiences; however, the ability to express their thoughts in writing may be the most complex. Writing is an essential tool for communication and an important tool for learning. When a writer creates a message, he or she must orchestrate a wide spectrum of physical and mental processes including *planning* what to say; *generating* text through handwriting, dictation, or electronic means; and *reviewing* the text to make improvements (Flower & Hayes, 1981). Each of these processes requires high levels of skill and will by a writer to do well.

A writer who can compose effectively has developed a writing tool kit stocked with knowledge of how to complete writing tasks along with knowledge about the topic he or she wishes to write about. Such a writer complements the tools needed for the task with a strong motivation and sense of self-efficacy that provides the emotional and cognitive push he or she needs to complete a writing task despite the challenges and complexities encountered during the process. As a nod to the complexities involved in producing written language, researchers and teachers have placed writing at the pinnacle of the language hierarchy (Graham, 1997; Hillocks, 1986).

In the array of skills a writer must use effectively, one of the most important is the ability to construct sentences. The sentence, although a very basic syntactical structure of our language, can nevertheless provide profound compositional challenges for any writer. Each sentence a writer creates requires a construction process that parallels the tasks needed to create a composition. In fact, a sentence can require so much thought and planning that it resembles a "composition in miniature" (Flower & Hayes, 1981). For example, the last sentence you just read required that I formulate an idea ("I need to say how difficult a sentence is to create"), retrieve words to match my idea ("Should I use the word *require* or is that too strong?"), mentally arrange and rearrange words into grammatically acceptable syntactical structures "(I could start the sentence with "When a writer creates" and then build from there), translate those structures into readable text, and then manipulate the text as needed to fine-tune the message. At times, because of the multiple complexities involved, the construction of each sentence can test a writer's ability. But to create a composition, a writer has to continually perform such mental gymnastics while plowing through this process over and over, logically and creatively analyzing and manipulating each individual sentence along the way, until a satisfying end is reached.

Helping a developing writer learn to effectively craft sentences is a complex task requiring direct, systematic instruction. In this chapter I present a research-based method of systematic sentence-level instruction called "sentence combining." My goals for this chapter are to provide reasons for teaching sentence construction skills directly; to offer an explanation for why sentence-combining instruction is an effective technique; and to discuss methods and ideas for including sentence-combining practice within the overall writing program. I also provide two classroom examples to illustrate what sentence combining might look like within a classroom.

Rationale for Direct Instruction of Sentence Construction Skills

For a writer to construct sentences, he or she must have knowledge of "syntax," or how to effectively organize words within a sentence structure. Initially a child learns the syntax of a language (or how words are supposed to be put together) through oral communication with other language users. Later this oral knowledge is transferred to written language either before or during early school experiences. When more formal writing experiences commence, young writers learn that there are different syntactical "types" of sentences (simple, compound, complex, and compound-complex) and that sentences perform various functions within a composition (declarative, imperative, interrogative, exclamatory). However, writers need to go well beyond this basic awareness of what a sentence is and the functions a sentence performs. They must develop enough facility with controlling and manipulating syntax to generate sentences that are clear, energetic, forceful, interesting, coherent, grammatical, and (as many writers fondly remember being told by their teachers) revealing of a "complete thought."

Developing such syntactical facility begins with formulating basic noun–verb pattern sentences (*The dog ran*) and expands through the school years to include longer, more complex syntactical structures (*Although the dog ran away, we were unsure of exactly why he ran or where he was going*). Next the writer must take his or her knowledge of individual sentence construction and logically string together enough sentences to build a paragraph, paragraphs then turning into a composition. However, the flexibility that makes language beautiful also makes it tricky. The idea, word, and syntactical choices available in a given sentence can represent potential entanglements that can derail this process for any writer. In fact, many of the sentences in this chapter "derailed" my writing process as I stopped, searched, and considered better ways to say what I was thinking.

Sentence construction skills are essential for several reasons. First, knowledge of effective writing formats at the sentence level allows writers to translate their thoughts into text. Second, constructing well-designed, grammatically correct sentences may make the material students write easier for others to read. A story crafted with one simple sentence after another without variety quickly becomes boring. Likewise, a story written with excessively long, complex sentences can be difficult to follow. In either case, if grammatical issues are present because of malformed sentences, the reader's mind is distracted from the writer's intent (Saddler & Graham, 2005). Because of the importance of this skill and its inherent complexity, writers benefit when teachers provide direct and systematic practice in constructing sentences (Saddler & Graham, 2005).

Sentence Combining

Only one approach to teaching sentence construction skills has received the sustained attention of researchers. This approach, called sentence combining, was developed in the 1960s, when researchers and teachers were looking for alternatives to teaching formal grammar (parts of speech, sentence diagramming). Since then, more than 80 studies conducted during the last 40 years have demonstrated with few exceptions that sentence combining is an effective method for helping students produce more syntactically mature sentences (e.g., Cooper, 1973; Crowhurst & Piche, 1979; Hunt, 1965; O'Hare, 1973; Saddler & Graham, 2005). (*Syntactical maturity* is the ability to write a variety of complex and compound sentences within a story.)

As a curriculum supplement, sentence combining provides mindful practice in manipulating and rewriting basic phrases or clauses into more varied and syntactically mature forms. For example, if a student characteristically composes simple kernel sentences such as "My dog is fat. My dog is black," he or she can learn through sentence-combining practice to combine or embed these kernel sentences into more syntactically complex and mature sentences, such as "My dog is fat and black" or "The fat black dog is mine," depending on what idea in the sentence he or she wishes to emphasize. Likewise, if a student produces sentences that are overly complex or ambiguous, he or she can learn to decombine the sentences back into their basic kernels and then recombine them into a more cohesive and understandable whole.

Three theoretical principles support sentence-combining practice: first, writers need instruction in formulating a concept of what a written sentence is and the syntactical options that are possible when producing a sentence. Sentence-combining practice can help children develop a metalinguistic awareness about syntactical choices made when desiging a piece of writing by helping them mindfully think about the sound of their language. Second, once the sentence formation and reformation process becomes more familiar through sustained, systematic practice, the overall cognitive strain a writer experiences while writing is reduced, allowing attention to shift to other writing tasks such as awareness of audience needs, what constitutes good writing, or how to navigate writing processes. Third, gains in *syntactical fluency*, the ability to produce a variety of sentences, lead to quality writing by making a composition more enjoyable to read (Strong, 1986).

Sentence-combining practice is valuable for writers at all levels because it represents a unique type of "controlled composition exercise" that parallels tasks writers routinely perform while writing. Every writer has to convert mental ideas into syntactical arrangements, and the more knowledge a writer has of syntactical variety, the greater his or her ability with this task. Highly skilled professional authors who have spent many long hours working and reworking their syntax have internalized a vast array of syntactical options. During writing, these resources can be drawn upon as needed to help convey thoughts and ideas in a way that seemingly mere mortal writers cannot approach. Younger writers, less skilled writers, and writers with learning disabilities do not have this storehouse of syntactical forms for support.

When a writer does not possess well-formed knowledge of syntactical options that can be rapidly drawn upon when needed, two problems could occur in his or her writing: first, he or she may default to simpler, more familiar syntactical patterns, leading to writing filled with sentences that look and sound very similar. The writer could also attempt to create more complex syntactical constructions he or she is unfamiliar with forming, creating a tangled jumble of thought that is difficult for a reader to interpret.

Sentence-combining exercises can help with both of these situations by prompting students to use syntactical options in their writing through practice in consciously controlling and manipulating syntax (Saddler, 2005). The exercises provide a skill-based experience with syntactical manipulation that parallels what writers actually do when refining their text, namely, combine, change, add, rearrange, and delete words and ideas. Through the process of decombining and recombining sentences, students can learn to untangle, tighten, and rewrite sentences that may be too complex for a reader to easily understand. Instead of constructing longer sentences, the value of sentence combining may reside in making sentences and whole discourse better through employing a variety of syntactical forms—the goal being clarity of thought instead of complexity. Therefore, sentences can be shorter if they are more effective in getting the writer's message across to the reader.

Recognition of the importance of sentence construction skills is found in the Common Core State Standards (CCSS). For example, the CCSS suggest that writers should

> use words, phrases, and clauses as well as varied syntax to link the major sections of the text, create cohesion, and clarify the relationships between claim(s) and reasons, between reasons and evidence, and between claim(s) and counterclaims" and that they should "use a variety of transition words, phrases, and clauses to convey sequence, signal shifts from one time frame or setting to another, and show the relationships among experiences and events. (National Governors Association [NGA] & Council of Chief State School Officers [CCSSO], 2010)

The CCSS also suggest a second area of writing that sentence combining can directly effect: style.

Style in writing is literally a writer's way with words (Nemans, 1995). Deciding on the best syntactical arrangements in a given piece of writing relates directly to a writer's particular style. Five different writers, if given a particular topic and a specific set of data about that topic, would likely craft five uniquely formed compositions, each with a particular style. That style sets them apart from other writers. Hemingway's style, for example, plain and direct, is far removed from Hugo's intensely descriptive and expansive prose. For these writers, their prose has a certain rhythm and pattern of emphasis. Yet each is highly effective.

Style is prominently mentioned in the CCSS. For example, the CCSS suggest that writers in grades 6–12 should "produce clear and coherent writing in which the development, organization, and style are appropriate to task, purpose, and audience" (NGA & CCSSO, 2010). Furthermore, the

CCSS state that writers need to "establish and maintain a formal style and objective tone while attending to the norms and conventions of the discipline in which they are writing."

In the next section, I present two classroom vignettes of sentence-combining instruction at different grade levels to illustrate how such language experiences can be included in writing process classrooms. The first example depicts how sentence combining can be included in a 2nd-grade classroom, while the second illustrates a 10th-grade class.

Instructional Recommendations

Example 1: Second-Grade Class

This class consisted of children with a range of writing abilities including several children who struggled with various aspects of writing. The teacher, Ms. Asaro, instituted sentence-combining practice to help these children construct better sentences and better stories.

Many of the students in Ms. Asaro's classroom tended to create very short sentences that sounded similar. Not only were many of the students writing sentences that were short, simply constructed, and lacking in descriptive words, but many also used a very repetitive subject–verb–object pattern that gave the reader the impression of immature writing and made their stories choppy and difficult to read. Others produced massive run-on sentences connected by a long series of *and*'s, while still others scattered sentence fragments throughout their compositions.

These difficulties on the sentence level affected the overall quality of their stories. Although Ms. Asaro used a variety of writing prompts and always allowed the children a choice in what they wrote about, their stories were typically short and rather boring. She believed that many of her students could say more in their stories, but because they lacked the skill to write well-constructed, interesting sentences, they could not accurately translate their ideas and emotions into text. Based on her analysis of her students' writing strengths and needs, she decided to supplement her writing workshop time with sentence-combining instruction.

Ms. Asaro followed a learn–see–do structure in her lessons (see Figure 10.1 for a description of the overall instructional steps). She began by introducing the exercises as an activity that could help writers create more interesting sentences that sound better to readers. She suggested that skilled writers frequently rework their sentences to help convey their message better and explained that even in her own writing she would often change her sentences around to decide if she could write her ideas in a better way.

Teach sentence-combining exercises in a learn–see–do structure using these steps:

1. Teacher modeling of how and why combinations are made.

2. Scaffolded practice in which the teacher guides students to develop multiple solutions to a problem.

3. Independent practice during which the students are creating solutions to a problem that are discussed and supportively evaluated by the whole class.

FIGURE 10.1. Instructional steps.

She started with a whole-class discussion by projecting a pair of simple kernel sentences on the overhead projector and modeling how to combine them. To help everyone understand the basic process of combining sentences, she chose two sentences that were as similar as possible, except for the words to be combined: "The dog is little. The dog jumped high." She suggested that, for these exercises, there is usually more than one combination possible and not to worry about making mistakes because mistakes were opportunities for learning. Then she read both sentences out loud and said, "Hmmm . . . well, one way to put these two sentences together would be to say 'The little dog jumped high.' " She wrote the new sentence on the overhead transparency and explained her reasoning in combining the sentences in the way she chose and why she believed the new combination sounded better. She showed that, when she combined the sentences, she moved words or parts around, deleted or changed words or parts, and/ or added words or parts to the sentences to make them sound better and convey her ideas more clearly.

Ms. Asaro then performed several additional combinations while increasing the amount of discussion and quality judgments the students provided and decreasing her own input. Her goal was to prompt the students to rely on the knowledge of English they had developed from years of listening and reading to decide on the correctness and sound quality of a combination, which is exactly what she wanted them to do when they wrote stories. The discussion that commenced led to some interesting opinions about why a certain combination sounded better and why adding a word here or there made the thought clearer. Even students who seldom participated in class discussions added their ideas to the mix.

After this introductory session, Ms. Asaro began all of the subsequent sessions with oral practice. First, she reasoned that when combining sentences the ear must hear alternatives to be able to choose the sentence that sounds best (Strong, 1986). She realized that in her own writing she often reread a passage of text out loud to hear the sound. Second, her students' handwriting and spelling skills were still developing, and, as a result, the physical act of writing impeded the speed with which they could write sentences. Practicing orally circumvented this difficulty, saved precious class time, and allowed for additional practice opportunities with the skill being learned.

Oral practice was included by arranging her class in pairs, presenting kernel sentence clusters on the overhead, and asking the pairs to discuss the kernels and provide examples of combinations orally. She randomly called on pairs to give their combinations and wrote several different examples on the overhead. These were then read aloud to determine which sounded best.

Although writing is sometimes viewed as a solitary activity, Ms. Asaro believed that much of the potential power of sentence-combining exercises resided in playing with language within a group environment of idea exchanges. She felt that when many students approached an identical writing task at once, they became aware of the solutions available from other writers close to their level of maturity and experience, so, during these oral exercises, she always encouraged group discussions, feedback, evaluation, reflection, and praise.

Following oral practice, Ms. Asaro would have a brief partner practice session where students worked together to write out combinations for several additional kernel sentence clusters. The students frequently wrote their responses on a transparency and then presented their versions on the overhead. Ms. Asaro always asked for several possible solutions for each problem and discussed each thoroughly, praising success and supporting improvement as needed.

Sources for Material

Although Ms. Asaro's district did not possess a curriculum for sentence combining, finding sources for exercise content was actually fairly simple. Initially, she created kernel sentences from a collection of short stories the class was reading by reducing a passage into very simple short sentences (see Figure 10.2 for an example). Then the kernels were rewritten by students working in pairs. The new versions were read by each pair to the class and followed by group discussions of each version.

Ms. Asaro also found that classroom activities or school events could be sources of inspiration, along with the lives and interests of her students. Newspapers and magazines also furnished interesting content for her to develop sentence-combining exercises. Many of these sources offered a bonus by providing her students with information on a new concept or reinforcing a lesson from a science or social studies unit.

Any textual source can be developed into a sentence-combining exercise by reducing or "decombining" the passage into basic kernel sentences that can be easily recombined. Make kernels for each sentence in the original text straightforward and simple, and create logical cues to help with recombining. For example:

Original passage from *Les Misérables* by Victor Hugo (p. 55):

He seated himself near the fireplace and stretched his feet out towards the fire, half dead with fatigue.

Decombined passage:

He seated himself.

He sat near the fireplace.

He stretched his feet out.

He stretched them towards the fire.

He was half dead with fatigue.

FIGURE 10.2. Decombining textual passages.

Types of Exercises

When developing exercises from these sources, Ms. Asaro followed two guidelines (Strong, 1976, 1986). First, she set up the exercises so that the base clause came first, followed by one or more modifying sentences. For example:

Base sentence: The bird flew.
Modifying sentence: The bird was blue.
Combination: The blue bird flew.

Second, she used two types of clues to prompt or focus the children on the important information they needed to keep from the second sentence. The first clue was an underlined word:

The professor had written many books.
The professor was wise.

This problem resulted in the combination:

The wise professor had written many books.

The second type of clue was a connecting word enclosed in parentheses at the end of the sentence to be combined:

> Kristie fell over the laundry basket.
> She lost her balance. (because)

This problem resulted in a combination such as:

> Kristie fell over the laundry basket because she lost her balance.

After the students were comfortable with these exercises, Ms. Asaro eliminated the clues. Without the clues, the students had to decide what important material in the second sentence to include within the first when the two were combined.

Once she realized that her students were comfortable with combining two sentences, she began to ask them to combine longer sequences of sentences (without clues) that could be combined in multiple ways. For example:

> The dog barked.
> The dog was brown.
> It was in a cage.
> It was angry.

This group of sentences elicited many interesting combinations and provided a fun conversation concerning which of the versions sounded best. For example:

> The brown dog barked because it was in a cage.
> The angry brown dog was barking in its cage.

When combining multiple sentences, Ms. Asaro prompted her students to add additional descriptive words to the completed sentence. For example:

> Barking angrily, the huge brown dog walked around his cage.

See Figure 10.3 for additional examples of exercises.

Skill Sequence

Initially, Ms. Asaro relied on skill sequence suggestions created by Cooper (1973; see Table 10.1) as a guide and adjusted the topics to coincide closely with the needs of her students within their own compositions. Ms. Asaro

Sentence-combining exercises move from basic problems that offer only a limited number of possible solutions to paragraph and longer problems that can be combined in many different ways. There are two types of exercises: cued and open.

Cued Exercises

Cued exercises are the most basic. They offer a specific clue in the form of an underlined or a key word or words placed in parenthesis that guide the student to combine the kernels in a particular way. For example:

Underlined clue:
The day was cold.
The day was <u>wet.</u>

Possible solution:
The day was wet and cold.

Key word(s) in parentheses:
The man wrote the story.
He had something to say. **(because)**

Possible solution:
The man wrote the story because he had something to say.

Open Exercises

Open exercises are generally more complex because they involve sets of kernels without any type of cue provided. Without cues a writer has to choose the information to keep and to discard. For example:

The boy swung the bat.
The bat was made of maple.

Possible solution:
The boy swung the maple bat.

Once students are comfortable with combining two kernel sentence clusters without clues, introduce exercises that require combining sequences of three or more kernel sentences without clues. For example:

The horn sounded.
The horn was shrill.
The sound startled Mary.
The sound made the cat run away.

Possible solution:
The shrill horn sounded, startling Mary and making the cat run away.

FIGURE 10.3. Types of exercises.

TABLE 10.1. Possible Sequence of Sentence-Combining Exercises

1. Inserting adjectives and adverbs
    Examples: The man ate the veggie burger.
    The man was <u>starving</u>.
    The starving man ate the veggie burger.

    The man ate the veggie burger.
    He ate <u>hungrily</u>.
    The man ate the veggie burger hungrily.

2. Producing compound subjects and objects
    Examples: Bruce wanted to read.
    <u>Mary</u> wanted to read.
    Bruce and Mary wanted to read.

    Kristie wanted pasta.
    Kristie wanted <u>broccoli</u>.
    Kristie wanted pasta and broccoli.

3. Producing compound sentences with *and* and *but*
    Examples: Maren wanted to play outside.
    Sarah wanted to play inside. (but)
    Maren wanted to play outside, but Sarah wanted to play inside.

4. Producing possessive nouns
    Examples: I like the kitten.
    It is <u>Kevin's</u>.
    I like Kevin's kitten.

5. Producing sentences with adverbial clauses using connecting words (*because*, *after*, *until*, and *when*)
    Examples: We went to school.
    We wanted to learn to read. (because)
    We went to school because we wanted to learn to read.

6. Producing sentences with relative clauses
    Examples: The student will be first.
    The student <u>is the closest to the door</u>. (who)
    The student who is the closest to the door will be first.

7. Inserting appositives
    Examples: Steve spoke to the class.
    Steve is <u>a great storyteller</u>.
    Steve, a great storyteller, spoke to the class.

Note. For a more detailed discussion on sequencing sentence combining exercises, see Cooper (1973).

believed that a writer's own work is the best arena to learn any writing skill. Although the contrived exercises were effective in increasing the variety and overall quality of the sentences her students wrote, she wanted to move away from this format as rapidly as possible. As soon as her students understood and were comfortable with combining sentences, she began asking them to work and rework the sentences within a current piece of their writing. Such tailoring of the skills she taught made her teaching time more effective and the skills themselves more relevant to her students at their individual stages of understanding and need.

To provide group practice that focused on a specific skill, Ms. Asaro projected a paragraph from one of her students on the overhead projector and asked the class to suggest ways the sentences could be improved. She paired up her students and provided a paper copy of the paragraph to each pair. She challenged them to talk together to discover how the paragraph could be changed. After they had written down their ideas, the class read various versions out loud and discussed how each was different from the original text.

Ms. Asaro believed that using her students' own work was the most natural way to engage them at their level of need and provide direct resolution of problems associated with a current piece of writing. In addition, since in any written work sentences build on one another to create a unified whole, her students could explore the effect a change in rhythm of one sentence might have on others. Also, because the answer to what makes a good sentence depends mostly on the purpose of that sentence within the context of a composition, allowing them to practice selecting options within their own writing made sense.

Judging Correctness

During the practice sessions, the concern Ms. Asaro most often faced was gauging "correctness." Her students wanted to establish objective criteria to help them test the correctness of different sentence combinations, perhaps because they were more familiar with being told something was right or wrong rather than being told, "That's good, but there might be a better way to say it."

Although our language does have rules that govern syntax, Ms. Asaro believed that using complex grammatical terminology to judge correctness would have been counterproductive. She stressed effectiveness as a much better indicator of merit than correctness. She felt that gauging effectiveness encouraged risk taking by welcoming mistakes as opportunities for discussion and problem solving. Within this context, mistakes became sentences that could be formed in better ways. This view was especially beneficial for her less skilled writers, who were often unwilling to take risks with their writing. In addition, emphasizing effectiveness helped her students understand that there is often not one right answer in writing; rather, there may be multiple solutions that require introspection to decide on the best option.

Ms. Asaro found three standards (Nemans, 1995) helpful in aiding her students to gauge the effectiveness of responses: clarity and directness of meaning, rhythmic appeal, and intended audience. Initially, she modeled and discussed the standards, then directed student pairs to use the standards to rate an exemplar paper followed eventually by each other's writing.

Measuring Improvement

Although Ms. Asaro felt that her students were improving, she began to look for evidence that sentence combining was making a difference and exactly what that difference was. In what ways was her students' writing changing? Was the time she was investing in sentence combining justified?

After analyzing her class's stories from before and after sentence-combining instruction, there were two areas in which Ms. Asaro noticed improvement. The first was a reduction of punctuation errors. As she had often taught, punctuation helps organize sentence elements. What she did not anticipate was that through the combining–decombining–recombining process her students would have hands-on practice using punctuation elements. As they increased the complexity of their sentences, they learned, for example, that commas were needed to set off elements from one another and that they could create rhythmic appeal within a sentence. They talked about when and where punctuation was needed and where it was not. Overall, their compositions became much cleaner in terms of punctuation and more appropriate usage, which led to a marked decrease in both fragments and run-on sentences.

The second benefit was in the overall quality of the stories they wrote. Her students' writing became more enjoyable for her to read. They had far fewer repetitive subject–verb–object sentences and run-ons, leading to a more satisfying rhythm to their writing and pieces that simply sounded better.

These improvements did not occur overnight. Sentence combining was not a quick fix; it took time and effort. Ms. Asaro had to dedicate instructional time to teaching sentence combining, but she did not allow the practice to detract from her other writing tasks. She kept the sessions short—no more than 10–15 minutes, several times per week—and the practice lively, believing that if the sessions became drudgery to teach, they would be even more so to learn.

Example 2: 10th-Grade Class

The second example involves teaching sentence combining to a 10th-grade social studies class. In this class, four students had identified disabilities, but many more struggled with various aspects of writing. The teacher, Mr. Thomas, wanted to improve his students' ability to write essays about historical figures and to help them remember more about the period of history they were studying.

Mr. Thomas realized that his students' writing needed assistance in several areas. Many of his students produced papers filled with run-on sentences and fragments. They frequently used the connectors *and, but*, and *or* to create long sentences or failed to include punctuation where it was needed. Few of his students invested effort in revising their papers.

Run-On Sentences and Sentence Fragments

Mr. Thomas realized that his students' run-ons and fragments might be occurring because they had difficulty understanding when and where to use punctuation. He analyzed their writing to determine the kinds of errors being made and found that the run-on sentence mistakes fell into one of two categories: failing to use periods to separate thoughts that could stand alone and using too many conjunctions to connect ideas within a single sentence.

He believed that his students often failed to add needed punctuation because they were trying to create sentence variety. As they did not understand or had not specifically practiced how to create grammatical complexity in stories, they ended up with run-ons. In order to provide support for teaching correct punctuation, he first explained to his class that a sentence is like an island that can stand alone (Saddler & Preschern, 2007). Then he provided the students with two sentences to combine and explained how each sentence could stand alone because it had a subject, a predicate, and modifiers. Next, he asked the students for examples of ways to combine the sentences without using a connecting word such as *and, but,* or *so*. This process was repeated during mini-lessons at least three times per week. In addition to his students' papers, he found that his social studies textbook provided great content for the creation of exercises.

Mr. Thomas used a similar activity to help eliminate run-on sentences that used conjunctions to connect too many ideas. When introducing the activity, he wrote the overused conjunction on a picture of a bridge (Saddler & Preschern, 2007). Then he explained to students that conjunctions, specifically *and, but*, and *so*, work as bridges to link ideas. When there are too many bridges in a sentence, it becomes difficult for the reader to cross and understand. He then wrote a run-on sentence (e.g., "George Washington went to the river and then he got into the boat and then he sailed across the wide river with his troops") on the board and replaced all the *ands* with pictures of bridges to help students visualize this. Once his students saw how run-ons could be confusing, they began to understand the purpose and function of these conjunctions. Mr. Thomas noticed that this realization caused a decrease in the number of run-on sentences his students wrote.

Revising

Mr. Thomas believed it was important to integrate the sentence-combining exercises with other components of the writing process as soon as possible because the quicker any learned skill taught during a mini-lesson was integrated into actual writing, the greater the likelihood that the skill would actually be adapted into his students' writing toolbox. One way he found to incorporate sentence-combining skills directly into the writing process in a meaningful way was during revising (see MacArthur, Chapter 9, this volume, on revising).

Before Mr. Thomas began sentence-combining practice, he believed that his students mainly saw the revision process as one of editing. They seemed to operate under a least-effort strategy, meaning they changed what was easiest to change. He noticed that they would conduct "housekeeping" by fixing spelling, capitalization, formatting, and perhaps punctuation rather than engaging in real revising—namely, molding the sound of text to make a message clearer or providing an audience with what they need to know.

He began to include lessons on revising using the sentence-combining skill being practiced. For example, he would place a student's writing sample on the overhead projector and look for specific places in the essay where a conjunction could be used to connect two shorter sentences or where a phrase could be embedded to create a better-sounding sentence or to add variety.

While conducting these lessons, Mr. Thomas would think out loud and model the thought process involved in choosing to make a certain combination. He used a variety of self-statements to help his students "see" what he was thinking. For example, he would say, "What do I have to do here?" to define the problem. He also used "Does that make sense?"; "Is that the best way that part can sound?"; and "Can I say that better?" as self-evaluations and "I really like the sound of that part" for self-reinforcement.

After modeling the revision process, Mr. Thomas began to have the students edit their own pieces of writing using the sentence-combining skills being practiced. The goal was for them to find two or three places to add sentence variety. For example, if a lesson had been taught on writing more sophisticated paragraphs through the use of participial phrases, he had the students either choose a sentence that could be embellished using a participial phrase or identify two sentences that could be combined to create one sentence with a participial phrase. If necessary, he would help them find places to make changes.

After his students had proofread a previous paper, he had them write a new one. In this new piece, he required students to include at least two sentences that targeted the writing goal. For example, if they were working on cause-and-effect subordinate clauses, he required them to include two sentences that correctly used either *because, since, so,* or *even though* for transition words.

Another great way Mr. Thomas found to have students increase their sentence-combining and revising skills was to have them proofread each others' work. He arranged students in pairs and had them search for one sentence they thought was well written in their partners' work and one place in which there could be a revision using the sentence-combining skill being practiced. He then allowed the students about 10–15 minutes to work as he circulated and provided assistance as needed. He then prompted the students to provide one positive comment and one suggestion to their partners.

After several weeks of brief sentence-combining practice sessions, Mr. Thomas noticed that the amount of revisions climbed in his students' work. Because he kept the rough drafts his students produced, he was able to notice that they were changing words, adding phrases and clauses, and reworking entire sentences far more frequently and effectively.

Conclusions

As the research suggests, sentence combining is an effective technique to increase students' ability to manipulate syntax. Fortunately, sentence-combining practice can be readily integrated into a classroom that employs a writing workshop approach, as these vignettes suggest. Keep in mind that developing "syntactic maturity" and an improved facility to select effective structures for a given rhetorical context calls for frequent time in your writing curriculum dedicated to systematic sentence-combining practice. Consider also that sentence combining is best used as a stylistic resource (Butler, 2011) added to regular composition work (Strong, 1976) and as a compliment for other research-validated writing practices.

Although sentence-combining exercises have proven effective in increasing the syntactical fluency of writers, they represent only one component within a writing program. They cannot meet every challenge writers will face during the composing process, nor can they help with other critical writing tasks such as planning. Therefore it would be a mistake to rely on them exclusively. However, even with these limitations in mind, when sentence-combining exercises are used as one component of a well-rounded writing program that includes ample time for writing, conferencing between peers and teachers, mini-lessons to increase skills, ample teacher modeling, and choice in writing assignments, they can provide essential knowledge for writers to use as they craft and shape their message.

References

Butler, P. (2011). Reconsidering the teaching of style. *English Journal, 100*(4), 77–82.

Czerniewska, P. (1992). *Learning about writing.* Oxford, UK: Blackwell.

Cooper, C. R. (1973). An outline for writing sentence combining problems. *English Journal, 62,* 96–102.

Crowhurst, M., & Piche, G. L. (1979). Audience and mode of discourse effects on syntactic complexity in writing at two grade levels. *Research in the Teaching of English, 13,* 101–109.

Flower, L. S., & Hayes, J. R. (1981). A cognitive process theory of writing. *College Composition and Communication, 32,* 365–387.

Graham, S. (1997). Executive control in the revising of students with learning and writing difficulties. *Journal of Educational Psychology, 89,* 223–234.

Hillocks, G. (1986). *Research on written composition.* Urbana, IL: ERIC Clearinghouse on Reading and Communication Skills.

Hunt, K. W. (1965). *Grammatical structures written at three grade levels* (Research Report No. 3). Champaign, IL: National Council of Teachers of English.

National Governors Association & Council of Chief State School Officers. (2010). *Common Core State Standards for English language arts & literacy in history/social studies, science, and technical subjects.* Washington, DC: Authors. Retrieved from *corestandards.org.*

Nemans, B. S. (1995). *Teaching students to write.* New York: Oxford University Press.

O'Hare, F. (1973). *Sentence combining.* Champaign, IL: National Council of Teachers of English.

Saddler, B. (2005). Sentence combining: A sentence-level writing intervention. *Reading Teacher, 58,* 468–471.

Saddler, B., & Graham, S. (2005). The effects of peer-assisted sentence combining instruction on the writing of more and less skilled young writers. *Journal of Educational Psychology, 97*(1), 43–54.

Saddler, B., & Preschern, J. (2007). Improving sentence writing ability through sentence-combining practice. *Teaching Exceptional Children, 39, 3,* 6–11.

Strong, W. (1976). Close-up: Sentence combining. *English Journal, 24,* 56–65.

Strong, W. (1986). *Creative approaches to sentence combining.* Urbana, IL: ERIC Clearinghouse on Reading and Communication Skills and the National Council of Teachers of English.

Chapter 11

Best Practices in Spelling and Handwriting

BOB SCHLAGAL

Spelling and handwriting, once staples of general education, now occupy an ever-smaller portion of the elementary school curriculum. And some educators view them as dying a slow but fitting death. Broadly speaking, two forces have helped push spelling and handwriting to the dusty corners of the classroom. The first was a shift in instructional priorities in the late 20th century that emphasized personal communication and deemphasized grammar, spelling, punctuation, and handwriting in composition. (These latter are sometimes regarded as surface features that have little to contribute to written communication itself.) The second and now more powerful force is a contemporary emphasis on electronic keyboard- and keypad-driven communication. Word-processing programs and spell-check functions have led some to believe that investing the time to teach children how to spell or write legibly is no longer particularly important—that is, that these skills will be taken care of in the natural course of things as children transition to keyboards. This is not the case.

There will continue to be many settings in which fluid, legible handwriting and correct, automatic spellings are essential; and there is evidence that these fundamental processes make important contributions to overall reading and writing ability. But these skills are not casually attained.

Spelling

Throughout much of U.S. educational history, spelling was a core element of literacy instruction. There was justification in this in that reading and writing are rooted in knowledge of the spelling system and its patterns. Currently, however, there is a degree of uncertainty among teachers about the English spelling system and methods for teaching it (Moats, 2005–2006). Most primary grade teachers appear to include spelling instruction in their curriculum, and most assign lists of words to be learned across a week. But there is a remarkable variety in their approaches to spelling as well as a strong tendency to neglect the needs of poor spellers (Graham et al., 2008; Johnston, 2001). Some teachers continue to believe that learning to spell is a rote memory process, drawing words from diverse sources, including basal readers, written work, and class readings, as well as student selection (Graham et al., 2008). When words are chosen from sources in this way, it is generally assumed that memorization is the key to learning to spell. When that is the case, the particular kinds of words students study are not important, as long as they further curricular goals. For this reason, some teachers choose to teach spelling through curricular vocabulary. The spelling words for a week might be drawn from new words introduced in a social studies unit, a science chapter, or a novel being read. Students are then responsible for both the spelling and the definitions of the words.

One problem with this approach is that it offers little information about the spelling system. Although curricular or self-selected words may at times be thematically related or personally useful, they seldom have any significant spelling relationship with one another. They are lists of orthographically unrelated words that must be memorized one item at a time. In this way, one learns to spell specific words, but these words reveal little about spelling as an orderly system. Further, curricular words present a high degree of challenge. Students not only must learn to spell them, but also to pronounce, read, and define them, creating multiple levels of challenge.

An example of this vocabulary approach could be seen in a very ordinary and predominantly middle-class school I visited several years ago. Curricular vocabulary was the customary method of teaching spelling throughout the school. In one third-grade class, for example, the weekly spelling test for the class had been drawn from a social studies unit on Native Americans. Four of the 10 words that I wrote down after leaving the class were these: *native, shaman, culture,* and *environment.* In later conversation, the teacher indicated that many of her mostly 8-year-old students struggled with spelling in her class and that their retention of the words studied was generally not good.

Interestingly, this vocabulary approach to spelling is an unconscious re-creation of a method commonly used in 19th-century U.S. schoolhouses—an approach that was later rejected and replaced by research-based lists that were carefully graded in difficulty. In the earlier vocabulary approach words were assigned that were not commonly evident in children's speech or writing, words that they might "grow into." Upper elementary children typically studied lengthy lists of complex and orthographically random words like *vicissitude, indictable*, and *convalescent*—words that in most instances would not be reflected in their normal writing and would not appear in their reading. In each case, contemporary or historic, the words to be learned are challenging for the target-age child to spell, challenging in meaning, and presented to be added one at a time to memory.

Given the broad variability in approaches to spelling (Graham et al., 2008), and given teacher uncertainty about the nature of English spelling (Moats, 2005–2006), it is useful to see how research has shaped materials and approaches—and how these speak to the new Common Core State Standards (CCSS; National Governors Associaion [NGA] & Council of Chief State Officers [CCSSO], 2010).

Early Spelling Research

Based on research undertaken in the 20th century (Schlagal, 2001), two very practical kinds of modifications were made to spelling books. The first was based on a widespread recognition that despite heavy emphasis on spelling in U.S. schools, the results were not pleasing (Hanna, Hodges, & Hanna, 1971). Word frequency was introduced as a way to create lists of study words that were easier to learn and more practical in use. The second was based on the demonstration that English spelling is more orderly and predictable than many had claimed.

Word Frequency

A major change was made to spelling books in the 1930s: the creation of word lists drawn from recently completed counts of the most commonly used words (Hanna et al., 1971). Words were selected based on the frequency of their appearance in the speech, print, and writing of children and adults and were presented in groups of slowly increasing difficulty. Attention was also paid to word length. That is, spelling lists were created so that younger children learned shorter, higher frequency words, while older children learned longer, lower frequency words. Thus second graders might be assigned words like *mask, first*, or *queen*, while fifth graders might be assigned words like *address, imitate*, or *apartment*. Organizing words this way provided a general control of difficulty, and it guaranteed that the words students studied for spelling were words they used and needed for their writing (Hanna et al., 1971).

The new approach made spelling lessons easier and more practical—a clear advantage over vocabulary approaches. Nonetheless, the learning strategy remained the same. Word lists presented in spelling books were still generally unrelated by pattern; therefore, each word was a separate item for memorization. At the same time, new research-based strategies were elaborated to support word learning and memory. One technique is the Look–Say–Cover–Write–Check *study method*, often recommended in basal spellers and used in multisensory remedial work. Also established in the 1930s and 1940s were the *weekly pretest–study–test* plan and the use of *periodic review*. In addition, it was established that *self-correction* of errors on pretests (copying the word correctly two to three times) further helped in attending to specific spellings. Each of these methods supports the learning and retention of words (Hanna et al., 1971; Schlagal, 2002).

It should be noted that grading words by frequency improved spelling materials for several reasons. First, word frequency has been shown to affect spelling performance (Treiman, 1993). Second, this approach provides information about the nature of the system, although in a broad and indirect way. That is, the progression of word difficulty across the grades generally captures the increasing patterns of complexity in the spelling system. In traditional spelling books words shift from the study of Anglo Saxon terms (*bed, farm, hand, milk*) to more sound-to-pattern Norman French words (*blame, crown, broil, royal, dinner, piece*) in the early to middle elementary years: this vocabulary embodies the foundation of Modern English and represents about 40% of our dictionary entries (Henderson, 1990) and much of our basic vocabulary for common speech and composition. Words of Latin and Greek origin increasingly occupy upper-grade-level spelling material—beginning in the fourth grade and taking strong root in sixth grade and beyond (*insane, ability, exist, meditate, extinguish*) (Henderson, 1990). This band of lower frequency words embodies the strong meaning/pattern component that informs the various academic disciplines and is needed in more learned and formal modes of expression. Students who learn to spell effectively across the grades in this way are likely to absorb information about the system, though in indirect ways.

This frequency-based presentation of words remains, in modified form, in many basal spelling programs today. And further, this general outline of word structure is echoed in the very general outline of spelling benchmarks stated in the CCSS.

Generalization

Due to the widespread belief that our spelling system is too complex and disorderly to teach, a memorization approach to spelling has often been dominant in U.S. education—and as we have seen (above) persists for some teachers today. A second important 20th-century innovation in materials and approaches came from a demonstration that English spelling possessed a far higher degree of order than many had thought. In the 1960s—assisted by newly available computer technology—researchers examined a large body of words by their direct letter–sound correspondences. But they did not stop there. Understanding the complex order of the system, they also examined letter sounds by their position in words (*kick* but not *ckik*), by the effect of stress patterns on spellings—consonants double, as in *omitting*, if the stress is on the syllable before the affix—and by the effect of meaning— past tense is spelled -*ed* regardless of sound, for example, /walkt/, /fannd/, /started/. Only a very small group of words was found to have any truly unpredictable letters. When rules such as these are factored into the study of English, it then appears to be a system that can be learned by and large through pattern generalization rather than strict memorization.

Since English spelling is largely systematic, many spelling basals began to offer lists of words that were organized to highlight patterns within the system. Control of difficulty was still maintained by word frequency and length, but the words were no longer structurally random. Word lists were formed with between one and four patterns, so that there would multiple examples of each spelling feature being taught. If learners grasped patterns taught in the word list, there was a good chance that they could generalize that knowledge to similar untaught words. Additionally, explanations were included in the text to help teachers and students understand the principles being demonstrated. This presentation of graded and structurally organized lists had an advantage over older lists: instead of memorizing 20 individual words, the student learned small clusters of related words, an easier burden on memory and a support for pattern learning.

Current spelling books remain organized around spelling patterns and generalizations and for the most part resemble their later 20th-century predecessors, although some have used developmental research to further refine word and word feature organization. Despite offering a clear advantage over the rote memory approach, however, they do contain an inherent weakness: spelling books are organized strictly by grade level. Although this organization may meet the needs of average learners, it is less likely to meet the needs of children at the top and bottom of their classes—that is, some may experience far too little challenge to promote learning, while some will experience far too much. These latter students have long been observed to retain little from their efforts without teacher adaptations and interventions (Schlagal, 2002; Graham & Harris, 2002). Additionally, teachers may choose not to teach the generalizations represented in the unit. This could be because the teacher does not prioritize spelling, or believes that spelling requires visual memorization, or because he or she lacks a clear understanding of the system and what can be and should be taught (Moats, 2005–2006).

A further difficulty with modern spelling books is that they are typically filled with activities and motivational games like *unscrambling words* that do not contribute to students' understanding of spelling patterns and drive low-achieving spellers to distraction (Schlagal, 2002). Nonetheless, well-structured basal spellers offer teachers a well-thought-out foundation from which to work *if* they are able to reach beyond the word lists to the principles they represent, and if they are able to think beyond the grade-level limits of the spelling book itself. (See discussion below.)

Developmental Spelling Research

Since the late 1970s, educational researchers have shifted their focus away from spelling materials and instructional plans and toward learners (Nelson, 1989; Schlagal, 2001). Working from linguistic insights provided by Charles Read (1975) and Henderson and Beers (1980; see also Templeton & Morris, 2000) demonstrated that young children's misspellings were neither random nor the result of faulty memory. Instead, they were shown to be ingenious and predictable. Errors like FEH (*fish*) could be explained by the fact that there is no single alphabet letter that represents the /sh/ sound, but the letter *h*, if pronounced slowly, contains it. Further, the short-*i* sound is closer by position in the mouth and by sound to the letter name *e* than the letter name *i*. These errors, therefore, were not based on imperfect memorization or faulty phoneme awareness but on accurate analysis of sounds and shrewd use of alphabet letters to represent them.

Here are a few compositions by kindergarteners. Each is a little more sophisticated in spelling development than the previous one. (Note: Students' inventions are capitalized.)

T D ES MI DLS BR DAY.
[Today is my doll's birthday.]

DER MAMA I DO NOT LIK THE WA U AR AKDN TO ME. LOVE ALICE
[Dear Mama, I do not like the way you are acting to me. Love, Alice.]

POLR BERS DIW NOT HIBRNAT IN WINTIR.
[Polar bears do not hibernate in winter.]

Henderson and others (see Templeton & Morris, 2000) have provided a description of spelling development as it changes over time. These changes initially reflect a growing control of sound or phoneme analysis. For example, the first child in the examples above shows only partial phoneme awareness in her spellings of *to* (T), *day* (D), and *dolls* (DLS). By contrast, the third child is showing very complete awareness of the phonemic structure of even complex words like *hibernate* (HIBRNAT) and *winter* (WINTIR). Despite the completeness of the child's analyses, the words are not spelled conventionally. Notice that the second child's spelling of *acting* (AKDN) is also phonemically complete (given her Southern accent) as are her spellings of *way* (WA) and *you* (U), but both show an undeveloped sense of the appearance of English words.

As children's ability to map sounds to letters grows through practice and by instruction and exposure to print, many of their direct letter–sound associations grow more conventional (Henderson & Beers, 1980; Read, 1975; Templeton & Morris, 2000). This growing ability to map sounds to letters becomes a kind of glue that helps hold words in memory. As their knowledge of words increases, children have more information from which to develop more sophisticated theories about the system. Invented spellings gradually become more conventional in appearance as children begin attending to how sounds are spelled, not just to single letters, but also to patterns of letters. Here is an example.

Let me stay up to MIDNITE PLEES, PLEES, PLEES! I won't make NOYSE.
I just want to jump on the bed down STARES like Bobbys TRAMPALEEN.

In this composition, the student shows a high degree of accuracy in basic letter–sound mapping. Consonant blends, short vowels, and basic high-frequency vocabulary are under control. Errors occur, however, as the child tries to spell vowel patterns, as in the words *midnight, please, stairs, trampoline*, and *noise*. (Earlier phonetically driven efforts at these words might have looked like these: MEDNIT, PLEZ, STARS, etc.)

As students learn basic long-vowel and vowel-blend patterns, they face problems caused by operations like *e*-drop and consonant doubling (Schlagal, 1992), and as these more dynamic ways of representing sound by pattern come under control, students struggle to sense how meaning is also represented by spelling patterns (Templeton & Morris, 2000). That is, students must learn to recognize that meaning relations take precedent over sound in upper-level vocabulary. These relations can be seen in word pairs like the ones below. Note that one word in each pair has a challenging element for which sound provides no reliable cue. These elements are indicated by brackets and clarified in the partner word indicated with **bold** print:

regul[a]r–regularity
colum[n]–columnist
compete–comp[e]tition
si[g]n–signature

To summarize, studies of spelling development have provided helpful descriptions of learning and of common error-types as they change across time. These changes reflect a broad movement from early, partial analyses of speech sounds to conventional sound-to-letter matching (phonemic) to sound-pattern representation (orthographic) and finally to the meaning-based patterns of upper-level vocabulary (morphemic). While there is debate about whether to describe this progress in terms like *stages* or *accumulative phases*, there is general agreement among educators that spelling development unfolds in the way described (Moats, 2005–2006). From a practitioner's point of view, this area of research opens up instructionally useful possibilities.

It should be said, however, that some critics object to the idea of a stage-like progression of word knowledge due to the fact that not all of a child's errors may fall into a single stage and that some words at a stage above may be spelled correctly. Although true, stages are not conceived of as ironclad categories, rather as organically evolving strategies that reflect learners' assumptions about the way that words are built. A study by Young (2007) found that only a very small portion of errors examined in spelling lists, compositions, and the like fell outside of children's identified stages. When errors did occur outside of a designated stage, they were almost entirely error-types from the previous lower stage of development. Correctly spelled words from a higher stage of word knowledge were minimal within the already small body of stage outliers. From the developmental position it is the preponderance of error-types that a child makes—errors at the appropriate level of challenge—that reveal the strategy used for building words when a specific spelling is unknown (Schlagal, 2001). And it is in this strategic terrain where instruction is most effective—in the terrain where spelling concepts are well structured but incomplete—not in working with outlying errors that may reveal slips of the pen, inattention, or frustration due to task difficulty. What is more, errors committed at a more primitive strategic level tend to be far easier to self-correct if attention is given to them.

CCSS and Guidelines for Spelling

Although the general CCSS contours relating to spelling loosely follow the path of development described above, there are several areas in which clarity is needed. One of these is the kindergarten standard that children learn to "associate the long and short sounds with common spellings (graphemes) for the five vowels." The terms "grapheme" or even better, *common letter*, can make developmental sense here—and is likely what was intended—but the phrase "common spellings" could be mistaken to imply that kindergarteners should be *taught* long vowel patterns in the ordinary course of things. Although long vowels are relatively easy to identify auditorily, *common spellings* for long vowels are more abstract, varied, and thus complex (*rain, boat, tape, keep, so* etc.) These are mastered at a slower rate than is typical for most developing kindergarteners (Schlagal, 1992).

On the other hand, learning the "spelling–sound correspondences for common consonant digraphs" is a basic alphabetic phoneme–grapheme concept and would be better placed in the standards for kindergarten rather than first grade (Invernizzi, 1992; Schlagal, 1992). There they do not make developmental sense.

Because reading and spelling are mutually supportive, it would be helpful to see more specificity related to spelling as the CCSS move up through the grades. For example, at grades four and five there is no practical information, the chief standard being "Spell grade-appropriate words correctly, consulting references as needed." But grade-level words are more complex and challenging at grade four than at grade three and more complex and challenging at grade five than at grade four. In grades six through eight the standards indicate only that the student is to "spell correctly," an ability that does not emerge spontaneously and ignores the fact that words continue to grow in complexity and diversity of pattern across these grades. The standards from grades four through eight appear to assume that students will have acquired nearly all the information they need in the first three grades to spell correctly or access correct spellings through other sources.

There is much that students need to learn about words at each of the grades four through eight in order to spell accurately "grade-appropriate words" or to be able to locate correct spellings elsewhere. In fourth grade, for example, students begin to confront in reading and writing a growing number of vowels in unaccented syllables as well as *r*-controlled vowels. These are words like *harvəst, cabbəge, caməl, doctər,* and *scərry.* (Although not difficult to read, they are tricky to spell.) The difficulty of these features increases as words become more syllabically dense. That problems with schwa and *r*-colored vowels continue into the middle school years and beyond are well documented (Gates, 1937; Schlagal, 1992). Similar schwa-based problems can be found in the *-able/-ible* and *-ance/-ence* endings that appear with increasing frequency in upper-level elementary vocabulary (along with the *-tion/-sion/-cian*). And schwa poses problems words like *justəce, populər*, and *norməl* (fifth grade by word frequency) or *hostiləty, accustəm*, or *combənation* (sixth grade by word frequency).

Beginning at grade 6 students confront a growing body of words with consonant doubling complexities due to affixing (*correspond, commotion, illustration, interrupt*) and due to stress and letter position (*committed* vs. *commitment*). No standards related to spelling appear again in the CCSS until grades 9 through 12 when, along with "spell correctly," standards state that students should correctly use "patterns of word changes"; that is, they should be able to use base words and their derivatives (grades 9–10: *analyze, analysis, analytical; advocate, advocacy*, or grades 10–12: *conceive, conception, conceivable*). However, to acquire this ability requires word study that would begin far earlier, typically in fifth grade for achieving grade-level learners.

For example, the concept of base and derived word forms can be introduced as early as third grade (for most children) with consonant doubling and *e*-drop sort (above). The idea of base and derived forms can then be extended in the upper elementary grades to help clarify schwa sounds by accessing multiple forms: *regulər—regularity, combine—combənation*; or to clarify silent letters: *colum(n)—conlumnist, si(g)n—signal*. In grade 6, many students are ready to be taught how prefixes that they have already learned often adjust their spelling to fit with the bases to which they are added. *Ad-* (to) and *sub-* (under), for example, are altered and create the doublings in *am*munition, *at*tempt, *as*sign, or *ar*rest and *suc*ceed, *sug*gest, *sum*mon, or *suf*fice. Word sorts can be created for such words as well as words with suffix endings that need study (e.g., *-able/-ible* or *-sion/-cian*).

It has been written in defense of the standards that they are designed as an "accessible roadmap" (CCSS) and not a set of prescriptions. In the case of spelling, however, the roadway vanishes from the map after the third grade. It is not until ninth grade that any destinations appear, but how the learner is to arrive at these destinations remains undefined.

Along with a need for expanded detail showing grade-level expectations for spelling, it would be important that the CCSS provide recommendations for addressing the needs of lower performing students. Research of various kinds supports the effectiveness of interventions in improving inadequately established foundations, whether in spelling, handwriting, reading, or writing (Graham & Harris, 2002).

Developmental Spelling Instruction

Based on research and clinical work with poor readers and poor spellers, the late Edmund H. Henderson (Henderson, 1990; Henderson & Beers, 1980) developed a systematic approach for teaching spelling without the use of traditional materials. The popular *Words Their Way* (Bear,

Invernizzi, Templeton, & Johnston, 2011) is a classroom adaptation of this approach. Because Henderson found that there was a strong connection between spelling and reading ability, he did not separate teaching spelling from word analysis and word recognition. Based on a systematic assessment of children's current word knowledge (Henderson, 1990; Schlagal, 1992), Henderson sought to improve students' word recognition and spelling ability in very precise ways. He elaborated a system of categorization tasks in which children compare and contrast spelling patterns within groups of words in order to highlight the features they may be using, but may be confused about. In other words, word-study activities are created to connect with and extend children's current grasp of the spelling system as well as to automatize word and pattern recognition.

A group of first graders, for instance, might be having difficulty spelling short vowels correctly. Therefore, they would be directed toward categorization activities involving the sorting of *known* single-syllable words using strongly contrastive short vowels. A sort might be constructed using the following words as *headers*. That is, the words below in italics establish the categories under which children will name and sort words into the short-*a*, -*i*, and -*o* columns. A completed sort might look like this:

mat	*sit*	*cop*
nap	big	not
rag	dip	dog
mad	lid	rob

In this activity, a child is given a word card. The child (1) *names* the word, (2) places it in the proper category, and (3) reads down the list of words in that category. (Reading down the list gives the student a chance to catch any mistakes and provides repeated experience reading the individual words.) Children take turns naming and sorting words until all words have been placed. At that time, the teacher guides the students as a group to read down a single list and tell "how all the words are the same." The children might say "They all have *a*." The teacher then asks, "What sound do you hear *a* making in these words?," and so on. This process is repeated for each list. Note that additional words with the same sound/spelling pattern can be added or substituted as a challenge across a period of study. These could involve not only different words but other features like consonant blends (beginning and/or ending), consonant digraphs, and the like.

Reading research indicates that basic print skills must be learned accurately but also learned to the point of being automatic (Perfetti, 1985). That is, all facets of letter–sound recognition, word analysis, word recognition, and text reading must be done quickly, accurately, and effortlessly. For this reason this word-sort activity (and its variants) is intended to be practiced over the course of a number of days until children can quickly name and sort each word. As this activity becomes automatic, students should be checked on their ability to spell the words correctly. The purpose of this short-vowel word study is to assist with automatic word recognition, enhance sensitivity to letter–sound relationships, and promote accurate spelling of the basic short-vowel word patterns.

When students become accurate and quick with the short-vowel sort above, an additional strategy can be helpful. In this activity, the teacher makes words for students to read, changing the elements to highlight the particular letter–sound structure with which they are working (Morris, 2005). (Pocket charts and letter cards, a Smart Board, or a magnetic surface and magnetic letters can be helpful here.) To begin, the teacher creates a short-vowel word and begins to manipulate beginning, middle, and final elements. For example, he or she might make and ask children to read the following word:

f-a-t

He or she might continue by changing beginning sounds (the easiest):

f-a-t→ b-a-t→ r-a-t→ m-a-t

and then move to final sounds (more difficult):

m-a-t→ m-a-p→ m-a-n→ m-a-d

and finally to the medial vowel (the hardest): s-a-t→ s-i-t→ s-o-t

Note that the teacher changes one letter sound at a time at first. If children can handle each of these manipulations, he or she can begin to change more than one, as follows:

r-a-t→ f-i-t→ b-a-g→ d-o-g

Blends and digraphs can be added for additional challenge: (flat→ slit→ slot→ shot)

In a reversal of this task, the teacher provides sets of letters to children, asking them to make words that he or she names. By dictating predictable short -a, -i, and -o words to students, the teacher can see more closely who is able to make and transform the words quickly and easily and who requires more time and practice. When students make words themselves in this way, they are forced into greater attention to details of sound and letter choice than is needed for the recognition of words. (Notice that the words represent only patterns that are currently being studied and never ones that have not yet been taught.)

When students have mastered short-vowel words and can handle most consonant blends and digraphs (like the writer of the trampoline story described earlier), they are prepared to move into the study of basic vowel patterns. Here, the student is introduced to the way a single vowel can represent different sounds based on the spelling pattern of the word. A completed sort for the *a*-pattern might look like this:

back	*came*	*card*
flat	tape	sharp
fast	flame	farm
slap	cake	hard

By comparing, contrasting, and sorting the above words, students can see that the letter *a* may take on different sounds based on the spelling pattern—c*ac*, c*ace*, or c*arc*—in which it occurs. It is important that students note both the sound that *a* makes in a correctly sorted column of words and the structure that cues it. The decision-making process in word sorts helps emphasize order within and across words and can assist with pattern generalization (Morris, 2005; Templeton & Morris, 2000).

Note that the *a*-pattern sort (above) contains the now well-known short *a*. It is important that students be able to contrast what is new with what is already understood. If too much new material is presented at once, confusion is often the result (Henderson, 1990; Morris, Nelson, & Perney, 1986). That is why only one long-vowel pattern at a time is typically introduced. Once the above patterns have been confidently mastered, another form of long *a* (e.g., *-ai-* or *-ay*) can be added.

Again, as a sort moves toward mastery, using the make-a-word activity can provide another important form of practice. To illustrate how this might work with vowel patterns, the teacher makes the following word:

f-a-d

After the children have read the word *fad*, the teacher might change it by adding a silent *e* (f-a-d-e) and asking what the word has become. The teacher might continue manipulating the target structures in a path like this:

f-a-d-e→ b-a-n-e→ b-a-n→ b-a-r-n→
b-l-a-m→ b-l-a-m-e→ a-r-m→ a-r-k→

b-a-r-k→ f-l-a-c-k→ f-l-a-k-e→ s-n-a-k-e→

s-n-a-g→ s-n-a-r-l→ n-a-p→ g-r-a-b

As before, reading the words should be followed by students making similar words themselves that the teacher dictates. The teacher can also make the operation more explicit by asking students to explain the transformations: "Why did the *a* change its sound here? What did the silent *e* do to the vowel? Can you hear the *a* when it's combined with an *r*?"

The basic *a*-patterns are typically easiest for most children. Once these are mastered, one can move through remaining vowel patterns. The following progression is typical and follows the *a*-pattern. (Items in parentheses can be substituted or included one by one after the previous patterns have been mastered. Note also that the *e*-pattern is generally taught last because the more common long vowel patterns are -ee and -ea rather than the more common silent-*e*.)

i-pattern: *swim drive girl (right, my, wild)*

o-pattern: *stop rope corn (boat, soon, sold, hook)*

u-pattern: *mud huge burn (few, blue, juice)*

e-pattern: *get need he (mean, deaf)*

Students who have gained control of basic short- and long-vowel patterns are developmentally ready to examine the operations involved in the addition of *-ed* and *-ing* endings. In this case, students are directed to become aware of the structure of the base word in order to determine whether modifications in spelling are needed. In other words, if you add *-ed* or *-ing* to one-syllable short-vowel words ending in two or more consonants *(back, blast)*, then you do nothing to the base word *(backing, blasted)*. If, however, the word ends in a single consonant, then you must double that consonant before the ending *(trap–trapping)*. If you add *-ed* or *-ing* to a long-vowel word with a vowel pair *(sleep, boat)*, then you do nothing to the base word *(sleeping, boating)*. If, however, the word ends in a silent *e*, then the *e* is dropped *(scrape–scraping)*.

Errors involving the joining of syllables may continue across grades if the correct strategies are not carefully taught and reinforced as two syllable base words enter the picture (Schlagal, 1992). Many spelling series present the doubling/*e*-drop principle by listing words in their completed form; although the text will give an explanation of it, there is likely to be no specific study of the principle *in action*. A word-sort approach engages children in the active manipulation of the words both in their base and inflected forms.

The consonant doubling/*e*-drop sort highlights the doubling/*e*-drop operation. In this activity, the teacher begins with the single vowel (*a*), as follows:

tape	*taping*	*tap*	*tapping*
s-h-a-p-e	shaping	g-r-a-b	grabbing
s-h-a-v-e	shaving	b-a-t	batted
t-a-m-e	taming	c-l-a-p	clapping
trade	t-r-a-d-i-n-g	fan	f-a-n-n-e-d

Headers for the base words are included in the doubling/*e*-drop table so that students have a point of reference. Each time a word is handed to a student, the student says the word, places the word in the correct column, indicates whether the vowel is long or short, and spells the base word. For example, the child might read *shaping*, place it under *taping*, then say, "long *a*; it comes from *shape*: s-h-a-p-e." In this way, the child has to remove the *-ing* and restore the *-e*. As students grasp the operation, the task can be reversed so that they sort the base word (e.g., *trade*), indicate whether it is short or long, then spell the inflected form (*trading*). These kinds of manipulations can lead to a practical understanding of these transformations.

Once the doubling/*e*-drop sort has been mastered, the teacher can guide students through the same operation with other vowels. As the principle is grasped in these single-vowel conditions, students can move to sorting with multiple vowels. (This is where understanding long vs. short is critical.) One can also sort two-syllable open and closed syllable words to highlight sound and syllable division patterns.

For older students, word sorts take on additional interest as meaning comes into play. This initially involves the use of simple prefixes (*un-, re-, ex-*) and suffixes (*-ful, -less,* and *-ness*) and moves on to roots like *-tract-, -spect-* and *-port-*. After a sort like the one below has been completed, students should examine the words, say what is the same in a column, and from their understanding of word meanings, try to guess the meaning of the roots.

tractor	*spectator*	*portable*
sub**tract**	in**spect**	trans**port**
at**tract**	**spect**acular	sup**port**ive
dis**tract**ion	**spect**acles	re**port**
traction	re**spect**	im**port**

This method parallels the follow-up activities above in which students are directed to discover the common spelling pattern and say how it functions in the target words. In this case, by trying to think through to the common root meaning, students begin to sensitize themselves to spelling pattern–meaning connections in upper-level vocabulary.

In sum, developmental spelling instruction has several advantages. First, if word study is adjusted appropriately, instruction is tailored to the specific needs of individual students (or groups) by means of ongoing observation and assessment. Second, it builds skill through specific word and word pattern recognition. Third, it develops spelling ability through the manipulation of patterns that may be generalized to other words of the same kind. Additionally, word sorts can be adapted to any number of interesting games and activities (Bear et al., 2011; Morris, 2005). And finally it can be extended to the manipulation of letter–sounds and patterns from parts-to-whole once key concepts have been grasped in the medium of known words and perceived patterns—that is, through quick, accurate sorting. In this way, word study allows one to combine analytic and synthetic phonics, using the strengths of each while avoiding their shortcomings as isolated approaches. The focus thus captures word, pattern, and sound in a very complete linguistic performance.

Of course, a difficulty that all teachers face is the varied levels of students in a given classroom. Individualizing instruction across several groups is an organizational challenge for the teacher. It requires appropriate assessment and the use or development of instructionally appropriate word-sort activities and routines. In addition, this approach requires teachers to learn something about children's spelling development, about the spelling system itself, and about word-study routines. Clearly, such knowledge is of value to both the teacher and the student (Moats, 2006), but not all teachers have the foundational knowledge needed or the means to acquire it.

Developmental spelling instruction is designed to aid students in progressively mastering the spelling system. Although this mastery is essential to becoming a skillful speller (as well as reader and writer), this approach does not generally include explicit instruction on high-frequency irregular words (*from, friend, have, been*, etc.). These kinds of words must be taught separately, although they can be examined usefully by their contrast with well-understood spelling patterns so that their idiosyncrasies can be highlighted. The *study method* (Look–Say–Cover–Write–Check) can be helpful when such words prove difficult.

Current Instructional Research

Many teachers wish to maximize student learning through appropriate instructional placement, but they may not have the time or experience to design a developmental spelling sequence. As an alternative, teachers can adapt well-organized basal spellers for that purpose. This approach draws on strengths of spelling books, while avoiding their primary weakness: the implication that one basal speller meets the needs of all students in a grade.

Spelling experts have long argued that a single grade-level spelling book does not meet the needs of every child in a class (Hanna et al., 1971; Schlagal, 2002; Templeton & Morris, 2000). Although many students will gain meaningfully from grade-level spellers, some (working with minimal challenge) will find little new to learn, while others (working at a frustration level) will find far too much that is unfamiliar to benefit from instruction. Of particular concern in this setting is the latter group of students.

Morris and his colleagues (1986) demonstrated that students working at a frustration level (scoring below 40% accuracy on a curricular spelling assessment) made errors in spelling that were far poorer in quality than students working above that level. Morris et al. further studied the gains of poor spellers after a year's worth of grade-level spelling book instruction in their classrooms (Morris, Blanton, Blanton, Nowacek, & Perney, 1995). Although the poor spellers did well on end-of-week tests, their long-term retention and mastery of spelling concepts was poor in comparison with their instructional-level peers, who made significant strides in both areas. Yet when poor spellers were placed in lower-grade-level books, where they had a better foundation of word knowledge, they performed just like their higher functioning peers. That is, when studying words at an appropriate level of difficulty, they retained the majority of the words they studied across the year, and they developed concepts that allowed them to spell words accurately that they had not studied, something their frustration-level peers were unable to do (Morris, Blanton, Blanton, & Perney, 1995). Further, these results were uniform despite marked differences in the amount of time different teachers gave to spelling or the varied methods (including word sorts) they used for teaching.

Adapting Conventional Materials to Meet Every Child's Needs

Contemporary spelling books provide a useful resource for teachers and, if used in innovative ways, can be an important component of instruction. Owing to their use of word frequency, organized lists, and a clear progression of difficulty, spelling books can be adapted in several ways to make spelling instruction more interesting and more effective, especially in meeting the needs of those experiencing difficulty.

Accurate placement is a key to success in spelling instruction. Instructional groups may be created by using a curriculum-based assessment: if one is not available with the spelling series, one can be made from a random selection of about 30 words from the master list taught across the year. A diagnostic developmental inventory like the Qualitative Inventory of Word Knowledge (Schlagal, 1992) may also be used. Students who score well below 40% in accuracy on such assessments should be placed at levels in which they are scoring above 40%. The errors of students who score between 30 and 40% should be examined carefully for quality. If their words are "off " by only one or two letters, then they may be considered teachable at grade level. If the errors reveal a greater loss of quality, then they should be considered at frustration level. Students who score 85% or above may be asked to search out their own lists of more challenging words with the same patterns as those in the grade-level list.

Monday:
1. Pretest of the week's new words without review
2. Students score and correct errors, writing the correct spelling twice.
3. The teacher leads instructional groups through a word sort to highlight the patterns for each group.

Tuesday:
1. Each child receives a copy of the week's words as enlarged words on a sheet of paper.
2. Words from the sheets are cut up individually and sorted into the same categories as Monday.
3. Individual sorts are checked by the teacher for correctness.
4. Children pair up and play Concentration (Memory) or any other game that requires matching words by spoken and written patterns.

Wednesday:
1. Students hunt for words with the same patterns in books or magazines.
2. Students do timed speed sorts with a partner to couple quickness with accuracy.

Thursday:
Students practice spellings with partners, with one student calling out the words and the other spelling them out loud (an example for each category may be given for reference) as they write them in appropriate columns on a dry-erase board or something similar.

Friday:
The weekly spelling test is given. Teachers may combine all the words into one list that each child tries (children are only graded on the words they studied that week). Other ways of giving separate tests can involve assistants, parent volunteers, or the use of recordings. A similar program to this one was subjected to careful research and found effective with struggling second-grade spellers (Graham et al., 2002).

FIGURE 11.1. A week's spelling activities.

Although the most important feature of this approach is appropriate placement, sorting activities can be used with the book's lists to help students grasp patterns that are being taught in a given week of instruction (Graham, Harris, & Fink-Chorzempa, 2002; Schlagal, 2002). The kinds of activities shown in Figure 11.1 can be lively, engaging, and instructionally powerful.

An advantage to adapting spelling books for instructional-level work—that is, using more than one grade level of spelling book—is that they provide a ready resource of graded and organized word lists from which to engage in developmentally appropriate spelling instruction. Because basal spellers typically have patterned lists, they can also be adapted for word-sorting activities (although sorting itself, though helpful, is not as important as placing children at the *right level of difficulty*—see Morris, Blanton, Blanton, Nowacek, et al., 1995). In addition, one can easily use research-based activities like the *study, self-correction*, and *practice methods* (described above) along with *periodic review*.

Spelling books can save a teacher considerable effort, eliminating the time needed to create or extract appropriate lists of words from some other source. Adjusting spelling instruction along students' instructional levels ensures that spelling instruction is developmentally appropriate, that is, that it is meeting the needs of all of the students, not just those for whom the grade-level book is a good fit. But any adaptation of this kind requires greater planning and organization on the part of teachers.

Handwriting

Historically and well into the 20th century, handwriting was viewed as an important component of literacy instruction, and efforts to develop both a fluent, legible manuscript and cursive writing spanned most of the elementary years. Currently, however, handwriting is minimally represented in elementary level curricula, and it is nearly nonexistent in teacher preparation programs. (Increasing contemporary use of keyboards and keypads in high-speed digital communication would seem to argue for keyboard primacy, while diminishing the usefulness of handwritten communication). This bias appears to be reflected in the CCSS. The CCSS does not mention cursive, and handwriting legibility and fluidity are confined to kindergarten and first-grade goals. There is no evidence that most children can achieve adequate competence in handwriting in the span of 2 years' focus. Recent articles and reports have appeared in various news and opinion outlets criticizing the general neglect of this subject area in the CCSS. Nor are these objections merely nostalgic and sentimental. There are good empirical reasons behind them.

Despite the diminished place of handwriting in the curriculum and the broad availability of word-processing programs, fluent and legible writing remains a necessary practical skill. In the academic world alone, it is needed for adequate note taking, state proficiency tests, and standardized tests requiring handwritten essays. And poor handwriting influences judgments about the quality of written work (Briggs, 1980) and even about the education, intelligence, or professional competence of writers. Students' perceptions of their own handwriting also affect their judgments about themselves as writers (Graham, 1992; Graham & Weintraub, 1996).

Recently, Graham, Harris, and Hebert (2011) combined the results of available studies of *presentation effects* on writing scores. Their analysis demonstrated the negative impact of noncontent factors (poor spelling, handwriting, grammar, or the use of word-processed text) on judgments of writing quality. Deficiencies in any of these factors led to harsher judgments on the writing of both school-age and college-age students. Although poor usage in any factor lowered the perceived quality of the writing, poor handwriting among school-age students had the largest negative impact.

Poorly developed handwriting, however, can affect more than judgments about written content and writing ability. In combination with poor spelling and by itself, it can contribute to disability in written expression (Graham, Harris, & Fink, 2000). Just as a failure to develop accurate and automatic decoding can impair comprehension in readers, failure to develop legible and automatic letter and word formation may interfere with content in writing (Jones & Christensen, 1999). Students who struggle to retrieve letters from memory, to reproduce them on the page, and to scale them to other letters have less attention available to spend on spelling, planning, and effectively expressing intended meanings (Hayes & Chenowith, 2006).

In contrast, when the component skills of writing are automatic, writers are free to devote their energy to the composition itself, although attention alone is not enough to guarantee improved content. Because of the excessive labor and unattractive results involved in such writing, students are more likely to avoid or minimize the process when possible (Graham & Weintraub, 1996).

Further, recent findings indicate that students across the elementary years write quicker and longer essays when using a pen as opposed to a keyboard (Berninger, Abbott, Augsburger, & Garcia, 2009), and that they contain more ideas (Hayes & Berninger, 2009). This finding contradicts the assumption that children will write more and faster if trained to keyboards. Indeed, as stated above, scorers of word-processed texts have also been shown to grade these products more severely than handwritten texts (Graham et al., 2011). More fundamental still, evidence suggests that learning letters and spellings by hand is superior to learning them with a keyboard (Longcamp et al., 2008). That is, the tactile feedback from forming letters and spellings by hand provides a firmer mental representation of the word for both recognition (reading) and spelling.

Finally, there is evidence that direct instruction and sufficient practice in handwriting can play a significant role in preventing the development of writing disabilities among younger students (Graham et al., 2000). This important fact should be considered from the point of view of both regularly planned instruction in the primary grades and of intervention among students who struggle with handwriting. Given these findings, it is important to examine issues and methods of handwriting instruction.

Issues in Handwriting

There is a long-standing controversy over the best way to teach the formation of letters. Should children be introduced to writing through a traditional manuscript alphabet and later to cursive, as was common throughout most of the 20th century? Should students begin with cursive to prevent the difficulties of learning a new way to write in later grades? Or should they be taught a slanted or italic version of print that is designed to connect with cursive and so ease the difficulty of transition?

Those who favor introducing writing through manuscript argue that vertical, lower-case letters are close to what children encounter in print and that printed letters in writing are easier for them to read (Sheffield, 1996). In addition, they argue that children who come to school with letter knowledge will have learned and been exposed to basic manuscript forms. By making explicit instructional connections with what children already know, teachers avoid the problem of having to revise or correct what their students may have already learned. Further, advocates argue that forming manuscript letters involves far fewer fine-motor movements than does forming cursive or slanted letters and is therefore easier for younger children.

Those who advocate beginning with cursive state that writing is more a kinesthetic than a visual act (Sheffield, 1996). Because an important element of word knowledge is motor memory (Hanna et al., 1971; Longcamp et al., 2008), it is said that developing memory for spellings is easier when words are written in a continuous flow rather than when composed of physically separated letters. Although teaching cursive may make greater demands on students in the beginning, it is also said that there are immediate benefits to this approach, even for beginners. For example, because *b* and *d* are formed differently in cursive and are not mirror images of one another, reversal problems can be avoided from the outset. Also, because letters within words are connected, children are said to be able to manage the problem of spacing *between* words more easily, and, as mentioned above, children do not have to make the time-consuming and often imperfect transition from manuscript to cursive in second and/or third grade.

Most advocates of the cursive-only approach are concerned primarily with disabled readers and writers (Sheffield, 1996). Teaching these students cursive is often part of the instructional retraining process. Tutors or therapists seek to undo the fixed, imperfect, partial learning that characterizes disabled reading and writing and to rebuild them on a firmer foundation. Training students in cursive is often an integral part of this process. Whether the experience of clinicians working with disabled writers provides the best insights for general education is unclear. Despite the logic of the cursive-only claims, there is too little research at this point to verify them, especially for normal populations (Graham & Weintraub, 1996), and the weight of contemporary attitudes and practices works against it (see CCSS). (One should note that some states like Massachusetts and California have supplemented the CCSS to include the teaching of cursive.)

Because of the difficulty that many children experience in making the transition from manuscript to cursive, some advocate the use of a slanted initial teaching alphabet that is more like cursive than vertical manuscript. It is claimed that this promotes easier and more complete adaptation to cursive. Many schools choose to use slanted or italic letter forms in their handwriting instruction precisely because of these transitional problems.

A shortcoming of a slanted or italic alphabet involves the increased number and complexity of strokes that young children must perform in order to make the letters (Graham, 1992). As a result, students are less able to produce consistently well-shaped and proportioned letters. In addition, evidence does not support the claim that slanted alphabets assist in the transition to cursive or result in quicker, more fluid, or more legible writing (Graham & Weintraub, 1996).

Due to its relative simplicity and comparative legibility, the evidence appears to support the use of the traditional manuscript form with a transition to cursive later in the primary grades. The question remains: What practices best assist students in developing good handwriting?

Handwriting Instruction

Because careful teaching and practice of handwriting can facilitate fluency in writing and may prevent writing disabilities (Berninger et al., 2009; Graham et al., 2000), it is important to provide explicit instruction and sufficient opportunity to practice correct letter formation. Short daily practice sessions are likely to be more effective (and more interesting) than longer, less regular sessions. Although there should be time to practice handwriting as a separate skill, it should not replace the time given to regular writing.

There should be abundant opportunity in the classroom for students to write meaningfully and purposefully so that they can apply and extend the skills they acquire through separate practice (Graham & Weintraub, 1996; Henderson, 1990).

How the alphabet is best introduced is not a settled matter, nor is the order in which letters are best taught. ABC order is not necessarily the most effective way to introduce letters, in part because the reversible letters *b* and *d* come so close to each other. (Thoroughly teaching one before teaching the other is likely to reduce confusion.) Further, if letter sounds are taught with letter names, the sounds for the vowels *a* and *e*—short sounds as in *s<u>a</u>d* and *b<u>e</u>d*—are initially confusing to young children (Read, 1975). Therefore, a teaching order in which confusable letters and sounds are carefully separated seems preferable to a strict ABC order.

Teacher modeling of correct letter formation is an important component of instruction. For beginners, both visual and verbal modeling (i.e., the teacher demonstrates how a letter is made correctly while describing how it is formed) appears to be the most effective means of introducing a letter prior to practice (Graham & Weintraub, 1996). Teacher explanations appear to be less effective for students in higher grades than modeling alone (Graham & Weintraub, 1996). Perhaps, already knowing the letters, older students find teacher explanations unneeded and distracting. Nonetheless, clear and correct models are an important ingredient in guiding students to effective practice.

Copying a letter from a correct model is helpful to students' practice, and it can be made more effective by adding several components. The teacher can provide a model in which numbered arrows indicate how the strokes are to be made (Berninger et al., 1997). After examining the model carefully, the student should cover it and write the letter from memory. Incorporating numbered arrows and adding a simple visual memory technique appears to be more effective than other forms of copying. This method parallels the helpful "look, say, cover, write, check" tradition in spelling practice (Henderson, 1990). Students can also benefit from learning to verbalize a set of rules for forming a letter so that they can guide themselves through the process, but the verbal guide should be one easily committed to memory (Graham & Weintraub, 1996).

Implementing research-based handwriting instruction need not be dull or routine. Some programs combine story- and song-based instruction with research-based methods in ways that are memorable, engaging, and pleasurable. An example of this is the British Letterland program (Wendon & Freese, 2003). In Letterland, an imaginary land where letters come to life, a letter is first introduced as a pictogram. That is, the outline of each letter is used to create a character. For example, the letter *c* is introduced as Clever Cat. Her face is drawn within the arc of the *c* and her ears above it. Once

Clever Cat has been examined, students are shown the plain letter *c* and told that much of the time she cannot be seen because she likes to keep it a secret that she is there. Students are then given a sheet of paper with a large letter *c* and invited to draw their own picture of Clever Cat's face like the one on the pictogram card.

Prior to learning to write the letter *c*, children are introduced to a song that explains how she likes to be stroked: "Curve round Clever Cat's face to begin. Then gently tickle her under her chin" (p. 35). The teacher then models slowly tracing the pictogram as students recite the verse. This is then repeated as the teacher traces over a letter C without the pictogram. Next, the teacher draws a large *c* on the board while the children trace it in the air, imagining that Clever Cat is still visible within her letter. Students then practice "stroking" Clever Cat on their own, working from arrow-guided models. Children may also animate the letters they have written by drawing in the characters they know.

The sounds of letters and letter combinations are also imaginatively taught in this program. When a minimum number of letters and sounds has been learned, students begin using the pictograms (and props) to act out the sounds of simple consonant–vowel–consonant words in "live spelling." Thus, letter formation, letter sounds, and phonemic analysis are carefully introduced and exercised from the beginning of the program.

For older students—and especially LD students (Graham & Weintraub, 1996)—with handwriting problems, strategies that emphasize neatness and self-monitoring have been shown to be helpful. These can include checklists, peer assistance, and praise. For more severe problems, reteaching letter formation using evidence based methods may be necessary.

Conclusion

More than anything else, contemporary research on spelling and handwriting tells us that these skills are not unimportant. In fact, they are fundamental building blocks. Neglecting them can lead to social, educational, and personal consequences; and poorly developed spelling or handwriting can affect the higher level literacy processes in which they are embedded. There is sufficient empirical evidence of their essential value to give them a more important role in the curriculum. Much that we know now can improve the quality and efficiency of spelling and handwriting instruction. By carefully considering the research, classroom teachers can find or create thoughtful programs to advance learning and increase engagement and interest in these core aspects of literacy. At this time, however, that means going beyond the marked limitations of the CCSS in these areas.

References

Bear, D. R., Invernizzi, M., Templeton, S., & Johnston, F. (2004). *Words their way: Word study for phonics, vocabulary, and spelling instruction.* Columbus, OH: Merrill.

Berninger, V. W., Abbott, R. D., Augsburger, A., & Garcia, N. (2009). Comparison of pen and keyboard transcription modes in children with and without learning disabilities. *Learning Disability Quarterly, 32,* 123–141.

Berninger, V. W., Vaughn, K., Abbott, R., Abbott, S., Rogan, L., Brooks, A., et al. (1997). Treatment of handwriting problems in beginning writers: Transfer from handwriting to composition. *Journal of Educational Psychology, 89,* 652–666.

Briggs, D. (1980). A study of the influence of handwriting upon grades using examination scripts. *Educational Review, 32,* 185–193.

Gates, A. I. (1937). *A list of spelling difficulties in 3876 words: Showing the "hard spots," common misspellings, average spelling grade-placement, and comprehension grade ratings of each word.* New York: Teachers College Press.

Graham, S. (1992). Issues in handwriting instruction. *Focus on Exceptional Children, 25,* 1–14.

Graham, S., & Harris, K. R. (2002). The road less traveled: Prevention and intervention in written language. In K. Butler & E. Stillman (Eds.), *Spelling, reading, and handwriting* (pp. 199–217). Mahwah, NJ: Erlbaum.

Graham, S., Harris, K. R., & Fink, B. (2000). Is handwriting causally related to learning to write?: Treatment of handwriting problems in beginning writers. *Journal of Educational Psychology, 92,* 620–633.

Graham, S., Harris, K. R., & Fink-Chorzempa, B. (2002). The contribution of spelling instruction to the spelling, writing, and reading of poor spellers. *Journal of Educational Psychology, 94,* 669–686.

Graham, S., Harris, K. R., & Hebert, M. (2011). It is more than just the message: Presentation effects in scoring writing. *Focus on Exceptional Children, 44,* 1–12.

Graham, S., & Hebert, M. (2010). *Writing to read: Evidence for how writing can improve reading* (A Carnegie Corporation Time to Act Report). Washington, DC: Alliance for Excellent Education.

Graham, S., Morphy, P., Harris, K. R., Fink-Chorzempa, B., Saddler, B., Moran, S., et al. (2008). Teaching spelling in the primary grades: A national survey of instructional practices and adaptations. *American Educational Research Journal, 45,* 796–825.

Graham, S., & Weintraub, N. (1996). A review of handwriting research: Progress and prospects from 1980 to 1994. *Educational Psychology Review, 8,* 7–87.

Hanna, P. R., Hodges, R. E., & Hanna, J. S. (1971). *Spelling: Structure and strategies.* Boston: Houghton Mifflin.

Hayes, J. R., & Berninger, V. W. (2010). Relationships between idea generation and transcription: How the act of writing shapes what children write. In C. Braverman, R. Krut, K. Lundsford, S. McLeod, S. Null, P. Rogers, et al. (Eds.), *Traditions of writing research* (pp. 166–180). New York: Routledge.

Hayes, J. R., & Chenoweth, N. A. (2007). Working memory in an editing task. *Written Communication, 24,* 283–294.

Henderson, E. H. (1990). *Teaching spelling* (2nd ed.). Boston: Houghton Mifflin.

Henderson, E. H., & Beers, J. W. (Eds.). (1980). *Developmental and cognitive aspects of learning to spell: A reflection of word knowledge.* Newark, DE: International Reading Association.

Invernizzi, M. A. (1992). The vowel and what follows: A phonological frame of orthographic analysis. In S. Templeton & D. Bear (Eds.), *Development of orthographic knowledge and the foundations of literacy: A memorial festschrift for Edmund H. Henderson* (pp. 32–52). Hillsdale, NJ: Erlbaum.

Johnston, F. R. (2001). Exploring classroom teachers' spelling practices and beliefs. *Reading Research and Instruction, 40,* 143–156.

Jones, D., & Christensen, C. A. (1999). Relationship between automaticity in handwriting and students' ability to generate written text. *Journal of Educational Psychology, 91,* 44–49.

Longcamp, M., Boucard, C., Gilhodes, J. C., Anton, J. L., Roth, M., Nazarian, B., et al. (2008). Learning through hand- or typewriting influences visual recognition of new graphic shapes: Behavioral and functional imaging evidence. *Journal of Cognitive Science, 20,* 802–815.

Moats, L. C. (1995). *Spelling: Development, disability and instruction.* Baltimore: York Press.

Moats, L. C. (2005–2006). How spelling supports reading. *American Educator, Winter,* 12–23.

Morris, D. (2005). *The Howard Street tutoring manual: Teaching at-risk readers in the primary grades* (2nd ed.). New York: Guilford Press.

Morris, D., Blanton, L., Blanton, W. E., Nowacek, J., & Perney, J. (1995). Teaching low-achieving spellers at their "instructional level." *Elementary School Journal, 96,* 163–177.

Morris, D., Blanton, L., Blanton, W. E., & Perney, J. (1995). Spelling instruction and achievement in six classrooms. *Elementary School Journal, 96,* 145–162.

Morris, D., Nelson, L., & Perney, J. (1986). Exploring the concept of "spelling instructional level" through the analysis of error-types. *Elementary School Journal, 87,* 181–200.

National Governors Association & Council of Chief State School Officers. (2010). *Common Core State Standards for English language arts & literacy in history/social studies, science, and technical subjects.* Washington, DC: Authors. Retrieved from *www. corestandards.org.*

Nelson, L. (1989). Something borrowed, something new: Teaching implications of developmental spelling research. *Reading Psychology, 10,* 255–274.

Perfetti, C. A. (1985). *Reading ability.* New York: Oxford University Press.

Read, C. (1975). *Children's categorization of speech sounds in English.* Urbana, IL: National Council of Teachers of English.

Schlagal, B. (2001). Traditional, developmental, and structured language approaches to spelling. *Annals of Dyslexia, 51,* 147–176.

Schlagal, B. (2002). Classroom spelling instruction: History, research, and practice. *Reading Research and Instruction, 42,* 44–57.

Schlagal, R. (1992). Patterns of orthographic development into the intermediate grades. In S. Templeton & D. Bear (Eds.), *Development of orthographic knowledge and the foundations of literacy: A memorial festschrift for Edmund H. Henderson* (pp. 32–52). Hillsdale, NJ: Erlbaum.

Sheffield, B. (1996). Handwriting: A neglected cornerstone of literacy. *Annals of Dyslexia, 46,* 21–35.

Templeton, S., & Morris, D. (2000). Spelling. In M. L. Kamil, P. B. Mosenthal, D. P. Pearson, & R. Barr (Eds.), *Handbook of reading research* (Vol. 3, pp. 525–543). Mahwah, NJ: Erlbaum.

Treiman, R. (1993). *Beginning to spell.* New York: Oxford University Press.

Wendon, L., & Freese, G. (2003). *Letterland: Teacher's guide.* Cambridge, UK: Letterland.

Young, K. (2007). Developmental stage theory of spelling: Analysis of consistency across four spelling-related activities. *Australian Journal of Language and Literacy, 30,* 203–220.

Chapter 12

Best Practices in Promoting Motivation for Writing

PIETRO BOSCOLO
CARMEN GELATI

Learning to write is a complex journey, requiring a long apprenticeship with increasing levels of difficulty: from scribbles, through which preschool children discover a new means of expression; to writing words and simple sentences in early primary school; to high school compositions, in which students are expected to elaborate concepts and ideas in appropriate written language. During this apprenticeship, students learn to use genre structures and morphological and syntactic rules and acquire the cognitive and linguistic knowledge and abilities that characterize academic language. For many students, this apprenticeship is not only demanding, but—as language skills teachers testify—is often scarcely attractive for various reasons that will be clarified below. This chapter has two objectives. The first is to analyze, in the light of recent research findings, the meaning of motivation and lack of motivation to write in school, and of some constructs and adjectives frequently used in relation to this topic. The second is to outline and illustrate with examples some guidelines for instructional practice aimed at fostering student motivation to write.

Motivation—and Lack of Motivation—to Write as a Student Attitude toward Writing

Recent conceptualization of motivation has highlighted three main factors that influence a student's attitude to school learning (Brophy, 2008). The first factor is the value a student places on a learning activity, that is, the reason(s) he or she is more or less willing to engage in that activity or discipline. The second factor regards the student's expectancy and concern about his or her competence in a discipline and the possible outcomes. The third factor is the social environment in which the learning takes place: for instance, the classroom climate, peer relationships, and teachers' goal structure, that is, their emphasis on learning as a process (mastery goal) or as an outcome (performance goal). These factors contribute in different degrees to create and consolidate a student's stance toward a discipline. When learning a discipline, the student also learns a lot of things *about* it. In the case of writing, students come to assign a value to writing, that is, to construe it as an engaging or, alternatively, as a repetitive and boring activity; as a more or less important subject in the curriculum, and a more or less relevant one for future study and life. The way writing is taught and perceived in the classroom also influences a student's attitude. In sum, the student develops a set of beliefs, many of which are implicit, about the functions and role of writing in school instruction (Bruning & Horn, 2000). Consistent with this conceptualization, in this chapter we argue that motivation to write is an attitude to, or view of, writing. It is based on the set of beliefs that students develop through writing activities, that is, through the various situations and tasks in which they are asked to write and use written productions. In turn, students' attitude toward writing influences their approach to a specific writing task, and the degree to which they are willing to engage in it. A view of writing as mainly focusing on reproducing text types or, alternatively, on the student's personal elaboration of knowledge and experiences, has implications for the ways specific writing tasks are organized in the classroom, and how writing is related to other disciplines.

Lack of motivation to write can also be conceptualized in terms of attitudes and beliefs that develop through the school years as the result of repeated writing experiences. We may agree with Graves (2003) that at the beginning of elementary school children "want" to write, because before schooling they have experienced various forms of preconventional writing (Tolchinsky, 2006). Unfortunately, during their school years the will to write in many cases decreases and even disappears, and the child's discovery of writing as a way of expressing and communicating is often a promise that subsequent writing instruction does not live up to. There are several, nonmutually exclusive reasons that can explain many students' loss of motivation to write, all related to an "academic" view of teaching writing. First, writing is often taught in a rigid way, with the teacher emphasizing conformity to text types and writing conventions, rather than students themselves searching for meaning in writing (Oldfather & Shanahan, 2007). Unlike reading, which children are able to use in any subject quite early in primary school, writing is not usually perceived by students as a flexible tool for acquiring, elaborating, and communicating knowledge, but as a discipline in itself. Second, students are often given writing tasks as exercises detached from other classroom activities, and with little or no opportunity to interact with classmates when writing (e.g., to find ideas or revise written texts). Moreover, students today have many opportunities to write outside the school, thanks to computer technology and the Internet. The Internet has created a new literacy and provides people, particularly adolescents, with new possibilities of expressing themselves and communicating by writing. These possibilities may contribute to making school writing even less attractive. We will come back to this aspect of literacy later.

Lack of motivation, however, may not only be due to unattractive writing tasks. Together with beliefs about writing, students also develop self-perceptions and beliefs (expectancies) about themselves as writers, that is, about their writing competence and ability to manage writing tasks. Being motivated to write is closely related to a student's self-perception of writing competence. Many studies over the past two decades have analyzed the role of student self-perception of competence and self-efficacy in writing.[1] As Pajares and Valiante (2006) have persuasively pointed out, the degree to which an individual perceives him- or herself able to perform a task influences his or her performance. In turn, an improved performance makes a student feel more competent. From a motivational point of view, self-perception of competence is closely connected to an individual's involvement in writing as well as to the quality of his or her self-regulation. The relationship between these aspects is a bidirectional one: a student is unlikely to be involved in writing if he or she is not self-efficacious. In the same way, feeling competent about writing makes a student more willing to write. The availability of cognitive and metacognitive tools, such as

---

[1] The phrases "self-perception of writing competence" and "self-efficacy for writing" are often used as synonyms, although they refer to two different motivational variables: self-perception of writing is an individual's evaluation of his or her writing ability (e.g., "I am able to express my ideas clearly in written form"), whereas self-efficacy regards an individual's belief about his or her performance in a specific writing task (e.g., "I think that I'll write a good report").

strategies for generating ideas from memory or for self-monitoring while writing, helps a student feel competent and thus more willing to write. Unfortunately, these tools are not available to struggling writers; therefore, promoting the development of self-regulated strategies is a basic step toward improving students' ability to write, and also indirectly supporting their motivation to write (Harris, Graham, & Mason, 2006).

In sum, a motivated student can be defined as one who values writing and is willing to use it as a worthwhile activity or means of expression, communication, and elaboration. Motivated students are realistically self-confident about their ability to use writing successfully, and this sense of competence is a condition and a source for feeling satisfied when writing. The concept of motivation to write as defined above is different from the concept of intrinsic motivation to write adopted implicitly by the process approach and explicitly by some scholars (e.g., Oldfather, 2002). In general, behavior is intrinsically motivated when an individual is gratified for his or her own sake, not for external rewards, and basic psychological needs for competence, autonomy, and relatedness can be satisfied (Deci & Ryan, 1985). A behavior is extrinsically motivated if it is carried out under the promise of a reward or the threat of punishment. According to the self-determination theory within which intrinsic motivation is conceptualized, intrinsic and extrinsic motivation are not alternative poles, but should be viewed as lying along a continuum including different degrees of external regulation from extrinsic motivation ("I wrote this composition to avoid the teacher's punishment or to demonstrate that I am good at writing") to identification ("Writing is an important and worthwhile activity for me") to intrinsic motivation ("I enjoy writing"). A child is often intrinsically motivated to write in early schooling, but unsuccessful writing experiences due to the increasing complexity of writing through the school grades may transform his or her original "will to write" to extrinsic motivation, concerned with teacher evaluation rather than with the process of writing. This attitude may be difficult to change, as shown by some intervention studies in which writing activities were extensively used in learning various subjects at different school grades: history and science in elementary school (Boscolo & Mason, 2001) and literature in high school (Boscolo & Carotti, 2003). The results of these studies confirm the positive effects of writing on learning already emerging from research on writing to learn. In general, after the interventions, participants reported that they felt more competent in writing and considered it as more useful, but did not report liking it more. Therefore, a student's intrinsic motivation often leaves room for a more complex view of writing that implies his or her realistic self-perception of competence as well as an awareness of the difficulty of writing. This attitude should not be considered as negative since the student is willing to engage in writing. However, it can hardly be called intrinsic motivation. In conclusion, we think that a motivated-to-write student is not necessarily eager to write, but, with differing degrees of awareness, wants to write because he or she thinks that writing is a worthwhile activity (although not always an enjoyable one).

About Authentic and Interesting Writing Tasks

In defining motivation to write as basically a student's attitude, we have pointed out that this attitude influences involvement in a writing task. Of course, a student's involvement in a task is not only a consequence of positive beliefs, but also of the attractiveness of the writing task. What does "attractive" mean when related to a writing task? In recent years, several adjectives, including "authentic," "interesting," and "challenging," have been used to qualify the writing tasks and activities that students feel most involved in. The meanings of the first two adjectives will be analyzed here, while "challenging" will be considered later. "Authentic" has been used in relation to writing with two different meanings. The first meaning has recently been underlined in relation to the need to involve students in authentic writing tasks (Bruning & Horn, 2000). According to Hiebert (1994), authentic literacy tasks are those that involve children in immediate uses of literacy for enjoyment and communication—for example, fifth graders' writing a petition to the city council seeking more traffic lights near their school, including a report compiled by them. Hiebert (1994) also gave examples of unauthentic tasks, citing ones in which literacy exercises, such as the use of compound words or sentence combining, are practiced for some undefined future use (p. 391). While agreeing with Hiebert (1994) on the need to underline the authentic dimension of school writing, we wish to add some comments about the meaning of this adjective. The example of a fifth-grade petition may lead to thinking that authenticity could be a synonym for "practical relevance." Of course, writing in a classroom may be relevant to the degree to which students are faced with a real problem that can be solved using writing, such as writing a petition or a protest letter to a newspaper. Authentic writing, however, is not only aimed at achieving a practical goal. Stressing the communicative function of writing might lead to quite "unauthentic" writing activities, such as communicating in written form with school fellows (it is so much easier to talk or phone!), or writing a "journal" that will not be read by anybody. Studies in writing mostly conducted from a social constructivist perspective have emphasized the social dimension of writing, and the importance of making students aware, at different school levels, that writing is a fundamental tool of communication. However, we think that stressing the social dimension of writing does not only mean emphasizing communication. Writing is a social activity because we can share our writing with others and discuss and comment on it, as well as using it to communicate.

The second meaning of "authentic" is related to the student's expression of a personal point of view or feeling: the so-called writer's voice. One of the prominent aspects of the process approach has been the emphasis on the importance of expressing one's thoughts and feelings through writing. According to Elbow (e.g., 1981), a well-known exponent of this position, writing instruction should enable students to discover their voice, which results in "authentic" writing. We have already mentioned the opportunities for authentic writing outside the school provided by computer technology and the Internet. A new expression has been coined: *media literacy*, which includes a set of abilities and skills in which aural, visual, and digital literacy overlap. The features of writing according to a media literacy perspective are analyzed elsewhere (see Karchmer-Klein, Chapter 13, this volume). Here we wish to underline the point that even younger students are motivated to write when they feel freed from the formal constraints of academic writing and that teachers should not view these "writings" with hostility or concern, but as tools in allowing students to construe the different meanings of writing.

What children should realize in primary school is that writing is a flexible tool by which many functions can be realized and goals achieved. Any writing task can be authentic: for example, an e-mail message is authentic as a quick way of communicating. However, a formal letter is also authentic, although in another context. Both literary and everyday writing can be used fruitfully to make students aware of the different ways in which thoughts and feelings can be authentically expressed. Whereas a comment on the Web does not imply particular concern with the formal aspects of writing, a comment on a poem or story written in the classroom implies more attention to academic writing rules (and the teacher's evaluation!). A useful practice may consist in a class discussion about the similarity or difference between various texts: an e-mail, a formal letter written to or by the teacher, or a debate on the Web. All these messages, although different from one another, have a communicative function. In the discussion, students can be invited to express their comments on these texts, and discover something new about tone, use of words, and voice: in sum, about writing as a way of communicating.

Another adjective used in relation to writing tasks is "interesting," the meaning of which, unlike "authentic," has been analyzed in depth in psychological and educational studies on interest over the past two and half decades. From these studies a basic distinction between two types of interest has emerged: situational and individual (or personal) interest (Hidi, 1990). Situational interest is generated by particular conditions and/or objects in the environment that attract attention because of their novelty. This type of interest is usually transitory, as is the situation from which it arises. Individual or personal interest is a relatively enduring disposition to attend to objects and events and to reengage in certain activities over time. Both types of interest are related to writing in school. Many teachers think that giving students interesting topics for compositions or allowing them to choose their own topics, as suggested by the process approach, is a useful way to promote motivation to write. Interesting topics are those related to students' personal experiences and interests (e.g., sport, games, TV, problems of adolescence), about which they are presumed to have a lot to write about. This instructional practice is based on the unwarranted assumption that the "interestingness" of a topic can be transferred to writing on that topic. In fact, being interested in, say, baseball does not necessarily mean being interested in writing about baseball. The problem is not finding an *interesting topic* or event on which to make students write, but *making writing interesting*. An interesting topic is a good starting point, but what can motivate students to write is the awareness that writing on that topic is worthwhile. For instance, writing an account of an event (interesting topic) may be aimed at collecting and comparing the different ways in which the students in a class have perceived and construed that event. In this case, writing represents a first instance, which might be followed by students' analysis of their own, and classmates' narratives, and a discussion of the differences and similarities in narrating, also compared with a narration external to the class (e.g., a newspaper). In research conducted with primary and middle school students, Gelati (2012) found that interest in an event positively affects writing personal accounts. In the study, two events were planned to provide contrasting kinds of experience: one more interesting for boys (soccer) and the other for girls (dance). The topics of dance and soccer had been previously rated for interest by girls and boys. All students participated in both experiences and wrote their related personal accounts. Results showed that, independently of gender, students produced more complete texts and enriched texts with more personal and higher quality evaluations when they wrote about the experience that they found more interesting. An increased interest in writing was also found.

Writing about the event may be an occasion for helping students to express their voices and to become aware of a new, and authentic, function of writing. Written narratives might be used a few weeks later to allow students to elaborate their previous thoughts and feelings in rereading their work. This effort may contribute to creating a "literate community" in the classroom (Nolen, 2007), which we will return to later. From this community, we would expect students' positive attitudes about writing to develop, that is, their willingness to view and use writing as a real communicative, elaborative, and expressive tool. This implies using the attractive features of a situation as a regular, rather than an exceptional, strategy, on the one hand, and helping each student search and develop a personal meaning of writing through classroom activities, on the other.

Developing Motivation to Write

In the previous pages we have argued that a basic source of students' lack of motivation is the writing tasks themselves, which may be perceived by students as boring, difficult, and/or detached from their personal experience in and out of the classroom. In the following pages we outline a framework for instructional practices aimed at avoiding these shortcomings and leading students of different grade levels to perceive writing as a worthwhile and attractive activity. The frame consists of three guidelines based on the conceptualization and findings of recent research on motivation and writing (Boscolo & Gelati, 2008; Bruning & Horn, 2000; Hidi & Boscolo, 2006, 2007).

Helping Students Experience Writing as a Useful Activity

The adjective "useful" may not seem very appropriate to writing, whose instrumental value does not need to be underlined. In fact, "useful" has two meanings related to writing activities in the classroom. The first is that what is written, individually or in collaboration, should have a value or relevance for the students. We will present later an example of useful writing in the form of devising rules for group formation in a fourth-grade class. Such a project, which does not pertain to a specific discipline, is aimed at producing a text that is the result of collaborative work. Another example is related to students' attempts to play with genres, to which we will return later, under the heading "challenging tasks." In some cases creative texts can be obtained from this "play" by students involved in modifying and renewing old texts, such as stories. Over the past two and a half decades writing researchers have emphasized processes rather than products, in part as a reaction to traditional writing instruction aimed at making students write "good" texts. Also, students' planning and revisions have often been considered more important than their written productions. While agreeing with the theoretical and educational relevance of the process approach to writing, we argue that a motivating aspect of writing is related to the student's production of a "useful" text, where "useful" means that it has an informative, practical, or aesthetic value. Students should be taught to value writing as an activity; however, its products too must be valued, particularly when they are the result of collaborative work.

The usefulness of writing does not only regard the production of a text, such as rules, that can be used in the classroom. There is another, less obvious form of usefulness, which regards writing as a tool for learning. In recent years the elaborative function of writing has been highlighted, although there are very few studies on the motivational aspects of writing-to-learn. We will present later examples of writing activities closely connected to the study of literature in a ninth-grade class (Boscolo & Carotti, 2003).

Fostering the Communicative Function of Writing

Writing is usually a solitary behavior, through which a student can demonstrate what he or she has learned for later evaluation by the teacher. Over the past two and a half decades, the social dimension of writing has been greatly stressed by the social constructivist approach to literacy and literacy learning. This approach has argued that writing is a social activity not only because what one writes can be read by somebody else (in the classroom, usually the teacher), but also because writing can be performed in an interactive context. The social dimension of writing is clearly related to reading: in co-constructing a text, as in classroom collaboration, as well as in sharing written ideas and thoughts with schoolmates, the two literate practices are closely related. Writing is a communication tool not only because what one writes can be read by somebody else, but also because writing can be performed in an interactive context. When the production of a text is aimed at achieving a common objective (e.g., preparing a brochure for an exhibition organized by the school, or a playbill for a school performance), the planning, writing, and revising of this text can be done in collaboration. The final text is communicated, as well as the salient phases of its production. Communicating may regard the production of a common document and also, less obviously, forms of individual writing, such as those used by many students to learn. This includes the moments when students take notes during a classroom discussion or lecture to prepare a report or just record some concepts emerging from the discussion which they have been impressed by. These forms of writing may turn out to be useful in subsequent classroom discussions, as elements for giving students a first idea of community of discourse. Showing them that individual writing, such as note taking, also has an interactive component, may help them understand the close connections between writing and classroom activities.

Nolen (2007) uses the notion of "literate community" to describe those classrooms in which literacy activities establish and maintain the relationship between individuals. Literate communities have social norms that facilitate the development of interest in literacy by establishing the group's shared identity as readers and writers. In these classrooms, reading and writing provide opportunities to experience writing as a tool for self-expression and communication, whereas in traditional classrooms writing is basically an individual activity. Writers and readers switch roles frequently, and the resulting communication of feedback and ideas provides multiple opportunities for interest development. In contrast, traditional writing instruction focuses more on teaching the skills of writing, and the main purpose for becoming literate is that it is an important school subject. In literate communities, students develop their identities as writers through writing activities in which they are involved with teachers in producing worthwhile material or expressing and sharing their own ideas with schoolmates.

Giving Students Novel and Challenging Tasks

In an interesting study, Miller and Meece (1999) showed that third graders preferred high-challenge to low-challenge reading and writing tasks. High-challenge academic tasks were considered those that required writing multiple paragraphs, that involved student collaboration, and that lasted longer than a single lesson, whereas low-challenge tasks were completed individually, lasted for a single lesson, and required writing single words or phrases. From the study, conducted with 24 third graders of different achievement levels and from classes with different levels of exposure to high-challenge tasks, it emerged that students at each level who were familiar with high-challenge tasks and high-achievers in classrooms with minimum exposure preferred high-challenge academic tasks, whereas the low and average achievers in the minimum exposure classrooms felt less confident in dealing with more complex tasks. However, regardless of exposure, all students generally disliked low-challenge tasks. A task can be considered challenging according to the degree to which it stimulates a student's cognitive involvement in a collaborative context (Miller, 2003). More specifically, a challenging task requires students to assume increasingly higher levels of responsibility for learning, that is, autonomy in carrying out a task as well as elaboration, not only retrieval, of prior knowledge. A collaborative context facilitates and stimulates students' involvement. Challenge, however, is not the same as complexity: a challenging task may present some difficult aspect, but it also stimulates a student's will to engage in it.

The cognitive approach has conceptualized writing as a problem-solving process, where the solution is the production of a text that fulfills the writer's communicative goal. This problem-solving dimension is emphasized in two writing activities: when students' writing is aimed at achieving a goal, as in the case of the petition, and when students have the opportunity to play with genres. The teaching of genres is a problem that has led to heated debate for decades. Through various reading and writing experiences, students get to know genres. A possible challenging task is rewriting a text (e.g, a poem that students know, a story, a fairy tale), changing some elements (e.g., the protagonist, the setting, or the goal of a story), and rewriting it. Rewriting is seldom an enjoyable task; in this case it may be enjoyable if the challenging objective is to invent a new story or a new poem. Two conditions have to be satisfied; first, respecting the structure of the original text; second, the introduction of new elements—for example, a character— must be consistently integrated in the whole composition. In the classroom, this work can be carried out in small groups, each involved in producing the best new text. In primary school, "playing" with writing is an activity students are willing to engage in. Playing means, for instance, manipulating stories by changing characters, motives, or the sequence of episodes to obtain new, more amusing, or curious endings, albeit within the constraints of text coherence. It may mean rewriting a short text and avoiding certain word categories; or composing a meaningful short text (a "cento") using words taken from titles of newspaper articles and reading passages; or creating images and metaphors with colors to describe the seasons. This writing is called "creative" because it is aimed at creating "new" meanings, that is, having children discover novel and challenging uses of language (Boscolo, Gelati, & Galvan, 2012). This is also children's first contact with intertextuality in which they realize that new meanings are usually constructed by means of old words and phrases. Children not only enjoy themselves practicing it, but also test and increase their linguistic competence, obviously under the teacher's guidance. Moreover, their efforts may produce texts that merit being collected in a classroom *portfolio*. Of course, the use of challenging tasks may contribute to motivation to write if children are able to manage them, as recent studies on interest have shown, and the results are pleasing. Later, in high school, this type of play may become a fruitful tool for de-composing and analyzing (no longer for fun!) literary texts in greater depth, as we show later in the chapter. For older students, competence is also the motivational basis for working, and playing, with texts.

Writing Different Text Types in Elementary and High School: Some Examples of Motivating Lessons

So far, we have analyzed the concept of motivation to write and the meaning of words and concepts related to this topic. In the following pages two examples of writing instructional interventions aimed at promoting motivation to write through useful and enjoyable collaborative classroom activity are presented. The first instructional intervention was conducted in fourth-grade classes (Boscolo & Cisotto, 1997), the second in a ninth-grade class. Although conducted at different school grades, the two instructional interventions shared the following features:

1. The role of the teacher. All the writing activities included collaborative work in which the teacher's role was to facilitate collaboration among students in small and large groups. For the younger students, facilitation included providing help when requested.
2. The classroom as a writing environment in which ideas and written productions are shared.
3. Writing and writings. In both elementary and high school writing may include a variety of genres. Although writing instruction, starting from primary school, focuses on a few text types, teaching writing also makes students experience, and later use, the flexibility of writing.

Writing Different Types of Texts in Primary School

An instructional intervention was designed to encourage children to experience writing as a useful and enjoyable collaborative classroom activity (Boscolo & Cisotto, 1997). It had three major features. First of all, writing took place throughout all the learning activities from the very start. In elementary school children are often asked to write a report on a scientific activity or a classroom discussion as a means of concluding the activity and producing final material for a teacher to evaluate. In the intervention, writing was used extensively during an activity, not only at the end of it. The teacher was focused, therefore, on presenting writing as a flexible and multipurpose tool, not on making the children conform their texts to "good" text types. Second, writing was proposed as an activity connected to crucial classroom situations. The different functions of writing in meaningful classroom activities, such as science experiments and classroom discussions, were stressed. This approach contrasts with more typical instruction in which writing is taught as a skill related to other language skills, but separate from other subjects. Third, writing was performed as a collaborative activity. Students worked in groups during the various phases of the learning activities, and produced collaborative texts. Even the writing they did individually—such as taking notes—was used for participation in group activities. This perspective had important implications for the teacher's evaluation of children's texts. The written work of the experimental group children was revised by the teacher and schoolmates. Revision by schoolmates was carried out in a collaborative activity in which each writer was also a reviser. The relationship between writer and reader/reviser was therefore symmetrical, and revision was not perceived as "risky" or threatening. On the other hand, the teacher did not emphasize and correct children's mistakes, but facilitated self-correction and helped them improve their productions. It should be emphasized that the extensive use of collaborative writing did not exclude individual writing in situation-oriented classes. Individual writing was aimed at consolidating children's writing ability by having them practice writing on topics closely connected to the classroom activities in which they were engaged—for instance, organizing notes taken during a discussion, exposing the phases of a common project, highlighting the positive and negative aspects of discussing. Individual writing was therefore an occasion for practice, through which the children could also reflect on classroom collaborative activities.

The intervention was articulated into three segments, focusing first on argumentative, then narrative, and finally expository discourse. Each segment had a common sequence:

1. *Problem presentation.* The starting point for classroom activities was a stimulating problem that children had to solve. The problem might concern some aspect of classroom life (e.g., how to form groups), text production for a real audience (writing the plot for a play to be performed), or a learning experience (a science experiment).

2. *Idea generation.* The children contributed to solving the problem by expressing their ideas in classroom discussion. The generation of ideas was facilitated by a set of writing activities aimed at allowing the children to regulate their participation (e.g., note taking, recording impressions, and regulating speaking turns).

3. *Discussion and evaluation.* The ideas recorded were discussed, compared, and evaluated. Writing was still used as a regulation tool, but children's activities also focused on text production.

4. *Synthesis and production.* The children's ideas became a product, that is, they were used to compose a collaborative text (in the case of argument and narrative) or to check understanding (in the case of exposition).

We illustrate this sequence in relation to three text types: argumentative, narrative, and expository.

Argumentative Text: Writing the Rules for Group Formation in the Classroom

Problem Presentation. The teacher proposed some stimulating and involving questions. The most popular of these was: What should the criteria be for group formation in the class? (The teacher explained that the criteria adopted would be used for forming groups in the class.) Other questions that were considered included whether homework is useful to learning, and whether a recent and very popular series of stories for children, including horror and sex elements, could be considered appropriate reading material for young readers.

Idea Generation. Collective discussion followed the question, combined with writing, to serve the following functions: (1) as a tool for regulating turn taking ("While waiting, write your idea on a sheet of paper so you will not forget it"); (2) as an informal tool for recording ideas expressed by other students as well as oneself; (3) as a tool for determining the most important points during the discussion; and (4) as a tool for summarizing the results of the discussion. The children were encouraged to formulate their first conclusions and use their informally written ideas to dictate the points of agreement on the criteria of group formation to the teacher, who wrote them on the blackboard.

Discussion and Evaluation. Children discussed in small groups one of the conclusions during idea generation (i.e., a criterion proposed for group formation). They used their notes to recall the previous points and to guide the discussion. They also took new notes on colored paper, according to a strategy suggested by the teacher where one color was used for a positive contribution, another for a negative suggestion, and another for a "stroke of genius." For example, for the argument that "groups should be formed with children of different competence levels" a positive contribution was "If a child is in a trouble, he or she can be helped by the other group members"; a negative suggestion was "If a child isn't specialized in anything, he or she can do nothing for the group"; a stroke of genius was "All children have to learn." This phase ended with the construction of the first draft of text in small groups.

Text Production. The work of each group was read to the whole class, and a composition was written collectively. For each group a child read the draft, soliciting comments and requests for clarification from the other children, while other members of the group made a note of suggestions for how to improve the text, as well as informal comments and reflections. The drafts of each group were used for the collective composition, which was carried out through self-dictation; that is, the children discussed and selected the best criteria, formulated them orally with the teacher's help, and then wrote them in their notebooks. The formulated criteria then were written on a poster that was hung in the classroom.

Narrative Text: Creating a Narrative

Problem Presentation. The children had to find interesting topics with concrete objectives on which to write for a real audience. In this case, it was to prepare a booklet of stories as a Christmas gift to their parents. Other possibilities were to write a funny story for pen pals or the plot for a play to be performed at the end of the school year.

Idea Generation. In collecting ideas for a story the children freely expressed their ideas, which the teacher wrote on the blackboard. The children also wrote their own and their classmates' ideas on cards.

Discussion and Evaluation. The collected ideas were analyzed and evaluated in a collective discussion. For example, the class agreed on a narrative core: "A girl who can express five wishes for Christmas." Children recorded comments, doubts, and suggestions. The ideas about characters, location, episodes, and sequence were organized, and several alternatives regarding the sequence of episodes were explored in collective or small-group discussions. The children used the phase 2 notes to propose changes and/or to plan story development.

Text Production. The collaborative construction of the plot and the first sketch of the narrative were performed as a writing workshop:

- The material generated in the planning phase was used to construct the text.
- When in doubt, the children used a dictionary and asked the teacher and other children for advice.
- The children showed their written material to classmates to check clarity and coherence. Classmates' advice on how to improve the materials stimulated the writer to revise and try a new, more satisfactory elaboration.
- Children read their own stories, and others were invited to make comments and criticism. Sometimes it was the writer who expressed his or her doubts.
- The stories of several children and/or groups were integrated and connected.

Expository Text: Checking a Hypothesis

Problem Presentation. Some scientific topics (e.g., the transformation of corn into popcorn; how sugar is transformed in water) suggested by meaningful situations (e.g., a school party) were proposed to the class.

Idea Generation. The teacher invited the children to write some questions (e.g.: What inside a head of corn becomes popcorn?) in order to:

- Explore their previous knowledge of the phenomena.
- Guide their first discussion and observation during the experiment.

Discussion and Evaluation. What children had written about their knowledge was read and discussed. During the discussion, a child could change his or her hypothesis (the answer to the question) by correcting with a different color. During the experiment, writing was used to:

- Describe the procedure, materials, and conditions.
- Collect data (e.g., about weight and water level) to be reported in a table (numbers and drawings were used, as well as words).
- Record comments about what was happening. Since the children paid great attention to the experiment, systematic recording was difficult (and probably boring) for them.

Text Production. Children used all their written comments concerning previous knowledge and setting up the experiment. They modified what they had written by adding or replacing information, added their comments on what they had understood about the observed phenomenon, and corrected their initial hypotheses. In this phase writing was used to check their understanding.

In the intervention the teacher had several roles, which included having children "discover" a problem, stimulating idea generation, and regulating discussion. There were two main functions regarding writing in particular; the first was to introduce children to the uses of writing in new and meaningful situations. The teacher suggested how to use writing (e.g., showing how to use note taking to remember or record salient ideas in a discussion), modeled the writing behavior, and helped solve problems in collaborative composition. The second function was to help children become self-regulated writers. The teacher discussed writing difficulties with them, both individually and in small groups, suggested solutions and strategies, and gave feedback on ongoing and final productions. At the end of the two semesters of the school year, the children were evaluated by the teacher, who took into account the collaborative texts as well as other texts written individually during school time, but outside the experimental intervention.

Writing as a Learning Tool in High School: An Example Related to the Study of Literature

Motivation to write has a different meaning for primary and high school students. Primary school students learn to use writing in different genres: to express their feelings, to narrate episodes of their family life, to comment on what happens in the classroom, and to set rules for classroom life. From a motivational point of view, the problem is basically to provide students with writing tasks that they can perceive as meaningful, that is, related to classroom activities in which writing has a real function, or which represent a challenge for students. In sum, to motivate primary school student to write means to provide them with opportunities to use writing in attractive and useful ways.

Instead, high school students do not have to discover the functions of writing: they are—or should be—aware of the potentialities of writing for personal expression and interpersonal communication, particularly outside school. They already know that through writing they can express their ideas and organize their knowledge of subject matters; they also know how to employ the "subsidiary" uses of writing, such as note taking and schematizing. What they need is to find other "meanings" in the academic writing they have been dealing with for so long time. Thus, motivating high school students to write means helping them realize the relevance and usefulness of academic writing as a way to express and communicate one's ideas, on the one hand, and as a powerful instrument through which learning can become more personal and effective, on the other: that is, writing as a tool for learning. In other words, motivating high school students to write means leading them to discover the conceptual valence of writing. Therefore, meaningful writing tasks, through which students can view writing as closely connected to the activities that are relevant to the classroom life, are also needed in high school.

In an intervention study conducted for one school year with ninth graders, two ways of teaching literature were compared (Boscolo & Carotti, 2003): one using writing for traditional composition on various topics, including literary ones, the other as a tool for understanding literary texts. Both groups used several forms of writing, but the traditional one mainly focused on composition and writing for note taking, schematizing, and summarizing, whereas the writing-oriented class used writing as a tool for understanding literature better. The main hypothesis of the study was that using various forms of writing as elaborative and communicative tools would have positive effects on students' attitudes to writing and literature as well as on their ability to understand the meaning of a literary text—that is, students' attitude to literature should be more positive in that experiencing various writing genres should enable them to appreciate literary reading more. Moreover, writing should have an effect on both students' literary understanding and their ability to write a commentary on a literary text. Thus, our emphasis was on the effect of various writing genres in high school, as compared with a more traditional writing instruction, mainly based on composition. The study was made possible by the syllabus of "language skills" that in the first year of high school does not include the study of Italian literature according to its chronological development (from the Middle Ages to the present) as in subsequent years; thus teachers are free to select novels, stories, and passages from all Italian literature. Passages from foreign literature translated into Italian are also presented.

There are a lot of writing activities that can be carried out in the teaching/learning of literature. Some activities are traditionally used in school—for instance, summarizing, schematizing, taking notes. Other activities are carried out when students "work" on the text: analyzing the text structure, paraphrasing, recording personal comments or reflections, commenting on an author's thoughts in written form. As in primary school, writing also can be manipulation: for instance, changing the register of a literary text, or rewriting a story from a different character's perspective. For instance, in Stevenson's *Treasure Island*, rewriting the story from Long John Silver's perspective implies introducing and understanding the pirate's point of view. Differently from primary school, however, text manipulation is not an "instructional play," but a tool for better analyzing a literary text. There is also personal writing, such as a diary or narration of personal events. Last, there is collaborative writing, such as writing a report on literary work with one or more schoolmates. In the study, students were presented with a list of traditional and innovative writing activities and asked to rate each of them for liking ("Do you like?"), self-perception of competence ("How able are you to . . . "), and perception of usefulness before and after the intervention. Out of the quasi-experimental perspective of the study, we think that the writing activities used in the study of literature could be used as self-evaluation tools for students and a basis for discussion after classroom work on literature.

The teaching intervention for the writing-oriented group was as follows. First, the teacher assigned reading a novel or story as homework with a deadline, and periodically reminded students. At least two novels and 10 short stories were read during the year. Students read literary texts at school only when they had to focus on some aspects emerging from classroom discussion. On the set date, students expressed an initial appreciation of the text they had read. It was an occasion for pointing out the difference between *understanding* and *enjoying* a literary text, a difference that is not simple for ninth graders and can be considered in a greater depth over several years (from grades 9 to 13), as it includes reflection and discussion about reading and comparisons between texts (intertextuality). Thus, the instructional intervention described in this chapter should be viewed as part of a longer one, lasting the 5 years of high school.

Through questions and classroom discussion the teacher checked whether the literal meaning of the novel or story had been understood, also using, if necessary, specific short-answer questions. The students were invited to propose the topics to be discussed in the classroom—for instance, in the case of Stevenson's *Treasure Island*, the narrator's role, the description of the island, the characters, and their division into gentlemen and pirates. The teacher organized activities that were carried out individually and/or in groups, either as classwork or homework. For instance, students were guided to identify the physical and moral aspects of "good" and "bad" characters, and to reflect about the rough nature of these distinction through a more careful analysis of characters.

Writing was used in various ways as a tool for literary comprehension:

1. The students were invited to express and justify their reactions to reading a literary text assigned as individual homework. The reactions were usually expressed orally during classroom conversations, but sometimes the students themselves preferred to write them down. Students noted their impressions and reflections during literary reading in the classroom, as well as the teacher's comments, to be able to recall their "response" to literary text in future discussions and elaborations. The notes were discussed and integrated by new teacher's comments. Organizing these notes was assigned as homework. Students had to put their notes in order according to different criteria: emotional reaction, conceptual understanding, reference to other literary texts, points to be clarified in further classroom discussions, and so on.

2. The students were invited to find significant keywords to describe characters or places and events in the literary text they were reading. This was a type of "card indexing," which required the students to personally elaborate a text. For instance, in a novel by Italian novelist Italo Calvino the theme of hybridity was emphasized and discussed. Students then used this theme to interpret the text. It was a selective reading through which they discovered and practiced tools useful also for future text analysis, when they would be able to compare texts and understand the meaning of intertextuality.

3. Text analysis was usually followed by a synthesis, in which students were asked to give a synthetic representation of the text. Synthesizing is quite different from summarizing. Whereas a summary is aimed at "objectively" identifying the most relevant ideas or events of a text, a synthesis reflects a reading aimed at highlighting specific aspects of a literary text, emerging also from the teacher's explanation and students' discussion.

4. The students wrote the "minutes" of some particularly interesting lesson by organizing their notes.

5. The students wrote a final report of their work, which was discussed in the classroom.

6. Some of the tools used for text analysis (e.g., the role of irony in an author's voice) were "transferred" to a new literary text—that is, students

were asked to use the concepts they had learned, and this task was also an occasion for raising their awareness of the elaborative function of writing.

Students' Personal Comments on the Study of Literature and the Use of Writing

At the end of the intervention—that is, at the end of the school year—both traditional and writing-oriented group students were asked questions about their experiences with writing and literature. The analysis of students' responses showed some interesting results. We report some of these results because we think that an instructional intervention should be accompanied and followed by the monitoring of students' responses and reactions to the teacher's suggestions. Participants in the traditional group, where writing was basically limited to composition, identified the story or novel they liked more, focusing on content, whereas the writing-oriented-group students focused on specific procedures, that is, the types of analysis conducted on literary texts (e.g., comparison of different texts, aspects of characters, and the use of discussion). Moreover, the writing-oriented group underlined the importance of literature in helping students understand literary meanings, look at reality from different points of view, and make a student more mature. A comment on schematizing:

> "Schematizing is a way to discuss and clarify for ourselves and the teacher. Using a schema we can summarize the topics, but each of us in our own way, highlighting what has interested us more."

Regarding the types of writing viewed as most useful for the study of literature, while the traditional group participants sustained the usefulness of academic writing (notes, summary, composition, paraphrase, report, outline), the writing-oriented group (namely, male students) emphasized writing aimed at text analysis and comments on text as well as, although to a lesser degree, text manipulation (e.g., rewriting a passage by adopting the perspective of another character)—that is, types of writing most closely related to the study of literature. Both groups listed note taking and schematizing.

Most students in the writing-oriented group mentioned the uses of writing experienced in their literature class as novel functions, such as changing the register of a narration or the perspective of a description. Whereas the traditional-group students replied they had experienced no novel function, the others wrote that they had learned to use academic writing (including composition on literature!) more consciously.

Regarding the question of whether writing is an interesting activity or a "duty," the traditional group either replied generically ("writing is really interesting") without any justification, or mentioned personal writing, in which one can express and relieve his or her feelings. The writing-oriented-group students gave more mature answers, and about half of them underlined the dual aspect of writing in school, that is, writing is both a "duty," a mandatory activity, and a possible source of interest. Only a few students mentioned personal and relaxing types of writing. A few answers of the writing-oriented-group male students follow:

> "I think that if a writer is a person—and therefore has ideas—writing is a duty because ideas and opinions cannot be forgotten and must be communicated."

> "Writing is unavoidable as well as useful. It is interesting for me to study various types of writing, which help us express ourselves better, also orally. Writing is a way of expressing yourself, and everybody uses the way which is more appropriate to him/herself."

Last, about the usefulness of writing in studying various school subjects, the traditional group underlined instrumental uses of writing (e.g., writing as a tool for recording and facilitating remembering, increasing one's culture and reasoning and reflection abilities, improving one's oral and written expression), whereas a few writing-oriented-group students underlined the cross-disciplinary functions of writing, and the relationship between writing and reading. Several responses of this group underlined the role of writing in expanding and integrating knowledge. A female student wrote:

> "Taking notes when reading and elaborating them later is very important for me, because these activities also help me if I have to do a quick review before an oral test. The integration of notes taken in the classroom with homework is even more productive for learning."

And a male student:

> "Writing can help a student report on a scientific topic or explain a mathematics or physics problem, but above all it is a person's wealth."

The Role of the Teacher in Promoting Motivation to Write

The role of the teacher is crucial in promoting motivation to write, for two reasons. The first is that as students' beliefs influence their approach to writing, a teacher's beliefs about writing influence the ways in which he or she organizes the writing setting and instructional practices. Making students aware of the multiple functions of writing in a literate community, which we have considered a necessary step in promoting a positive attitude toward writing, requires the teacher's belief that writing is not only an essential subject or ability in the curriculum, but an important experience through which students should be helped to find a personal meaning in literate practices. Moreover, the teacher's view of writing also influences his or her view of motivation to write. If the teacher views writing as a basically individual skill, he or she will tend to promote motivation mainly through assigning, when possible, interesting topics. If, instead, motivation is viewed—and valued—as a students' attitude to be developed and improved through meaningful activities, the assignment of writing will clearly be a different one.

The second reason is that writing instruction is a complex matter, which requires the teacher to choose tasks, activities, and strategies carefully. This complexity involves, in particular, the following aspects related to motivation to write: interest, collaboration, and evaluation. First, writing tasks cannot always be novel, or interesting, or aimed at successfully achieving tangible results. Becoming a competent writer requires a balance of more involving moments, when writing appears novel and interesting, and less involving ones, when a student organizes his or her learning experiences through writing. We think that while students view writing in the classroom as consisting of meaningful experiences, they may also view less challenging tasks as important, not necessarily boring, aspects of their becoming writers.

This balance should also regard the use of group versus individual writing in the classroom. The examples of good practices in this chapter all regard collaborative writing, or writing in a collaborative context. We view collaborative writing as an essential element for leading students to appreciate and enjoy writing as a process and a product. However, collaborative and individual writing should be viewed and adopted in a dynamic relation. Opportunities for collaborative writing may be those in which ideas are generated, written texts are compared and revised, and a common product is obtained and evaluated. Individual writing, on the other hand, is the moment in which each student expresses his or her thoughts and voice, being aware that a collaborative experience of reading and writing converge in his or her writing, and that what one writes individually may be the source of other collaborative experiences with classmates.

The third aspect, the teacher's evaluation of student writing, is also related to the individual–collaborative dimension of writing in the classroom. We do not ignore that poor evaluation may be unavoidable in a class and may lower students' self-efficacy beliefs and self-perception of competence, and subsequently their interest in writing. A writing *portfolio*, through which students may become aware of their advancement in writing, is now a self-evaluation method adopted in schools. It documents the development of writing competence, as well as motivation to write, through students' narration and description of their involvement, satisfaction, and also frustration in the various writing experiences (Calfee, 2000). We think that by learning to view writing as a meaningful activity, students should also be helped to recognize and face its complexity. Being motivated to write also means being able to manage the challenges and difficulties of writing: giving students the necessary tools to face the challenge requires the teacher to carefully analyze task difficulty and students' levels, as well as self-perceptions of competence.

A Concluding Remark

This chapter was based on two main assumptions. The first was that, although young children may be intrinsically motivated to write, through the various writing activities over the school years they often develop a negative attitude toward writing and a negative attitude toward themselves as writers. The second assumption was that instructional practices may influence a student's attitude either positively or negatively. Promoting motivation to write means reconstructing students' attitudes toward writing through activities from which a view of writing as a meaningful activity can emerge. In other words, motivating students to write means helping them construct positive beliefs about writing and replace negative ones. It should also be clear that this construction is neither quick nor easy, and during the long apprenticeship of learning to write students—and teachers—may find several occasions for disappointment. Teachers, in particular, should be aware that the development of beliefs may not be linear, and that students should be supported in their efforts to become competent and motivated writers. The scaffold function of teaching has been highlighted over the past decades, also in relation to writing instruction. We wish to conclude this chapter by applying the concept of motivational scaffolding (Renninger, 1992) to writing. Interest in writing, not only learning, should also be supported. The meaningful writing activities that a teacher organizes to stimulate and sustain students' motivation to write may be isolated moments of classroom life for students, interesting and enjoyable but not sufficient to create an enduring attitude toward writing. It is up to the teacher to create continuity among these moments, for instance, by reminding students of their individual contributions, outlining the value of the results they attained, and inviting students to find new and challenging writing tasks.

References

Boscolo, P., & Carotti, L. (2003). Does writing contribute to improving high school students' approach to literature? *L1—Educational Studies in Language and Literature, 3,* 197–224.

Boscolo, P., & Cisotto, L. (1997, August 26–30). *Making writing interesting in elementary school.* Paper presented at the 7th biannual meeting of the European Association for Research on Learning and Instruction, Athens, Greece.

Boscolo, P., & Gelati, C. (2008). Motivating reluctant students to write: Suggestions and caveats. *Insights on Learning Disabilities: From Prevailing Theories to Validated Practices, 5(2),* 61–74.

Boscolo, P., Gelati, C., & Galvan, N. (2012). Teaching elementary school students to play with meanings and genre. *Reading and Writing Quarterly: Overcoming Learning Difficulties, 28,* 29–50.

Boscolo, P., & Mason, L. (2001). Writing to learn, writing to transfer. In P. Tynjälä, L. Mason, & K. Lonka (Eds.), *Writing as a learning tool: Integrating theory and practice* (pp. 83–104). Dordrecht, The Netherlands: Kluwer.

Brophy, G. (2008). Developing students' appreciation for what is taught in school. *Educational Psychologist, 43,* 132–141.

Bruning, R., & Horn, C. (2000). Developing motivation to write. *Educational Psychologist, 35,* 25–37.

Calfee, R. C. (2000). Writing portfolios: Activity, assessment, authenticity. In R. Indrisano & J. R. Squire (Eds.), *Perspectives on writing* (pp. 278–304). Newark, DE: International Reading Association.

Deci, E. L., & Ryan, R. M. (1985). *Intrinsic motivation and self-determination in human behaviour.* New York: Plenum Press.

Elbow, P. (1981). *Writing with power: Techniques for mastering the writing process.* New York: Oxford University Press.

Gelati, C. (2012). Female superiority and gender similarity effects and interest factors in writing. In V. W. Berninger (Ed.), *Past, present, and future contributions of cognitive writing research to cognitive psychology* (pp. 153–174). New York: Psychology Press.

Graves, D. H. (2003). *Writing: Teachers and children at work* (2nd ed.). Portsmouth, NH: Heinemann.

Harris, K. R., Graham, S., & Mason, L. H. (2006). Improving the writing, knowledge, and motivation of struggling young writers: Effects of self-regulated strategy development with and without peer support. *American Educational Research Journal, 43,* 295–340.

Hidi, S. (1990). Interest and its contribution as a mental resource for learning. *Review of Educational Research, 60,* 549–571.

Hidi, S., & Boscolo, P. (2006). Motivation and writing. In C. A. MacArthur, S. Graham, & J. Fitzgerald (Eds.), *Handbook of writing research* (pp. 144–157). New York: Guilford Press.

Hidi, S., & Boscolo, P. (Eds.). (2007). *Writing and motivation.* Oxford, UK: Elsevier.

Hiebert, E. H. (1994). Becoming literate through authentic tasks: Evidence and adaptations. In R. B. Ruddell, M. R. Ruddell, & H. Singer (Eds.), *Theoretical models and processes of reading* (pp. 391–413). Newark, DE: International Reading Association.

Miller, S. D. (2003). How high- and low-challenge tasks affect motivation and learning: Implications for struggling learners. *Reading and Writing Quarterly, 19,* 39–57.

Miller, S. D., & Meece, J. L. (1999). Third graders' motivational preferences for reading and writing tasks. *Elementary School Journal, 100,* 19–35.

Nolen, S. (2007). The role of literate communities in the development of children's interest in writing. In S. Hidi & P. Boscolo (Eds.), *Writing and motivation* (pp. 241–255). Oxford, UK: Elsevier.

Oldfather, P. (2002). Students' experiences when not initially motivated for literacy learning. *Reading and Writing Quarterly, 18,* 231–256.

Oldfather, P., & Shanahan, C. (2007). A cross-case study of writing motivation as empowerment. In S. Hidi & P. Boscolo (Eds.), *Writing and motivation* (pp. 257–279). Oxford, UK: Elsevier.

Pajares, F., & Valiante, G. (2006). Self-efficacy beliefs and motivation in writing development. In C. A. MacArthur, S. Graham, & J. Fitzgerald (Eds.), *Handbook of writing research* (pp. 158–170). New York: Guilford Press.

Renninger, A. (1992). Individual interest and development: Implications for theory and practice. In K. A. Renninger, S. Hidi, & A. Krapp (Eds.), *The role of interest in learning and development* (pp. 361–395). Hillsdale, NJ: Erlbaum.

Tolchinsky, L. (2006). The emergence of writing. In C. A. MacArthur, S. Graham, & J. Fitzgerald (Eds.), *Handbook of writing research* (pp. 83–95). New York: Guilford Press.

Chapter 13

Best Practices in Using Technology to Support Writing

RACHEL KARCHMER-KLEIN

> If our schools continue to limit the literacy curriculum to reading and writing traditional, alphabetic, printed texts, then our children will be well prepared for 1950 but ill prepared for 2050.
> —BAKER, PEARSON, AND ROZENDAL, (2010, p. 2)

As a teacher educator I spend a lot of time in local schools. Over the past 15 years I have seen technology take a more prominent role in education. Computer labs, digital cameras, interactive whiteboards, and mobile learning devices are fixtures in many schools. Further, approximately 69% of teachers report using these tools for instructional purposes such as preparing written text (61%), creating graphics or visual displays (53%), contributing to blogs or wikis (9%), and corresponding with others (31%) (National Center for Education Statistics, 2010). Yet, concurrent to my observations of technology-infused lessons, I observe very little change in literacy instruction. That is, most teachers continue to emphasize traditional conceptions of literacy; teaching kids to read and write left to right and top to bottom using static, one-dimensional materials (Davies, 2006; Karchmer-Klein & Shinas, 2012a). This is not surprising, especially in light of the political pressures associated with nationwide education legislation, such as No Child Left Behind and Race to the Top. In fact, teachers have voiced this concern to me when I approached them about this topic. Susan, a third-grade teacher in an inner-city low-performing school told me:

"I wish I had the luxury of thinking about how technology changes literacy and then rethinking my whole literacy curriculum. But at this school we are told what to teach and how to teach it. If the administrators want to change what we do in the classroom then you might see a change."

While I certainly do not recommend we stop teaching how to read and write traditional, linear texts, I do suggest we prepare students to read and write dynamic, multimodal, electronic texts—the very texts they interact with daily outside of school (Lenhart, Arafeh, Smith, & MacGill, 2008). And, the accessibility to technology tools in most schools, coupled with a shift to the Common Core State Standards (CCSS; National Governors Association & Council of Chief State School Officers, 2010), provides fertile ground for preparing our students with 21st-century literacy skills.

The purpose of this chapter is to encourage educators to think differently about writing and its relationship to technology. The most common perspective of technology is that it is a tool used to support pedagogically sound research-based instructional activities (Harris & Hofer, 2009; Yancey, 2005). I would like to challenge readers to also consider technology as a change agent, one that requires a reconceptualization of writing instruction (Herrington, Hodgson, & Moran, 2009; Karchmer-Klein, 2007a). In fact, I argue that before technology can be used effectively as a tool to support writing, one must recognize how technology changes writing.

To this end, the chapter is divided into three sections. First, I provide an overview of how writing should be reconceptualized in the 21st century. Second, I share a range of technology applications along with examples of how they can be used to support 21st-century writing skills in K–12 settings. Third, I conclude the chapter with final thoughts related to curriculum standards and professional development.

Reconceptualizing Writing

Technology is increasingly recognized for its potential to support K–12 writing instruction. Research indicates the positive effects of word processing (e.g., Goldberg, Russell, & Cook, 2003), spell-check (e.g., MacArthur, Graham, Hayes, & De La Paz, 1996), speech synthesis (e.g., Kelly, Kratcoski, & McLain, 2009), and multimedia software (e.g., Dalton, Smith, & Alvey, 2010) on different stages of the writing process. Until recently, computers tended to be the tool used in research studies examining issues related to technology and writing. This made sense given the increase in computer availability in K–12 schools in the last 20 years (NCES, 2010). However, the large-scale educational purchases of new technologies, such as tablets, e-readers, and interactive whiteboards, have shifted some of the focus. As of January 2012, 1.5 million iPads are in use in educational settings (Apple, 2012) and 30 million students worldwide have access to SMART Board interactive whiteboards (SMART Technologies, 2012). Additionally, the CCSS encourage the education community to take a closer look at devices other than computers. Beginning in kindergarten, students are expected to explore and use a variety of digital tools for writing. This is especially exciting because it not only emphasizes the importance of a range of writing-related technology tools in K–12 education, it also encourages schools to get these tools in the hands of their youngest students (Karchmer, Mallette, & Leu, 2002; Larson, 2010; Marsh, 2011).

Although computers, tablets, e-readers, and interactive whiteboards are different devices, they share a common medium: electronic text. Electronic text has several unique attributes that have implications for writing. First, electronic text can be composed of numerous modes. Modes, such as words, audio, images, hyperlinks, and video, are signs that carry meaning (Bezemer & Kress, 2008). When writers effectively integrate these modes, they develop a multimodal ensemble that conveys a unified message (Jewitt, 2011). Traditionally printed texts, like picture books, incorporate multimodality (i.e., pictures and words). In fact, literacy instruction in the early years focuses on teaching students to glean meaning from picture cues if they are unable to make meaning from words. However, somewhere along the line, traditional literacy instruction shifts the focus from utilizing multiple modes to a primary focus on static words (Daiute, 1992). This shift is short-sighted given the importance of interacting with multimodal electronic texts in digital environments.

Second, electronic text can be nonlinear. By incorporating hyperlinks and other modes, writers can guide their readers down varying paths. Alternatively, readers can develop their own reading path, perhaps leading them to a different understanding of the text than the author intended. I found this in my own research when examining multimodal text designed by educators using a virtual poster tool (Karchmer-Klein & Shinas, 2012a). In this study several educators included arrows as textual scaffolds to identify the order in which the reader should follow the modes on the virtual posters (see Figure 13.1), sending the reader down the writer's path. However, some educators did not include textual scaffolds, leaving readers to develop their own reading paths, which in several instances hindered comprehension of the writers' intended meaning. To develop 21st-century readers and writers, we must prepare students to work within nonlinear writing structures so they understand how these dynamic texts affect comprehension.

Third, electronic text is malleable, enabling writers to continuously revise content. They can also change background colors, font styles, and

FIGURE 13.1. Example of a virtual poster using arrows to direct reading path.

the placement of graphics to determine the best format for their writing; this is a much different capability than traditionally printed prose that is typically sent to editors for proofreading and formatting. In digital environments, what one person reads on Monday may be different from what another reads on Tuesday.

Fourth, electronic text is the medium by which we communicate over the Internet, the global computer network serving billions of users. This connection to the Internet has profound implications for writing (Leu, Kinzer, Coiro, & Cammack, 2004). It enables writers to present their work to authentic audiences. This is beneficial to writers who want to project their message to a large audience or for those whose work is rarely shared with outside readers. In fact, teachers report an increase in students' motivation to write well when they know their work will be published on the Internet (Karchmer, 2001). It seems that Internet publishing encourages students to pay more attention to spelling conventions and the overall appearance of their final products. Publishing on the Internet also provides writers with opportunities to interact with their audience. Research on students' writing has shown that teachers' comments focus mostly on proofreading concerns. Students then tend to make peripheral revisions to their work, concentrating on mechanics rather than on substantive changes (Matsumura, Patthey-Chavez, Valdés, & Garnier, 2002). By inviting critique from outside audiences via the Internet, writers may recognize the social context of their work, leading them to consider different perspectives on their ideas and to think more deeply about how best to approach revision (Beach & Friedrich, 2006).

The next section of this chapter presents a range of technology applications along with examples of how they can be used to support 21st-century writing skills in K–12 settings. The section is organized by Internet-based applications, mobile educational applications, and how these types of applications can be combined to create a 21st-century recursive writing process.

Internet-Based Applications That Support Writing

Since its creation, the Internet has so far been defined by two iterations of web applications. Web 1.0 was characterized by its one-way delivery. Writers, with knowledge of html code, could compose and publish information through read-only websites. Anyone with Internet access could read the websites, but fell short of communicating with the authors. Conversely, Web 2.0 applications, such as blogs, have been defined by the transactional relationship they allow between readers and writers. That is, readers are encouraged to contribute by becoming active coauthors rather than passive audience members.

Collaboration is perhaps the best way to think about Internet-based writing practices. A variety of tools are available to foster such activities and new technologies continuously emerge, requiring careful thinking about how they can and should be used in classroom instruction. In the following section I highlight some of the most popular tools currently used to support students' writing development.

Blogs

Weblogs, also known as blogs, are electronic journals created with Web 2.0 tools. They are virtual spaces where writers share thoughts, ponder ideas, and pose questions using compilations of words, images, video, and audio. Two unique aspects stand out about this form of digital writing. First, blog authors take on the role of both writer and editor, making decisions about the content, layout, and language of their electronic text. This differs greatly from the traditional publication process where editors dictate the presentation. Second, blogs enable readers to comment on entries, allowing relationships to form between readers and writers. This is an especially powerful affordance from a pedagogical perspective as it provides writers access and interaction with a wide range of audiences.

Some experts estimate there are over 450 million English language blogs (Technorati, 2011), and they vary widely in purpose and content. My previous work identified three types of education-related blogs (MacArthur & Karchmer-Klein, 2010). First, there are those blogs written by educators about the highs and lows of teaching. A wonderful example is *teacher tom (http://teachertomsblog.blogspot.com)*, the winner of the Edublog 2010 Best Teacher Blog. A preschool teacher from Seattle, Washington, teacher tom shares anecdotes about his work in a cooperative preschool and his views of education in general. Michael Smith shares a superintendent's point of view on his blog, *Principal's Page (www.principalspage. com/theblog)*. He chronicles his experiences discussing a range of issues from small-town education to mediocre teaching. Some bloggers choose to remain anonymous so they can share their stories while maintaining their privacy. For example, Mimi's blog, *It's Not All Flowers and Sausages (http://itsnotallflowersandsausages.blogspot.com)*, and Edna Lee's blog, *Regurgitated Alpha Bits (http://regurgitatedalphabits.blogspot.com)*, tell of true stories and the frustrations of life as elementary school teachers. Although these blogs detail personal experiences in education, their stories are relatable to many educators.

A second type of educational blog includes those in which teachers and students work together to share content. *Ms. Mac's Website (http:// kmcfadzen.wordpress.com)* is a great example of this. On the blog you will find videos of students displaying their work accompanied by assignment descriptions, providing contexts from which to understand what takes place in Ms. Mac's art room. Especially exciting is the Art Talk section in which students write entries in response to art-related issues. Readers are encouraged to comment. Likewise, Mr. Avery's Classroom Blog shares students' stories created with the tool *Storybirds (http://storybird.com)*. *Storybirds* is a Web 2.0 publishing tool that allows authors to write a story using preset images and templates. Authors then invite others to compose the story with them, resulting in a collaborative piece. You can read fun examples of these at Mr. Avery's blog *(http://mravery.edublogs.org/projects/storybirds)*.

While one of the benefits of blogs is the interaction between reader and writer, many bloggers are disappointed by the low numbers of comments they receive about their posts. David Mitchell, the deputy headteacher at Heathfield Primary School in the United Kingdom, found this to be true when his students published work on their class blog. He found the majority of comments came from inside his school with few, if any, outside comments. In response, he created the concept of *Quadblogging (http://*

quadblogging.net). Quadblogging connects four classrooms from around the world. Each week one of the four classes is the focus, and the students in the other three classes read and make "quality comments" on the classroom's posts. The students get to know each other and also learn about different places, customs, and cultures. Since September 2011, 50,000 students have participated in quadblogging. You can go to the Quadblogging site to sign your class up to participate in this innovative collaborative project.

Third, there has been a recent explosion of educational blogs written by educators to share advice and reviews of educational resources. Teachers are sharing ways of integrating new devices such as tablets and e-books into instruction and also offering reviews of different applications. For example, the *Collegiate iPad User Group (http://blogs.collegiateschool. org/ipad/about)* shares information about a new iPad initiative. Students and teachers are encouraged to read about the implementation and share comments in response to the postings. Moreover, posts include instructions on how to conduct a number of different functions on the device such as configuring a Bluetooth keyboard and downloading PDF books. Katherine McNight, a former high school teacher, maintains a blog sharing important ideas and lessons about how to use technology to support writing development *(http://katherinemcknight.com).* And *teacherwithapps (http://teacherswithapps.com),* written by two teachers, developed their blog to "help parents, grandparents, teachers, administrators, and anyone else, wade through the vast number of 'educational' apps being introduced. . . . "

Educators' perspectives should not be undervalued when it comes to understanding technology integration. In fact, most of what we know about best practices in using the technology to support reading and writing comes from the good work of classroom teachers who use technology on a regular basis (Karchmer, Mallette, Kara-Soteriou, & Leu, 2005). Their daily interactions with students along with their interest in technology puts them in an exceptional position to share critical insight into how the Internet can support writing as well as other disciplines.

Wikis

A wiki is a digital collaborative writing space. Similar to blogs, writers can incorporate a range of modes to share thoughts and ideas about different topics. *Wikipedia* is probably the most recognized wiki. Created in 2001, it is an online encyclopedia meant to be revised by its readers. Similarly the DAVISWiki *(http://daviswiki.org)* and the RocWiki *(http://rocwiki. org),* focused on their respective cities, can be edited by anyone interested in adding important information about Davis, California, or Rochester,

New York. Unique to wikis is their powerful collaborative nature. That is, they create a networked space where people from all over the world can work together to compose content. From a pedagogical perspective, they are especially useful tools because they maintain records of development and revisions, enabling teachers to document students' participation.

Innovative teachers integrate wikis into classroom instruction in many ways. For instance, Craig Kemp, a fourth-grade teacher in Singapore, maintains an exciting wiki where students engage in a Mind Create three times a week *(http://weare4k.wikispaces.com/home)*. Mr. Kemp posts a picture or video and students respond to it in a genre of their choice, posting their writing on the wiki for others to read. *Greetings from the World (http://greetingsfromtheworld.wikispaces.com)* is a collaborative writing project that uses wikis and a virtual poster tool to share important content. Arjana Blazic, the creator, wanted to share her students' experiences in her home country of Croatia with the rest of the world. To do so, her students created glogs using *Glogster*, a Web 2.0 tool that allows users to create virtual posters combining text, video, images, and music (Karchmer-Klein & Shinas, 2012a). She embedded these glogs on her classroom wiki and invited other schools to view them. She also invited students and teachers to create their own glogs about their home countries, states, and cities and post them to the wiki so her students could learn about different places and cultures. As of March 2012, 520 students from 19 different countries have created 300 glogs representing their home countries. Together, they have developed a dynamic compilation of resources from which others can learn.

Wikijunior (http://en.wikibooks.org/wiki/Wikijunior) captures the essence of true collaborative writing. It is a project geared toward children from babyhood through age 12. Here you will find hundreds of books in various stages of the writing process. Students can choose one and add, delete, and revise sections to make it better. The site encourages writers to fact-check, proofread, and also create their own books. There is also a *Wikijunior talk page* where students can discuss changes and content with others.

This is certainly not an exhaustive list of ways to integrate wikis, but is meant to provide ideas to get you thinking about how to do so in your writing classrooms. It is also important to keep in mind that along with using this collaborative tool comes a number of issues. My colleague Skip MacArthur and I highlighted these issues in previous work and they are worth mentioning here (MacArthur & Karchmer-Klein, 2010). First, teachers must consider carefully what it means to collaborate on writing assignments in the classroom and how they will prepare students to divide the responsibilities associated with the tasks. Second, given the open nature of the writing process when using wikis, students must learn how to respectfully respond and revise their classmates' work. Third, teachers must consider appropriate evaluation methods when assessing collaborative writing pieces. While there are no definitive ways of negotiating these issues in all classrooms, I strongly encourage you to develop a plan for responding to them before you consider using wikis in your instruction.

Other Collaborative Tools

In the first edition of this book, I recommended that teachers engage their students in collaborative Internet projects (CIPs), a practice in which two or more classrooms study similar topics and share their findings through writing and visual arts over the Internet (Leu, Leu, & Coiro, 2004). I explained that those who regularly participate in CIPs do so for three reasons. First, most projects focus on connections between content and students' background knowledge, something teachers believe is important for making learning concrete. Second, teachers value CIPs because they allow students to participate actively in their own learning. And third, CIPs help students recognize and appreciate differences among their peers (Karchmer-Klein & Layton, 2006). These reasons still hold true. However, the ways in which classes are collaborating have changed dramatically in the last 5 years. Whereas most early collaboration took place via e-mail, teachers are now using micro-blogging and social networking tools to examine issues and share perspectives with other students. Although there is little research supporting the use of these tools in academic settings, it is important to acknowledge their use in K–12 environments, especially since they rely upon the ability to communicate effectively with electronic text.

Micro-Blogging

Micro-blogging uses an Internet application (e.g., Twitter, Plurk, Tumblr) that allows writers to post short messages, pictures, and video. School districts across the country have been utilizing micro-blogs for several years to keep parents, teachers, and students in direct communication with school-related events (e.g., Thorpe, 2012). It seems teens are slowly migrating toward Twitter accounts, with 16% of 12–17-year-olds using the service in 2011 compared to 8% in 2009 (Irvine, 2012). Likewise, teachers are beginning to imagine the affordances micro-blogging brings to the classroom. Specifically, teachers seem excited to use micro-blogging in at least two ways to support writing.

First, *Twitter*, probably the most popular micro-blogging service, asks users to answer the question "What are you doing?" in 140 characters or less. Teachers and writing organizations are taking advantage of this feature to help students practice writing concise messages that convey important points. Steve Rayburn, a college English teacher, engaged his students in a Twitter activity that required them to take on a character's persona. As they read *Dante's Inferno*, students posted tweets from Dante's perspective to his love interest Beatrice. The assignment required students to hone their writing skills by composing concise messages that conveyed deep meanings (Ladd, 2009). Similarly, students at the San Francisco School of Arts were encouraged to enroll in a Twitter Micro-Lit Contest, hosted by Unstuck, a nonprofit annual publication. Contestants could write a nonfiction, fiction, or poetry entry of 12 separate tweets of 140 words or less. The winning piece would be posted on the publication's Twitter account. These types of activities require students to think deeply about the words they choose and participate in active language building.

A second way teachers are integrating micro-blogging in their instruction is by backchanneling, a real-time digital stream that allows students to respond to classroom discussions. Elementary, middle, and high school teachers are encouraging students to use classroom Twitter accounts and other backchannel tools (e.g., TodaysMeet, Google Moderator) to respond to, query, and summarize class content (Gabriel, 2011). For example, Chris Webb, a middle school teacher, explained on his blog how he observed sixth graders backchanneling as they watched a 50-minute video. The students were required to post questions they had about the content presented and also summarize portions of the video.

I observed Mrs. Arenstad's fifth-grade class engaged in backchanneling during a class read-aloud of Lois Lowry's *Number the Stars*. Mrs. Arenstad told me that she liked backchanneling because "it motivated the students and at the same time engaged them directly in the lesson, requiring them to think about the content and report on it during class time." The day of my observation the students were already familiar with backchanneling and using *TodaysMeet*, a free program that creates a safe space for students to discuss relevant content. The purpose of the lesson was to reinforce note-taking skills by summarizing and paraphrasing important episodes in the narrative text to recognize sequence and main ideas. Students were asked to listen to Mrs. Arenstad read aloud two chapters of the book and backchannel main ideas in the order they happened. At the start, Mrs. Arenstad reminded the students of her guidelines. These included:

1. Be respectful of your classmates' comments.
2. Stay on topic.
3. Do your best to use conventional spelling but it is not required.
4. Focus on multitasking: listen, summarize thoughts, write.
5. Pose questions you have about the text.
6. Paraphrase your ideas in 140 characters or less.
7. Add something new. Don't repeat what others have said.

As the teacher read the chapter, I watched as students listened intently and typed directly onto their laptops. At the end of the first chapter, Mrs. Arenstad projected the transcript onto the whiteboard so the class could review the notes so far:

- Annemarie is upset she does not know everything—Joyce
- She is upset but she is figuring out that it is part of being an adult—Mike
- I'm not sure she knows why. I think she is confused by what Uncle says—Lauren
- Annemarie was confused early in the day but as the day goes on she seems to put two and two together—Kirsten
- She is becoming like her mother; an adult—Joyce
- Annemarie is also learning what it is like to say goodbye to someone who dies. They are making food and preparing the living room—Nathan

Together they prioritized the most relevant comments by developing a timeline of events from the chapter. They also highlighted questions that still needed to be answered from the text. Mrs. Arenstad then read the second chapter and the students continued to backchannel. At the end of the reading, she again projected the transcript and the class reviewed the comments. Once this was completed, the students worked in small groups to compose summaries of the chapters. This example of backchanneling illustrates how it can be an integral part of the lesson by reinforcing content through collaborative meaning making. Backchanneling has become more popular recently because teachers recognize how technology can facilitate class discussions.

Social Networking Sites

Social networking sites (SNS) are defined as "supportive systems of sharing information and services among individuals and groups having a common interest" *(dictionary.com).* Researchers have begun to look at the educational significance of social networking sites on student learning (e.g., Coutts, Dawson, Boyer, & Ferdig, 2007; Fewkes & McCabe, 2012). Although this line of study is in its infancy, providing little empirical evidence from which to draw conclusions, many teachers seem to embrace SNS to build collaborative learning communities.

Edmodo, an SNS for educators, seems to be one of the most popular because it is a closed system. Unlike Facebook, teachers can create their own password-protected Edmodo site and invite only the participants they want included. Once connected, students can participate in a range of collaborative literacy activities given the number of tools available. In fact, Edmodo could be considered a portal or "instructional hub" (Dobler, 2012) because it allows teachers to store a range of resources in one location.

I observed a seventh-grade teacher engage his students in an Edmodo-based lesson. The topic was the Mexican–American War. To begin, the students opened their laptops and their class Edmodo site as Mr. Reilly projected the site on the whiteboard and introduced the lesson. He explained that they would be using a variety of activities to think deeply about the conflict. The class reviewed the content covered the previous day, including an overview of the war and who was involved. Next, Mr. Reilly opened a link he had embedded in the Edmodo site, and as a class the students listened to "Saint Patrick's Battalion," a song about the Irishmen who fought against the U.S. army during the war. When the song was over, Mr. Reilly gave the students 2 minutes to use what they learned from the song to decide which side of the war they would fight on. Next, the students used the polling tool on Edmodo to post their decision. As a class they reviewed the poll's results and discussed the different perspectives. To close the lesson, the students were required to post a note explaining their position along with one reason to support their view. Tyler, one of Mr. Reilly's students wrote:

I would not switch sides. You can call me a coward, but the United States had a much stronger army. I would be too afraid to move to a weaker military. It is also cowardly to leave your own country.

Edmodo can be used in a multitude of ways to support writing including activities such as literature circle discussions, peer editing, and pen pals. However, it is only as powerful as the teacher makes it. This point will be further explored in the next section.

Mobile Educational Applications That Support Writing

Unique to the tablet is the mobile educational application (or "app"), a software program designed to support user productivity, presentation, and/or gaming in the content areas. There are currently more than 20,000 educational apps available for use with the iPad (Apple, 2012) and approximately 800 are characterized as writing-focused.

As I write this chapter I am working in two schools in the midst of schoolwide iPad integrations: one elementary and one middle school. Part of my role at both schools is to help teachers identify useful apps related to their content areas. At the start of this work, I developed an application log where I document different types of apps, their cost, how teachers use them, how other educators review them, and my own analysis of their effectiveness. This examination led me to categorize educational apps in one of two ways.

Category 1

One category of educational applications includes those that independently teach or reinforce content. Characterized by gameplay environments, these apps assess skills as users complete different levels of difficulty. For example, based on the CCSS, *iTooch-English* incorporates a plethora of multiple choice content-area questions organized by grade level within an interactive interface. Third grade, for instance, includes questions related to choosing words and phrases for effect, introducing a topic, stating and supporting an opinion, vocabulary usage, and parts of speech. Students can work in practice or test mode and the app maintains a running progress report. Additionally, the app provides instructional support if the student struggles with content. Recent research indicates that student learning is greatest when content scaffolds are available before and during gameplay (Tsai, Kinzer, Hung, Chen, & Hsu, 2011). *iTooch-English* is an especially promising app given the interface, direct correlation to the CCSS, and the content support available to students.

I have seen this category of apps used in many of the classrooms I observe, and students' reactions seem to be positive. This is not surprising given research indicating gameplay environments are motivational (e.g., Aliya, 2002; Boyle, 1997). From my discussions with teachers, I noticed that those who were new to technology integration relied on these apps more than the more experienced technology users. It seems they are the easiest apps to integrate because they are, in essence, a method of drill and practice. As a seventh-grade teacher told me,

> "I am just learning how to work in a 1 to 1 technology environment. It is difficult to figure out how to get students to work independently on the iPad, so for now I am only using apps that teach content and don't require them to make content."

Additionally, teachers expressed excitement over these types of apps because they helped differentiate instruction, providing extra practice for those students who still struggle with a concept and more complex tasks for those who need to be challenged. For instance, a first-grade teacher integrated the *Drag and Tag (Nouns at Home)* application into her center time. Students practiced identifying nouns in game-like environments and the application progressed based upon the users' success. Kirstin, the first-grade teacher, explained:

> "Apps like this one allow me to work with a small group of students while the other kids are using an app to reinforce a skill at their own pace. It is the kind of tiered activity that helps me manage the classroom."

A list of noteworthy apps that fit into this category can be found in Table 13.1.

Category 2

The second category of educational applications includes those designed to be embedded within teaching practices. The application does not teach a skill or present information on its own. Instead the teacher or student

TABLE 13.1. Noteworthy Apps in Category 1

Title	Level	Cost	Description
iTooch English	Elementary	$5.99	Reinforces English skills based upon the CCSS. Uses a practice-and-test mode in a multiple-choice game-like environment.
Word BINGO	Elementary	$0.99	Reinforces DOLCH sight word list using a variety of interactive games.
Drag and Tag	Elementary	Free	Reinforces knowledge of nouns using a practice-and-game mode.
Shake-a-Phrase	Elementary	$1.99	Teaches vocabulary and parts of speech for ages 8+. It creates a new random sentence whenever students shake their iPads. Students can check the definition of a new word by just tapping it and can take quizzes about parts of speech.
SAT Vocab Cards	Middle/high school	Free	A flash card activity reinforcing a range of vocabulary
Basic English	All	Free	Teaches vocabulary using pictures and audio

must utilize the application to experience, conceptualize, analyze, or apply content (Kalantzis, Cope, & Cloonan, 2010). "Experiencing" refers to the learners' reflections on their own knowledge as well as their exposure to new ideas and situations. "Conceptualizing" refers to active thinking, or making mental and theoretical connections between concepts. "Analyzing" requires critical thinking by drawing inferences and establishing functional relations such as cause and effect. "Applying" refers to the application of knowledge in real-world situations in both predictable and creative ways. These four dimensions provide a framework from which to consider how technology, specifically mobile applications, can innovate content and support student writing within classroom environments. See Table 13.2 for a list of noteworthy applications in this category

Presentation Applications

Presentation applications fall in this category. For example, *Show Me* is similar to a whiteboard where users can draw, color, and insert images and audio to represent ideas. I have seen *Show Me* used in the classroom at a simplistic level to experience knowledge, and I have also observed more complex integration, encouraging analysis of concepts and inferencing. For example, a basic use of *Show Me* was observed in a fourth-grade writing class where students were reviewing grammar rules. The teacher wrote a series of sentences on the whiteboard and asked students to "Show Me" the different parts of speech. The teacher called out a word and told the students to write verb, noun, adjective, pronoun, or adverb on their iPad. This method of using *Show Me* allowed the teacher to evaluate all of the students' knowledge of the topic at the same time since they were responsible for independently documenting their responses.

An example of a more complex use was observed when seventh-grade students developed *Show Me* presentations to illustrate the transformation of North America into the postapocalyptic world of Panem in Suzanne Collins's *The Hunger Games*. Students studied the geographical descriptions of the 12 districts presented in the book. Using the *Show Me* app, they presented their interpretations to the class in two ways. First, they drew concept maps, showing the relationships between the author's descriptions of the districts and the characteristics of the current North America. Second, they projected a map of North America and using the drawing features, drew lines to represent the district boundaries. In this example, the app's affordances allowed students to conceptualize the content and visually represent their interpretations in meaningful ways. Other examples of *Show Me* presentations on a range of topics can be found at the *Show Me Open Community* website *(www.showme.com)*.

TABLE 13.2. Noteworthy Apps in Category 2

Title	Level	Cost	Description
Build a Story	Elementary	$3.99	Allows writers to create personalized storybooks using preset themes and character categories.
Puppet Pals HD	Elementary	Free	A digital storytelling tool with saved characters and images or users' pictures. Students can record their voice and save it.
Toontastic	Elementary	Free	A cartoon-making app including preset characters and backgrounds with audio capabilities.
SundryNotes Pro	Middle/ high school	$7.99	A note-taking tool that can record voice and audio notes and import images or pdf files. In addition to the functions of Evernote, students can create tables and change the background/border colors.
Writing Prompts	Middle/ high school	$1.99	Writing prompt generator using current events, scene elements, words, sketches, colors, genres, and writing types to motivate and direct writers.
Evernote	Middle/ high school	Free	A note-taking tool that can record voice and audio notes and import images. Notes can be exported to other apps or e-mail.
Popplet Lite	All	Free	A concept-mapping tool that allows users to insert images while they write and organize ideas.
StoryKit	All	Free	Create digital books with sound, images, and text. Users can write their own books or rewrite preloaded books like *The Three Little Pigs*.
Show Me	All	Free	A personal interactive whiteboard. It allows people to record voiceover whiteboard tutorials and to share them online. People can insert images, write texts, and draw lines.
Book Creator	All	$4.99	Digital book-making app with text, images, videos, and sound capabilities. Books made can be exported as pdf and be read on iBooks. Layout format is not fixed so students can make personalized books.
iMovie	All	$4.99	Video-making and presentation tool with photos, music, and sound effects. Students can use some samples of trailers as a frame to make their own video clip.

Writing Applications

There are also many writing-focused educational apps that fit within this category. For example, one of my observations brought me to a first-grade classroom where students were using the *Rory's Story Cubes* app. This app has cubes covered with different images. Students role the cubes by shaking the iPad, and then apply their writing knowledge to develop a story based upon the combination of images that appear. There are over 10 million possible combinations of story starters.

Similarly, the *Writing Prompts* app for older students generates thousands of story starters using different approaches. There is a scene section, for instance, that includes a place, a character, an object, and a smell, mood, weather, or time. The student shakes the iPad and different combinations appear such as:

Place: in another galaxy

Character: a confused ghost

Object: two new lightbulbs

Smell: fresh roses

Additionally, there is a words section that presents five to six words that students must incorporate into their writing and a scenes section that provides a scenario such as "You find a package at your door with nothing on it but your name." There is also a news section that provides students with a current headline from a national newspaper as well as a direct link to the article. Students use these prompts in the different sections to compose stories from perspectives they may not have considered.

I observed eighth-grade students using the news section from this app in their writing course. The class had been discussing critical reading skills and what writers need to know about presenting effective messages on the Internet, beginning with succinct titles. Working independently, the students used the *Writing Prompts* app to identify a headline. They shook their iPads and generated news headlines. Some examples include:

Spaceship Lands in a Faraway Place

Pumpkin Seed Oil Is a Valuable Wisconsin Product

Future of Store Unknown

Next, they took on the role of reporter. Drawing inferences from their headline, they wrote one-page news articles about their topic. Next, they connected to the actual article through the link on the app. As they read it, they compared and contrasted what they had written with the actual source and then presented their findings to the class. Afterward, the teacher led a conversation about the importance of deep reading and looking beyond Internet headlines to understand the real stories.

Digital Storytelling

Digital storytelling apps are a third example of this category. Digital storytelling is the practice of composing multimodal texts that share narratives in dynamic ways. They can be personal accounts, professional presentations, or interactive stories and can require students to conceptualize content and apply what they have learned about genre. Digital stories are becoming a staple in many writing classrooms now that the process of integrating audio, video, graphics, and text has become less cumbersome. Most exciting, there are apps for all age levels, enabling even the youngest writers to create dynamic multimodal ensembles.

If you teach young children or are apprehensive about implementing digital storytelling in your classroom, I recommend starting with structured apps. These provide support to the writer by including preset themes, images, and characters. They also take the writer through the process of creating a digital story, teaching students how to combine different modes to compose the narrative. For example, the *Build a Story* app begins by prompting the writer to choose a setting such as a jungle, circus, or farm. Next, writers choose the pages they want to include. The options are designed to compliment the chosen theme. On each page, they can choose from a selection of images organized by category such as food, animals, weather, and people. Writers can also add speech bubbles where they can type text to represent dialogue between characters. Completed stories can be printed or e-mailed to the teacher. Similarly, *Toontastic*, a cartoon-creator app developed in partnership with Stanford University's Graduate School of Education, is organized by story grammar. Audio support leads the writer through the composing process, defining concepts such as conflict, climax, and resolution, and explaining how to navigate through the site. Especially exciting, *Toontastic* allows writers to animate their scenes by moving characters and adding audio dialogue and mood music.

Once students and teachers become more comfortable with utilizing different modes to tell stories (e.g., audio, video, images), they can transition to less-structured storytelling apps, ones that allow writers to develop their own content and are not confined by the choices provided by the app. The recently released *iBook Author* app is a powerful example of how authors can compose dynamic multimodal stories. The writer begins by choosing a preset page layout. However, the remainder of the composition is left to the author to determine. You can easily embed interactive graphics, text, video, and 3-D objects. Of particular interest is the ability to insert text saved as a Microsoft Word or Pages document. For instance, I created a new book and inserted this chapter into the app. In seconds I had a professionally formatted text that could be read on the iPad. *Story Kit, SonicPics*, and *StoryRobe* are other apps that fit within this category. A group of Apple Distinguished Educators created exceptional tutorials on how to use each of these apps. The tutorials can be found on the website *Digital Storytelling with the iPad (https://sites.google.com/site/digitalstorytellingwiththeipad/resources)*.

It is critical to add a word of caution about such powerful tools and digital storytelling in general. In order for students to compose effective multimodal ensembles, they must understand that each mode carries meaning (Kress, 2003). They must be aware of audience and consider alternative reading paths so that their message is unified and comprehensible (Karchmer-Klein & Shinas, 2012a). Similar to issues with PowerPoint, we want to steer students away from the bells and whistles of the tool (Baker et al., 2000) and toward purposefully selecting modes to develop unified messages.

Integrating Category 2 Apps

This second category of applications is more complex because it relies on the teacher's ability to integrate the apps effectively within the context of instruction. If you are hesitant to take this step, it may be beneficial to organize your instruction using Harris and Hofer's (2009) approach to grounded technology integration. This approach encourages teachers to first identify content. Once the learning goals are clear, teachers can make important pedagogical decisions related to the classroom environment such as whether the lesson is teacher- or student-centered, if it requires few or more prior experiences, and if it should be completed individually, in small groups, or as a whole class. Once these goals are established, teachers can then choose an educational application that provides support to student learning within the context of the learning goals. By following this process of lesson development, the focus remains on how students can experience, conceptualize, analyze, and apply curriculum content through meaningful technology-integrated activities.

Digital Recursive Writing

Tablets, such as the iPad, were never intended to replace desktop or laptop computers. Rather they were developed "for browsing the web, reading and sending e-mail, enjoying photos, watching videos, listening to music, playing games, reading e-books" (Apple, 2010). However, there are many writers who have transitioned to composing directly on the iPad because of the fluidity it offers to the writing process. Consider the following example from an eighth-grade classroom. The teacher introduced an assignment that required students to research a poet, choose and interpret a favorite poem written by the poet, describe how the poem appealed to the five senses, and present the findings to the class in a cohesive presentation. Students were encouraged to compose a digital story incorporating multiple modes, but also had the option of writing a traditional paper. All of the students chose the former. Edward, a relatively tech-savvy student, used a combination of educational applications to develop his assignment.

Edward began by using his iPad to connect to the Internet to conduct his research. Using the web browser, he found two websites about his poet. The first was his poet's personal website and the second was a blog that reviewed poems by different authors. Edward examined the poet's site and as he identified key facts, he toggled between the browser and *Evernote*, a free note-taking app, where he documented things like birthdate, hometown, and stories behind the poems. He then moved to the blog, skimming for poems written by his poet. This site included audio clips of the author reading a selection of his own poems. Edward plugged his headset into the iPad and listened to several until he identified his favorite. Again, he opened *Evernote* and took notes interpreting the poem, specifically the senses it evoked, as per his teacher's instruction. Next, Edward opened *Popplet Lite*, a free mind-mapping app, to create a visual representation of his response. He created a graphic organizer, much like a storyboard, to represent how his final presentation would look. Although he still had more brainstorming to do, Edward chose to begin his presentation using *Wix*, a free web-building tool. He opened the website, created the project, and began to insert content. He continued to transition between the different applications, over the course of 3 days, until he completed it. Edward's example is one of 21st-century digital recursive writing.

This form of digital recursive writing is not limited to older students. Teachers at the Martin J. Gottlieb Day School in Florida are implementing a schoolwide iPad integration beginning with first graders. A primary goal is to teach students to "fluently switch between apps, then insert, embed, share, and disseminate their creations." To do this, they begin by providing students with opportunities to learn how to use apps independent of each other. For instance, students use *Doodle Buddy*, a presentation tool, to practice writing their Hebrew letters. Next, students practice taking pictures of themselves using the built-in camera features on the iPad. They learn to save and retrieve the images from the Photo Gallery and edit as needed. Teachers then connect these two features by showing the students how to upload their photos into *Doodle Buddy* and then practice writing their name in Hebrew using colored markers. Clearly, students are given ample opportunities to build procedural knowledge of these technology tools so they learn the complexities of electronic text before combining the apps to build meaningful presentations. Ms. Tolisano, the technology specialist, explains on her blog:

> It is crystallizing itself clearly, that the iPad lessons are building on each other. The best success, I have been able to observe, is when students had explored an app in one class, worked with the app to create in another class, and finally pulled the sequence together for a larger project by remixing, sharing and collaborating.

Admittedly, digital recursive writing is difficult to master. It is time-intensive, requires thoughtful planning, and demands mastery of writing and technology tools. However, it embeds technology into the writing process in a way that makes the devices meaningful. That is, technology and its capabilities become integral components of the writing process rather than peripheral tools.

Final Thoughts

Teachers are more inclined to integrate technology when there is a clear connection between technology-based activities and curriculum standards (Karchmer-Klein, 2007b). Fortunately, technology is embedded within the CCSS for writing. When I was asked to write this chapter, I took a closer look at the standards and found that while the degree and complexity to which technology is included at each grade level varied, there were four common threads. Students are expected to (1) use a variety of digital tools, (2) produce and publish electronic text, (3) interact and collaborate with others on their writing, and (4) use multimedia (i.e., modes) to scaffold comprehension of their texts. The applications and examples presented in this chapter illustrate how students can use technology for these purposes.

In conclusion, writing instruction must prepare students to communicate effectively in the 21st century. The affordances of Internet-based and mobile educational applications enable teachers to recognize how technology changes writing while also using technology as a tool to support pedagogically sound research-based instruction. Perhaps the most important lesson to be learned from this chapter is that the teacher is the most influential player when it comes to utilizing technology in the classroom to support writing instruction. That is, technology integration is only as effective as the lesson constructed by the teacher. Yet teachers must be given adequate professional development to think deeply about new technologies and how they influence writing instruction (Karchmer-Klein & Shinas, 2012b). I hope the tools and examples discussed in this chapter empower educators to try them out and further explore best practices.

References

Aliya, S. K. (2002). The role of computer games in the development of theoretical analysis, flexibility and reflective thinking in children: A longitudinal study. *International Journal of Psychophysiology, 45*, 149.

Apple. (2012). Apple reinvents textbooks with iBooks 2 for iPad [Press release]. Retrieved from *www.apple.com/pr/library/2012/01/19Apple-Reinvents-Textbooks-with-iBooks-2–for-iPad.html*.

Baker, E. A., Pearson, P. D., & Rozendal, M. S. (2010). Theoretical perspectives and literacy studies: An exploration of roles and insight. In E. A. Baker (Ed.), *The new literacies: Multiple perspectives on research and practice* (pp. 1–22). New York: Guilford Press.

Beach, R., & Friedrich, T. (2006). Response to writing. In C. A. MacArthur, S. Graham, & J. Fitzgerald (Eds.), *Handbook of writing research* (pp. 222–234). New York: Guilford Press.

Bezemer, J., & Kress, G. (2008). Writing in multimodal texts: A social semiotic account of designs for learning. *Written Communication, 25*, 166–195.

Boyle, T. (1997). *Design for multimedia learning.* London: Prentice Hall.

Coiro, J., Knobel, M., Lankshear, C., & Leu, D. J. (Eds.). (2008). *Handbook of research in new literacies.* Mahwah, NJ: Erlbaum.

Coutts, J., Dawson, K., Boyer, J., & Ferdig, R. (2007). Will you be my friend?: Prospective teachers' use of Facebook and implications for teacher education. In C. Crawford et al. (Eds.), *Proceedings of Society for Information Technology and Teacher Education International Conference 2007* (pp. 1937–1941). Chesapeake, VA: Association for the Advancement of Computing in Education.

Daiute, C. (1992). Multimedia composing: Extending the resources of the kindergarten to writers across the grades. *Language Arts, 69*, 250–260.

Dalton, B., Smith, B.E., & Alvey, T.L. (2010, December). *5th grade students compose and reflect on their multimodal stories.* Paper presented at the annual meeting of the National Reading Conference, Fort Worth, TX.

Davies, J. (2006). Nomads and tribes: Online meaning-making and the development of new literacies. In J. Marsh & E. Millard (Eds.), *Popular literacies, childhood and schooling* (pp. 161–173). London: Routledge.

Dobler, E. (2012). Flattening classroom walls: Edmodo takes teaching and learning across the globe. *Reading Today, 29*, 12–13.

Fewkes, A. M., & McCabe, M. (2012). Facebook: Learning tool or distraction? *Journal of Digital Learning in Teacher Education, 28*(3), 92–98.

Gabriel, T. (2011). Speaking up in class, silently, using social media. *New York Times.* Retrieved from: *www.nytimes.com/2011/05/13/education/13social.html?pagewanted=2&_r=1.*

Goldberg, A., Russell, M., & Cook, A. (2003). The effect of computers on student writing; A meta-analysis of studies from 1992–2002. *Journal of Technology, Learning and Assessment, 2*(1), 3–51.

Harris, J., & Hofer, M. (2009). Grounded tech integration. *Learning and Leading With Technology, September/October*, 22–25.

Herrington, A., Hodgson, K., & Moran, C. (2009). *Teaching the new writing: Technology, change, and assessment in the 21st century classroom.* New York: Teachers College Press.

Irvine, M. (2012). Teens on twitter: They're migrating sometimes for privacy. *Huffington Post.* Retrieved from *www.huffingtonpost.com/2012/01/30/teens-on-twitter_n_1241109.html.*

Jewitt, C. (2011). An introduction to multimodality. In C. Jewitt (Ed.), *The Routledge handbook of multimodal analysis* (pp. 14–27). New York: Routledge.

Kalantzis, M., Cope, B., & Cloonan, A. (2010). A multiliteracies perspective on the new literacies. In E. A. Baker (Ed.), *The new literacies: Multiple perspectives on research and practice* (pp. 61–87). New York: Guilford Press.

Karchmer, R. A. (2001). The journey ahead: Thirteen teachers report how the Internet influences literacy and literacy instruction in their K–12 classrooms. *Reading Research Quarterly, 36*, 442–466.

Karchmer, R. A., Mallette, M. H., & Kara-Soteriou, J., & Leu, D. J. Jr. (Eds.). (2005). *New literacies for new times: Innovative models of literacy education using the Internet.* Newark, DE: International Reading Association.

Karchmer, R. A., Mallette, M. H., & Leu, D. J. Jr. (2002). Early literacy in a digital age: Moving from a singular book literacy to the multiple literacies of networked information and communication technologies. In D. M. Barone & L. M. Morrow (Eds.), *Literacy and young children: Research-based practices* (pp. 175–194). New York: Guilford Press.

Karchmer-Klein, R. A. (2007a). Audience awareness and Internet publishing: Factors influencing how fourth graders write electronic text. *Action in Teacher Education, 29*(2), 39–50.

Karchmer-Klein, R. A. (2007b). Re-examining the practicum placement: How to leverage technology to prepare preservice teachers for the demands of the 21st century. *Journal of Computing in Teacher Education, 23*(4), 121–129.

Karchmer-Klein, R. A., & Layton, V. (2006). Literature-based collaborative Internet projects in elementary classrooms. *Reading Research and Instruction, 45*(4), 261–294.

Karchmer-Klein, R. A., & Shinas, V. H. (2012a). 21st-century literacies in teacher education: Investigating multimodal texts in the context of an online graduate-level literacy and technology course. *Research in the Schools, 19*(1), 60–74.

Karchmer-Klein, R. A., & Shinas, V. H. (2012b). Guiding principles for supporting new literacies in your classroom. *The Reading Teacher, 65*(5), 285–290.

Kelly, J., Kratcoski, A., & McClain, K. (2009). The effects of word processing software on the writing of students with special needs. *Journal of the Research Center for Educational Technology, 2*(2), 32–43.

Kress, G. (2003). *Literacy in the new media age.* London: Routledge.

Ladd, D. (2009). Anonymous fame: Steve Rayburn's "Twitter in Hell" project gets national attention. *The Online Gargoyle.* Retrieved from *www.uni.illinois. edu//og/news/2009/04/anonymous-fame-steve-rayburns-twitter.*

Larson, L. (2010). Digital readers: The next chapter in e-book reading and response. *The Reading Teacher, 64*(1), 15–22.

Lenhart, A., Arafeh, S., Smith, A., & MacGill, A. R. (2008, April). *Writing, technology and teens.* Pew/Internet and American Life Project. Retrieved from *http://pewinternet.org/pdfs/PIP_Writing_Report_FINAL3.pdf.*

Leu, D. J. Jr., Kinzer, C. K., Coiro, J., & Cammack, D. W. (2004). Toward a theory of new literacies emerging from the Internet and other information and communication technologies. In R. B. Ruddell & N. Unrau (Eds.), *Theoretical models and processes of reading* (5th ed., pp. 1570–1613). Newark, DE: International Reading Association. Retrieved from *www.readingonline.org/ newliteracies/lit_index.asp?HREF=leu.*

Leu, D. J. Jr., Leu, D. D., & Coiro, J. (2004). *Teaching with the Internet: Lessons from the classroom* (4th ed.). Norwood, MA: Christopher-Gordon.

MacArthur, C. A., Graham, S., Hayes, J. B., & De La Paz, S. (1996). Spelling checkers and students with learning disabilities: Performance comparisons and impact on spelling. *Journal of Special Education, 30,* 35–57.

MacArthur, C. A., & Karchmer-Klein, R. A. (2010). Web 2.0: New opportunities for writing. In G. A. Troia, R. K. Shankland, & A. Heintz (Eds.), *Writing research in classroom practice* (pp. 45–69). New York: Guilford Press.

Marsh, J. (2011). Young children's literacy practices in a virtual world: Establishing an online interaction order. *Reading Research Quarterly, 46*(2), 101–118.

Matsumura, L. C., Patthey-Chavez, G. G., Valdés, R., & Garnier, H. (2002). Teacher feedback, writing assignment quality, and third-grade students' revision in lower-and higher-achieving urban schools. *Elementary School Journal, 103*(1), 3–25.

National Center for Education Statistics. (2010). *Teachers' use of educational technology in U.S. Public Schools: 2009.* Washington, DC: Author. Retrieved from *http://nces.ed.gov/pubsearch/pubsinfo.asp?pubid=2010040.*

National Governors Association & Council of Chief State School Officers. (2010). *Common Core State Standards for English language arts & literacy in history/social studies, science, and technical subjects.* Washington, DC: Authors. Retrieved from *www. corestandards.org.*

SMART Technologies. (2012). SMART board™ interactive whiteboard reaches 20–year milestone. [Press Release]. Retrieved from *www.smarttech.com/us/ About+SMART/About+SMART/Newsroom/Media+releases/English+US/ Releases+by+year/2011+media+releases/2011/SMART+Board+Interactive+ Whiteboard+Reaches+20–Year+Milestone.*

Technorati. (2011). *State of the blogosphere.* Retrieved from *http://technorati.com/ state-of-the-blogosphere.*

Thorpe, B. (2012). More K–12 schools embrace texting, social media to share information. *MLive.* Retrieved from *www.mlive.com/news/flint/index. ssf/2012/02/more_k-12_schools_embrace_text.html.*

Tsai, F., Kinzer, C., Hung, K., Chen, C. A., & Hsu, I. (2011). The importance and use of targeted content knowledge in educational simulation games. In M. Chang, W. Hwang, M. Chen, & W. Muller (Eds.), *Sixth International Conference on e-learning and games* (pp. 245–247). Berlin: Springer.

Yancey, K. B. (2005). Using multiple technologies to teach writing. *Educational Leadership, 62,* 38–40.

Chapter 14

Best Practices in Writing about Text

TIMOTHY SHANAHAN

Scholars have long known that learning to read and learning to write are related processes (Tierney & Shanahan, 1991). Reading and writing each depend on learning slightly different versions of the same linguistic and cognitive information (Fitzgerald & Shanahan, 2000), including metaknowledge (e.g., understanding the functions and purposes of reading and writing, monitoring comprehension and production); knowledge about substance and content (e.g., world knowledge, domain knowledge, content knowledge); knowledge about universal text attributes (e.g., graphophonics, syntax, text organization), and the knowledge and skill needed to negotiate reading and writing (e.g., procedural knowledge, communication strategies). Thus, both reading and writing depend on a mastery of sound–symbol relationships (for decoding in reading or for spelling in writing), vocabulary, grammar/syntax, text organization, and the like. They both require knowledge of the world, the content of what we read and write about. Readers and writers both must recognize they are in a communicative relationship with the other, writers by anticipating the readers' needs for information, readers by thinking about the author's choices, and both need to be self-aware, monitoring their own actions and effectiveness.

As similar as reading and writing are, however, it is essential to recognize they are also different. Reading and writing depend on highly *similar* information, not *identical* information. That means being good at reading does not guarantee a student will be equally good at writing: someone can be a good reader and a poor writer, or vice versa (Stotsky, 1983). For example, both reading and writing require knowledge of the world; writing requires it as the basis of what the writer will write about, while reading requires it as a tool for making sense of the information the writer provides. While it may seem like the knowledge base would be exactly the same, it is not. Readers and writers have to be able to start from different places. The reader has to follow an author's lead, using prior knowledge on a topic to draw inferences or to fill gaps that the author leaves. The writer, on the other hand, has to be able to initiate the "conversation," which requires a greater degree of explicitness and a more thorough and complete grasp of the same information. (It is sort of like the difference between recognizing which choice is right on a multiple-choice test and being able to produce an answer to a question with a cogent and complete statement of information.) Knowing a topic well enough to read about it successfully pales before the more onerous demands of writing; more extensive and better organized knowledge is required for someone to write about it with sufficient depth. Similarly, it has been shown that there are different, though overlapping, cognitive paths from sound to letter than from letter to sound; spelling and decoding are not just mirror images of each other (Fitzgerald & Shanahan, 2000).

The separation of reading and writing argues for the teaching of both reading and writing, the only way to ensure that both will be learned. However, their separability is also why reading and writing can be combined so effectively to support learning (Tierney, Soter, O'Flahavan, & McGinley, 1989). Because reading and writing differ, by combining them or, more accurately, by combining their cognitive operations, they are able to offer alternative perspectives to the learner. Reading about a topic and writing about the same topic require somewhat different perspectives on the information, and thus doing both activities together tends to provide a richer learning experience. Similarly, exploring language both through reading and writing helps to build an understanding of how language works— whether the focus is on graphophonemic relations, vocabulary, syntax, organization, or genre—as we explore these aspects of language somewhat differently in reading and writing. Gaining a slightly different angle on the same information provides one with greater perspective and awareness.

Importantly, research has shown that the connections of reading and writing can be successfully exploited, allowing for the enhancement of literacy learning experiences (Graham & Hebert, 2010; Tierney & Shanahan, 1991). Of all the instructional approaches to connecting reading and writing studied so far, writing about text has been the most successful as an avenue to improving reading achievement, and such integrated approaches have been valuable in stimulating higher quality writing outcomes too. This chapter explores four research-supported approaches to guiding students to write about text in literacy-enhancing ways.

Writing to Text Models

One way writing about text can be used to deepen children's reading and writing skills is to have students read model texts and then to imitate some aspects of the model text through their own writing. Such modeling is a very common approach to teaching writing at the college level, where 76% of instructors report using it regularly (Stolarek, 1994). However, there are persuasive examples of text modeling with elementary (Cramer & Cramer, 1975) and secondary students too (Shields, 2007). The idea of text modeling is that students must carefully and analytically read texts to identify the key features of the text to produce their own version of a genre or a text feature. By engaging in such reading—with an eye aimed specifically at identifying features of craft and structure—students can sharpen both their reading and writing tools.

Modeling or imitative writing has not been studied often, but studies of the efficacy of writing to text models have found small, though positive, effects. Graham and Perin (2007), in an extensive review of studies of what improves writing achievement, found the study of text models to be an effective, albeit limited, approach to improving writing quality. Their review examined six studies focused on grades 4 through 12 that compared the performance of students who examined model pieces of writing to guide the construction of their own compositions with the performance of students who had not received such modeling support. The average effect size for modeling was 0.25; the experimental students received a quarter of a standard deviation advantage from modeling. If the control group performed at the 50th percentile at the end of the study, the modeling groups would have performed at the 60th percentile. There were no differences in the effectiveness of modeling procedures across the studies due to demographic or treatment variations.

What does text modeling instruction look like? Basically, the idea is that to teach students about a genre, say the fairy tale genre, it is necessary to engage them in the reading and writing of fairy tales. Necessarily, the reading of the texts to be imitated must come first since without a model students would not have a clear idea of what to focus on in the production of their own versions. For such reading (or listening), teachers need to select appropriately strong or salient texts, An exemplary version of a fairy tale, one that is prototypical of the genre, and that would be easy to recognize as a fairy tale, would be a good choice. There is some evidence that model quality may not matter particularly when multiple examples are used (Charney & Carlson, 1995). However, such evidence comes from older student writers who might be better able to identify essential text characteristics on their own, without much teacher support.

Fairy tales usually focus on a quest of some kind and they tend to pit good against evil. Such tales always include magic, often, though not always, with talking animals or other "strange" creatures. Frequently fairy tales include royalty (kings and princesses), and the tales customarily take place in somewhat exotic or distant settings ("at the edge of a dark wood," "in a kingdom," "across the seven seas") far away and long ago ("once upon a time")—and, presumably, emotionally at a safer distance for young readers who may be reassured that such events cannot befall them. The plots of fairy tales often include instances in which various events reoccur three or seven times.

To teach students to write in the fairy tale genre, the teacher would have the children read or listen to such stories, followed by some kind of guided analysis—breaking the stories down into their elements. Thus, in *Goldilocks and the Three Bears*, we have a story that takes place "once upon a time" in a "large forest." Goldilocks sets off on an adventure. She enters the home of a family of three bears (who amazingly enough talk and comport themselves like people). This story has a lot of threes in it: three bears, three bowls of porridge, three chairs, three beds, and most important, Goldilocks attempts to figure out what is "just right for her" three times. By reading and rereading such tales, and discussing them and even charting out their elements, the students come to recognize the recurring text features. For example, the wolf in the *Three Little Pigs* tries to get the pigs three times before he gets his ultimate lesson, and the queen in *Rumpletstiltskin* attempts to guess Rumpletstiltskin's name three times as well.

Once the students are conversant with the essential elements or characteristics, then they are ready to attempt to produce their own fairy tales, complete with the essential fairy tale genre features they have identified. Initially, the teacher might provide a template for the children to fill in or complete with their own versions of the key features, but over time such scaffolding is removed and the children create their tales with less support or constraint.

Modeling can focus on genre, as in this example, but there are many other features of text that could be replicated as well. Thus, students might try to write their own version of *Brown Bear, Brown Bear* investing its predictable literary pattern with their own content (Cramer & Cramer, 1975). Similarly, students might take the structure of a text comparing crocodiles and alligators, trying to imitate its informational text structure in their own reports on lions and tigers or frogs and toads or Democrats and Republicans.

Imitation of text models is even emphasized in the upper grades in the Common Core State Standards (CCSS; National Governors Association Best [NGA] & Council of Chief State School Officers [CCSSO], 2010), in which students are expected to study how Shakespeare used Ovid as the source material for *Romeo and Juliet* and how Jerome Robbins, Arthur Laurents, and Stephen Sondheim later used *Romeo and Juliet* as the basis for *West Side Story*. Anyone who studies a text or some aspect of a text so carefully that he or she can use it as the basis for their own written inventions truly understands and appreciates the original work and is better situated to take on similar texts in the future, influencing both reading and writing. Of course, modeling requires readers to read like writers, with an eye not only to what the text says, but to how it works (Tierney & Pearson, 1983).

Summarizing Text

Another way reading can be a valuable basis of writing is to have students summarize texts, condensing the information into an essentialized but shorter version of the original (Brown & Day, 1983). To write an effective summary, of course, readers must recognize which ideas are indispensable to the original text, and which ones can be dropped altogether or combined within collective statements or generalizations. As such, summarization entails many important reading and writing skills including paraphrasing. Research shows summarization instruction improves both writing quality (Graham & Perin, 2007) and reading comprehension (Graham & Hebert, 2010; National Institute of Child Health and Human Development, 2000; Shanahan et al., 2010) across a wide range of ages; summarization has been found to exert large and consistent positive impacts on student outcomes with both reading and writing performance. Across 19 studies of the effects of summary writing with students in grades 3 through 12, the average effect size was .52. The summary writers ended up at the 70th percentile, while the control groups would have ended at the 50th percentile.

Although studies have shown summarization to improve reading and writing at a variety of grade levels, the effects are markedly larger (0.79) with younger students—those in elementary school—than with older ones (0.33) in the middle and high school grades (Graham & Hebert, 2010).

Good readers (or listeners) usually find that if they stop occasionally to sum up the information as they progress through a text or presentation they end up with better comprehension and recall (National Institute of Child Health and Human Development, 2000). But the *writing* of summaries appears to be even more powerful. "Writing summaries about a text proved to be better than simply reading it, reading and rereading it, [and] reading and studying it" (Graham & Hebert, 2010, p. 16). Along the same lines, summarization of multiple sources is a vital step in the process of academic research.

To summarize effectively, students need to recognize main ideas and key details, disregard unimportant or repetitive ideas, construct topic sentences, paraphrase, and collapse or combine lists or events into general statements. Thus, if someone were retelling the story of *Goldilocks and the Three Bears* he or she would likely write something like, "Goldilocks tried out the Bears' breakfasts, chairs, and beds, always with the same result: the baby bear's stuff was just right for her," rather than retelling each episode in its entirety.

As with modeling, to teach summarization effectively, the instructional texts should be carefully selected. For instance, summarizing a brief text, like a paragraph, is a very different experience than summing up a more extensive text, like a chapter or a book. It usually is best to start with shorter texts and as students become proficient with them, to then move on to the challenge of longer texts. Similarly, it is best to start out with relatively easy-to-understand texts, particularly with regard to how clear, explicit, well organized, and straightforward they are in style. Again, it is not that summarization should not be applied to more complicated texts, only that students will likely do better if they have the chance to build up to dealing with higher levels of complexity.

Another idea for dealing with the summarization of longer text is to use the GIST approach (Cunningham, 1982; Frey, Fisher, & Hernandez, 2003). With GIST students initially read a brief text, perhaps a couple of paragraphs, and then write a single-sentence summary of the information, limiting the summary to 20 words or less. When students become proficient with one-sentence summaries, the teacher then provides students with more extensive texts that have been marked with stopping points. Students are to read to the designated stopping points and to write the brief GIST summaries they have been practicing. By the time they complete a full article they will have written perhaps five or six sentence summaries of the various sections of the text, and then they combine these brief summaries and craft them into an overall summary.

Teacher guidance is also essential in effective summarization teaching. There are two approaches that have been tried successfully. In one approach, the teacher provides students with a partial graphic summary of a text and the students' initial task is to fill in the missing information. As the students complete the summary, they work with less supportive summaries, filling in more of the information on their own, until they can write an entire summary independently (Chang, Sung, & Chen, 2002).

See Figure 14.1 for an example of a summarization template that could be used. It is a fairly simple example in which the text expresses one main idea and three supporting ideas. In this one, none of the structures are filled in, but with such a simple text, providing the structure alone might be sufficient to meet many students' needs. Even with a bare-bones template

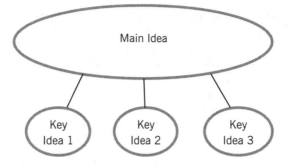

FIGURE 14.1. Graphic summary support.

like the example, it is possible to gradually withdraw support with practice. Finally, it would also be reasonable for the teacher to provide students with the beginnings of a summary statement: "The author's main idea was _____, and he or she supported his or her idea with three key pieces of evidence. . ."

In the other successful approach to summarization, students are taught the summarization process itself (Bean & Steenwyk, 1984; Brown & Day, 1983). Specifically, the teacher scaffolds the summarization process by taking students through each step with increasingly more student input. To do this, it can help if the text itself can be projected for analysis. Initially, the teacher might guide students to identify the main ideas, either helping them to state the major ideas or to locate the ideas in the text itself if the author stated them explicitly. Then, the text can be examined sentence by sentence to delete unnecessary, repetitive, or trivial information. Replacing extensive events, processes, or lists with summary statements is another step in the process. Finally, the teacher shows students how to translate the marked-up text into a summary statement of an appropriate length. Such practice can be fortified through the use of skeleton outlines that facilitate student identification of key information (Taylor & Beach, 1984). For more details on how to teach students to summarize, see Shanahan et al. (2010).

Writing about Text

Another way writing about text can improve reading and writing achievement is to engage students in responding to questions about text, especially questions that require more extensive and extended analyses and critical evaluations of the texts. "Answering questions about a text can be done verbally, but there is a greater benefit from performing such activities in writing. Writing answers to text questions makes them more memorable, as writing an answer provides a second form of rehearsal" (Graham & Hebert, 2010, p. 16). Writing answers to questions about text has a small but consistently positive effect on reading comprehension (grades 2–12). Graham and Hebert (2010) reviewed eight such studies with students in grades 6–12, and all had positive impacts for having students write questions about text or write answers to such questions. The average effect size was 0.40, meaning, on average, the students who wrote about text scored at the 66th percentile, while the control group ended up at only the 50th percentile.

However, when questions required more extensive responses—involving personal reactions, interpretation of a text's meaning, analyses of a text's craft or content, or critical evaluation of a text—then the effect sizes grew in magnitude (Graham & Hiebert, 2010; McGee & Richgels, 1990). The average effect size for the more extensive writing was 0.77 across nine studies, meaning students who were engaged in writing more extensive responses to text ended up at the 78th percentile, while the control group stayed at the 50th percentile. Graham and Hebert (2010) concluded that writing more extensive responses to text was particularly effective in improving reading achievement, and that it was more effective than reading alone, reading and rereading, reading and studying a text, or reading and discussing a text (all of these were used as control group conditions in the various studies). Again, the specificity and explicitness required by writing are believed to be the source of this substantial and consistently positive effect, so drawing evidence from a text to explain and support one's responses to the text are valuable processes in which we need to engage students, especially as they move up through the grades. Many of these studies were conducted within content-area classes, such as social studies and science, suggesting the broad utility of combining reading and writing in these ways.

Extensive analytical writing has been shown, through research, to have a positive impact both on reading and writing achievement, as well as on knowledge of the content in the texts (Shanahan, 2004). Questions that only ask students to summarize or repeat information from a text do not have as powerful an effect on reading and writing ability as do questions that require a more extended and transformative treatment of the material (McGee & Richgels, 1990). This is particularly true as students progress through the grades; thus summarization and note taking have a bigger impact on reading achievement during the earlier years, but as students gain in proficiency and language sophistication, having them write longer and more analytical or evaluative pieces about what they read has a more profound effect on learning outcomes.

The idea here is neither for students to mimic an author's style or approach or to recognize or summarize an author's major points, but for the students to react to and to transform the author's ideas. For example, a student might be asked to write a personal response to the information, even comparing it to his or her own life experiences. Or the writing assignment might require the reader to analyze a character's actions or to evaluate an author's analysis of the information in terms of its clarity, accuracy, thoroughness, or value.

Extensive analytical and evaluative writing is valuable because it promotes a critical understanding of a text and often requires readers to revise their understanding as they read and write. Additionally, such writing requires readers to use their own knowledge and bring it to bear on the information in the text. Such writing tends to be longer, and the extendedness of it likely plays an important role in the students' growing writing abilities.

How can teachers frame questions about texts that will require sufficiently thorough and high level responses? One way to do this would be to use the new CCSS (NGA & CCSSO, 2010) as a basis for questions. For example, the CCSS lays out reading standards for grades K–5; although these are reading standards, they nevertheless provide useful guidance for appropriate questions to frame writing responses to text:

- How does Mr. Plumbean's point of view about freedom in "The Big Orange Splot" differ from your own point of view? Use evidence from the text to support your claims about Mr. Plumbean's views. (Grade 3)
- What are the similarities and differences between "A Special Place for Charlee" and "The Tenth Good Thing about Barney?" Provide evidence from both texts to show the specific similarities and differences. (Grade 4)
- How do the visual images of "Point Blanc" contribute to the meaning and tone of the text? Be specific in your use of examples from the text. (Grade 5)

Each question requires readers to think deeply about the texts, and as such, they would obviously make appropriate high-level reading comprehension questions. However, by requiring the students to write answers to such questions, and to provide evidence from the texts in support of their answers, the cognitive demands rise, as do the potential impacts of the questions on student learning. Other ways of encouraging students to engage in formulating an extensive response is to provide sufficient space and time for students to answer the questions. These questions would demand at least a half-page to a page for students to respond; physically providing sufficient space between such questions is necessary. Similarly, students often try to hurry through their responses, giving quick and incomplete answers, rather than thorough or extensive ones. It is helpful to talk to students about what such answers require in terms of time commitment, and teachers may even want to scaffold some model answers, demonstrating for the students how elaborate the review of the text information has to be and how lengthy the responses might be. Some writing teachers insist teachers attempt to write answers themselves to such questions, to determine what quality of answer is possible and to gain purchase on what it is the students will need to do to be able to write an adequate response. Armed with such information, it is possible for the teacher to decide what the most appropriate supports might be.

Text Synthesis

Text synthesis, or writing from sources, is the most demanding and elaborate approach to writing about reading, but it is one that plays an important role in communication and learning, and it too can have big learning payoffs (Spivey, 1991; Spivey & King, 1989). "Synthesis" means combining ideas from many sources together into one essay or presentation. After reading several articles, watching multiple videos, or conducting multiple experiments or observations, the students create their own texts based on the information drawn from the original materials. Syntheses are more than summaries, however; they require writers to create their own arguments and to use the source materials as evidence to support their claims and to refute counterclaims.

To synthesize text effectively, writers have to become researchers, not just casual readers. They may have to conduct research, to search for the information they need, and to recognize similarities and differences among the information that appears in the source texts (younger readers do not easily recognize that repetition of an idea across multiple sources is an indication of the relative importance of the idea). Authors may echo each other, but they also may contradict each other, or simply present nonoverlapping information; the accumulation of discrete facts from multiple sources may require some attention as well. Readers have to recognize conflicts among sources and then they must transform the materials for their own use, capturing the most important ideas and making sense of the contradictions and unique mentions. Students often think they have to decide which source is correct, and that can be an exciting adjudication process. However, it is just as reasonable to write about the discrepancies, documenting them and exploring the disagreements of opinion or points of view. Not surprisingly, much of the variation in how well students synthesize is due to variations in their reading proficiency (Spivey & King, 1989). When introducing students to text synthesis it is probably a good idea to limit the difficulty and the numbers and lengths of the initial source materials to be used, and to provide scaffolding and support to readers in making sense of the texts. Sometimes when teachers introduce writing about reading, they fail to provide the same level of reading support that they would usually offer in a more self-contained reading lesson.

Why is synthesis such a powerful learning task? Wiley and Voss (1995) shed some light on this process. Working with college students, they assigned groups either a single history chapter to write a report about or a "text set" that they had created by dividing up the chapter into seemingly independent pieces. The students in both groups were able to produce the requisite writing with similar levels of quality—these were proficient readers and writers after all—but they learned the material better when they had to coordinate the separate pieces themselves through synthesis. Specifically, the students who were required to synthesize did better at learning the causal and explanatory relationships among the ideas than did the students who simply had to summarize this information. This effect is likely because the writing synthesis task, unlike the summarization task, required the readers to construct the relationships themselves—which developed stronger memories and understandings of the information.

Engaging in synthesis writing experiences sharpens the reader's eye and gives the writer an opportunity to state his or her own ideas and positions (Graham & Hebert, 2010). It is helpful if teachers provide tools to guide the students' research, such as teaching them how to use some kind of note-keeping form that supports the organization and comparison of information. For example, a social studies support form might guide students to record key information about the countries the students are researching from their sources, with spaces to record information on economics, culture, government, language, religion, and geography (see Figure 14.2 for an example). With such a guide, a student can learn to track the sources of information in a manner that allows easy comparison and should facilitate the discovery of discrepancies of sourcing and fact, and will make it easy to see what important information is repeated again and again. Finally, it can be useful to provide students with templates that help them to transform such inert information into their own essays or articles (De La Paz, 2005). Such templates can teach students how to organize their key information into a report or essay, showing where to record their own topic sentence, providing transitions and connecting information between sections, giving guidance as to the extent and placement of information to be provided, and so on.

Writing from sources is demanding because it requires the simultaneous use of a number of sophisticated reading, writing, and thinking skills. For example, to engage in such writing successfully, students have to be able to cogently state their own premises, beliefs, or opinions and then must find evidence in support of their claims. Teachers can undermine the quality of

	Text 1	Text 2	Text 3
Geography			
Economics			
Government			
Language			
Religion			
Culture			

FIGURE 14.2. Text synthesis guide.

their students' synthesis work by having them write on topics rather than on positions, themes, or arguments. Although it might seem appropriate to have students write from multiple sources about New York, Babe Ruth, endangered species, or other subjects of interest, it is usually more effective to have them take a position and then seek evidence in support of that position. The difficulties students have in locating information are usually pretty obvious ("Mrs. Jones, I can't find anything on dolphins"), but many times a synthesis task fails because students have difficulty taking a clear position or anticipating quality counterarguments. Without a clear and meaningful argument or opinion, every other aspect of the synthesis becomes more problematic. For example, if the student doesn't have a clear position to articulate, it becomes more difficult to identify which evidence to include in the resulting report. Having students practice stating arguments and counterarguments can be a useful exercise. Here are some examples:

- *Argument:* The environment suffers because people destroy habitat.
- *Counterargument:* It is sometimes necessary to damage the environment for economic reasons.

- *Argument:* Football should be banned because it causes concussions.
- *Counterargument:* Football can be dangerous, but it is possible to make it safe.

- *Argument:* School uniforms make students safer and improve learning.
- *Counterargument:* School uniforms are not necessary for either school safety or improved learning.

As should be evident from the examples, counterarguments are not necessarily just negative restatements of the original argument. Encourage your students to work collaboratively to turn topics into postions and then to formulate counterarguments to these positions. Many students get used to the "read–retell" sequence so ubiquitous in reading lessons. But just regurgitating what a text said becomes harder if the students are reading the texts with real purposes (to formulate their positions) and if they are trying to negotiate multiple texts rather than single ones, especially when the sources disagree.

There are many other skills entailed in such writing projects as well. One of the hardest for students seems to be using information from original sources without plagiarizing. Students are not dishonest, but the citation system of using and crediting information is subtle and complex. Students need to be apprenticed into it carefully and intentionally. Often students struggle even to record information from a text without copying. A good way to build discipline around this skill is to have students practice recording information without looking. When students are recording information from a text, their tendency is to copy word for word. But if they are required to read a section and then to close the book and try to write down the key information without immediate access, they are forced to put the information into their own words (a great reading skill). If they can't remember what to write once they have closed the source, then they are to put down their pencils and read it again, putting away the text and picking up the pencil when they are, again, ready to record.

Of course, there are times when a writer does want to quote from an original source (and such demands are common in schools from grade five up). To take an actual quote, the student does have to copy exactly from the original source, but how much quoting is appropriate and how to balance quotes with one's own statements requires practice and teacher guidance.

Another aspect of making use of information from source materials is the need to mark a text up, to be able to note contradictions, useful information, and the like. It helps if students have access to versions of the materials on which they can write—underlining, circling, adding notes, drawing connecting arrows, and so on. This, of course, is not always possible in a school situation, but Post-it notes can be a big help in this regard. They allow students to write notes about the text at the points in the text where the notes would be helpful, without much expense and without damaging expensive textbooks and reference sources.

Of course, not all the information students will use comes from texts. Often the essential information a writer wants to draw from might be from a scientific observation or experiment, a field trip, a video, an online source from the Internet, or even personal experience. Each source poses different problems for the budding writer, but again they require active summarization, appropriate use of paraphrase, crediting, and the like. Moreover, the information drawn from these sources must be accurately recorded and organized along with the other information sources.

Final Thoughts

Research has shown that writing about reading can have a powerful and positive impact on learning. Students who engage in writing about reading usually improve their reading and writing skills, as well as increasing their knowledge of the content. Having students creating their own texts based on existing models, summarizing what they read, writing answers to questions about texts that require extended analysis or evaluation of the text information, or synthesizing multiple texts to write reports and essays based upon the combination of information from those sources into original compositions—all exert powerful impacts on student reading and writing achievement.

Teachers need to give such assignments and to support students in negotiating these tasks successfully, by managing and slowly extending the complexity and extensiveness of the texts used, by guiding the reading so students start with a deep understanding of the texts to be written about, by demonstrating and explaining how to conduct the various steps of the tasks, and by structuring the work or providing templates or other guides that encourage early success.

Not much has been included in this chapter about other kinds of supports that are often included in writing and that are treated elsewhere in this volume. For example, revision is very important in all of the forms of writing about reading. Students should not be expected to end up with cogent and well-formed stories, summaries, answers to questions, or synthesis papers on a first draft. Such tasks are demanding and each will require students to try and try again to achieve real proficiency. One way of stimulating and supporting such outcomes is by making students privy to audience reactions to their work. Is a synthesis too choppy, moving from one idea to another without careful transition? Is a story or article too imitative or repetitive of the original text? Is a summary too extensive or too brief to serve the purpose? It is easiest to identify such problems and to respond to them with improved drafts when someone reads your papers and reacts to them honestly and thoughtfully.

Similarly, all these approaches to writing are both complicated and enhanced by the addition of technology. Being able to search for information on the Internet should provide students with a richer collection of source materials to use as the basis of synthesis papers, but the use of such materials complicates things by making source credibility a big issue, and by possibly making the source sets too extensive and diverse to manage easily. Computers are great for keeping track of information as well, but they require technical skills for managing spread sheets or other data or information summarization tools. Research reveals that writing with computers is superior to writing without them (Graham & Perin, 2007) as they allow students greater flexibility and make revision less cumbersome. However, most schools make computers available for writing mainly through school computer labs, often far from the texts students need to write about. It requires real effort on the part of teachers to make the various materials—texts and technology—available simultaneously so students can better write about what they read.

Finally, all of these tasks are challenging and all require that students put forth concerted effort over time to accomplish them successfully. It is hard to imagine any of these being done well from the beginning. Such effort (and dealing with such frustration) requires motivation. Teachers need to encourage students and to keep them actively engaged. Explaining the importance of each activity and revealing to the students the value such activities have in their learning and work is a valuable support, as is engaging students in metacognitive discussions in which they explore their own insights about how the processes work. Also, finding ways for students to use these various tasks to pursue ideas they themselves are curious about is beneficial (if someone is fascinated by penguins, then allowing him or her to write summaries of penguin texts is a reasonable support), as is engaging students collaboratively in the various activities (there is no reason why a synthesis paper or even a critical response has to be researched and written alone). Certainly, given the challenge level of these activities, it is wise to acknowledge to the students how difficult the tasks are and to find ways to document student progress toward meeting them. Writing about reading is worthwhile, but it is only likely to lead to learning when students are actively engaged in the reading and writing tasks—recognizing the value of the activities and meeting their challenges with determination and self-awareness.

References

Bean, T. W., & Steenwyk, F. L. (1984). The effect of three forms of summarization instruction on sixth graders' summary writing and comprehension. *Journal of Reading Behavior, 16,* 297–306.

Brown, A. L., & Day, J. D. (1983). Macro-rules for summarizing text: The development of expertise. *Journal of Verbal Learning and Verbal Behavior, 22,* 1–14.

Chang, K. E., Sung, Y. T., & Chen, I. D. (2002). The effect of concept mapping to enhance text comprehension and summarization. *Journal of Experimental Education, 71,* 5–23.

Charney, D. H., & Carlson, R. A. (1995). Learning to write in a genre: What student writers take from model texts. *Research in the Teaching of English, 29,* 88–125.

Cramer, R. L., & Cramer, B. B. (1975). Writing by imitating language models. *Language Arts, 52,* 1011–1015.

Cunningham, J. (1982). Generating interactions between schemata and text. In J. A. Niles & L. A. Harris (Eds.), *New inquiries in reading research and instruction* (pp. 42–47). Washington, DC: National Reading Conference.

De La Paz, S. (2005). Effects of historical reasoning instruction and writing strategy mastery in culturally and academically diverse middle school classrooms. *Journal of Educational Psychology, 97,* 137–156.

Fitzgerald, J., & Shanahan, T. (2000). Reading and writing relations and their development. *Educational Psychologist, 35,* 39–50.

Frey, N., Fisher, D., & Hernandez, T. (2003). "What's the gist?": Summary writing for struggling adolescent writers. *Voices in the Middle, 11*(2), 43–49.

Graham, S., & Hebert, M. (2010). *Writing to read: Evidence for how writing can improve reading.* New York: Carnegie Corporation. Retrieved from *www.all4ed.org/files/WritingToRead.pdf.*

Graham, S., & Perin, D. (2007). A meta-analysis of writing instruction for adolescent students. *Journal of Educational Psychology, 99,* 445–476.

McGee, L. M., & Richgels, D. J. (1990). Learning from text using reading and writing. In T. Shanahan (Ed.), *Reading and writing together: New perspectives for the classroom* (pp. 145–169). Norwood, MA: Christopher-Gordon.

National Governors Association & Council of Chief State School Officers. (2010). *Common Core State Standards for English language arts & literacy in history/social studies, science, and technical subjects.* Washington, DC: Authors. Retrieved from *www.corestandards.org.*

National Institute of Child Health and Human Development. (2000). *National Reading Panel–Teaching children to read: Reports of the subgroups* (NIH Pub. No. 00-4754). Washington, DC: U.S. Department of Health and Human Services. Retrieved from *www.nationalreadingpanel.org/publications/subgroups.htm.*

Shanahan, T. (2004). Overcoming the dominance of communication: Writing to think and to learn. In T. L. Jetton & J. A. Dole (Eds.), *Adolescent literacy research and practice* (pp. 59–174). New York: Guilford Press.

Shanahan, T., Callison, K., Carriere, C., Duke, N. K., Pearson, P. D., Schatschneider, C., et al. (2010). *Improving reading comprehension in kindergarten through 3rd grade.* Washington, DC: National Center for Education Evaluation and Regional Assistance, Institute of Education Sciences, U.S. Department of Education. Retrieved from *http://ies.ed.gov/ncee/wwc/pdf/practice_guides/readingcomp_pg_092810.pdf.*

Shields, J. S. (2007). The art of imitation. *English Journal, 96,* 56–60.

Spivey, N. N. (1991). Transforming texts: Constructive processes in reading and writing. *Written Communication, 7,* 256–287.

Spivey, N. N., & King, J. R. (1989). Readers as writers composing from sources. *Reading Research Quarterly, 24,* 7–26.

Stolarek, E. (1994). Prose modeling and metacognition: The effect of modeling on developing a metacognitive stance toward writing. *Research in the Teaching of English, 28,* 154–174.

Stotsky, S. (1983). Research on reading/writing relationships: A synthesis and suggested directions. *Language Arts, 60,* 627–643.

Taylor, B. M., & Beach, R. W. (1984). The effects of text structure instruction on middle-grade students' comprehension and production of expository text. *Reading Research Quarterly, 19,* 134–146.

Tierney, R. J., & Pearson, P. D. (1983). Toward a composing model of reading. *Language Arts, 60,* 568–580.

Tierney, R. J., & Shanahan, T. (1991). Research on the reading–writing relationship: Interactions, transactions, and outcomes. In R. Barr, M. L. Kamil, P. Mosenthal, & P. D. Pearson (Eds.), *Handbook of reading research* (Vol. 2, pp. 246–280). New York: Longman.

Tierney, R. J., Soter, A., O'Flahavan, J. F., & McGinley, W. (1989). The effects of reading and writing about thinking critically. *Reading Research Quarterly, 24,* 134–173.

Wiley, J., & Voss, J. F. (1995). The effects of "playing historian" on learning in history. *Applied Cognitive Psychology, 10,* 1–10.

Chapter 15

Best Practices in Writing Assessment for Instruction

ROBERT C. CALFEE
ROXANNE GREITZ MILLER

When we prepared this chapter several years ago for the first edition of *Best Practices*, we felt that we were pushing the envelope. We proposed (1) that teachers give high priority to writing as an essential part of a balanced literacy program, (2) that writing be linked to the content areas to "make thinking visible" (Miller & Calfee, 2004; Richart, Church, & Morrison, 2011), and (3) that teachers develop classroom-based writing assessments tailored to their specific settings, their students, and their own learning priorities. We set the stage with three portraits drawn from observations of excellent teachers, illustrating the flow of formative writing assessments across the developmental span from kindergarten to high school. We then spelled out ways in which our proposals might be implemented, cautioning readers about barriers posed by No Child Left Behind (NCLB) accountability and standardized tests.

As we complete revisions for the second edition, a glimmer of light appears in the east, a portent of forthcoming changes in the nation's schools. Recommendations in the Common Core State Standards (CCSS) call for substantial modifications in both reading and writing. The full title warrants close reading: *The Common Core State Standards for English Language Arts & Literacy in History/Social Studies, Science, and Technical Subjects* (National Governors Association [NGA] & Council of Chief State School Officers [CCSSO], 2010). The CCSS call for integration of reading and writing, and for integration with the subject matter areas. These ideas are truly radical!

Our editors asked authors to incorporate the CCSS in their chapters, and to discuss "how the Standards might be expanded." We take full advantage of this opportunity, envisioning a time when classroom teachers will enjoy substantial professional freedoms and responsibilities. The themes from our earlier chapter foreshadowed what will now become "best practice." The chapter begins with a review of ways in which the CCSS are going to handle writing assessment, and of the work of two consortia (the Partnership for Assessment of Readiness for College and Careers (PARCC) and the SMARTER Balanced Assessment Consortium (SBAC), that are constructing assessment systems for implementation of the CCSS (cf. Educational Testing Service [ETS], 2012). Three portraits then set the stage for core sections on *literacy for learning, text-based writing*, and *teacher-based classroom writing assessment*. The focus throughout the chapter is on formative assessment, where the purpose is to monitor and guide instruction. External testing will clearly continue to be part of the school year, but the door seems to be opening for teachers to take a greater role in assessing student learning. Our aim is to encourage and support such activities.

Writing in the Age of New Standards

The CCSS were developed by the Council of Chief State School Officers and the National Governors Association to establish nationwide expectations for student achievement. Information about the CCSS is spread over dozens of sources, hundreds if not thousands of pages, with changes almost daily (ETS, 2010). The CCSS set forth *content expectations:* What essential domains in literacy (and mathematics) should be the target of student learning? The assessment consortia are establishing *performance expectations* for the CCSS; if a standard requires students to learn to jump, the performance assessment lays out details for "how high?" Several groups are playing support roles for implementation, including the Achieve group, which is developing implementation packages, and the assessment consortia. Publishers, state departments of education, and local districts are hard at work deciding how to respond to mandates. The entire program is to be in place in 2015, but many educators are already "doing the Standards."

Several features of the CCSS promise to make a big difference for K–12 teachers in the literacy arena—in reading and writing; in the relations among curriculum, instruction, and assessment; and in linkages between literacy and the content areas.

■ The CCSS are anchored in "college and career preparedness"; they "define general, cross-disciplinary literacy expectations that must be met for students to be prepared to enter college and workforce training programs . . . " (p. 4).

■ The CCSS propose an integrated literacy model: "The Standards are divided into Reading, Writing, Speaking and Listening, and Language strands for conceptual clarity, [but] the processes of communication are closely connected . . . " (p. 4). For the past 25 years, the spotlight has been focused on reading.

■ The description of literacy in the CCSS is quite broad. For reading: "Students who meet the Standards readily undertake the close attentive reading that is at the heart of understanding and enjoying complex works of literature. They habitually perform the critical reading necessary to pick carefully through the staggering amount of information available today in print and digitally. They actively seek the wide, deep, and thoughtful engagement with high-quality literary and informational texts that builds knowledge, enlarges experience, and broadens world views. . . . [They] develop the skills in reading, writing, speaking, and listening that are the foundation for any creative and purposeful expression in language" (p. 4).

■ Students are expected to become self-motivated and to make full use of the tools of literacy, independently and habitually—they are to become literacy experts.

■ Basic skills are to serve higher level activities; a brief section on Foundational Skills in K–5 Reading covers outcomes from the National Reading Panel (phonological awareness, phonics, and vocabulary; National Institute of Child Health and Human Development [NICHD], 2000).

■ Literacy standards are linked to major content areas in both elementary and secondary grades; students are supposed to learn to read and write about *things that are really important—for college and careers!*

■ The CCSS repeatedly call for a balance between informational and literary texts, between reports and stories, between fact and fiction.

■ The CCSS encourage extensions to the multimedia dimensions of contemporary literacy, to "print and non-print media forms, old and new" (p. 4).

Several matters are *not* covered by the CCSS that seem important to us:

■ The CCSS describe learning to read words, paragraphs, and pages (Richards, 1942), but do not say much about *how to read a book* (Adler & van Doren, 1967).

■ These are content standards, not performance standards; they describe what students should know and be able to do, but leave open how well students should "know and do."

■ The CCSS do not recommend how students are to be helped to meet the CCSS; "Teachers are free to provide students with whatever tools and knowledge their professional judgment and experience identify as most helpful for meeting these goals . . . " (p. 4). Teachers' professional judgments and experiences will be critical for supporting the CCSS. The challenge is to reempower many who have spent years following scripts and pacing charts. We think that an enormous reservoir of "professional judgments and experiences" is in place, ready to be tapped.

Numerous implementation issues must be addressed as the program rolls out. Here are three examples that are roiling the water as we complete this chapter:

■ A mismatch between what is taught and what is tested—and what counts. Summative standardized testing of the CCSS is difficult to reconcile with the image of students spending the year working collaboratively on multiweek projects in the content areas.

■ The emphasis on "informational" text is taking shape as disconnected snippets of nonfiction writing. A more positive example comes from page 33 of the CCSS, where *Staying on topic within a grade and across grades* lists almost 40 trade books on the human body spanning kindergarten through fifth grade. These books are a good start for studying human biology, but more is needed than a collection of titles.

■ "Close reading" is probably a passing fad, but as of this writing is being presented as an essential feature in implementation of the CCSS. The idea is that reading means a detailed study of a short passage (a paragraph or page), in which the reader attends only to the printed material, trying to ignore previous experience. The CCSS mention close reading as one of several strategies for handling a text, and by the time you read this chapter this idea may been placed in perspective. But be on the alert for other fads.

Pulling these pieces together, here is our status report on current events, along with our wish lists. First, summative tests will include *extended performance tasks* extending over a week or more (ETS, 2010). Students from third grade through high school will be given a topic to study, and then assigned a writing task. They will have time to review and polish the final product. For our wish list, we hope that these performance tasks will "really count." The summative package will also contain multiple-choice tests, and if the latter are more heavily weighted, then content coverage will continue to be emphasized. Our hope is that student writing (and thinking) will be an important part of the final score, making it worthwhile for teachers to devote instructional time to these goals.

Second, the assessment consortia are developing *digital libraries* to help teachers in planning and conducting formative assessments. The libraries are to contain "released items; formative assessments; model content frameworks; instructional and formative tools and resources; student and educator tutorials and practice tests; scoring training modules; professional development materials; and an interactive report generation system" (ETS, 2010). Our hope is that the libraries will emphasize the professional development and teacher collaboration items rather than test items. Formative assessment is a dynamic process, which Cizek (2010) describes as "administered midstream, in the course of instruction . . ., [in order to] (1) identify the student's strengths and weaknesses; (2) assist educators in planning subsequent education, (3) aid students in guiding their own learning, revising their work, and gaining self-evaluation skills, and (4) foster increased autonomy and responsibility for learning on the part of the student" (p. 4). We can imagine situations in which the teacher might decide to conduct something like a "test," but these are likely to be rare events. What is most needed are examples of how to tap student knowledge and understanding on the fly, taking student responses as the cue for action. We can imagine "local libraries" that start with materials from the libraries, but are then populated with twitter and blog fests reflecting local contexts. These libraries will not turn out to be test collections, but living repositories of techniques for conducting dynamic assessments (Popham, 2008; Chappuis, Stiggins, Chappuis, & Arter, 2012).

Third, states, districts, and teachers are looking to publishers to develop *curriculum and instruction packages* to help students "meet the standards." The idea of "teaching to a test" is not that bad if the tests are worthwhile. Large publishers are presently adapting reading series to incorporate more informational texts and promote high-level reading comprehension strategies. There will be new opportunities for supplemental publishers to develop curriculum packages that complement the basal series, especially in the areas of the reading–writing connection and integration of literacy and content areas. Today's basal readers include embedded end-of-unit tests to check on student learning. We hope that the new materials will feature embedded formative assessment models, along with text-based writing activities. We also hope that the new materials will incorporate formative assessment modules, with "starters" embedded at multiple levels throughout the lesson plans, to check prior knowledge, monitor progress along the way, review achievement at the end of each unit, and assess transfer to related activities later in the year. Such modules can be educative for teachers.

Finally, the consortia have funding to construct *professional development programs* for the CCSS. Details have yet to be announced, but our hope is that these activities will be school- and district-based, with opportunities for individuals to use online activities and webinars. We can imagine a revival of activities such as summer "Chatauquas," and participation in professional events (e.g., convention workshops jointly sponsored by the International Reading and National Science Teachers Associations). The CCSS have the potential to reform public schooling by helping practitioners integrate curriculum, instruction, and assessment around high-level, "college- and career-ready" goals that mesh with the local contexts.

It is with these activities and aspirations in mind that we now turn to the assessment of writing under the new CCSS, where writing will permeate the entire school curriculum, from the earliest grades through the high school years. We believe that the spirit of the CCSS will prevail and that the new programs will provide teachers with exciting new tools for ongoing classroom-based assessments. In this spirit, our chapter moves forward from the previous edition to this brave new world.

Three Portraits

This section presents three snapshots that place formative assessment within best practice in today's classrooms. Each snapshot combines several observations into a single portrait. We begin with Samuel, a kindergartener, who delivered his first show-and-tell report earlier that morning. Now he sits beside Ms. Hancock as she reviews her notes. Sam is small for his age, and a bit shy. Facing the entire class had been a challenge, but he had done it! His topic had been his new baby sister. After announcing that she had come home from the hospital, he was at a loss about what to say next. Ms. Hancock prompted him. What did her hair look like? What noises did she make? What did she do? Samuel had something to say about each question. During the conference, Ms. Hancock writes four sentences using Samuel's words: "Martha is my new sister. She is bald. She gurgles. She mostly sleeps." Samuel has just completed his first project, which will be published in the weekly parent newsletter. At home, his parents are delighted as he reads his report, which later serves as the centerpiece of the parent–teacher conference.

Samantha, a fifth grader, has been a voracious reader since preschool. She became a "real writer" in second grade when she was encouraged to begin a personal journal. She had composed brief papers in the earlier grades, but now she faces a new challenge. Her teacher, Mr. Buchers, has announced that, in preparation for middle school, the March assignment will be a research paper. Students must first select a "current events topic" and locate background reading. Mr. Buchers is a history buff, and in the fall he introduced students to historical analysis. Now the class will study history in the making! Mr. Buchers recognizes that he is pushing the students; this type of writing is usually introduced in middle school. But he is confident that they can handle it and will benefit from a head start. Students work in small groups on the assignment, which should take 2 or 3 weeks to complete. Mr. Buchers reviews the basics: find resources in the library and on the computer, take notes for the report, and prepare an outline—actually a graphic web. Samantha has chosen "Now is the time for a woman to be elected president." Her father likes the idea, but her mother is less sure. Samantha agrees with her father but realizes that she must consider both sides of the issue. She is quite excited by the project.

Tom and Chizuko have been good friends since ninth-grade math. As seniors, the SAT writing test looms large on the horizon. They both enjoy math and science but are less comfortable with writing assignments. Neither did especially well on the PSAT writing test. They are studying together, using materials from the College Board website as a guide: "Brainstorm, collect information, organize, do a rough draft, revise and refine, read more, and write more" (College Board, 2006). Great advice, but how to apply it for an on-demand timed test? Math is much simpler— analyze the problem, work out the answer, and that's it. Writing is mushy, with never enough time to make sure that everything is exactly right. And no one teaches writing! English classes are about novels and plays, and other teachers expect students to already know how to write. Their parents are no help.

These snapshots capture the variety of writing scenarios experienced by today's students. There are writing standards, but the responsibility for acquiring skills rests largely on students' shoulders. In the elementary grades, reading is the top priority; as much as half the school day is spent in the basal reader. By middle school and high school, teachers deal with more than 100 students every day, which means little opportunity for grading compositions. As the CCSS are implemented, these situations will need to undergo substantial change.

Literacy for Learning

Why, when, and how should students learn to write? In reading, the contrast has been made between learning to read and reading to learn (Chall, 1995). A similar distinction can be made for writing, but we think that the idea is questionable in both instances. From the earliest stages, both reading and writing should be embedded in the purposes of literacy: to think and to communicate. Students must acquire skills and strategies for handling print, which requires time (and patience) from both teacher and student, but learning is more effective when motivated by a clear purpose. Learning to write makes most sense when the student is writing to learn (Zinsser, 1988). In school, this means that writing and writing assessment are linked to meaningful academic outcomes. Writing instruction should engage students with topics that have a long-term payoff, rather than writing simply to write.

For Samuel, the kindergarten show-and-tell report helps him to focus on a topic (his new sister), and to elaborate it with a few sentences. He can apply this strategy to the rock in his pocket, the snake in the terrarium, and (later) the causes of the Civil War. Samantha and her classmates are learning new skills and strategies, including the mechanics of the five-paragraph essay, but they are acquiring these skills while working on *something* that matters for an assignment that they have helped to shape. Tom and Chizuko have learned to write following the College Board guidelines. The SAT situation will be quite different. Instead of approaching the test feeling confident and self-assured, able to apply their learning to the situation, they suddenly confront a high-stakes task for which they feel ill prepared. If they are fortunate, their teacher (or tutor) will help them to handle the SAT situation, partly because it matters, but also because they are likely to encounter similar situations throughout life.

In each of these portraits, student compositions are evaluated in some fashion. Samuel was aware that Ms. Hancock was judging his report; in fact, everyone in the class knew that he had not produced the "three things" that were the standard for a show-and-tell presentation. He had failed, but suddenly the situation changed, and he had succeeded! For Samantha, her writing project will eventually be graded, but Mr. Bucher has posted the grading criteria (the rubrics) for the assignment on the classroom wall. Since September, Samantha has gone through the process: (1) think about the rubrics in preparing the draft, (2) run your work by a peer, and (3) show it to Mr. Bucher before the final revision. In Samantha's school, the report card uses rubrics rather than grades, and parents are familiar with the system. Tom and Chizuko confront a different challenge. They know how to write for school, and they can judge the quality of their writing. In preparing for the SAT, they confront a different situation—they are taking a *test!* They have one chance to prepare a composition about an unknown topic that will be graded by a stranger, and the grade will "matter"; it will influence decisions about college admissions. They will use their previous experiences in judging their own performance to do the best that they can, but it is a new situation for them, and they are both anxious.

The scenarios span a range of evaluation experiences from what is called *formative assessment* to *summative assessment* (Andrade & Cizek, 2010). You are familiar with summative assessments if you have ever taken a standardized test. It is a "bottom-line" experience. How well can you do filling in the multiple-choice bubbles under time pressure and circumstances that make you anxious? The stated purpose is to find out what students have learned at the end of a course of study, but the more important purpose is to compare students, to rank them. Formative assessment is generally described as "assessment that guides instruction" (Popham, 2008). In this category are assessments of skill and knowledge at the beginning of a school year, monitoring of individual progress, and even evaluation of instruction. We will focus on formative assessment that is teacher-based, that aims to improve student performance, and that is not used to grade or rank. Formative assessment is about tracking progress rather than accomplishment, making a movie rather than taking a snapshot (Calfee, 1997; Kellogg, 2008).

Best practices in formative writing assessment as defined above begin with an authentic task, where purpose and audience are clear and meaningful, where support and feedback are readily available, and where the final product has both personal and academic value for the student. Contemporary approaches to writing assessment (Black, Harris, Lee, Marshall, & William, 2003; Chappuis, Stiggins, Arter, & Chappuis, 2005; Chappuis et al., 2012; Harp, 2006; Stiggins, 2004) typically employ a conceptual framework similar to Figure 15.1, which shows how a teacher can view assessment as *inquiry*, as action research. The figure portrays formative assessment as a dynamic process rather than a routine activity. *Inquire* means to "look into, to seek, to search, to investigate." It begins with identification and analysis of a problem. For Samuel, the challenge for the teacher was to determine conditions under which he could meet the kindergarten standard: three things about the topic. What might be going on when he stopped? Perhaps he didn't really have three things to say about his sister. That seemed unlikely. Perhaps he was flustered. Perhaps he didn't want to say anything. Perhaps he was overwhelmed by the situation.

Thinking through the problem generates hypotheses, hunches about what might be going on, and actions. In the second stage, the teacher conducts an experiment and collects data. If Samuel had nothing to say about the topic, or didn't want to say anything, that was one thing. But if he was overwhelmed or flustered, then a *scaffold* should help. A few suggestions were enough to get him going. The joining of *instruct* and *assess* in the figure is intentional. When a problem arises, when a student is stymied, then the goal is to determine the conditions under which the student can perform, rather than stopping with failure. The assessment happened in the blink of an eye. The "intervention" was instantaneous—Ms. Hancock's three leading questions. The evidence was equally immediate. Ms. Hancock evaluated Samuel's responses and found them on target. The weekly newsletter provided her report.

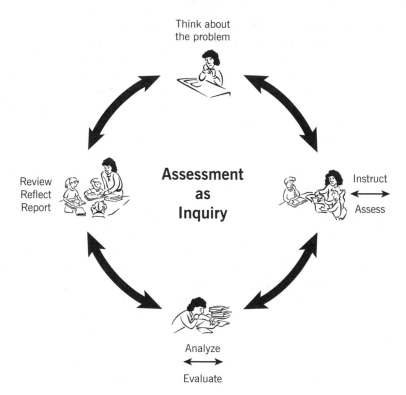

Think about
the problem

Review
Reflect
Report

**Assessment
as
Inquiry**

Instruct
⟷
Assess

Analyze
⟷
Evaluate

FIGURE 15.1. Literacy assessment as a process of teacher inquiry.

The experimental element in the figure is *instruct*, a word with the same root as *structure*, which carries the connotation of building, designing, framing, and completing. Teachers guide young people through increasing elaborate academic edifices across the school years—designing complex structures, engaging in a variety of construction tasks, checking their work along the way, and inspecting the final product. We can imagine them working in the "construction zone" (Newman, Griffin, & Cole, 1989). Literacy provides an essential tool kit (or machine shop) for the construction process. Best practices for writing assessment check the status of the kit: the tools need to be in good shape, and the user must know how to use them effectively. But authentic curricular goals are critical—building is more than learning how to hammer and saw. *Assess* is coupled with *instruct*, in the sense that, as the construction process moves along, there is continuous monitoring of the work by both the builder and the "supervisor." Formative assessment is continuous and interactive; student-workers are expected to check their progress as they move along, and to be able to explain what they are doing and why.

Analyze and evaluate in Figure 15.1 capture the task of reviewing evidence to make judgments about learning. When Ms. Hancock takes notes on Samuel's words during his report, these serve as evidence, as does the scaffolding she provides along the way. Samuel was clearly eager to tell classmates about his new sister, but leading questions were necessary to keep him going. He was still learning his ABCs and, from one perspective, was a "nonreader." When Ms. Hancock wrote his sentences in the newsletter, however, he could read his report on his own. These observations provide evidence for an evaluation that often takes shape as a story. What does the story tell about what Samuel knows and can do? What might be the most useful next steps instructionally? Such questions exemplify the evaluation process, which requires reflection and debate. The point is not to decide whether the performance is good or bad but to consider alternative interpretations that suggest various instructional responses—to think like an experimenter (Calfee & Hiebert, 1990). The question is not "Can Samuel compose/write a show-and-tell report?," which implies a yes-or-no response. Rather, it is "Under what conditions can Samuel produce a show-and-tell report with particular characteristics?" (e.g., three ideas related to a central theme). The evidence in this case suggests that Samuel has not yet learned this task to the point where it has become automatic. On the other hand, with a bit of guidance he was able to complete the task and was enthused about his accomplishment. He was engaged, he could talk about the results, and the event set the stage for his future learning activities and provided a model for the entire class.

Best practices for writing assessment call for reviewing and reflecting on what has happened and then preparing a *report* of the event. The basic idea is to document the activity. In fact, classroom assessment is often on the fly, with the results recorded mentally; where the evidence is oral, memory may be all that is possible. An important feature of written material is that one does not have to rely on memory—there is a concrete record. The question is how to make effective use of the information. The most important record in formative assessment is one that serves the teacher in documenting student learning and steering instructional decision making. The student is clearly an important audience for such information, which can provide feedback, encouragement, guidance, and sometimes grades. Other audiences include parents, administrators, and other teachers. Reporting, except for formal mandates like report cards, tends to receive relatively little attention in educational situations, which is somewhat strange when you think about it. If you visit your doctor or auto mechanic, you expect assessment and evaluation to be part of the process, typically as a basis for subsequent action. You also expect a record of the entire process: what was checked, what was found, and what was done. Best practices for writing should follow the same model, to monitor and shape student learning, and to improve the "curriculum in practice."

Samantha's teacher, Mr. Buchers, is tuned in to this principle. The class assignment is to write a research paper about a significant curriculum goal, the analysis of historical happenings. The task requires both reading and writing, but, most important, it requires thinking. Samantha will report regularly to the class about her project, and Mr. Buchers will gently but firmly model and shape questions during these discussions. What evidence does Samantha offer for her claims about a woman president? What about other interpretations? Lessons from previous decades? Possibilities for the future? Samantha's written record informs Mr. Buchers about her progress in dealing with these questions. Tom and Chizuko, in contrast, feel that they are working in the dark. Their English teacher administers biweekly practice exams and offers suggestions for self-assessment. The opportunity to practice helps, but it is up to the students to review their progress and decide what they need to do to improve. In their case, the inquiry loop is broken.

Text-Based Writing

What should a developing writer write about? One answer, which seems rather obvious, is something with which he or she is familiar. Although "obvious," this answer is problematic for several reasons. One is the enormous variation in the experiences that students bring to a task. "Write about your favorite animal" seems a reasonable request. But some students may not know much about any animals, favorite or otherwise, whereas others have choices ranging from home menageries to zoos, museums, and Dr. Seuss stories. Yet another reason is that the familiar may not seem worth writing about, or may lead to informal writing, of the "ya know what I mean" variety. Finally, students can approach this kind of writing from a variety of perspectives—stories, anecdotes, essays, descriptions—only some of which may be appropriate for the assignment.

The CCSS issue a clear call for writing to texts. At the outset, the CCSS require students "to write arguments to support claims from an analysis of substantive topics or texts . . . ; to write informative/explanatory texts to examine and convey complex ideas and information . . . through the effective selection, organization, and analysis of content [presumably from texts]; and to write narratives to develop real or imagined experiences or events . . . " (p. 18). This task begins in kindergarten, where youngsters are to "use a combination of drawing, dictating, and writing to compose opinion pieces in which they tell a reader [audience] the topic or name of the book they are writing about and state an opinion or preference" (p. 19), and similarly for informational works and narratives.

If this seems like a lot of writing, that is clearly what the writers intend: "To build a foundation for college and career readiness, students need to learn to use writing as a way of offering and supporting opinions, demonstrating understanding of the subjects they are studying, and conveying real and imagined experiences and events. . . . They need to appreciate that a key purpose of writing is to communicate clearly to an external, sometimes unfamiliar audience, and to adapt the form and content of their writing to accomplish a particular task and purpose. . . . Students must devote significant time and effort to writing. . . . " The authors probably intend for this work to be evaluated both summatively and formatively, to determine how well the CCSS are being met, and to guide instruction.

In text-based writing, students read one or more passages in preparation for writing to a prompt based on the text material.

> "You are going to read *My Pet, Bobby the Boa*, which tells about a young girl, Susan, whose pet is a boa constrictor. It describes what it is like to own a pet snake, to take care of it, and ways in which it can be fun. Suppose your parents have given you a pet snake. Based on Susan's story, describe what it would be like to take care of the snake, and to have fun with it as a pet."

This writing allows students to express their individualities, but also grounds the task in the text. The source text can require more or less attention from the writer. For example, consider this prompt:

> "When she wrote *Silent Spring* in 1962, Rachel Carson warned about the dangers from environmental pollution [extract]. Below are two editorials, one claiming that this threat has been lifted, the other arguing that the situation has worsened. What do you see as the strengths and weaknesses of the two editorials?"

When writing has become a commonplace of daily life in the classroom, as should happen under the new CCSS, the teacher confronts both opportunities and challenges. Evidence of student learning is available everywhere: reports on chapter books and short stories; summaries of science articles; editorials about historical events; essays about current events, and so on. These compositions display how well students handle both content and style. It is clearly impossible for teachers to grade every piece of student work, but neither can they ignore students' efforts. The resolution of this conundrum is to select for formative evaluation those student works that are most useful for guiding instruction and documenting growth. Students will soon take for granted the conditions of authentic writing, which allow time and offer support (from the teacher and other students). They also need to learn about the realities of on-demand writing typical of standardized test like the SAT. Each situation offers opportunities to review the distinctive features of best practices.

Text-based compositions generate information about both *content* and *quality*, about what students have learned and how well they can communicate it. One aim of the CCSS is to encourage teachers to consider writing as an integral part of learning for all curriculum domains, where the *what* is especially important. This chapter centers around the *how well* question, essential for effective communication. How are students to communicate what they know about a "subject matter"? One answer is through classroom discussions and teacher questioning. These are problematic for several reasons. They are often one-sided, with teacher talk dominating and student talk sparse, offering students limited opportunities to "compose." Small-group techniques offer another option, but management poses a challenge, as does documentation.

Writing provides a practical answer to most of these problems—students can all write at the same time, and the information does not disappear into the air. But (1) students must write well enough to capture what they have to say, and (2) someone has to handle evaluation tasks. We do not have space to lay out the range of writing tasks that can fulfill these functions, but they include simple note taking (a lost art in today's classrooms), reading notes (students write reactions to interesting or important points as they read), quick writes, and group projects, among others. These suggestions illustrate ways in which students can "devote significant time and effort to writing," from the earliest grades onward, as called for by the CCSS. These tasks all provide opportunities for evaluation and feedback, but can easily overwhelm teachers if they have to bear the entire burden. We suggest that these are also opportunities for students to learn to take responsibilities.

Separating content and writing quality is an important first step in evaluation of text-based compositions. A student has produced a marvelous piece of writing, but the content shows little grasp of the topic or is completely off topic. Another student turns in a piece that is a real mess—poorly organized, full of misspellings, marred by grammatical flaws—but you can tell that the student is deeply engaged and has something to say about the passage. The challenge here is to appreciate the substance despite the mechanical problems.

The combining of content and literacy in the CCSS poses new challenges for writing assessment. In the past, students were given "writing tests" and writing quality was what mattered. The trait rubrics described below were developed to handle this facet of a composition. Students were also asked to show what they knew about the various subject matters, sometimes by writing, but more often with multiple-choice questions. Under the CCSS, the goal is for students to learn to demonstrate their knowledge about school subjects by composing well-written essays. For classroom assessment, teachers will need to prepare well-crafted "questions," and to think about answers that are well crafted when viewed through both content and writing lenses.

This chapter is about writing assessment, and that will be our focus. Here are a couple of practical ideas about how the teacher can deal with both content and quality. First, holistic grading is probably not the best tactic, even if it seems the easiest and quickest. Assigning a single score, grade, or judgment leaves the student unsure about both quality and content. One simple approach is to give a composition one grade for content coverage and a separate grade for writing quality. To be sure, a paper may be so poorly written that the content cannot be judged, in which instance that message is the best feedback. Second, the more clearly the content expectation is laid out in the writing prompt, the easier it will be to assess the composition. With text-based assessments, the prompt can be explicit about the function of the passage in drafting the composition: "Summarize the passage; relate the information to your experience; criticize the argument; point out the strengths and weaknesses." Each of these prompt elements provides guidance for the writer, and the assessment can be tailored to how the writer responds.

Now let us turn to evaluation of writing quality, and the *analytic* or *trait rubrics* (Spandel, 2008; Culham, 2005), which are widely used at present. Most popular is the "Six Traits (Plus One)" approach:

- *Ideas:* The composition includes a central focus or theme, which is elaborated with relevant details, anecdotes, and similar features.
- *Organization:* The order and layout of the paper are coherent, with a clear sense of direction in communicating the focus or theme.
- *Voice:* The writer speaks directly to the reader and communicating a sense of purpose and an awareness of audience.
- *Word choice:* The vocabulary is precise, appropriate, and rich.
- *Sentence fluency:* One finds flow, connectedness, and variety in the construction of sentences; note that grammatical conventions are covered in the next trait.
- *Conventions:* Attention to mechanical features, including spelling, grammar, punctuation, and paragraphing.
- *Presentation:* A new facet that covers appearance, including handwriting, effective use of layout, and well-chosen illustrations, reflecting the emerging use of computers for polishing a work.

Numerous resources are available for this multitrait system, including rubrics for each trait, and examples of student writing that illustrate different levels of accomplishment for each facet (Northwest Regional Educational Laboratory [NWREL], 2012). Best practices in writing assessment are well served by these resources, which prepare the student for accomplished writing, from the elementary grades through high school into college and on to the variety of professions where writing is either central (newspaper reporters, magazine and book editors) or essential (anyone who prepares memos or documents as part of his or her job). Recall that the CCSS emphasize "college bound and career ready."

The multitrait system works quite well, and is relatively simple to use. Computer supports are also available for scoring and for tailoring rubrics to particular applications, which promises to be quite helpful (e.g., CTB, 2012). But a few cautions deserve mention. *Voice* is both important and challenging in classroom writing. For serious writing in high school and beyond, a clear sense of purpose and awareness of audience are critical requirements for any writing assignment. Unfortunately, most writing prompts do not adequately address these two features. The audience is either the teacher (implicitly) or an artificial entity ("Write a letter to your parents"), and purpose is missing or artificial. As a result, student compositions lack an authentic voice—but the problem is the prompt rather than the student. The assignment is just an assignment. Under these conditions, expecting students to infuse their composition with personal voice—with an authentic sense of purpose and audience—is unrealistic. An honest voice might lead the student to begin, "I'm writing this paper for Ms. Martin because I have to. I only need a B, so I'm not going to really do my best, but hope this is good enough." This problem can be handled in a couple of ways. One is use situations *within* the classroom that are as genuine and engaging as possible (some topics are more interesting and personally relevant than others). The other is to look for opportunities *outside* the classroom; with the arrival of the Internet, despite limited access in many schools, students can engage others from around the world in authentic dialogues.

A second point that deserves mention is *length*. Writing experts are conflicted about this feature; indeed, some think it is a mistake even to mention it. More is certainly not necessarily better, but students should know about the perils of "not enough," and situations where "too much" can be a problem. Teachers routinely include expected length as part of an assignment (five paragraphs, two pages, etc.). If length is not included, it often matters nonetheless. The fifth grader who hands in three sentences when everyone else is filling a page is likely to receive a low grade, even if the sentences are well crafted and on topic. In the elementary grades, "more" is probably a positive outcome, certainly for a first draft. In the later grades, the nature of the assignment may be important. Even here, it is worth remembering that the best predictor of scores on most college entrance writing exams is neither content nor style, but length.

The third point centers on *genre*, the type of writing called for by the assignment (Schleppegrel, 2004). Distinguishing between narrative and informational writing, between stories and reports, is an important first step, and students could benefit from greater clarity in the distinction between these two, especially given the emphasis on this distinction within the CCSS. In addition, we think that it will become increasingly important for students to learn about distinctions within the informational genre. For example, we have seen rubrics for narrative writing that emphasize topical focus, introduction, conclusion, and so on. This language is a mismatch to the narrative form, which builds on concepts like theme, setting, and resolution (Lukens, 2002). For informational texts, planning a simple descriptive piece around the five-paragraph essay is quite different from laying out a compare-and-contrast analysis, a process explanation, or a persuasive argument (Chambliss & Calfee, 1998).

The fourth point centers on the *content* or *substance* of a composition, which we covered earlier, but is not part of the six-trait system. What rubrics might be used to evaluate content? One approach uses coverage of the topic as the criterion. If the assignment is about earthquakes, did the student stick with earthquakes? From one perspective, this point is simple, but staying on topic can take many forms. The student can reproduce material from various sources, from paraphrasing to outright cutting and pasting. A student can develop the topic as a story, recounting his experiences during the San Francisco Loma Prieta quake. Other students can demonstrate understanding by transforming resources and experiences into a genuine composition—the building of something new from a collection of basic elements. Best practices in writing assessment should distinguish among these activities. Summarizing and note taking are important skills for students to learn to the point of fluency and as a context for practicing conventions. Storytelling is an engaging activity and provides another opportunity for practicing skills. To be sure, relatively few storytelling jobs are available for college graduates, but education should be about more than jobs.

At a practical level, we think that text-based writing assessments should also include a rubric that gauges students' capacity to *transform* the substance of the topic (Bereiter & Scardamalia, 1987). The challenge is how to handle this task at a classroom level. Ideally, the teacher has led students through a topic like earthquakes (or a more general domain like plate tectonics), and individuals or small groups have conducted additional reading and research, exploring the domain along paths that may be new to the teacher. Teachers cannot be experts on everything, and don't need to be. But how can a teacher offer students the freedom to explore and judge the quality and accuracy of diverse reports, without losing their way in unknown territory?

In a project on reading and writing about science (Miller & Calfee, 2004), we and our colleagues spent considerable time and energy wrestling with such questions. On the one hand, it is important for the student to include fundamental concepts and relations in his or her composition, what are referred to as *schemata* (Anderson, Spiro, & Anderson, 1978), or sets of ideas and words connected in particular ways, which can serve as a template for evaluating presentations. For instance, volcanoes, an engaging topic across the grades, take two wildly different forms in classrooms: (1) the vinegar-and-soda version in which these ingredients, along with red dye, are poured into a clay model to generate an eruptive fizz; and (2) the plate-tectonics account, which suggests that the earth is cracked into great chunks by the roiling of magma, where volcanoes emerge as "blurps," like in a kettle of thick pea soup. However, a student decides to treat the topic of volcanoes, a composition that captures the scientific content must include the pea-soup model in some form. An enlightening example comes from observation of a small-group project by students at a school near Honolulu. The students had prepared a lengthy report for the weekly news magazine on the difference between the vinegar-and-soda exercise in the classroom and what they had discovered from reading about the volcanic terrain on which they walked. Their report displayed evidence of deep, transformational learning.

Constructing Classroom-Based Writing Assessments

As noted earlier, the CCSS will offer significant opportunities for teachers to track learning literacy and learning content from kindergarten through high school—and to engage students as partners in the process. The assessment consortia are creating formative assessment packages, which should provide models for teachers. But progress depends on teachers taking charge of the process, which means creating performance assessments tailored to individual classroom situations. This notion is clearly "possible," as can be seen by what happened in the 1980s and 1990s: performance-based assessments (Finch, 1991), writing portfolios (Calfee & Perfumo, 1996), and the California Learning Assessment System (CLAS; Ormsby, 1994). Reviving these accomplishments will be essential if the CCSS are to help all students to be "profession and career-ready" when they leave high school.

This final section describes ways to create dynamic assessment systems for curriculum-embedded writing (Calfee & Miller, 2005). The facets covered in this section are important for any writing assessment. The purpose here is to place these facets within the context of the classroom teacher's daily work across the content areas. When a testing company or state develops a large-scale writing assessment, it calls upon teams of experts, conducts pilot runs, computes complex statistics, and so on. It is another thing for the classroom teacher to prepare a writing task that is relatively spontaneous, intended for a one-time, low-stakes formative assessment. The second scenario is actually more critical for learning, assuming that the teacher actually uses the results to inform his or her judgments about student learning. The stakes may not seem "high," but they can be significant. Before discussing our ideas about classroom-based assessment, let us note the distinctions with other programs that look similar on the surface. District interim benchmarks are now employed in many schools to "monitor student progress," often with the announced goal of using the results to inform instruction. Interim benchmarks will be part of the CCSS assessments. But benchmarks resemble standardized tests and are identical for practical purposes. They are administered on a preset schedule, are standardized, and generate reports that are too generic to guide specific instructional decisions. Textbook packages often include end-of-unit tests, which are virtually identical to benchmark tests. Finally, response to intervention (RTI; Lipson & Wixson, 2010) sounds like it might fill the bill—intervene and then decide how to respond to student needs. But again the tests are generic, as is the typical intervention. Classroom-based writing assessments are anything but routine. They are tailored to a specific situation, based on an activity either designed by the teacher or significantly adapted from an existing model.

What are some ways in which a (busy) classroom teacher can approach this task? The basic building blocks needed to construct a writing assessment are similar for virtually any scenario, formative or summative: *prompts, procedures*, and *rubrics*. We assume a text-based setting, but the principles also apply to open-ended situations. Let us review each of these constructs, emphasizing the application to formative assessment in classroom settings.

The *prompt* sets the stage for the writing task. Rather surprisingly, relatively little research has been reported on how variation in prompt design affects the quality of student writing. Constructing a prompt is almost like writing a passage. In a brief amount of space, the teacher has to cover the following points:

■ Develop a *focus statement* that directs students' attention to the key topic for the composition, activates prior knowledge (including the target text), and guides thinking about the task.

■ Present, as clearly as possible, the *purpose* of the composition. Words like *tell, describe, explain, convince,* and *illustrate* serve this purpose, especially if students have received prior instruction on these terms.

■ Identify the *audience* for the work. This is a challenge in school writing because everyone knows that the teacher is the real audience, but students can learn to imagine various audiences. Indeed, writers often have to rely on imagination. Freedman (1997) gives an informative account of the ways in which high school students in San Francisco and London handled audience in writing to one another. With a little creativity, local audiences can be identified: the principal, the mayor, the editor of the newspaper. Writing for nobody can be discouraging.

■ Where appropriate, specify the *form* of the product, such as a paragraph (or more) or a letter (a favorite because of the style).

■ Tell the writers as much as possible about the *criteria* to be used in judging the work. How important are supporting details? If a text is provided, how should it be used? Is the work a draft, or should the student attempt a polished product? Ideally, for classroom assessments, criteria have been defined early in the school year and practiced (with feedback) regularly. If the multitrait system is being used, give it away—discuss the traits and rubrics with the students. If content is important (and it should be), review the main points with the class.

■ Think about possible *answer spaces* for each prompt, the ideas that students might generate in response to the prompt. Think about ways in which students might be directed toward productive paths or how they might be stalemated or led astray. For example, consider the following prompt:

> "Describe the differences between evergreen and deciduous trees. Based on your personal experiences, what is your favorite kind of tree for each type?"

When students are asked to build a composition around personal experience, which appears frequently in writing prompts, the way is open for them to move in any of a wide range of areas or nowhere, depending on the topic. We are not suggesting that prompts never invite students to draw on personal experience, but rather that the ground rules for such invitations require careful attention.

The *procedure* for a writing assessment builds, in the ideal situation, on what we know about the writing process (Gray, 2000). Students need time, information about the topic, scratch paper, support and advice, and a writing strategy. *Time* is arguably the most precious classroom commodity—there is never enough time, even for basic writing. Time is needed for reading and scoring, for discussing and reviewing, and for handling the needs of individual students. No wonder many teachers assign writing a low priority. We offer two suggestions in this arena. The first is never to ask students to write about nothing. The second is to engage them in the assessment process. By "writing about nothing," we mean exercises (including district assessments) that are solely designed for writing. The result is akin to taking a driving test; you drive to show that you can drive, but you cannot go anywhere! School subjects provide a plethora of openings for students to demonstrate knowledge, reasoning ability, and communicative capacity by composing, both orally and in writing. Especially when embedded in an authentic project, writing tasks evoke imagination and force that is otherwise totally lacking.

Information about *topic* was mentioned earlier in the distinction between text-based and stand-alone writing. Most readers can remember the closed-book exams of days past (they can still be found, of course). The contrast with writing tasks in life after school is striking. Seldom does a professional writer approach a problem (or write about it) with a closed book. Imagine a doctor, about to operate on you, announcing, "This is a closed-book operation!" We also suggest that information be made as public as possible. Walls in tomorrow's classrooms should be covered with notes, graphs, and pictures.

What a writer needs most are *words*. Students will write more compelling and better organized papers when they can lift their eyes to the classroom walls and find words and phrases that jumpstart them. Those who write for a living depend on this approach and rely on scratch paper and room to spread it out.

High-tech colleagues often puzzle about how *computers* might be used for writing in the classroom. They notice that students prepare a draft on paper, then use the computer for revision and publication, and ask, "Why don't they write on the computer from the beginning, like I do?" In fact, many of these same colleagues rely on paper to get started. Printed pages can be spread out for scribbling and sketching. It takes experience and practice with the computer screen to write exclusively on a computer (Whitham, 2005; Herrington, Hodgson, & Moran, 2009; Huot & Neal, 2008).

How the teacher arranges the social context for writing can play a significant role as a procedural facet for both instruction and assessment. Writing can be a lonely task. The two of us have written together, and we know the joys (and occasional frustrations) that come from collaboration. We mention *social support* partly to encourage teachers to consider group writing projects. To be sure, it is important to counsel students about how to work together in constructing a composition, and to monitor the group process. But a good deal of writing in college and in careers is collaborative, and so these activities promise long-term benefits. The CCSS call for collaborative work in both the writing and the speaking–listening domains. The last element in procedure is strategy, the process that a student writer moves through in creating a composition (Tompkins, 2011). You can find numerous variations on process, but the main ideas are captured by three two-part alliterative phases: (1) *develop* and *draft*, (2) *review* and *revise*, and (3) *polish* and *publish*. Not every writing assessment incorporates all of these elements, but best practices start with this design as the foundation. In standardized stand-alone tests, for example, the writer generally has time only to develop and draft.

The third element in creating a classroom-based assessment focuses on the bottom line. How well has the student completed an assignment? What grade should you assign to the work? "Grades" have been largely replaced by a new concept, the *rubric*. We have used this term earlier in the chapter, assuming that you have probably heard the word, but let us briefly take a closer look. Note that rubrics are often assigned after a composition is completed, and often as a holistic judgment, which is probably not best practice. It makes more sense to begin the task with the criteria in mind and to review progress throughout the process, so that the final ratings come as no surprise.

Advice about appropriate rubrics for writing assessment can be found in a variety of sources (e.g., Arter, McTighe, & Guskey, 2001). The primary division is between *holistic* and *analytic trait* strategies. In holistic scoring, which dominates large-scale assessment, the rater gives the composition a brief reading (a few minutes at most) and assigns it a single score. Raters undergo intense training for this task, during which they review *anchors*, prototypical papers in each of the score categories. To check consistency, benchmark papers are inserted during the scoring process, and raters are recalibrated as necessary. This process leads to reasonably high interrater reliability, which means that judges agree with one another, both overall and in judging individual students. The problem, of course, is knowing what the ratings mean and what to do with the information. For practical purposes, a holistic rubric acts like a grade, or a summative measure. The strategy is poorly suited to classroom assessment.

Analytic rubrics may be more useful to both teacher and student for understanding what is working and what needs fixing, but they are more complex and take more time. What can be done to lighten the load? One answer relies on technology, where computer-based text analysis can do the heavy lifting. Programs like Intelligent Essay Assessor, E-Rater, and Coh-Metrix (Ericsson & Haswell, 2006; Graesser, McNamara, & Kulikovich, 2011; Hagerman, 2011; Shermis & Daniels, 2003) provide students and teachers with a rapid evaluation of the quality of a composition. Some programs even provide an analysis of the match to the content schemas. Which critical concepts and relations from the topic are found in the composition, and which are missing (e.g., Pearson Publishing, 2012)? If this idea seems far-fetched, remember that, not too long ago, calculating the readability for a passage required a fair amount of work. Now it requires only a keyboard click in Word to determine that the Flesch–Kincaid readability for this chapter is 10.5—a bit higher than intended.

The second way to deal with grading, one that applies to all facets of composition assessment, is to give away the writing task, in part or whole, to students. The teacher can accomplish this goal in a variety of ways, including cooperative learning and peer review. What could be more sensible than teaching students to collaborate on projects, including writing tasks, and to learn to critique their own work? The main advice here centers on teaching students about the concepts of genre, traits, and rubrics. This strategy offers at least two clear advantages. One is that students become independent learners in the fullest sense, responsible for handling all aspects of communicating their mastery of a topic. The other is that the teacher no longer bears sole responsibility for student learning; in particular, he or she does not have to read and review every piece of student writing in detail. Rather, his or her task is to monitor and discuss the students' reading of their work. Student-led parent conferences in the elementary grades can serve to further extend this principle by engaging parents in the dialogue.

Two potential problems might seem worrisome. First, what if students do a poor job of evaluating their work? Or what if they cheat? Second, might it not be easier for the teacher to do the work rather than spend the energy needed to teach students how to handle the task? The response to both questions is the same: teaching students to become independent and responsible learners is difficult, but addressing this challenge is critical for reform of schooling in our country. These issues emerge with special clarity for content-area writing. When the conditions are right, writing reveals thinking with unusual clarity. The results show up partly as scores and grades, but more important are the portraits that students construct in demonstrating their understanding of topics and tasks and in revealing their capacity to "go beyond the information given" (Bruner, 1973).

Challenges and Opportunities

Basic skills in reading and mathematics have held center stage since the advent of NCLB. The basics cannot be ignored, but if the nation's students are to meet the new CCSS, then teachers need to meet the challenges of helping all students become proficient writers in the content areas. The principle here is that writing reveals thinking, that the capacity to lay out one's understanding in a clear, organized, and compelling fashion is an essential tool for thinking and for communication.

Effective and efficient formative assessment is a critical requisite for achieving this goal. Writing assignments are of limited value unless they are accompanied by informed and informative feedback on both the process and the content of the compositions. The techniques for planning and conducting such assessments are not mysterious; we know a great deal about best practices from both research and practical experience. As the CCSS point out, fulfilling these practices depends on classroom teachers who possess appropriate knowledge and skill, and who have opportunities for professional dialogue on these matters, much as physicians have opportunities for medical rounds. Classroom teachers also need the institutional support that recognizes the validity of assessments grounded in genuine performance activities. They can then pass on to their students the benefits of these opportunities and resources.

We hope that, as you reflect on the array of topics covered in this chapter, you will envision the planning and management of a writing assessment as an organic exercise, where you begin with an overarching design, realizing that, much like an orchestra conductor, your role is not to tell the harpist when to pluck a particular string or the timpanist when to strike a drumhead. Rather, your task is to listen to the ensemble, your baton guiding the tempo, but more often pointing to individuals to refine details that might otherwise go unnoticed. The metaphor appears in the CCSS, where a concluding statement brings together the numerous parts into a challenging whole: "For students, writing is a key means of asserting and defending claims, showing what they know about a subject, and conveying what they have experienced, imagined, thought, and felt" (p. 63).

References

Adler, M. J., & van Doren, C. (1967). *How to read a book*. New York: Touchstone Books.

Anderson, R. C., Spiro, R. J., & Anderson, M. C. (1978). Schemata as scaffolding for the representation of information in connected discourse. *American Educational Research Journal, 15*, 433–440.

Andrade, H. L., & Cizek, G. J. (Eds.). (2010). *Handbook of formative assessment*. New York: Routledge.

Arter, J. A., McTighe, J., & Guskey, T. R. (2001). *Scoring rubrics in the classroom: Using performance criteria for assessing and improving student performance*. Newbury Park, CA: Sage.

Bereiter, C., & Scardamalia, M. (1987). *The psychology of written composition*. Hillsdale, NJ: Erlbaum.

Black, P., Harris, C., Lee, C., Marshall, B., & William, D. (2003). *Assessment for learning: Putting it into practice.* Buckingham, UK: Open University Press.

Bruner, J. S. (1973). *Beyond the information given: Studies in the psychology of knowing.* Oxford, UK: Norton.

Calfee, R. C. (1997). Assessing development and learning over time. In J. Flood, S. B. Heath, & D. Lapp (Eds.), *Handbook for literacy educators: Research on teaching the communicative and visual arts* (pp. 144–166). New York: Macmillan.

Calfee, R. C., & Hiebert, E. H. (1990). Classroom assessment of reading. In R. Barr, M. Kamil, P. Mosenthal, & P. D. Pearson (Eds.), *Handbook of research on reading* (2nd ed., pp. 281–309). New York: Longman.

Calfee, R. C., & Miller, R. G. (2005). Breaking ground: Constructing authentic reading–writing assessments for middle and secondary students. In R. Indrisano & J. Paratore (Eds.), *Learning to write, writing to learn: Theory and research in practice* (pp. 203–219). Newark, DE: International Reading Association.

Calfee, R. C., & Perfumo, P. (Eds.). (1996). *Writing portfolios in the classroom: Policy and practice, promise and peril.* Mahwah, NJ: Erlbaum.

Chall, J. S. (1995). *Stages of reading development.* New York: Harcourt College Publishers.

Chambliss, M. J., & Calfee, R. C. (1998). *Textbooks for learning: Nurturing children's minds.* Oxford, UK: Blackwell.

Chappuis, S., Stiggins, R. J., Arter, J., & Chappuis, J. (2005). *Assessment for learning: An action guide for school leaders.* Portland, OR: Assessment Training Institute.

Chappuis, S., Stiggins, R. J., Chappuis, J., & Arter, J. (2012). *Classroom assessment for student learning: Doing it right—using it well* (2nd ed.). New York: Pearson.

Cizek, G. J. (2010). An introduction to formative assessment. In H. L. Andrade & G. J. Cizek (Eds.), *Handbook of formative assessment* (pp. 3–17), New York: Routledge.

College Board. (2006). *The keys to effective writing.* Retrieved March 13, 2006, from *www.collegeboard.com.*

Culham, R. (2005). *6 + 1 traits of writing: The complete guide.* Portland OR: Northwest Regional Educational Laboratory.

Educational Testing Service. (2010). *Center for K–12 assessment and performance management.* Austin, TX: Author. Retrieved April 22, 2012, from *www.k12center.org.*

Ericsson, P. F., & Haswell, R. (2006). *Machine scoring of student essays: Truth and consequences.* Logan: Utah State University Press.

Finch, F. L. (Ed.). (1991). *Educational performance assessment.* Chicago: Riverside.

Freedman, S. W. (1997). *Exchanging writing, exchanging cultures.* Cambridge, MA: Harvard University Press.

Graesser, A. C., McNamara, D. S., & Kulikovich, J. M. (2011). Coh-Metrix: Providing multilevel analyses of text characteristics. *Educational Researcher, 40,* 223–234.

Gray, J. R. (2000). *Teachers at the center.* Berkeley, CA: National Writing Project.

Hagerman, C. (2011). An evaluation of automated writing assessment. *JALTCall-Journal, 7*(3), 271–292.

Harp, B. (2006). *The handbook of literacy assessment and evaluation.* Norwood, MA: Christopher-Gordon.

Herrington, A., Hodgson, K., & Moran, C. (Eds.). (2009). *Teaching the new writing: Technology, change, and assessment in the 21st-century classroom.* New York: Teachers College Press.

Huot, B., & Neal, M. (2008). Writing assessment: A techohistory. In C. A. MacArthur, S. Graham, & J. Fitzgerald (Eds.), *The handbook of writing research* (pp. 417–432). New York: Guilford Press.

Kellogg, R. T. (2008). Training writing skills: A cognitive developmental perspective. *Journal of writing research, 1*(1), 27–52.

Lipson, M. Y., & Wixson, K. K. (Eds.). (2010). *Successful approaches to RTI: Collaborative practices for improving K–12 literacy.* Newark, DE: International Reading Association.

Lukens, R. J. (2002). *Critical handbook of children's literature.* Boston: Allyn & Bacon.

Miller, R. G., & Calfee, R. C. (2004). Making thinking visible: A method to encourage science writing in upper elementary grades. *Science and Children, 42*(3), 20–25.

National Governors Association & Council of Chief State School Officers. (2010). *Common Core State Standards in English language arts/literacy for social studies/history, science, and technical subjects.* Washington, DC: Authors. Retrieved from *www.corestandards.org.*

National Institute of Child Health and Human Development. (2000). *Teaching children to read: An evidence-based assessment of the scientific research literature on reading and its implications for reading instruction.* Washington, DC: Author.

Newman, D., Griffin, P., & Cole, M. (1989). *The construction zone: Working for cognitive change in school.* New York: Cambridge University Press.

Northwest Regional Educational Laboratory. (2012). *6 + 1 trait writing.* Portland, OR: Education Northwest. Retrieved April 21, 2012, from *http://education-northwest.org/traits.*

Ormsby, M. (1994). *Preparing students for CLAS (California Learning Assessment System).* Forestville, CA: Catalysts for Learning.

Pearson Publishing. (2012). *WriteToLearn.* New York: Author. Retrieved April 21, 2012, from *www.writetolearn.net.*

Popham, W. J. (2008). *Transformative assessment.* Alexandria VA: Association for Supervision and Curriculum Development.

Richards, I. A. (1942). *How to read a page.* Boston: Beacon Press.

Richart, R., Church, M., & Morrison, K. (2011). *Making thinking visible.* San Francisco: Jossey-Bass.

Schleppegrel, M. (2004). *The language of schooling.* Mahwah, NJ: Erlbaum.

Shermis, M., & Daniels, K. E. (Eds.). (2003). *Automated essay scoring: A cross-disciplinary perspective.* Mahwah, NJ: Erlbaum.

Spandel, V. (2004). *Creating writers through 6–trait writing assessment and instruction.* Upper Saddle River, NJ: Pearson Education.

Stiggins, R. J. (2004). *Student-involved assessment for learning.* Upper Saddle River, NJ: Prentice Hall.

Tompkins, G. E. (2011). *Teaching writing: Balancing process and product* (6th ed.). Upper Saddle River, NJ: Merrill.

Whitham, C. (2005). *Teaching and evaluating writing in the age of computers and high-stakes testing.* Mahwah, NJ: Erlbaum.

Zinsser, W. (1988). *Writing to learn.* New York: Harper.

PART IV

Special Populations

Chapter 16

Best Practices in Teaching Writing to English Learners

Reducing Constraints to Facilitate Writing Development

CAROL BOOTH OLSON
ROBIN SCARCELLA
TINA MATUCHNIAK

The Common Core State Standards (National Governors Association [NGA] & Council of Chief State School Officers [CCSSO], 2010) call for all students, including students who are "English learners" (ELs), to meet rigorous writing standards. Although the architects of the standards acknowledge that ELs may need additional time and instructional support as they acquire English language proficiency and master content knowledge, they look to teachers to provide "whatever tools and knowledge their professional judgment and experience identify as most helpful for meeting the goals set out in the Standards" (p. 4). In this chapter, we describe effective practices and teaching tools to enhance the writing of ELs and help them reach these ambitious standards. We first explore the characteristics of ELs and the constraints they face as they compose written texts in English.

Who Are ELs?

Who are ELs? ELs are variously called many names—newcomers, English language learners, limited-English-proficient students, second language learners, generation 1.5 students, long-term English learners, multilingual students, and so forth. Thirty years ago, many viewed them as a relatively homogeneous group with similar instructional needs. However, as immigration patterns have changed, the EL population has become more diverse. For example, ELs may come from homes where the primary language is not English, but they themselves may speak English only or they may switch between multiple languages *and* still have features in their writing attesting to their multilingual status (Valdés, 2001). Some may enter classrooms with knowledge of the academic registers of a variety of languages and a wide range of background knowledge on scholarly topics, while others may be highly limited in their knowledge of academic registers in any language and have little knowledge of the world.

Examining the Constraints Faced by EL Writers

In order to better contextualize the particular needs of diverse groups of ELs who must, at once, grapple with the demands of learning an additional language, negotiate the nuances of academic discourse, and master core subject matter, it is useful to describe the constraints that they face in learning to write. When composing, all students face the challenge of simultaneously juggling a number of demands that call for their attention. For inexperienced writers, juggling too many constraints can cause "cognitive" or "emotional" overload (Flower & Hayes, 1980, p. 32). The challenges are magnified for ELs. Not only do they face the cognitive, linguistic, communicative, contextual, textual, and affective constraints that all writers face (Frederiksen & Dominic, 1981), but they also face additional cultural and language development constraints unique to language learners. The constraints overlap and vary in importance as a function of distinct learner needs and characteristics.

Cognitive Constraints

ELs are often cognitively overloaded, especially in mainstreamed classrooms where they are held to the same performance standards as native English speakers (Short & Fitzsimmons, 2007). Skilled writers must coordinate a number of tasks within working memory, including planning for both the process of composing and for the product (i.e., the written text), all the while trying to retrieve words to express content as well as trying to organize those words into coherent text (Flower & Hayes, 1980). Complex thoughts do not necessarily translate into appropriately parallel complex sentences; in order for writing to be effective, the oral "utterance" has to be transformed into fully contextualized "text," which places additional constraints on cognition (Olson, 1977). In their meta-analysis of the key elements of effective writing instruction for students in grades 4-12, Graham and Perin (2007) identified teaching students strategies for planning, revising, and editing their compositions as having "a dramatic effect on the quality of student writing" (p. 15) because they help students manage the cognitive task of composing. A number of instructional frameworks support approaches that incorporate strategy instruction to advance ELs' development of English (Goldenberg, 2008; Schleppegrell, 2009). These frameworks explore the work of a wide body of research on what experienced native English-speaking student readers and writers do when they construct meaning from and with texts compared to ELs.

Linguistic Constraints

Adding to cognitive constraints is the constraint of mastering the constellation of language knowledge necessary to successfully participate in school. When ELs write, they draw on the sum of their language experiences. When they focus on overcoming constraints they face in writing, such as how to spell a word, where to place a period or an adjective, how to introduce a character, or how to organize supporting details, they utilize their metalinguistic awareness, or conscious attention to the ways in which language is used and conveys meaning. Whereas many ELs may have good oral language proficiency, most lack the academic language proficiency necessary for success in school (Biancarosa & Snow, 2006). Academic language, sometimes defined as a set of linguistic "registers" associated with academic disciplines (Scarcella, 2003; Schleppegrell, 2009), is precisely the type of specialized knowledge that novice writers (and ELs in particular) lack. Understanding academic registers, which can be difficult and confusing even for native English-speaking students, are especially challenging for ELs (Schleppegrell, 2009). Yet research shows that control of such academic language is one of the key determiners of success in developing academic writing proficiency (Christie & Macken-Horarik, 2007).

Communicative Constraints

In addition to the constraints imposed by language and cognition, students are also subject to communicative constraints, or the constraints imposed by the need to write for a specified audience and purpose. Just as when we talk to others in face-to-face situations and we adapt our language to their communicative needs, so too good writers modify their language to meet the needs of different audiences. Effective writers are able to construct rich and detailed representations of the audience to themselves, which, in turn, informs their composing processes in equally rich and elaborate ways. Novice writers, in contrast, have a limited ability to "assume the point of view" of the reader and consequently struggle to produce the reader-based prose that is so important for successful writing (Flower, 1981). As mentioned previously, ELs have an added burden because they are in the process of learning the linguistic features that constitute the *registers* or varieties of language used for particular purposes and in specific social settings.

Contextual Constraints

Contextual constraints involve the circumstances in which writing takes place. The context or situation in which students write, including the writing assignment, the topic, and the intended audience, can exert a strong influence on their composing processes. For example, are they in a timed-on demanding writing situation responding to an unfamiliar prompt with high-stakes consequences? Or are they writing on a topic of their choice in a succession of drafts that will evolve over time with supportive feedback from their teacher and peers? Do they have opportunities to collaborate with one another or are they expected to work in isolation? Is their audience themselves, a peer, a trusted adult, the teacher, or unknown audiences? The particular context can influence how writers decide what information is relevant, how they construct meaning, and the voice or register they adopt (Gutiérrez, 1992).

Textual Constraints

Students bring to the mental or written texts they are composing the influence of the content and the form of all prior texts they have written. Expert writers not only have a great deal of such knowledge, but their knowledge is highly organized and conceptually integrated such that they are able to rapidly recognize familiar patterns of information. These patterns, often stored in the form of automatic condition/action responses, can be useful in that they relieve, to some extent, the burden placed on working memory (Glaser, 1992). Novice writers (and ELs in particular), in contrast, may have neither the domain-specific knowledge nor the available working memory to process such knowledge. In addition, ELs often have less practice in the more academic genres of writing than their native-speaking peers, and hence face textual constraints when called upon to write in those genres. Particularly since the Common Core State Standards (NGA & CCSSO, 2010) call for all students, including ELs, to write well-reasoned text-based argumentative essays, ELs need more exposure to and practice in writing in a variety of genres.

Affective Constraints

Students need both the skill and the will to develop as writers (Gambrell, Malloy, & Mazzoni, 2007). A growing number of researchers recognize the affective and motivational dimensions of academic literacy, asserting that there is a social as well as a cognitive dimension of literacy (Greenleaf, Schoenbach, Cziko, & Mueller, 2001). Based on their review of adolescent literacy research, in general, as well as research on the literacy of adolescent ELs, in particular, Meltzer and Hamann (2005) recommend three primary instructional practices to reduce the affective constraints for ELs: (1) making connections to students' lives, thereby connecting their background knowledge to the content they are learning in school; (2) creating responsive classrooms that acknowledge students' voices, giving them an element of choice in learning tasks, and strengthening their literacy skills (Valdés, 2001); and (3) engaging students in collaboration where they interact with each other about texts they are reading and writing .

For many students who lack confidence and have low literacy self-esteem, the motivation to read and write can depend on their judgment concerning whether their teacher will give up on them or demonstrate their belief that they are worth the investment of the teacher's time and encouragement (Guthrie & Wigfield, 2000). ELs, in particular, need to be in safe classroom spaces where it is okay to participate, even with less-than-perfect English (Meltzer & Haman, 2005), and where teachers provide clear expectations and supportive feedback that is appropriate for their students' level of English language proficiency.

Cultural Constraints

Students bring rich and varied cultural knowledge to the task of writing. When we ignore our students' cultures, we miss valuable opportunities to connect with our students and motivate them (González, Moll, & Amanti, 2004). Moreover, we are unable to build our students' knowledge of the cultural information required to write effectively. English learners who have not lived in the United States very long may not know how to write about Halloween trick or treating, camping, or other topics. Further, they may lack the vocabulary, grammar, and rhetorical features to write about such topics as well as critical knowledge and experiences.

Best Practices for Facilitating ELs' Writing Development

The constraints reflect diverse language and literacy barriers faced by ELs as they develop as writers. Let's now take a look at some time-tested, research-based practices to enhance writing instruction and explore how they can help alleviate some of the constraints faced by ELs when they compose. Although we have organized the examples based on grade level, most, if not all, practices could apply equally for lower as well as upper grade levels, depending on the English proficiency of the student. Further, these practices could also be used with monolingual students.

Using Strategy Instruction to Reduce Cognitive Constraints

What follows are two specific strategies for reducing the cognitive constraints for EL writers, one geared for elementary students and one for middle and high school students.

The POW + WWW, What = 2, How = 2 Strategy for Narrative Writing for Elementary ELs

Planning and goal setting are overarching cognitive strategies that help writers establish a purpose for writing as well as enable the learner to determine priorities in writing. One pedagogical strategy to help elementary students plan, set goals, and compose narratives is the POW + WWW, What = 2, How = 2 strategy (Graham, Harris, & Mason, 2005). Students are first taught a general procedural planning strategy represented by the mnemonic POW: Pick my idea (i.e., decide what to write about), Organize my notes (i.e., organize possible writing ideas into a writing plan), Write and say more (i.e., continue to modify and upgrade the plan while writing). After discussing the characteristics of a good story, students are introduced to a substantive planning strategy specific to narrative writing represented by the mnemonic WWW, What = 2, How = 2. Using a graphic organizer to jot down their story ideas, students respond to the following questions: Who are the main characters? When does the story take place? Where does the story take place? What do the main characters want to do? What happens when the main characters try to do it? How does the story end? How do the main characters feel? Teaching general and genre-specific planning strategies has been shown to benefit ELs (Peregoy & Boyle, 2000).

A Color-Coding Strategy for Revising Analytical Essays for Secondary ELs

From sixth grade on, students are expected to read complex texts closely, make logical inferences, draw conclusions about them, and develop analytical essays in which they present their interpretations, citing textual evidence to support their analysis (NGA & CCSSO, 2010). One cognitive strategy to help students make their thinking visible and analyze whether they have simply fallen back on retelling or truly analyzed and interpreted a text is to have them color-code their essays. Teachers explain to students that three types of assertions make up an analytical essay and they designate a color for each. For example, they might say:

> "Plot summary reiterates what is obvious and known in a text. Reiterate means to repeat in order to make something very clear. Plot summary is *yellow* because it's like the sun. It makes things as plain as day. We need some plot summary to orient our reader to the facts, but we don't need to retell the entire story. Commentary is *blue* like the ocean because the writer goes beneath the surface of things to look at the deeper meaning and to offer opinions, interpretations, insights, and 'AH-HAs.' Supporting detail is *green* because it's what glues together plot summary and commentary. It's your evidence to support your claims."

Teachers can model how to color-code by guiding students through the process with sample weak and strong papers to help students internalize the coding. Then, working with a partner, students code their own first drafts and use their coding to visibly see where they need to add evidence and commentary when revising their essays. This visualizing strategy has helped mainstreamed ELs in grades 6–12 improve their analytical essay writing (Olson, et al., 2012).

Reducing the Linguistic Constraints in Writing for ELs

The following two instructional strategies reduce the linguistic constraints for EL writers. One is designed to build the language required to complete specific writing assignments at the elementary level, and the other is designed to build editing skills required at the secondary level. Both are useful when teaching ELs with an intermediate level of English proficiency.

Writing Word Banks, Learner Dictionaries, and Word Study Books for Elementary ELs

A number of educators have reported that word banks lessen the linguistic constraints on ELs while at the same time developing their knowledge of linguistic features (Zwiers, 2008). Writing word banks provide students with a teachable list of key vocabulary that relate to the writing assignments the students undertake. Key words are displayed, often alphabetically, pre-taught to students (e.g., through explicit instruction, choral repetition, and group and individual practice), and used by students when writing. Writing word banks can contain a number of word types, including sensory and active words, transition words, academic words used across subject areas, content-specific words, and fixed expressions such as "first of all." Using fixed expressions (also called collocations) correctly is an important step in learning to write well in a second language because they serve as "markers" of being able to write like a native speaker.

Many ELs, especially recent arrivals to the United States, also benefit from making their own word study books or notes, containing the words from their word banks and other words that they find useful in their writing. Their notes include the word and their personal definition of the word, along with translations, and memorable pictures or symbols to help them remember the word. A number of studies have demonstrated the effectiveness of the types of vocabulary activities described here (Fisher, Frey, & Rothenberg, 2008).

Editing Activities for Secondary ELs

All ELs, especially long-term ELs who have not made much progress improving their knowledge of English, require editing instruction so that they become skilled self-editors. Expert teachers model and sequence editing activities to help their students critically evaluate their own writing, demonstrating how skillful editors edit their own writing by modeling the questions they ask themselves: If I switched verb tense, do I have a good reason for doing so? Have I used modal auxiliaries like *might* to avoid making overgeneralizations? Does each pronoun refer to a specific noun in the preceding sentence? In the following activity, learners practice editing using a limited number of corrective feedback symbols (see Figure 16.1).

During editing activities, teachers should point out a few patterns of error, rather than each and every error the students produce. Instead of correcting student errors for the students, they show them how to correct their own errors. The effectiveness of using writing activities that explicitly teach grammar to EL students has been documented in a series of research studies (Ellis, 2000).

Helping ELs Juggle Communicative Constraints in Writing

To write well, learners must know how to write for different audiences and purposes. Early on, teachers can get ELs accustomed to the notion that they need to vary the linguistic and rhetorical features they use depending on the communicative context. Teachers can use a variety of means to support their students' development of such features, including teaching the features explicitly, repeatedly exposing the students to the features, and calling on students to use them. What follows are two research-based instructional practices, one involving autobiographical writing for elementary students of a beginning proficiency level in English, and another focusing on text

Symbol	Meaning	Example
cs	Comma splice	I had a question, I asked the teacher.
frag	Fragment	If you were a scientist.
num	Number	He finished his *researches*, but now he needs more *equipments* and *times*.
p	Punctuation	Though odd this story is true.
ref	Unclear pronoun reference	My essay and my keys are in my car. Will you please bring *it*?
ro	Run-on	No one knows the answer it is hard to solve each problem.
sp	Spelling	*Acheiving* dreams is *important*
s-v	Subject–verb agreement	Everybody *have* traditions.
t	Tense	I *will* be in class yesterday.
wf	Word form	We will become *independence* thinkers and writers.
ww	Wrong word	He was *very* tired that he left.
id	Idioms/fixed expressions	He was involved *on* the math projects.

FIGURE 16.1. Sample correction symbols.

analysis activities for secondary students with intermediate and advanced levels of English proficiency.

Autobiographical Writing for Elementary ELs

Educators and researchers have demonstrated the efficacy of using auto-biographical writing activities to develop EL writing skills (Cummins et al., 2005). For example, in oral history projects, ELs write biographical narratives about the life stories of the important people in their lives. They interview family members and record and analyze the interviews. The oral history projects provide valuable opportunities for students to collect and record life stories, transcribe them, and interpret their significance in writing. In other autobiographical activities, students write narratives, poems, and reports about their own personal experiences, for example, coming to the United States or learning English. One reason for the efficacy of auto-biographical activities is that they build on ELs' prior knowledge, including beliefs and concepts, and significantly influence learners' writing development as well as affirm student identities. Sharing their autobiographical texts with multiple audiences—like peers, teachers, parents, grandparents, sister classes, and web viewers—helps ELs learn to shape their writing to the needs of diverse audiences.

To help newcomers complete autobiographical writing activities while they are in the process of learning to read and write in English, teachers may ask community volunteers, parents, and older students who are literate in the students' home languages to transcribe students' dictated texts and later help the students to translate their texts into English. In this way, ELs produce dual language texts. Let's look at some steps for implementing autobiographical writing with ELs in their first languages. First, help students find a partner who can transcribe their oral stories. Give the partners some guidelines and a concept to investigate or story prompts. If possible, model the process to the partner to help the partner elicit language using simple words that are familiar to the partner. Use a Think–Pair–Share approach in which the student completes the story, the partner writes it down, and the two of them work to revise and refine the work in writing. Allow partners to work at their own pace. When the writing is completed, ask the partner to read it aloud to the student and ask the student to follow along, tracking with his or her eyes. When both are finished, read the story to the class and publish the story on the web or in a book of students stories. Here is a sample:

Cuando vine a los estados unidos, tuve mucho miedo porque no quise ir pero tuve que irme. Mi mamá me dijo, "Cuídate mi hija. Nos vemos pronto." Lloré y lloré y luego me dejó en la calle solita, sin familia. Vine caminando con una muchacha y unos señores con quien vivo hasta ahora. Todavía estoy esperando ver a mi mami.

Translation: When I came to the United States, I was afraid because I did not want to go. My mother told me, "Be careful, my daughter. We will soon see each other." I cried and cried and then she left me in the street alone, without family. I came walking with a girl and some men that I live with even today. I am still waiting to see my mother.

Text Analysis Activities for Secondary ELs

ELs benefit from the explicit instruction of academic language (August & Shanahan, 2007). A necessary first step before such instruction takes place is making ELs aware of the differences between informal text and academic text, which requires a close analysis of the linguistic features of texts (Scarcella, 2003). One useful type of text analysis for ELs with intermediate and advanced levels of English proficiency involves comparing informal and academic texts. Teachers provide two student-produced texts, one academic and one informal, on the writing prompt to which they will soon be writing as in Figure 16.2.

After students read the two texts closely and discuss them in small groups, teachers can ask them to underline the features that make the first text informal and the second text academic. Students can then discuss the

---

Student Text 1: Informal English

Main premise: *The government should introduce tighter gun controls.*

Donald Brown thinks that the government should have the right to own a gun but I don't. People like him sort of think that the government is stepping on our rights if it stops gun ownership. They think that most people who own guns are kind of good guys and they keep the guns for sport, recreation and other stuff. They also think that the police can't stop bad crime and we need guns to protect ourselves. But I think he is wrong. I agree with Maria Ramos. Maria thinks that guns increase the crime. I also think that human life is worth more than giving shooters the right to go shooting on the weekend. And I also think that many of the guns around the house end up used in gang fights or suicides.

Student Text 2: Academic English

Main premise: *The government should introduce tighter gun controls.*

Donald Brown maintains that the government should allow individuals the right to own guns. This position asserts that the government is infringing on our democratic rights when it restricts gun ownership. Most people who own guns, so the argument goes, are responsible citizens who keep the guns for sport and recreation. It is further contended that the police are unable to stop violent crime and therefore we might need guns to protect ourselves. However, as Maria Ramos states, guns increase the amount of violent crime in the community. Moreover, human life is worth more than individuals' right to own guns for recreational purposes. In addition, many of the guns that are kept around the house end up being used in violent domestic disputes or teenage suicides.

Informal and Academic Language	
Informal language	**Academic language**
Uses hedges such as *sort of* and *kind of.*	Uses hedges such as *might* judiciously.
Uses the word *I.*	Does not use *I.*
Uses the informal term *good guys.*	Uses a more formal term *responsible citizens.*
Uses informal transition *and I also think.*	Uses a more formal transition *In addition.*

FIGURE 16.2. Informal and formal academic English.

features of formal and informal texts and complete a graphic organizer such as the one in Figure 16.2.

Teachers can then repeat this exercise with numerous texts until students are able to recognize the differences between social and academic language. This type of comparison text analysis can be followed by activities that ask learners to revise and edit writing to make it more academic.

When asking students to convert informal text into academic text, it is useful to give them instructions, such as delete unnecessary words (e.g., hedges like *sort of*); replace informal words with more academic ones; identify grammatical problems and correct them; add transition words and other cohesive devices when needed, replacing the words *and, so,* and *but* with more sophisticated ones when required; combine ideas and sentences, whenever appropriate, replacing simple sentence structures with more complex ones; and reduce the length of the text. A number of national reports and studies have documented the effectiveness of teaching ELs the features of academic language, especially in the area of academic vocabulary (Snow, 2010).

Helping ELs Juggle the Contextual Constraints of Writing in School

For EL students to become confident and competent writers, they need experiences writing in a variety of contexts, including writing that evolves over time in stages and writing under timed writing conditions. Let's look at two best practices—one to help elementary students experience writing as a process and the other to help adolescent ELs juggle the constraint of deconstructing an on-demand writing prompt.

How Does Your Cookie Crumble?: A Process Approach to Writing for Elementary ELs

This lesson uses a concrete, learn-by-doing approach to introduce ELs to the concept of writing as a process (adapted from Opfell, Simpson, & Willett, 1992). Explain to students that they are going to get to write about what makes a good cookie and, at the same time, learn about the writing process. In the prewriting stage, the teacher can generate the students' interest in the topic by asking them to brainstorm qualities of their favorite cookie, including types, shapes, ingredients, and so on. A word bank with vocabulary (e.g., chocolate chip, crunchy, sweet, animal-shaped, ginger, round) can be posted and added to throughout the lesson. Next, students can taste-test several cookies (for instance, Animal Crackers, Oreos, and Fig Newtons), selecting words from the word bank to describe the taste, smell, texture, and so on, and use their notes to generate "I like [Oreos, Animal Crackers, Fig Newtons] because _____" sentences.

In the planning stage of writing, students can select the cookie they want to write about, draw a picture of it, and generate a list of words describing it, as in the illustration in Figure 16.3. During the writing stage, students can use the class word bank as well as their drawings as a source of ideas and vocabulary. Depending on the level of English proficiency of the students and the grade level of the class, the teacher can provide an open-ended prompt like "Write a letter to a friend describing your favorite cookie." Students who need more scaffolding can be presented with a writing frame that can be very simple or more complex as in the example in Figure 16.3. Teacher models, such as the one below, can also give students a point of departure as they compose.

> "I think Oreos are great! They are crispy and chocolatey on the outside and have a creamy white filling on the inside. Their round shape is another reason why they're my favorite. Best of all, you can pull them apart and lick off the filling. Yum!"

During sharing, revising, and editing, students can help each other turn ordinary words like "nice" into million dollar words (Graham et al.,

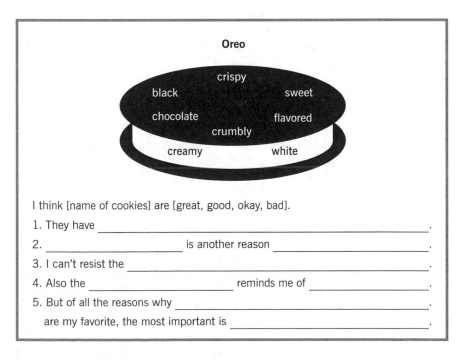

FIGURE 16.3. Cookie illustration and writing frame.

2005) like "delicious," "mouth-watering," and "yummy." The teacher can also conference with students and help them review their sentences to make sure they are correct.

DO/WHAT Charts: Responding to Timed, On-Demand Writing Prompts for Secondary ELs

In timed writing conditions, students often fail to respond to the prompt adequately because they haven't taken the time to thoroughly examine what they are being asked to do. Further, many struggling students and ELs who have limited practice may fall back on retelling or summarizing instead of presenting the required interpretation of a text during a timed writing test. Teaching students to analyze the prompt and construct a DO/WHAT chart can help students reduce the contextual constraint timed writing can pose because it can give them a roadmap for composing.

Teachers will need to model how to construct a DO/WHAT chart with students before the students can construct one independently. For example, teachers can provide students with a prompt such as the one on analyzing the theme in *The Horned Toad* by Gerald Haslam in Figure 16.4. They can guide students through the prompt and demonstrate how to underline verbs that describe what the student needs to *do* in the prompt in green and words that indicate *what* the task is in blue. Students then construct a DO/WHAT chart beneath the prompt. Such a chart will give students a roadmap for composing.

Helping ELs Juggle Textual Constraints in Writing

Let's explore one sequence of activities designed to give elementary ELs practice in writing in a variety of genres (ie. text types and structures for different purposes) and another geared toward helping secondary ELs grasp the structure of an introduction to an analytical essay. Both sequences help ELs learn to juggle textual constraints.

Operation Robot: An Exercise in Genres for Elementary Students

Teachers can tell students that over the next 2 weeks they are going to have an opportunity to create their very own robot and then write about it in a variety of genres or text types. To generate interest and build background knowledge, the teacher can ask students to bring in magazine pictures, advertisements, or toy robots from home. They can also discuss robots seen on television, in the movies, or online, and brainstorm things a robot could do if it had specialty parts (such as a vacuum cleaner arm). Students can

---

Prompt

After reading *The Horned Toad*, select one important theme to write an essay about. Create a specifically worded theme statement that expresses the author's main point, message, or lesson in the story.

Explore how the author communicates this theme through the relationships between the characters as the story unfolds. Pay special attention to:

- How the narrator reacts to the arrival of his great-grandmother
- How he interacts with Great-Grandma based on how he views her
- The symbol or symbols the author uses to reveal one character's traits or values and/or the changing relationship between the characters
- What the narrator learns by the end of the story

Through the interaction of his or her characters, an author is able to convey a message about life that is clearly important. Explain why the theme the author communicates is especially significant. Throughout your essay, use specific references to the text to support your ideas and follow the conventions of standard written English. Remember: There is no one theme and therefore no "right" answer to this prompt. What is important is to support your ideas with evidence from the text.

DO/WHAT Chart

DO	WHAT
Select	One important theme
Write	An essay
Express	The author's main point, message, or lesson
Explore	How the author communicates this theme
Pay	Attention to:
(Discuss)	• How the narrator reacts to Great-Grandma
(Discuss)	• How the narrator interacts with Great-Grandma
(Interpret)	• How the symbol or symbols that reveal their changing relationships
Explain	• What the narrator learns
Explain	Why the theme is significant

FIGURE 16.4. Prompt and DO/WHAT chart for *The Horned Toad*. Reprinted from Olson (2011, p. 343). Copyright 2011 by Pearson Education.

then collect construction materials (shoe boxes, pipe cleaners, aluminum foil, buttons, toilet paper rolls, etc.) and can share their supplies and ideas as they construct their special robots.

First, students are asked to *describe* their robot so clearly that another classmate can pick their robot out from the collected robots on a table. The teacher can model the descriptive process by constructing his or her own robot and sharing a sample description with the students in order to acquaint students with the features of the genre as well as create a class word bank with color, size, shape, and special feature words that students can draw from as they compose. After students write and exchange their descriptive papers and take turns trying to select another student's robot based on the description, students can write a *narrative*, recounting an adventure they imagine experiencing with their robot. Again, the teacher can model the conventions of the genre (character, plot, setting, dialogue, transition words, etc.) before students complete a story map and write narratives involving their robot. Next, students are invited to create a *practical/informative* booklet, complete with illustrations, on the care and feeding of their robot, hypothetically assuming that they need to leave their robot with a robot-sitter for a time. The teacher, once again, can model a step-by-step approach to writing instructions, emphasizing the importance of clarity and details. Finally, students can write a *persuasive* paper explaining why their robot is the best robot in the world, justifying their claim with evidence. Depending on the level of the class, the teacher can model formulating a claim and presenting reasons or even introduce the concept of acknowledging and overcoming a counterargument (adapted from Gatlin & Krebs, 1992). Engaging students in Operation Robot will not only introduce elementary ELs to writing in four different genres but help them form a community of learners as they brainstorm, write, share, and celebrate their creations, both physical and written, while having fun.

HoT S-C Team: Teaching Secondary ELs to Write Introductions to Analytical Essays

One of the textual constraints EL students face when they are writing to teacher-directed prompts is how to begin. A strategy that can help students envision what to include in an introduction to a text-based essay is HoT S-C Team (*Hook/TAG/Story–Conflict/Thesis*) as in Figure 16.5.

Students can then be given a number of sample introductions to essays on similar topics and be asked to identify the hook, TAG, summary statement/conflict, and thesis. While some might see this approach as somewhat formulaic, ELs need to be exposed to form making, in order to lower the textual constraints of essay writing, before they can engage in form breaking.

? How Do I Begin ?
✎ **The Introduction to Your Interpretive Essay** ✎

4 Parts: HT S-C T
(Ho T S-C Team) = (Hook/TAG/Story-Conflict/Thesis

1. Hook: Begin your introductory paragraph with an attention grabber or "hook" to capture the reader's interest. *It might include* <u>one</u> *of the following:*

   - Opening with an exciting moment from the story
   - An interesting description
   - Dialogue
   - Quotation from the text
   - A statement to make people think
   - An anecdote (a brief story)
   - A thought-provoking question (a question that makes people think)

2. TAG: Follow the "hook" with a TAG (title/author/genre = type of literature such as short story, narrative, novel, play, poem) that identifies all three parts of TAG for the reader.

3. Summary Statement-Conflict: As a part of the TAG, or right after the TAG, include a brief summary of the story and its conflict. Usually two or three sentences are enough to give background information to the reader about the story and the conflict.

4. Thesis Statement: The thesis statement in an essay is the claim the writer makes in response to the prompt. The thesis statement is the "key" that will "drive" your essay. Do people go on a trip with no idea of where to go? No, they look at a map or check the Internet for driving directions. Your job as a writer is to "map" your essay for the readers. Tell your readers where you will take them.

FIGURE 16.5. HoT S-C Team.

Helping ELs Reduce Affective Constraints in Writing

The two activities that follow demonstrate how the teacher can enable students to interact in a safe classroom space, produce writing that builds on something familiar (themselves), and be validated by being "published" on the class bulletin board.

The Important Book for Elementary ELs

The Important Book, by Margaret Wise Brown, takes a subject (a spoon, daisy, the sky, the wind, a shoe, etc.) and offers three or four sentences in a

The important thing about _____ is _____.

He/she loves to _____.

Also, he/she _____ enjoys _____.

But the important thing about is _____.

FIGURE 16.6. The Important Book paragraph.

predictable pattern about why that particular subject (or object) is important. As a get-acquainted activity, *The Important Book* can be used as a frame for students to interview one another about favorite pets, hobbies, sports, vacations, and the like and write paragraphs about each other that can be displayed on the class bulletin board along with their photographs or made into a class big book. The pattern can be adapted but looks something like the example in Figure 16.6. The simple frame makes the activity manageable for ELs even in the early weeks of school and can help boost self-esteem and classroom community.

My Name, My Self: Using Sandra Cisneros's "My Name" to Explore Identity

Writing about names in secondary school can be especially effective because it can "save students from feeling unimportant or not valued when no one knows their names" (Tchudi & Mitchell, p. 122). Sandra Cisneros's vignette "My Name" from *The House on Mango Street* works particularly well with English learners because the speaker, Esperanza, struggles with how her name is pronounced in English "as if the syllables were made out of tin and hurt the roof of your mouth" rather than the softer sounds "like silver" of her name in Spanish.

After reading "My Name," discussing how Esperanza feels about her name, and noticing how Esperanza compares her name to a song, an object, a color, and so on, students can fill out a sentence frame like the ones below comparing Esperanza's name to other things:

If Esperanza were an animal, she would be a *chameleon* because *she's looking for a name to change and match her mood.*

If Esperanza were a plant, she would be *a dandelion* because *she sometimes wants to let go and fly away from her sad name.*

Subsequently, students can create sentence frames about their names and a coat of arms for themselves like the one by Henry Nuñez, a sixth-grade

EL in Figure 16.7. Using their coat of arms as a planning strategy, students can then write paragraphs about their names that can be posted along with their illustrations. (For a detailed prompt, see Olson, 2011, p. 87.)

Concluding Thoughts

All learners face constraints when they are writing. However, ELs are affected by the constraints to a greater extent than their monolingual English-speaking classmates. Further, they must deal with additional constraints related to the development of English. For instance, ELs sometimes transfer linguistic and rhetorical features from their first languages to communicate in writing. Also, culture has an enormous effect on EL writing. Because it is so important and conceivably affects all instructional

Henry Nuñez

Coat of Arms

The animal that is most like me is a **wolf** because it symbolizes **how fierce I am**.

The plant that is most like me is a **Venus fly trap** because it symbolizes how my mouth is always open when I talk.

The object that is most like me is a **Arrowhead** because it symbolizes how sharp I am.

FIGURE 16.7. Coat of arms for sixth grader Henry Nuñez. Reprinted by permission.

practices, we deliberately incorporated culturally responsive instructional practices throughout this chapter, rather than address it separately in a section on "cultural constraints."

ELs are not a homogenous group; they have distinct needs and face distinct obstacles. Teachers who understand the constraints ELs juggle as writers and the research-based practices outlined here for reducing these constraints will be better able to make professional decisions about how best to serve the English learners in their classrooms. Additionally, teachers who also recognize and acknowledge the distinct resources ELs bring with them to school and create an inviting school environment where students can feel safe to participate in a community of learners will motivate ELs to do their best and enhance their development as writers.

References

August, D., & Shanahan, T. (2007). *Developing literacy in second-language learners: report of the National Literacy Panel on Language Minority Children and Youth.* Mahwah, NJ: Erlbaum.

Biancarosa, C., & Snow, C. E. (2006). *Reading Next—A vision for action and research in middle and high school literacy: A report to Carnegie Corporation of New York* (2nd ed.). Washington, DC: Alliance for Excellent Education.

Brown, M. W. (1949). *The important book.* New York: HarperCollins.

Christie, F., & Macken-Horarik, M. (2007). Building verticality in subject English. In F. Christie & J. R. Martin (Eds.), *Language, knowledge, and pedagogy: Functional, linguistic, and sociological perspectives* (pp. 156–183). London: Continuum.

Cisneros, S. (1984). *The house on Mango Street.* Houston, TX: Arte.

Cummins, J., Bismilla, V., Chow, P., Cohen, S., Giampapa, F., Leoni, L., et.al. (2005). ELL students speak for themselves: Identity texts and literacy engagement in multilingual classrooms. Retrieved April 26, 2012, from *www.achievementseminars.com/seminar_series_2005_2006/readings/ed.leadership.pdf*

Ellis, R. (Ed.). (2000). *Form-focused instruction and second language learning.* Special issue of *Language Learning.* Oxford, UK: Blackwell.

Fisher, D., Frey, N., & Rothenberg, C., (2008). *Content area conversations: How to plan discussion-based lessons for diverse language learners.* Alexandria, VA: Association for Supervision and Curriculum Development.

Flower, L. (1981). Revising writer-based prose. *Journal of Basic Writing, 3,* 62–74.

Flower, L. S., & Hayes, J. R. (1980). The dynamics of composing: Making plans and juggling constraints. In L. Gregg & E. Steinberg (Eds.), *Cognitive processes in writing* (pp. 31–50). Mahwah, NJ: Erlbaum.

Frederiksen, C. H., & Dominic, J. F. (1981). *Writing: The nature, development and teaching of written communication* (Vol. 2, pp. 17–20). Hillsdale, NJ: Erlbaum.

Gambrell, L. B., Malloy, J. A., & Mazzoni, S. A. (2007). *Evidence-based best practices for comprehensive literacy instruction.* In L. B. Gambrell, L. M. Morrow, & M. Pressley (Eds.), *Best practices in literacy instruction* (3rd ed., pp. 1–29). New York: Guilford Press.

Gatlin, P., & Krebs, E. (1992). Operation Robot: How we made thinking/writing our own. In C. B. Olson (Ed.), *Thinking/writing: Fostering critical thinking through writing* (pp. 411–417). New York: HarperCollins.

Glaser, R. (1992). Expert knowledge and the processes of thinking. In D. F. Halpern (Ed.), *Enhancing thinking skills in the sciences and mathematics* (pp. 63–75). Hillsdale, NJ: Erlbaum.

Goldenberg, C. (2008). Teaching English language learners: What the research does—and does not—say. *American Educator, 32,* 7–23, 42–44.

González, N., Moll, L., & Amanti, C. (Eds.). (2004). *Funds of knowledge: Theorizing practices in households, communities, and classrooms.* Mahwah, NJ: Erlbaum.

Graham, S., Harris, K. R., & Mason, L. (2005). Improving the writing performance, knowledge and motivation of struggling young writers: The effects of self-regulated strategy development. *Contemporary Educational Psychology, 30,* 207–241.

Graham, S., & Perin, D. (2007). A meta-analysis of writing instruction for adolescent students. *Journal of Educational Psychology, 99,* 445–476.

Greenleaf, C. L., Schoenbach, R., Cziko, C., & Mueller, F. (2001). Apprenticing adolescent readers to academic literacy. *Harvard Education Review, 71*(1), 79–129.

Guthrie, J. T., & Wigfield, A. (2000). Engagement and motivation in reading. In M.L. Kamil, P.B. Mosenthal, P. D. Pearson, & R. Barr (Eds.), *Handbook of reading research* (3rd ed.). New York: Longman.

Gutiérrez, K. (1992). A comparison of instructional contexts in writing process classrooms with Latino children. *Education and Urban Society, 24*(2), 244–262.

Haslam, G. (1995). *The horned toad.* Petaluma, CA: Thwack! Pow!

Meltzer, J., & Hamann, E. T. (2005). *Meeting the literacy development needs of adolescent English language learners through content area learning, part two: Focus on classroom teaching and learning strategies.* Brown University: Education Alliance. Retrieved June 17, 2010, from *www.alliance.brown.edu/topics/curriculum.shtml#item12630702a.*

National Governors Association & Chief Council of State School Officers. (2010). *Common Core State Standards for English language arts & literacy in history/social studies, science, and technical subjects.* Washington, DC: Authors. Retrieved from *www.corestandards.org.*

Olson, C. B. (2011). *The reading/writing connection: Strategies for teaching and learning in the secondary classroom* (3rd ed.). New York: Pearson.

Olson, C. B., Kim, J. S., Scarcella, R., Kramer, J., Pearson, M., Van Dyk, D., et al. (2012). Enhancing the interpretive reading and analytical writing of mainstreamed English learners in secondary school: Results from a randomized field trail using a cognitive strategies approach. *American Educational Research Journal, 4*(2), 323–355.

Olson, D. (1977). From utterance to text: The bias of language in speech and writing. *Harvard Educational Review, 47,* 257–281.

Opfell, L., Simpson, J., & Willett, S. R. (1992). How does your cookie crumble? In C. B. Olson (Ed.), *Thinking/writing: Fostering critical thinking through writing* (pp. 335–342). New York: HarperCollins.

Peregoy, S. F., & Boyle, O. F. (2000). ELs reading English: What we know, what we need to know. *Theory into Practice, 39*(4), 237–247.

Scarcella, R. (2003). *Academic English: A conceptual framework* (Tech. Rep. No. 2003–1). Irvine: University of California, Irvine, The University of California Linguistic Minority Research Institute.

Schleppegrell, M. J. (2009, October). *Language in academic subject areas and classroom instruction: What is academic language and how can we teach it?* Paper presented at workshop on *The role of language in school learning* sponsored by the National Academy of Sciences, Menlo Park, CA. Retrieved August 18, 2010, from *www7.nationalacademies.org/cfe/Paper_Mary_ Schleppegrell.pdf.*

Short, D., & Fitzsimmons, S. (2007). *Double the work: Challenges and solutions to acquiring language and academic literacy for adolescent English language learners: A report to Carnegie Corporation of New York.* Washington, DC: Alliance for Excellent Education.

Snow, C. E. (2010). Academic language and the challenge of reading for learning. *Science, 328*(5977), 450–452.

Tchudi, S., & Mitchell, D. (1999). *Exploring and teaching the English language arts* (4th ed.). New York: Longman.

Valdés, G. (2001). *Learning and not learning English: Latino students in American schools.* New York: Teachers College Press.

Zwiers, J. (2008). *Building academic language: Essential practices for content classrooms.* San Francisco: Jossey-Bass.

Chapter 17

Writing Instruction within a Response-to-Intervention Framework

Prospects and Challenges for Elementary and Secondary Classrooms

GARY A. TROIA

The passage of the 2004 Individuals with Disabilities Education Improvement Act ushered in responsiveness to scientific, research-based interventions (response to intervention [RTI]) as a potential alternative to aptitude–achievement discrepancy in the evaluation of children suspected of having learning disabilities. In other words, part of the evaluation process for learning disabilities diagnosis might entail consideration of whether the child referred for evaluation has made expected growth in response to interventions provided through general education that are, to the extent possible, firmly grounded in research. At the same time, RTI was viewed by school leaders as an opportunity to institute multilevel models of prevention and intervention for problem behavior and poor academic performance in the general education population to avert the need for unnecessary referrals to special education, to decrease the disproportionate representation of some minority students in special education, and to consolidate the fragmented supports for the many children who struggle in schools for a variety of reasons. There is no universally accepted RTI model, but in any given model there are several common operational features (see Johnson, Mellard, Fuchs, & McKnight, 2006), including:

▪ Universal screening with cut scores to triage individuals into low- and at-risk groups. Universal screening may occur more than once a year depending on the nature of the outcome being measured with the screening instrument, which is brief, simple, reliable, and repeatable. The data yielded by the screening predict future performance on other assessments and are collected under standardized conditions (i.e., the data are collected each time using the same method under similar circumstances and the score is derived each time using the same process).

▪ For those individuals in the at-risk group, there is more frequent monitoring of progress than for those in the general population. In some cases, this frequent monitoring may simply be just that—monitoring without any intervention per se. In most cases, however, the progress monitoring is used to identify how the individual responds to some specific treatment. This monitoring may employ a robust screening instrument, or perhaps some other assessment or combination of assessments that provide more diagnostic information.

▪ The multiple levels are encapsulated by three tiers of service: (1) a primary tier in which core general education programming is provided to all individuals, (2) a secondary tier in which targeted interventions and supports are put into place to address the needs of at-risk individuals (multiple levels may exist within this tier), and (3) a tertiary tier designed to provide intensive and specially designed individual treatments to those who do not adequately respond to targeted interventions in the secondary tier or who are identified as high risk and in need of immediate specialized treatment (i.e., they are eligible for special education).

▪ The general education core programming, targeted interventions, and specialized treatments applied at each tier incorporate evidence-based practices, which represent the integration of the best available scientific evidence, clinical expertise and authoritative opinion, and client and family values (Sackett, Rosenberg, Gray, Haynes, & Richardson, 1996). This view of evidence-based practices is not trivial because available scientific evidence may be limited, weak, or nonexistent, and research findings must be reconciled with social, political, and structural exigencies.

▪ Assessments and interventions, as well as the RTI process itself, are used with fidelity at all levels, meaning that they are used as designed for the purposes intended with adequate consistency, intensity, and integrity (i.e., the essential components are present). Fidelity is critical because poor fidelity leads to misdiagnosis, mistreatment, and potentially adverse outcomes. This implies that frequent monitoring of fidelity takes place.

Unfortunately, although we have some good models of RTI for the academic domain of reading, at least in elementary school settings, this is not the case in the area of writing, perhaps one of the most difficult areas of teaching and learning because of its complexity. One reason for this lack of applied knowledge in RTI for writing (RTI-W) is that existing writing assessment methods are not well developed to fulfill the many necessary functions of assessment in an RTI model (screening, progress monitoring, diagnosis). Another reason is that much of the research on RTI has focused on reading because of federal research funding priorities and the thrust of federal and state initiatives such as Reading First and Early Reading First. If RTI is to have the widespread impact on school organization, student success, and disability identification procedures many envision, then it will need to be applied across academic domains, including writing. This chapter describes how RTI-W might be implemented, with the caveat that the assessment recommendations in particular are speculative. Additionally, the contextual influences of large-scale assessments and the Common Core State Standards (CCSS) in the deployment of RTI-W are described because educators and administrators make decisions about classroom instruction and assessment in light of these educational policy elements.

RTI-W: Primary Core Writing Instruction and Universal Screening and Progress Monitoring

If students are expected to become competent writers and meet local and state standards for performance, then writing instruction must be approached in highly orchestrated ways by all teachers who expect writing in their classrooms and must be sustained across the grades to support students as they gradually become accomplished writers. Writing workshop is a prevalent instructional model in which the process of writing is emphasized more than the written product and which highly values students' interests and autonomy. Some of the most important attributes of this approach include a predictable routine; explicit modeling of skills, strategies, and the writing process; regular conferencing with students and families; high expectations with appropriate scaffolding; authentic audiences and purposes for writing; lots of encouragement and concrete feedback; flexibility in pacing and assignment parameters; cooperative learning arrangements; and ample opportunities for self-regulation (e.g., Cutler & Graham, 2008; Gersten & Baker, 2001; Graham & Perin, 2007; Rogers & Graham, 2008). An excellent primer on evidence-based core elementary writing instruction practices derived from research can be found in an educator's practice guide from the What Works Clearinghouse (Graham et al., 2012). Based on the synthesis of research findings examined by the panel that wrote the practice guide, there are four essential recommended practices: (1) provide daily time for students to write (minimal evidence); (2) teach students to use the writing process for a variety of purposes (strong evidence); (3) teach students to become fluent with handwriting, spelling, sentence construction, typing, and word processing (moderate evidence); and (4) create an engaged community of writers (minimal evidence). The guide gives helpful suggestions for implementing these four practices. Additionally, much of this volume contains information about effective instructional practices for teaching writing mechanics, sentence construction, various genres, and strategies to support the writing process. What is likely the most pressing need among general education teachers and those who collaborate with them is an understanding of how best to evaluate the writing performance of students within an RTI framework.

Assessing Writing in the Classroom

The assessment of writing is a frequently vexing issue for teachers—good writing is simply hard to define and even more difficult to measure accurately. Although a number of assessment methods applicable to the classroom context (i.e., other than large-scale tests) exist, no single one appears adequate for the goals of reliably judging student writing performance and monitoring student progress in written expression in response to instruction. These methods include (1) a direct or on-demand writing assessment in which students are asked to respond to a prompt to construct a written composition and the product is evaluated using some form of rubric (Benson & Campbell, 2009); (2) an indirect writing assessment in which the students respond to multiple-choice, true/false, or error correction items to demonstrate their writing knowledge (Benson & Campbell, 2009); (3) portfolios in which students gradually accumulate a varied collection of authentic writing process and product artifacts (these may include actual compositions in various stages of completion with or without peer/teacher comments, planning notes, completed revising and editing checklists, personal reflections and self-evaluations, responses to questionnaires, teacher and parent observations, etc.), and the artifacts are evaluated using externally established criteria, usually collaboratively developed with each student (Gearhart, 2009); (4) a curriculum-based measurement (CBM) of writing in which students copy or produce a text in a brief period of time under standardized conditions and the product is evaluated using one or more measures that are generally predictive of overall writing quality— samples of writing are taken at regular intervals and the results are compared to track student growth (Benson & Campbell, 2009; McMaster & Espin, 2007); and (5) automated essay scoring (AES; e.g., E-rater®). Each of these assessment methods has benefits and constraints; these are summarized in Table 17.1. Of course, direct and indirect writing assessments also are frequently employed in large-scale accountability systems, but in the

TABLE 17.1. Assessment of Writing

Assessment method	Benefits	Constraints
Portfolios	Provide opportunities for assessment conversations to consider readers' interpretations	Judgments of writing performance too often based on highest quality pieces rather than entire body of work
	Focus on authentic writing tasks rather than writing in response to assessment-driven prompts	Samples written and selected under diverse conditions and levels of support, rendering judgments difficult to interpret
	Accommodate evaluation of writing knowledge, skills, and processes as well as writing outcomes	Wide array of portfolio models can obfuscate alignment between portfolio design, data collection and analysis, and assessment purposes
	Can represent a balanced view of communicative competence because oral and visual performances can be included	Tensions between assessment and learning functions of portfolios can negatively impact reliability and validity of evidence
Indirect	Measurement reliability is enhanced through ease of scoring and high degree of consistency across test items	Lack content and face validity because tasks do not evaluate application of writing knowledge, skills, or processes
	Permit large-scale assessment in a single session	Do not reflect real-world writing demands
Direct/ on-demand	Assessment conditions and writing measures can be standardized	Measurement error is introduced through poorly written prompts; presentation effects (e.g., legibility, spelling mistakes) and writer identity lead to scoring bias
	Holistic, analytic trait, and primary trait rubrics are robust for evaluating multiple aspects of written composition in multiple forms for multiple purposes	Rubrics tend to not be sensitive to small increments of change and are difficult to use reliably; analytic trait rubrics tend to produce undifferentiated scores (i.e., few students score low on some traits and high on others)
Curriculum-based measurement	Brief, repeated sampling of timed on-demand writing (for young writers, copying of text is acceptable); performance is standardized, as are scoring procedures	Brevity of writing sample influences validity of inferences regarding writing performance— older students need longer sampling periods

(continued)

TABLE 17.1. *(continued)*

Assessment method	Benefits	Constraints
	Several writing measures can be applied to a given sample, including total words written, words spelled correctly, correct letter sequences, and correct word sequences	No single measure is sufficiently reliable and valid for all students at all grades; more complex measures appear to be better predictors of writing competence
	Progress monitoring of individual students for evaluating responsiveness to intervention is permitted	Though long-term gains are found, research has yet to identify how frequently samples should be collected, the rates of growth that can be expected, or how these measures are impacted by instruction
Automated essay scoring	Significantly reduces investment of time and effort required to score papers by hand; scores yielded are similar to those assigned by human raters	Scoring software programs require training on a corpus of sample texts on a specific topic (up to 500 in most instances) prior to being used; some are designed for the expository genre only
	Some scoring software programs are capable of providing native language diagnostic feedback	Not all scoring software programs provide meaningful diagnostic feedback on varied aspects of writing

classroom context the focus is on using data derived from these measures to provide immediate feedback to students, to adjust instructional foci and supports, and to identify students who require higher tiers of service.

How should these varied methods of writing assessment be used to support RTI-W? I propose in Figure 17.1 a plausible assessment system that addresses universal screening and progress monitoring with a combination of the assessment methods described above (for all tiers, not just Tier 1). Most important, no single source of data serves as the sole determiner of a student's placement in an RTI framework. Also, although the methods do not differ across grades, there are differences between elementary and secondary school settings with respect to precisely which outcomes should be evaluated and what task demands should be employed during testing. This is because, as written expression becomes more sophisticated as students grow older, task demands and outcomes also need to become more complex to accommodate students' growth. For CBM in particular, research (e.g., McMaster & Espin, 2007) has demonstrated that longer sampling periods

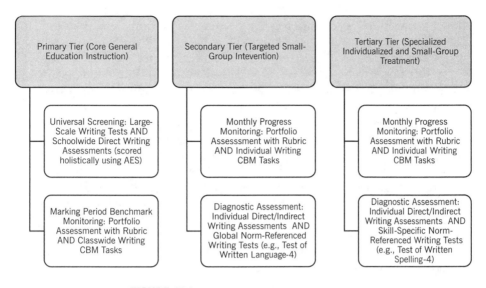

FIGURE 17.1. Assessment system for RTI-W.

(7–10 minutes or more, as opposed to 3–5 minutes) produce more technically adequate (i.e., reliable and valid) results for older students and that simple countable outcome measures such as total words written (TWW) and words spelled correctly (WSC), while adequate for differentiating good and poor writers in the elementary grades, are inadequate for doing so among older writers. For secondary school students, outcome measures such as correct word sequences (CWS) and percentages (%CWS, %WSC) appear to produce more technically adequate results, though no outcome measure for CBM has proven to be adequate for frequent progress monitoring purposes because none are sensitive enough to detect small increments of change in writing. Additionally, CBM outcome measures tend to exhibit stronger reliability than validity, meaning that they yield repeatable findings but the results do not predict performance on other writing assessments well.

To illustrate how such an RTI assessment system could work, let us take the fictional case of Mrs. Hammond's sixth-grade general education class at Clarksville Elementary. In the state where Clarksville Elementary is located, students in grades three through eight are assessed in the spring of each year with an on-demand writing assessment that requires students to respond to both narrative and expository prompts, and their responses are scored with a 6-point holistic rubric. Mrs. Hammond is provided with her sixth graders' scores from the previous year at the beginning of each school year. Nearly a quarter of her class receive scores designated to be below grade-level expectations, but because of the inherent limitations of large-scale tests (discussed later), Mrs. Hammond's school also relies on a combination of direct writing assessments scored holistically using AES software to ease the scoring burden on school staff and hand-scored brief multiple-choice indirect writing knowledge tests administered early in the school year. Thus, genres of writing not tested by the state and developmental aspects of writing knowledge are evaluated, rounding out the profile of individual writers in each grade. Together with the state writing performance assessment data, Mrs. Hammond (and all teachers at her school) can more precisely identify which students are likely to be at risk for not responding to instruction. With the additional schoolwide data, Mrs. Hammond identifies a third of her class as potentially struggling writers. Although one might expect additional data to reduce the number of identified at-risk students, because the school is more thorough in its assessment efforts, a greater number of students are identified as such. However, it is likely that some of these students identified at the beginning of the school year as "at risk" are false positives and will, in fact, respond adequately to core instruction. Hence, periodic benchmark assessment using portfolio work collected through standardized procedures and evaluated with a common holistic rubric created by teachers, in conjunction with standardized writing CBMs (these can be part of a portfolio for each student) can help establish over the course of a marking period which students, in fact, are not responsive to Mrs. Hammond's evidence-based writing instruction. Based on the progress-monitoring data, it turns out that only a few students in her class remain at risk by the end of the first marking period and consequently require supplemental Tier-2 writing instruction using targeted interventions.

The handful of high-risk students in Mrs. Hammond's class, now receiving Tier-2 targeted interventions, switch to more frequent (monthly) progress monitoring of their writing performance to help determine their responsiveness to the core writing instruction plus the supplemental writing intervention. Progress would be measured through standardized writing samples and individually administered writing CBM probe tasks. The writing samples and CBM probe responses would probably be collected and scored by the interventionist providing Tier-2 services, though kept by Mrs. Hammond in the students' writing portfolios. The rubric used to score the samples would aim to provide more discrete information about specific aspects of writing, such as content, style, and conventions (note that using too many traits is ill-advised because the separate traits do not discriminate well) or better yet, genre-specific expectations (e.g., story grammar elements or functional persuasive argument elements). In addition, the interventionist would attempt to connect information from the progress-monitoring writing samples collected under standard conditions with results obtained from (1) skill-focused (e.g., spelling) direct or indirect writing assessments and (2) a global norm-referenced standardized writing assessment administered close to the end of an intervention period (e.g., two marking periods—one must keep in mind that progress in writing may be much slower to manifest than progress in reading). If a student scored 1 standard deviation or more below the mean of the norm-referenced test, information from the analytically scored writing samples and the more skill-focused individualized direct or indirect writing assessments can help to illuminate *why* the student performed so poorly in comparison to same-age peers. Additionally, below-average performance on the test following a period of Tier-2 intervention would perhaps suggest a student was in need of Tier-3 specialized treatments through special education.

For the small number of students who, despite receiving Tier-2 services for writing, fail to show adequate response to intervention, then Tier-3 services likely are warranted. In Tier 3, the same approaches to writing assessment as employed in Tier 2 are enacted, except that at this point it becomes much more important to reliably pinpoint the subcomponents of writing with which a student is struggling to tailor individualized treatments; thus, skill-focused norm-referenced assessments rather than global writing tests are required.

RTI-W: Secondary Targeted Writing Interventions

For those students who are designated as at risk through universal screening efforts, student and teacher assistance teams might consider differentiated instruction through strategic instructional grouping arrangements (whole class, small group, and individual teaching during writing conferences), the application of universal design for learning principles (providing multiple means of representation, expression, and engagement; for in-depth information, visit the National Center on Universal Design for Learning website at *www.udlcenter.org*), and learner-centered adaptations and enhancements. A list of adaptations and technology enhancements for struggling writers is provided in Table 17.2 and includes accommodations in the learning environment, instructional materials, and teaching strategies, as well as more significant modifications to task demands and actual writing tasks. Effectively selecting, implementing, and monitoring the impact of any adaptation or enhancement will rely heavily on the advice of educators with expertise in writing instruction for students who struggle, such as literacy coaches, remedial tutors, special education teachers, speech–language pathologists, school psychologists, and other individuals who regularly serve on student and teacher assistance teams. Differentiated instruction can and should be implemented in the core general education classroom, but it also will be

TABLE 17.2. Adaptations for Struggling Writers

Learning environment accommodation

- Increase instructional time for writing
- Provide quiet and comfortable spaces for students to work

- Provide unimpeded access to writing tools
- Let students identify and select meaningful reinforcements for achieving writing goals (e.g., a reinforcement menu)

- Consult with an occupational therapist to identify specialized adaptations (e.g., chair and desk height)

Instructional materials accommodation

- Simplify language of writing prompts
- Highlight (e.g., color-code) key words and phrases
- Transition from simple to more elaborate graphic organizers and procedural checklists

- Post strategies, graphic organizers, and checklists in classroom and give students personal copies
- Have students keep a personal dictionary of "demon" words and frequently used spelling vocabulary

- Provide pencil grips for students
- Provide raised- or colored-lined paper
- Provide students with personal copies of alphabet strips
- Provide paper positioning marks on students' desks
- Develop individualized spelling lists

Teaching strategies accommodation

- Provide physical assistance during handwriting practice
- Reteach writing skills and strategies
- Expect and support mastery learning of skills and strategies (e.g., memorization of strategy steps)
- Use cross-age peer tutors to reinforce skills and strategies
- Assign homework designed to reinforce writing instruction
- Help students develop self-instructions (e.g., "I can handle this if I go slow") and self-questions (e.g., "Am I following my plan?") that focus on positive attributions for success and task progress

- Help students set specific and challenging yet attainable goals for the writing process (e.g., completing a planning sheet before beginning to draft) and written products (e.g., a quantity goal of including 10 descriptive words in a story, which is perhaps linked to a quality goal of improving word choice by 2 points on an analytic quality scale)
- Teach students to evaluate and adjust their writing behaviors and writing strategy use to improve their writing productivity and performance

- Promote maintenance and generalization of writing strategies by doing the following:
  o Model and discuss how strategies may be used in multiple contexts
  o Relate writing performance to strategy use
  o Have students teach others how to use strategies
  o Have students keep a strategy notebook they can consult at any time
  o Ensure all staff and caregivers are familiar with and prompt use of strategies
  o Reviews strategies often

(continued)

TABLE 17.2. *(continued)*

Task demands modification

- Increase amount of time allotted for completing written assignments
- Decrease the length and/or complexity of written assignments
- Have students complete text frames (i.e., partially finished texts)
- Reduce or eliminate copying demands (e.g., teach students abbreviations for note taking, supply worksheets with math problems from textbook)
- Allow students to use temporary/invented spelling

- Preteach spelling vocabulary for assignments
- Evaluate spelling using correct letter sequences (e.g., *hopping* has 8 possible correct letter sequences) rather than number of words spelled correctly to measure and reward incremental progress attributable to partial correct spelling
- Permit students to dictate written work to a scribe
- Selectively weight grading for content, organization, style, and conventions

- Grade assignments based on the amount of improvement rather than absolute performance
- Assign letter grades for body of work collected over time (i.e., portfolio assessment) rather than for each paper
- Provide feedback on content, organization, style, and conventions for some rather than all assignments (which may reduce students' anxiety about writing)
- Provide feedback on targeted aspects of writing rather than all aspects to avoid overwhelming students

Learning task modification

- Permit students to dramatize or orally present a written assignment in lieu of writing

- Assign students suitable roles (e.g., brainstorm manager) for creation of group paper

Technology enhancement

- If students have adequately developed keyboarding skills, permit them to write papers with a word processor
- Permit students to use outlining and semantic mapping software to facilitate planning

- Permit students to use voice recognition technology to facilitate text transcription
- Permit students to use integrated spell checker and/or word prediction software to facilitate correct spelling

- Permit students to use speech synthesis technology to facilitate revising and editing

Note. These accommodations and modifications possess face validity, but many of them have not been empirically validated for struggling writers.

used when providing targeted writing interventions to students through Tier-2 services that supplement the core program. In fact, for some at-risk students, differentiated instruction in the general education classroom with frequent progress monitoring may be what constitutes their Tier-2 services. For others, Tier 2 may encompass differentiated instruction plus targeted writing strategy interventions (hence, the multiple levels at Tier 2 noted at the beginning of the chapter).

Targeted strategy interventions for students who struggle with writing typically entail explicit, systematic, and comprehensive instruction in planning and revising strategies, the two aspects of the writing process that trouble struggling writers most. Fortunately, numerous studies have examined the effectiveness of various planning and revising strategies for students with and without writing difficulties in multiple educational contexts (i.e., whole classrooms, small-group instruction, individualized tutoring). Two excellent resources that describe this research and give advice on how to teach the many available strategies are *Writing Better: Effective Strategies for Teaching Students with Learning Difficulties* (Graham & Harris, 2005) and *Making the Writing Process Work: Strategies for Composition and Self-Regulation* (Harris & Graham, 1996). Prior to introducing any of these strategies, it is important to consider the role of self-regulation in writing, as successful writers are highly aware of themselves as writers and of the factors that influence their writing performance, and how to effectively manage these factors using diverse strategies. Self-regulation in writing includes at least four coordinated components (Graham et al., 1992): (1) goal setting, (2) self-talk, (3) self-evaluation, and (4) self-reinforcement. Generally speaking, the incorporation of self-regulation components in writing instruction has been shown to have a strong positive effect on strong and weak writers' composing abilities (e.g., Gersten & Baker, 2001; Graham & Perin, 2007). However, it is likely that structured and explicit self-regulation opportunities occur infrequently in most classrooms because of the highly individualized nature of self-regulation, so a focus on this aspect of writing can supplement core instruction in small-group encounters during intervention for nonresponsive struggling writers.

Self-Regulation for Writing

Setting goals enhances attention, motivation, and effort and facilitates strategic behavior (e.g., planning in advance of writing) through the valuation of goal attainment. In other words, if a goal is sufficiently important, the student will do all that is necessary to attain it. Research has demonstrated that goal setting improves writing skills in struggling writers (De La Paz, 2007; Graham, MacArthur, & Schwartz, 1995; Graham et al., 1992; Page-Voth & Graham, 1999; Schunk & Swartz, 1993). For goals to have the most beneficial impact on writing behavior and performance and to encourage students to marshal sufficient effort, they should be challenging (i.e., just beyond the student's current level of writing skill), proximal (i.e., attainable within a short period of time), concrete, and self-selected or collaboratively established (because real or perceived control boosts achievement motivation). Goals can focus on a writing process or on an aspect of the product. For writing product goals, quality and quantity goals can be established and explicitly linked. Examples of process goals might include:

1. Complete a planning sheet/graphic organizer using words or short phrases before writing—the use of single words or phrases to note planning ideas helps students feel less wedded to their initial plans because these plans do not become first drafts of whole texts.
2. Revise at least three times, once with a checklist, once with a peer, and once during a conference with the teacher before turning in the paper—setting up multiple "passes" at a composition with different tools and individuals helps establish an expectation that meaningful changes to one's goals, plans, and text will be made.
3. Use the spell checker on the computer plus backward read-aloud to correct spelling mistakes, followed by use of a peer editor—spell checkers catch a fairly limited number of spelling errors made by struggling writers, so rereading the text aloud (backward reading decouples orthographic recognition from linguistic processing, which tends to filter information and make mistakes harder to detect) and asking a peer to check for mistakes can facilitate editing.

Examples of product goals (a quality goal linked with a quantity goal aimed to make the quality goal more concrete) might include:

1. Increase organization score by 1 point → include an initiating event, a character goal, then two actions to achieve the goal, and finally a consequence.
2. Increase content score by 2 points → include five main ideas in an informational text with at least two supporting details for each main idea.
3. Increase word choice score by 2 points → include at least 15 action helpers, descriptive words, or transition words per page.
4. Increase conventions score by 1 point → have no more than three errors per page on the final copy.

Self-talk (instructions, questions, affirmations, or exhortations directed to oneself) helps orient attention to relevant information, organize thoughts, plan actions, and execute behaviors. Additionally, self-talk helps one cope with anxiety, frustration, self-doubt, and impulsivity, which tend to plague struggling writers and even those who are more accomplished writers. Self-talk has been widely investigated for several decades by researchers in many areas of psychology—sports, counseling, psychotherapeutic, and educational—with promising results: adaptive self-talk is a powerful mediator of human performance (e.g., Hamilton, Scott, & MacDougall, 2007; Manning & Payne, 1996). With respect to teaching struggling writers to use self-talk, it is most effective when (1) the content is tailored to the demands of the task and the individual's needs; (2) it is rehearsed aloud to automaticity and then used as a form of "inner speech" to control thoughts, feelings, and actions; and (3) it is monitored for fidelity of use by the teacher. Examples of self-talk include, "Have I used my revising checklist to check my work?," "This is hard, but I can do it if I try my best," "I'm good at coming up with ideas, so I'll turn in a good paper," and "Keep concentrating so you don't get distracted!"

Self-evaluation comprises both self-monitoring and self-recording of behavior and can be used to assess one's attention, strategy use, and task performance. Frequently, self-evaluation is accomplished through the graphic representation of a target behavior's occurrence in relation to a goal (thus, these two aspects of self-regulation are functionally interdependent). For instance, students might quantify their use of story grammar elements in fictional narratives produced over time on a chart that has the maximum score at the top (the goal). Likewise, students can track how many words they have written per time interval with the goal of increasing their productivity by 25% over baseline. Self-evaluation has been found to produce positive effects on behavior and academic performance in students with language and learning problems (e.g., Harris, 1986; Lloyd, Bateman, Landrum, & Hallahan, 1989; Maag, Reid, & DiGangi, 1993). Self-evaluation helps students establish worthwhile goals because the concrete data collected during this process gives feedback on their status relative to an external benchmark or a personal goal.

Finally, self-reinforcement can be enacted when students attain a performance criterion while self-evaluating their work. This component of self-management is just as powerful as external inducements to motivate behavior and can boost the efficacy of self-evaluation in writing (e.g., Ballard & Glynn, 1975). Reinforcement might take the form of self-congratulatory remarks, the procurement of tangible rewards, or participation in a preferred activity. Students with language and learning challenges likely will require guidance in forming accurate judgments about their performance, adhering to stringent guidelines for the application of contingencies, and selecting acceptable reinforcements.

To illustrate what differentiated instruction plus targeted writing strategy instruction might look like for a struggling writer, let's take the case of Emilio, a fourth grader who is a bilingual speaker of Spanish (his first language) and English and who has struggled with all aspects of writing (productivity, accuracy, and complexity) for at least 2 years according to his report cards. Emilio makes his dislike of writing known just about any time a writing assignment is given, and he perceives himself as "just no good at writing." He rarely plans in advance of writing, makes only superficial changes (focusing on word substitutions or correcting, often unsuccessfully, errors in conventions) when asked to revise, and generates short texts, often only half a page in length, bereft of detail despite his wealth of background knowledge about many topics (he is an avid web surfer and reader). His papers are often riddled with spelling, capitalization, and grammatical errors and tend to lack conceptual and linguistic sophistication—he writes much like a second grader. His handwriting is slow, labored, and difficult to decipher.

His teacher and the school's student and teacher assistance team (which includes a literacy tutor provided through Title I funding and the special education teacher) meet to identify appropriate adaptations to be implemented in the core writing program. The team notes that Emilio's struggles with sophistication in his writing are due, in part, to limited use of transition words and phrases to link ideas within text (e.g., *for instance, additionally, therefore*). Accordingly, the team identifies three adaptations that might support Emilio's use of more and varied transitional structures in his writing: (1) devote additional time to explicitly teach a list of high utility transition words and phrases for the genres of narration, exposition, and persuasion with a small group of students who have similar needs (an accommodation in the learning environment, the least-intensive and easiest-to-implement adaptation); (2) highlight, both visually and verbally, transitions in reading materials to provide concrete examples of how such verbiage is used by authors (an accommodation in instructional materials, somewhat more time-consuming to implement); and (3) establish a goal for Emilio to use at least two transition words or phrases correctly in each paragraph, with no two being alike in a text (an accommodation in teaching strategies that will require an investment of time and effort to monitor by the teacher and Emilio). The team also notes that, because Emilio's handwriting and spelling difficulties are likely hampering his written expression, a technology enhancement involving the use of a word processor with a spell checker (he already has excellent keyboarding skills) for all writing assignments is in order. They also believe personalized spelling vocabulary for weekly study (an accommodation in materials) would support Emilio's development as a speller. Additionally, the state standards at the fourth grade specify that, with guidance and support from adults, students should use technology to produce and publish writing and collaborate with others and demonstrate a command of keyboarding skills to type a minimum of one page in a single sitting. Thus, the team suggests that his writing productivity be increased to at least one page using the word processor, an easy enough goal to monitor. Finally, the team is greatly concerned by Emilio's poor use of planning and revising tactics to help him write more elaborate texts that display his knowledge about the world. Here the team decides that small-group targeted intervention (provided by the Title I literacy tutor) to supplement core writing instruction is in order. This intervention will be more intensive strategy training (that incorporates aspects of self-regulation) than could typically be provided in a Tier 1 context. The team determines that the intervention should focus on explicit teaching of genre-specific (narrative, expository, and persuasive) planning strategies with the aid of graphic organizers that will help Emilio generate and organize writing content ahead of writing and a generic but dynamic (i.e., items are added to the list as Emilio demonstrates advancing skills) revising and editing checklist that will help him upgrade his error detection and correction capacities. In addition, the Tier-2 intervention will incorporate mastery-based process and product goals with self-evaluation of goal attainment rather than time-based lessons, linking the mastery of strategies with increased writing performance, and include expectations of strategy generalization and maintenance across tasks and teachers (with a strategy notebook and frequent discussion of the impact of strategies on his writing performance). Obviously, the Tier-2 services integrate a number of adaptations listed in Table 17.2. Although there are many other problems in Emilio's writing to tackle, these initial steps should help him begin to achieve success and feel less abhorrence for writing tasks.

RTI-W: Tertiary Specialized Treatments

It is likely that students who have failed to thrive in the primary and secondary tiers of RTI-W will require highly specialized treatments to address writing at multiple levels of language organization (sublexical, word, sentence, paragraph, and text levels) with the input of knowledgeable professionals in the special education system. Mastery-based small-group or individual lessons at this tier place a high premium on skill- and strategy-based instruction with hierarchically sequenced steps derived from careful task analysis. Because a student in Tier 3 exhibits significant writing problems that impede productive participation in general education writing activities, it may be the case that the student with a writing disability will receive a specialized writing treatment that supplants rather than supplements the typical classroom writing instruction and that the student works on alternate writing standards (e.g., off-level or a more functionally oriented set of expectations). In any case, a RTI-W Tier-3 student will need many more modifications (and accommodations) to experience success (see Table 17.2 for suggestions).

A case involving a high school student named Tanisha illustrates how specialized treatments in Tier 3 might be used to assist a chronically poor writer who has been diagnosed with a writing disability based on progress monitoring data and norm-referenced test data. Tanisha's spelling is much like that of an elementary-age student in that she spells a majority of words phonetically, though she also frequently makes indecipherable errors. Her handwriting is slow but legible and she prefers to type rather than compose by hand. She possesses a firm grasp of basic capitalization and punctuation conventions, but more sophisticated grade-level applications of rules for writing conventions challenge her. Her sentences are structurally simplistic and lack variety; likewise, her paragraphs are simple, brief, devoid of detail, and sometimes out of sequential order. She often struggles with using precise and interesting word choices to communicate her ideas. The special education staff, after consultating with her general education teachers and using data from skill-based assessments, have determined that Tanisha's main problems include poor oral vocabulary knowledge (which limits her written expression), limited orthographic awareness (i.e., explicit knowledge about the spelling rules of English), and limited grammatical and syntactic development in spoken and written language. Not unexpectedly, Tanisha does not use advance planning strategies or revising strategies because she treats writing as a passive rather than an active process and because she lacks metacognitive awareness and actions during writing.

To address these significant issues, Tanisha's multidisciplinary special education team (including Tanisha and her parents) determines that she should receive 90 minutes per week of writing treatment from the special education teacher. The special education teacher, knowledgeable about evidence-based practices for students with writing difficulties, designs a specialized treatment consisting of (1) self-regulated strategy development (SRSD; see Chapters 1, 8, and 9, this volume) for planning and revising, which involves explicit and intensive mastery-based strategy plus self-regulation instruction with gradual release of teacher control; (2) multiple adaptations and technology enhancements with comprehensive training in the use of advanced technologies to aid written expression (e.g., word prediction software to bypass poor spelling, speech-to-text/speech recognition to fluently produce text yet reinforce explicit knowledge of capitalization and punctuation rules because these aspects must be dictated separately, speech synthesis/screen readers to check and correct text); (3) highly focused combined spelling and vocabulary instruction to build capacity for generating texts about high school subject matter (e.g., morphological patterns for Greek and Latin roots, base words, and affixes frequently used in courses); (4) sequential instruction in spelling increasingly longer, more orthographically dense words (e.g., consonant blends and digraphs and vowel diagraphs and diphthongs) as well as frequently confused homographs and homophones; and (5) intensive instruction in the recognition and production of the four basic sentence types (simple, compound, complex, compound-complex) along with embedded sentence-combining activities to produce more complex and varied sentences in writing.

Educational Policy Elements That Shape RTI-W

One must consider the operation of system-level policies in the implementation and scaling of RTI-W as well as the characteristics of RTI-W itself. Two important policy elements that directly impact classroom instruction and assessment decisions are content standards and large-scale assessments. Research suggests that state writing standards and large-scale assessments appear to influence both what is taught and how it is taught. According to studies, in response to changes in their state standards and assessments for writing, (1) teachers reportedly increased their instructional emphasis on writing for specific audiences and purposes (Stecher, Barron, Chun, & Ross, 2000); (2) schools included more writing across the curriculum (Stecher, Barron, Kaganoff, & Goodwin, 1998; Taylor, Shepard, Kinner, & Rosenthal, 2002) and increased the amount of daily writing in which students engaged (Stecher et al., 2000); and (3) teachers reported incorporating more reform philosophies related to portfolio-based instruction and assessment as compared to traditional skill- and task-focused classroom writing practices (Stecher et al., 2000). However, the impact of these changes on actual student writing performance was negligible. One potential explanation for this finding may be related to the degree to which writing standards reflect evidence-based instructional practices; effective writing instruction is more likely to occur in states where standards incorporate evidence-based writing practices. It is also likely that standards that include a greater proportion of best practices along with sufficient detail to guide instruction (thereby improving fidelity of implementation) increase the probability of improved teaching of writing, resulting in better student writing outcomes. Unfortunately, little is known about the degree to which writing standards reflect research, although the evidence does not suggest a strong alignment with current state standards (e.g., Duke, 2001). Moreover, according to research examining a sample of seven states' writing standards conducted by Troia et al. (2012), there appears to be a wide variability in states' attention to diverse writing purposes, generally poor specificity related to the knowledge and skills required at each grade, and large differences in explication of environmental supports for helping students attain mastery of writing skills and strategies.

The Common Core State Standards

The CCSS have been formally adopted by 46 states and the District of Columbia at the time of this writing. Those states that have adopted the standards are in various phases of rolling them out for implementation, with some states using a staggered rollout by grade level. Virtually all adopting states intend to completely phase in the new standards by the 2014–2015 school year, the year in which the two federally funded assessment consortia, the Partnership for Assessment of Readiness for College and Careers (PARCC; 24 member states) and the SMARTER Balanced Assessment Consortium (SBAC; 28 member states), plan to deploy fully operational next-generation assessments aligned with the CCSS. With this widespread adoption, variability across states like that described above will be greatly reduced. However, the CCSS, although vetted by a large number of stakeholders, need to be thoroughly evaluated for content clarity, breadth, emphasis, and rigor. Standards can be expected to effectively guide curriculum and instruction only if they are well articulated, comprehensive, and derived from theoretical models of learning specific to the content being taught.

In a study examining the breadth of content coverage, the frequency with which content was referenced, and the balance of content coverage of the CCSS for writing and language, Troia et al. (2012) found several strengths and weaknesses in the core standards. As for strengths, the CCSS are succinct as shown by the relatively low frequency with which the range of content addressed in the standards is referenced within each grade level or grade band, which is consistent with the intent of the National Governors Association and the Council of Chief State School Officers to create standards that are precise and yet interpretable by the public at large. A high degree of repetitiveness could logically impede interpretation by teachers and others because they would have to sift through redundancies to isolate kernels representing the core knowledge and skills expected of students. Also, the relative emphasis on the range of content within the standards appears to be well balanced, and the standards are consistent with respect to coverage of content from one grade to the next once an aspect of writing is introduced. Such consistency provides a coherent framework that guides instruction and assessment and may help to ensure greater opportunities for student mastery of writing expectations because the content does not drastically change across grades and all expectations receive relatively equal emphasis. As might be expected, the CCSS reflect spiraling standards, in that the range of expectations in many areas increases across grades. For instance, in the early elementary grades, fewer aspects of the writing process and fewer components of written texts are expected of students, but in later grades more aspects of the writing process and more components of text are required. Perhaps not surprisingly, writing conventions show a reverse pattern, with a higher number of conventions addressed in the early grades than in the later grades, presumably because it is important to master the conventions of writing early in development (e.g., Berninger & Amtmann, 2003).

As for weaknesses, the CCSS do not address (or do so in a very limited fashion) some aspects of writing that both represent current theoretical models of writing and have been shown through research to be strongly related to better student writing outcomes. For example, a recent meta-analysis by Graham, Harris, and Hebert (2011) found an average weighted effect size of 0.77 (a large effect) on the quality of students' papers associated with verbal and written peer or teacher feedback on students' texts or their attainment of writing skills or strategies. This effect size was derived from eight studies with participants from second through ninth grade. The CCSS address feedback in kindergarten and first grade, but not in later grades. Another recent meta-analysis (Graham & Perin, 2007) found a small but significant average weighted effect size of 0.25 on writing quality from six studies with preadolescent and adolescent participants for the study of text models. The CCSS barely make reference to the use of text models. This same meta-analysis found a large effect (average weighted effect size of 0.82) for teaching strategies to support the writing process from 20 studies with participants in grades 4 through 10; the core standards do not refer to strategies at all. The CCSS devote considerable attention to grammar in grades K through 4, though traditional grammar instruction has consistently been found to yield negative effects on student writing performance (Graham, McKeown, Kiuhara, & Harris, 2012; Graham & Perin, 2007). However, the core standards cover very little specific content related to spelling, handwriting, and keyboarding (i.e., text transcription skills), which have been found to play a vital role in the development of accomplished writing (e.g., Graham, Berninger, Abbott, Abbott, & Whitaker, 1997; McCutchen, 1996); instruction in transcription skills has a moderate impact (average weighted effect size of 0.55) on writing quality (Graham et al., in press). Finally, the CCSS do not address writing motivation at all, though there is evidence that at least two aspects of motivation—goal setting and self-efficacy—directly impact writing performance and are amenable to instruction (e.g., Graham & Perin, 2007; Pajares, 2003; Schunk & Swartz, 1993).

Because the CCSS for writing and language will serve as the architecture for instruction in RTI-W and because all students, regardless of which tier of service they receive, will be held accountable for meeting the CCSS (via large-scale assessment), educators will need to be mindful of how to help struggling writers meet these new standards (and of how to fill in areas missing in the CCSS when conducting writing instruction, based on available research evidence, professional wisdom, and students' needs and values). Efforts to provide differentiated instruction across tiers through strategic grouping arrangements, universal design for learning features, and adaptations for the learner, as well as the delivery of targeted interventions and specialized treatments by highly qualified and effective educators, will need to be supported and coordinated by state, district, and school leadership because these individuals serve as linchpins for translating policy dictates for educators, students, and families.

Large-Scale Writing Assessments

Large-scale writing assessment instruments (e.g., multiple-choice or indirect writing tests and timed/untimed responses to writing prompts or direct assessments) are used to determine whether students have met content standards (and occasionally to determine grade promotion and graduation eligibility). In this way, state writing assessments serve as a sort of universal screening measure, in that they help identify students who may be at risk for writing difficulties because they have not attained grade-level content expectations. However, large-scale writing assessments are rather blunt instruments fraught with significant limitations (and thus should not be used as the only, or even the primary, source of data for making instructional decisions relevant to implementing RTI-W). First, state writing assessments may put undesirable constraints on core classroom instruction. Although some studies have found that writing assessments yield an increase in writing across content areas (Taylor et al., 2002) and in tested genres (Stecher & Chun, 2002), multiple-choice state writing tests are associated with an increased emphasis on grammar and usage and a decreased emphasis on actual writing in classrooms (Murphy, 2003). Likewise, single-sample timed writing prompts may result in a narrowing of the curriculum to address the type of writing included on the test (Hillocks, 2002; O'Neill, Murphy, Williamson, & Huot, 2006) and in teaching more formulaic approaches to composing (Johnson, Smagorinsky, Thompson, & Fry, 2003).

Second, state writing assessments typically have limited validity due to two problems: trait underrepresentation and construct-irrelevant variance (Messick, 1989), which mean that the result obtained for a given student is likely not to be representative of that student's true writing ability as seen across diverse circumstances. These threats to validity occur when a test is too narrow (ignoring important aspects of writing) and when extraneous factors resulting from test development invalidate the examinee's response, respectively. Indirect writing assessments such as multiple-choice tests can be scored reliably and quickly, but they underrepresent the trait of writing by focusing almost exclusively on mechanical aspects (Witte, Flach, Greenword, & Wilson, 1995). Direct writing assessments often introduce construct-irrelevant variance in which variation is attributed to factors other than the student's writing ability, such as when students are required to write in response to a text, thus introducing variance due to reading ability (Allen, Holland, & Thayer, 2005; Weigle, 2002). Additionally, direct writing assessments often only assess one genre of writing, leading to an underrepresentation of the writing trait. Given the complexity of writing, it is likely that "writing is not a single, global ability" (Williamson, 1993, p. 21); thus, single measures of writing cannot adequately assess a student's writing ability.

If large-scale assessments are to be used as one kind of universal screening instrument, which requires a high degree of validity in the inferences regarding the generalizability of the test score, then states will need to redesign their writing tests to accommodate concerns regarding trait underrepresentation and construct-irrelevant variance in the assessments of writing by (1) evaluating writing using more writing samples, (2) clearly defining what is meant by "writing" in their assessments, and (3) articulating that definition with writing theory and research. Although the next generation assessments being developed by PARCC and SBAC may address these concerns, these too will have to be carefully evaluated to be sure scores are valid for purposes such as educational accountability and universal screening. At this point, large-scale writing assessments have limited utility for implementing RTI-W.

Acknowledgments

Preparation of this chapter was supported in part by Grant No. R305A100040 from the U.S. Department of Education, Institute of Education Sciences, to Michigan State University. The content does not necessarily reflect the positions or policies of the agency, and no official endorsement by it should be inferred.

References

Allen, N., Holland, P., & Thayer, D. (2005). Measuring the benefits of examinee-selected questions. *Journal of Educational Measurement, 42*, 27–34.

Ballard, K. D., & Glynn, T. (1975). Behavioral self-management in story writing with elementary school children. *Journal of Applied Behavior Analysis, 8*, 387–398.

Benson, B. J., & Campbell, H. M. (2009). Assessment of student writing with curriculum-based measurement. In G. A. Troia (Ed.), *Instruction and assessment for struggling writers: Evidence-based practices* (pp. 337–357). New York: Guilford Press.

Berninger, V. W., & Amtmann, D. (2003). Preventing written expression disabilities through early and continuing assessment and intervention for handwriting and/or spelling problems: Research into practice. In H. L. Swanson, K. R. Harris, & S. Graham (Eds.), *Handbook of learning disabilities* (pp. 345–363). New York: Guilford Press.

Cutler, L., & Graham, S. (2008). Primary grade writing instruction: A national survey. *Journal of Educational Psychology, 100,* 907–919.

De La Paz, S. (2007). Managing cognitive demands for writing: Comparing the effects of instructional components in strategy instruction. *Reading and Writing Quarterly: Overcoming Learning Difficulties, 23,* 249–266.

Duke, N. K. (2001, April). What do we expect young children to know and be able to do with different genres of text?: An analysis of state standards. In C. C. Pappas (Chair), *Children, genre, and schooling.* American Educational Research Association, Seattle, WA.

Gearhart, M. (2009). Classroom portfolio assessment for writing. In G. A. Troia (Ed.), *Instruction and assessment for struggling writers: Evidence-based practices* (pp. 311–336). New York: Guilford Press.

Gersten, R., & Baker, S. (2001). Teaching expressive writing to students with learning disabilities: A meta-analysis. *Elementary School Journal, 101,* 251–272.

Graham, S., Berninger, V. W., Abbott, R. D., Abbott, S. P., & Whitaker, D. (1997). The role of mechanics in composing of elementary school students: A new methodological approach. *Journal of Educational Psychology, 89,* 170–182.

Graham, S., Bollinger, A., Booth Olson, C., D'Aoust, C., MacArthur, C. A., McCutchen, D., et al.. (2012). *Teaching elementary school students to be effective writers: A practice guide* (NCEE 2012-4058). Washington, DC: National Center for Education Evaluation and Regional Assistance, Institute of Education Sciences, U.S. Department of Education. Retrieved from *http://ies.ed.gov/ncee/wwc/publications_reviews.aspx#pubsearch.*

Graham, S., & Harris, K. R. (2005). *Writing better: Effective strategies for teaching students with learning difficulties.* Baltimore: Brookes.

Graham, S., Harris, K. R., & Hebert, M. A. (2011). *Informing writing: The benefits of formative assessment: A Carnegie Corporation Time to Act report.* Washington, DC: Alliance for Excellent Education.

Graham, S., McKeown, D., Kiuhara, S. A., & Harris, K. R. (2012). A meta-analysis of writing instruction for students in the elementary grades. *Journal of Educational Psychology, 104,* 879–896.

Graham, S., MacArthur, C. A., & Schwartz, S. S. (1995). Effects of goal setting and procedural facilitation on the revising behavior and writing performance of students with writing and learning problems. *Journal of Educational Psychology, 87,* 230–240.

Graham, S., MacArthur, C. A., Schwartz, S. S., & Page-Voth, V. (1992). Improving the compositions of students with learning disabilities using a strategy involving product and process goal setting. *Exceptional Children, 58,* 322–334.

Graham, S., & Perin, D. (2007). A meta-analysis of writing instruction for adolescent students. *Journal of Educational Psychology, 99,* 445–476.

Hamilton, R. A., Scott, D., & MacDougall, M. P. (2007). Assessing the effectiveness of self-talk interventions on endurance performance. *Journal of Applied Sport Psychology, 19,* 226–239.

Harris, K. R. (1986). Self-monitoring of attentional behavior versus self-monitoring of productivity: Effects on on-task behavior and academic response rate among learning disabled children. *Journal of Applied Behavior Analysis, 19,* 417–423.

Harris, K. R., & Graham, S. (1996). *Making the writing process work: Strategies for composition and self-regulation.* Cambridge, MA: Brookline Books.

Hillocks, G. (2002). *The testing trap: How state writing assessments control learning.* New York: Teachers College Press.

Johnson, E., Mellard, D. F., Fuchs, D., & McKnight, M. A. (2006). *Responsiveness to intervention (RTI): How to do it.* Lawrence, KS: National Research Center on Learning Disabilities.

Johnson, T. S., Smagorinsky, P., Thompson, L., & Fry, P. G. (2003). Learning to teach the five-paragraph theme. *Research in the Teaching of English, 38,* 136–176.

Lloyd, J. W., Bateman, D. F., Landrum, T. J., & Hallahan, D. P. (1989). Self-recording of attention versus productivity. *Journal of Applied Behavior Analysis, 22,* 315–323.

Maag, J. W., Reid, R., & DiGangi, S. A. (1993). Differential effects of self-monitoring attention, accuracy, and productivity. *Journal of Applied Behavior Analysis, 26,* 329–344.

Manning, B. H., & Payne, B. D. (1996). *Self-talk for teachers and students: Metacognitive strategies for personal and classroom use.* Boston: Allyn & Bacon.

McCutchen, D. (1996). A capacity theory of writing: Working memory in composition. *Educational Psychology Review, 8,* 299–325.

McMaster, K., & Espin, C. (2007). Technical features of curriculum-based measurement in writing: A literature review. *Journal of Special Education, 41,* 68–84.

Messick, S. (1989). Meaning and values in test validation: The science and ethics of assessment. *Educational Researcher, 18*(2), 5–11.

Murphy, S. (2003). That was then, this is now: The impact of changing assessment policies on teachers and the teaching of writing in California. *Journal of Writing Assessment, 1,* 23–45.

O'Neill, P., Murphy, S., Williamson, M., & Huot, B. (2006). What teachers say about different kinds of mandated state tests. *Journal of Writing Assessment, 2*(2), 81–108.

Page-Voth, V., & Graham, S. (1999). Effects of goal setting and strategy use on the writing performance and self-efficacy of students with writing and learning problems. *Journal of Educational Psychology, 91,* 230–240.

Pajares, F. (2003). Self-efficacy beliefs, motivation, and achievement in writing: A review of the literature. *Reading and Writing Quarterly: Overcoming Learning Difficulties, 19,* 139–158.

Rogers, L. A., & Graham, S. (2008). A meta-analysis of single subject design writing intervention research. *Journal of Educational Psychology, 100,* 879–906.

Sackett, D. L., Rosenberg, W. M., Gray, J. A., Haynes, R. B., & Richardson, W. S. (1996). Evidence-based medicine: What it is and what it isn't. *British Medical Journal, 312,* 71–72.

Schunk, D. H., & Swartz, C. W. (1993). Goals and progress feedback: Effects on self-efficacy and writing achievement. *Contemporary Educational Psychology, 18,* 337–354.

Stecher, B. M., Barron, S. L., Chun, T., & Ross, K. (2000). *The effects of the Washington state education reform on schools and classrooms* (RAND Report DRU-2263). Santa Monica, CA: RAND Corporation.

Stecher, B. M., Barron, S. L., Kaganoff, T., & Goodwin, J. (1998). *The effects of standards based assessment on classroom practices: Results of the 1996–1997 RAND survey of Kentucky teachers of mathematics and writing* (CRESST Tech. Rep. No. 482). Los Angeles: University of California, National Center for Research on Evaluation, Standards, and Student Testing (CRESST).

Stecher, B. M., & Chun, T. (2002). *School and classroom during two years of educational reform in Washington State* (CSE Tech. Rep. No. 550). Los Angeles: University of California, National Center for Research on Evaluation, Standards, and Student Testing.

Taylor, G., Shepard, L., Kinner, F., & Rosenthal, J. (2002). *A survey of teachers' perspectives on large-scale testing in Colorado: What gets taught, what gets lost* (CSE Technical Report 588). Los Angeles: Center for Research on Evaluation, Standards Student Testing.

Troia, G. A., Olinghouse, N. G., Wilson, J., O'Shea, K., Mo, Y., Hawkins, L., et al. (2012, April). The Common Core writing standards and state adoption: Are we moving in the right direction? In C. F. Vanover (Chair), *The question of coherence: Perspectives on curriculum coordination and alignment.* American Educational Research Association, Vancouver, BC, Canada.

Weigle, S. C. (2002). *Assessing writing.* Cambridge, UK: Cambridge University Press.

Williamson, M. (1993). An introduction to holistic scoring. In M. Williamson & B. Huot (Eds.), *Validating scoring for writing assessment: Theoretical and empirical foundations* (pp. 206–232). Cresskill, NJ: Hampton.

Witte, S., Flach, J., Greenword, C., & Wilson, K. (1995). More notes toward an assessment of advanced ability to communicate. *Assessing Writing, 2,* 21–66.

Index